Discovery Strategies
in the Psychology of Action

This is a volume in
EUROPEAN MONOGRAPHS IN SOCIAL PSYCHOLOGY

Series Editors: Richard Eiser and Klaus Scherer

(This volume was accepted by the founding series editor Henri Tajfel.)

EUROPEAN MONOGRAPHS IN SOCIAL PSYCHOLOGY 35

Discovery Strategies in the Psychology of Action

Edited by

G. P. GINSBURG

University of Nevada
Reno, Nevada

MARYLIN BRENNER

Department of Psychology
University of Reading
Reading, England

M. VON CRANACH

Psychologisches Institut
Der Universität Bern
Bern, Switzerland

1985

Published in cooperation with
EUROPEAN ASSOCIATION OF EXPERIMENTAL
SOCIAL PSYCHOLOGY
by
ACADEMIC PRESS
(Harcourt Brace Jovanovich, Publishers)
London   Orlando   San Diego   New York
Toronto   Montreal   Sydney   Tokyo

ACADEMIC PRESS INC. (LONDON) LTD.
24-28 Oval Road
LONDON NW1 7DX

United States Edition published by
ACADEMIC PRESS, INC.
Orlando, Florida 32887

BRITISH LIBRARY CATALOGUING IN PUBLICATION DATA
Discovery strategies in the psychology of action.
 — — (European monographs in social psychology;35)
    1. Human behavior
    I. Ginsburg, Gerald P.   II. Brenner, Marylin J.
    III. Von Cranach, Mario   IV. Series
    150   BF131

LIBRARY OF CONGRESS CATALOGING IN PUBLICATION DATA

Main entry under title:

Discovery strategies in the psychology of action.

    Includes index.
    1. Intentionalism.   2. Social action.   I. Ginsburg,
Gerald P. (Gerald Phillip), 1932-   . II. Brenner,
Marylin J.   III. Cranach, Mario von.
BF619.5.D57   1984   153.8   84-14641
ISBN 0-12-284760-1   (alk. paper)

PRINTED IN THE UNITED STATES OF AMERICA

85 86 87 88   9 8 7 6 5 4 3 2 1

European Monographs in Social Psychology

SERIES EDITORS: RICHARD EISER AND KLAUS SCHERER

Founding Series Editor: Henri Tajfel

E. A. CARSWELL and R. ROMMETVEIT (*eds*)
Social Contexts of Messages, 1971

J. ISRAEL and H. TAJFEL (*eds*)
The Context of Social Psychology: A Critical Assessment, 1972

J. R. EISER and W. STROEBE
Categorization and Social Judgment, 1972

M. VON CRANACH and I. VINE (*eds*)
Social Communication and Movement: Studies on Interaction and Expression in Man and Chimpanzee, 1973

C. HERZLICH
Health and Illness: A Social Psychological Analysis, 1973

J. M. NUTTIN, JR
The Illusion of Attitude Change: Towards a Response Contagion Theory of Persuasion, 1975

H. GILES and P. F. POWESLAND
Speech Style and Social Evaluation, 1975

J. K. CHADWICK-JONES
Social Exchange Theory: Its Structure and Influence in Social Psychology, 1976

M. BILLIG
Social Psychology and Intergroup Relations, 1976

S. MOSCOVICI
Social Influence and Social Change, 1976

R. SANDELL
Linguistic Style and Persuasion, 1977

A. HEEN WOLD
Decoding Oral Language, 1978

H. GILES (*ed*)
Language, Ethnicity and Intergroup Relations, 1977

H. TAJFEL (*ed*)
Differentiation between Social Groups: Studies in the Social Psychology of Intergroup Relations, 1979

J. JASPARS, F. FINCHAM and M. HEWSTONE
Attribution Theory and Research:
Conceptual, Developmental and Social Dimensions

E. R. SEMIN and A. S. R. MANSTEAD
The Accountability of Conduct:
A Social Psychological Analysis

P. HELMERSEN
Family Interaction and Communication in Psychopathology:
An Evaluation of Recent Perspectives

This volume is dedicated to
the memory of Michael Brenner

Preface

In 1981, an intensive working conference was held at Bad Homburg, Federal Republic of Germany, on the analysis of goal-directed human action. The conference participants included psychologists, sociologists, ethologists and philosophers. Some of the participants had been pursuing the study of action as a major research effort for several years, while others were only sceptically receptive to it. The discussions and challenges of that conference made clear that the study of human activity as action had great theoretical and empirical potential, and at the same time stood in complementary relationship to several of the established areas of psychological and social psychological research. For these reasons, Michael Brenner and Mario von Cranach, the conference organizers, decided to edit a book on the basis of some of the conference's topics. Michael's death interrupted the work for some time, until Marylin Brenner and G. P. Ginsburg decided to take charge of the unfinished task. In its final state, this is not a presentation of the conference proceedings; those conferences papers that were included were largely changed and updated, and new papers were introduced.

Now that the volume has been finished, we should like to express our gratitude to the Werner-Reimers-Stiftung, Bad Homburg, and to the Maison des Sciences de l'Homme, Paris, sponsors of the conference.

We appreciated the understanding shown by the publishers and wish to thank Audrey Connor and Logos Alpha (Reading) for secretarial assistance.

Contributors

Numbers in parentheses indicate the pages on which the authors' contributions begin.

Marylin J. Brenner (1), Department of Psychology, University of Reading, Reading RG6 2AL, Berks, England

Michael Brenner[1] (207), Department of Social Studies, Oxford Polytechnic, Headington, Oxford OX3 OBP, England

David Canter (171), Department of Psychology, University of Surrey, Guildford, Surrey GU2 5XH, England

J. P. de Waele (115), Vrije Universiteit Brussel, Faculteit voor Psychologie en Opvoedkunde, 1050 Brussel, Belgium

J. Richard Eiser (187), Department of Psychology, University of Exeter, Washington Singer Laboratories, Exeter EX4 4QG, England

G. P. Ginsburg (1, 255), Department of Psychology, University of Nevada, Reno, Nevada 89557

Winfried Hacker (63), Technische Universität Dresden, Sektion Arbeitswissenschaften, DDR. 8027 Dresden, German Democratic Republic

Adam Kendon (229), Department of Anthropology, Connecticut College, New London, Connecticut 06320

Ernst-D. Lantermann (85), Fachbereich 3, Psychologie Universität Kassel, D-35 Kassel-Oberzwehren, Federal Republic of Germany

Elfie Mächler (19), Psychologisches Institut, Universität Bern, 3012 Bern, Switzerland

Vera Steiner (19), Psychologisches Institut, Universität Bern, 3012 Bern, Switzerland

Mario von Cranach (1, 19), Psychologisches Institut, Universität Bern, 3012 Bern, Switzerland

[1]Deceased.

Contents

Preface   ix

Contributors   xi

1. Introduction
Marylin Brenner, G. P. Ginsburg, and Mario von Cranach

The Human Action Approach   1
Summary of Contributions   3
References   18

2. The Organisation of Goal-Directed Action: A Research Report
Mario von Cranach, Elfie Mächler, and Vera Steiner

The Bernese Research Project   19
Basic Features of a Theory of Concrete Goal-Directed Action   20
Selected Topics of Our Action Theory   24
Empirical Investigations   47
The Actor: Originator of Acts   57
References   58

3. On Some Fundamentals of Action Regulation
Winfried Hacker

Goal-Directed Action as a Relational Category   63
Some Problems of Models of Action Organisation   68
Taxonomy of Goal-Oriented Actions   73
Goals as the Decisive Regulation Instance   74
Global Dimensions of the Analysis, Evaluation, and
     Design of Activities   78
Analysing Jobs in Relation to Objective Job Conditions   80
References   82

4. **Cognition and Emotion in the Course of Action**
   Ernst-D. Lantermann

   Introduction   85
   Characteristics of Human Actions   90
   A General Model for Action Control   91
   Control Processes at a Medium Level of Arousal   105
   Control Processes at a High Level of Arousal   109
   Concluding Remarks   111
   References   112

5. **The Significance of Action Psychology for Personality
   Research and Assessment**
   J. P. de Waele

   Present-Day Problems of Personality Psychology   115
   Two Problem-and-Conflict Situations   132
   Interpretations of the Observations Made on Five Individuals   136
   Conclusions   151
   Appendix 1: Outline of the Focused Interview   155
   Appendix 2: Summaries of Two PCS Interpretive Protocols   158
   References   167

6. **Intention, Meaning, and Structure: Social Action
   in Its Physical Context**
   David Canter

   Action and Behaviour   171
   Environmental Links   172
   The Physical Context as Process Integration   174
   Environmentally Located Goals   175
   Situationally Located Meanings   177
   Cognitive Ecology   177
   Some Limiting Antecedents   178
   Ecology and Conceptual Systems   179
   An Obstetric Example   180
   Role and Setting   181
   Role and Satisfaction   182
   Place Rules   183
   Conclusions   184

Time, the Forgotten Dimension   184
References   185

7. **Social Cognition and Social Action**
   J. Richard Eiser

The Role of Theory   187
Relating Cognition to Behaviour   188
Balance and Cognitive Consistency   191
Attribution Theory and Research   194
Expectancy-Value Approaches   197
Scripts and Schemata   199
Conclusions   202
References   203

8. **The Analysis of Situated Social Action:**
   The Case of the Research Interview
   Michael Brenner

Introductory Remarks   207
Action-Psychological Assumptions   207
The Research Interview as Situated Social Action   216
Conclusion   227
References   227

9. **Behavioural Foundations for the Process of**
   Frame Attunement in Face-to-Face Interaction
   Adam Kendon

Introduction   229
Routinisation   231
Differential Attention in Interaction   232
The Communication of Attention   235
Spatial-Orientational Positioning   236
Formation Arrangements   238
Frame Attunement   242
Functions of Salutational Exchanges   247
Gradients of Explicitness   249
Conclusion   250
References   251

10. **The Analysis of Human Action:
Current Status and Future Potential**
G. P. Ginsburg

Central Themes in the Analysis of Human Action   255
Some Examples of Action Themes in Current
    Social Psychology   257
The Future of Action Analysis in Social Psychology   262
Some Problems in the Analysis of Action   264
Conclusion   275
References   275

Author Index   **281**

Subject Index   **287**

1

Introduction

Marylin Brenner, G. P. Ginsburg,
and Mario von Cranach

The Human Action Approach

The primary objectives of this volume are to familiarize a wider range
of behavioural scientists with the central themes and the empirical po-
tentials of the human action approach, and to place the human action
models into the wider contexts of personality and social psychology and
microsociology.

There is no one model that represents the human action approach,
but there are certain important themes that are common to all of the
action models. Among the most central is the conceptualization of action as hierarchically as well as sequentially organized. This means that
any action must be understood in terms both of (1) its component
movements and sequences, and the mechanisms by which those are
integrated, and (2) the larger acts that the actions being performed are
helping to accomplish. Closely related to this theme is an emphasis on
context, including the immediate context of the antecedent actions in
the sequence, the situational context, and the sociocultural background. Feedback and feedforward processes, and other features of
open systems, also are common to the models, as is an explicit interplay between cognitive and behavioural categories of activity. In addition, all of the models construe action as goal directed, a feature that
illustrates the commonality of ideas and problems across the varied
backgrounds from which the different human action models have
emerged, (for ethology, see Hinde & Stevenson, 1970; for experimental
psychology, see Osgood, 1953). Finally, the human action models in
general are more descriptive than causally theoretical, making them
complex rather than simplistically elegant in appearance. But the choice
of a descriptive emphasis was deliberate, since most action theorists
consider the adequate description of human action to be a necessary
prerequisite to any causal theory, and to be very long overdue. Con-

1

DISCOVERY STRATEGIES
IN THE PSYCHOLOGY OF ACTION

temporary theories of human behaviour in psychology, sociology, and ethology do not offer adequate conceptualizations of human action, thereby ignoring either the context of the action, its hierarchical nature, its temporal extensity, or the multiplicity of simultaneously present reasons for and consequences of any given action. The action models also construe persons as agents capable of planning and evaluating as well simply reacting, and they view actions as meaningful to the participants and as occurring as real-time processes.

The contributions to the present volume are written by authors from a variety of backgrounds, leading to some differences in the use of terms, the concrete activities of interest, and procedures and criteria of scientific investigation. They all share a concern with human action as a major and unifying focus of research, but the differences among them reflect the fluid state of contemporary action theory—an investigative orientation still in the process of active formation and change. The chapters by von Cranach (Chapter 2), Hacker (Chapter 3), Brenner (Chapter 8), and Lantermann (Chapter 4) are designed to explicate one or another model of goal-directed action, while those of Canter (Chapter 6), Eiser (Chapter 7), and De Waele (Chapter 5) suggest and illustrate complementary linkages between goal-directed action theory and environmental, cognitive–social, and personality psychology, respectively. Kendon's chapter (9) also deals with human action, but its focus is on the crucial but ancillary goal of establishing and maintaining a jointly shared set of expectations and understandings with one's interactional partner, rather than on the more specific goals on which the other chapters focus. Kendon's chapter shares much in content with the work of the late Erving Goffman, but only brief consideration is needed to realize that this indeed is a social psychological theory of human action, and that it concerns goal-directed action in which the goals are of the most ubiquitous sort. The final chapter of the book provides a critical review of the major tenets of action theory and a prognosis for its future.

Because the scope and vocabulary of action theory is likely to be unfamiliar to the Anglo-American reader (see chapters by Eiser and Canter, this volume), a detailed overview of the contributions probably would be helpful. It should be kept in mind that the recent developments in the psychology of action have been carried forward by particular individuals and research teams, and therefore it was thought desirable to personalise the book. That is, the works of particular people and groups is presented in their own right with the idea of contrasting, rather than harmonising, present developments in the psychology of action. The display of current work in the psychology of action give rise, however, to the emergence of some fundamental points of theoretical and empirical convergence.

Certain concepts, and their interrelationships, are commonly invoked. In this context, von Cranach suggests: "Scientists . . . are naive psychologists too, and there are many reasons to assume that it is their shared view, based on common sense psychology, which has led so many action theorists in different disciplines, from analytic philosophy to Marxist psychology of activity, to use similar concepts" (Chapter 2, p. 21). "Common sense psychology" refers here to Heider's (1958) work, which suggests that

> lay people in their everyday life make use of psychological explanations which contain, as their core, a well elaborated theory of action, comprising many important constructs also used in scientific theory: goal, equifinality, decision, resolution, habit, volition, motivation, emotion, etc. . . . only recently has the nature of his Naive Psychology been acknowledged as a proto-type of action theory.

Summary of Contributions

The main sets of constructs used by the contributors to capture the major action themes, mentioned earlier, concern motivation, emotion, cognition, action, knowledge, the individual actor, and social interaction. Different authors emphasise different constructs and their interrelationships. Propositions concerning the regulation of action by feedback circles or systems, the sequential and hierarchical organization of behaviour, are more prominent in some chapters than in others. Aspects of action that are treated cursorily in some chapters are focused on in others.

VON CRANACH, MÄCHLER, AND STEINER

The chapter most central in expressing the basic tenets of the psychology of action is that of von Cranach, Mächler, and Steiner. Apart from detailing the theoretical approach of their own group and describing their research work and findings, von Cranach and his colleagues set their theory within the perspective of related approaches, such as Hacker's (Chapter 3, this volume) action-regulation theory. Definitions of act and action, and of the attendant notions of actor, plan, and goal, are given. Furthermore, in an effort to facilitate conceptual distinctions, acts are classified according to several dimensions: abstract–concrete (mental–overt), solitary–interactive, short-term–

long-term, and routine–original. Von Cranach et al. direct their own theory "toward the description of the organisation of concrete goal-directed action in the social environment (i.e., concrete interactions)." By *organisation* (and this is of general relevance to the chapters in this volume) is meant the "interdependence of patterns of manifest behaviour, cognition and social meaning (as related to the actor)".

Action is assumed to involve "bidirectional adaptation": action is the link between the actor (his or her cognitions and needs) and the environment, and it is through that link that each affects and adapts to the other. Behaviour is sequentially and hierarchically organised, and complex actions show manifold nested structures. Cognitions play a crucial role in steering and controlling these complex actions, and von Cranach et al. offer a classification of action-related cognitions according to their function, their temporal relationship to action, and their degree of conscious representation.

Von Cranach et al. contend that phenomenal experiences are links in an information-processing chain, and are not mere epiphenomena. Furthermore, non- or sub-conscious cognitions become conscious through attention being focused on them, and it is assumed that what is made conscious by attention reflects these non- or sub-conscious processes. This assumption is basic to the self-confrontation interview method used in von Cranach's research and described later in their chapter.

Motivation, volition, and emotion are construed to have "energizing" (in contrast to "steering") functions. Social environment and others' behaviours are viewed as external sources of social influence on action, whereas scripts, norms, values, and so forth—reflecting social convention and summarised by the concept *social representation*—are seen as internal sources. Interactive action is characterized by the coherence of the concrete acts of two or more individuals by rules that the interaction partners must know; that is, they must share social conventions.

The exposition of von Cranach's theory is elaborate, and in many respects painstakingly exhaustive. The less-well-developed areas concern the nature of social influence and social interaction, the role of emotion, and the nature of the individual actor qua individual. However, like most of the contributors, von Cranach et al. have pointd to those concepts and theories of social interaction and social influence that they consider amenable to integration with, and appropriate for the development and broadening of, von Cranach's theory. In this context they make the important point that "action concepts *act back* on the organisation of action itself."

After presenting the outline and major theorems of von Cranach's theory, von Cranach et al. describe several empirical studies conducted by their group, each of which reflects the descriptive emphasis of the theory. For example, observation systems were developed and applied in a study of manifest behaviour of children fighting over toys. Another observational study concerned how adults arranged a room for children to play in. Considerable effort went into the development of situations suitable for use in the study of action-accompanying cognitions. The self-confrontation interview mentioned earlier is one. It requires actors to watch a videotape showing their previous actions and to describe the cognitions they had during that earlier activity. An alternative method is the "loud soliloquy" in which actors are trained to comment on their on-going action. Von Cranach et al. conclude from these studies that such reports on cognition are indicative of the cognitions actually involved in the production of action.

In a closely related study of interpretations of filmed social action, observers of the film were found to use descriptive and explanatory concepts similar to those of the theory in making their attributions about the filmed actors. A further study of the use of social representations to *organise* social action involved detailed work with psychotherapeutic sessions. All of these studies serve to elaborate the linkages between actions and action-related cognitions.

In the final part of the chapter, attention is shifted to the actor as the originator of acts. People are seen as active rather than simply reactive, although the link between action and the environment must not be lost. Nevertheless, people differ considerably from each other and they show stability over time, so we clearly must understand individuals in terms of their personalities; but von Cranach et al. stress that the individual's personality is expressed in the form of individual and social *action*.

Chapter 2, by its very emphasis on selected aspects of action and its acknowledgement of the importance of other features, raises important questions and indicates important lacunae, not only in our knowledge but also in our ability to conceptualise adequately the phenomena of action.

HACKER

In Chapter 2, von Cranach et al. noted the relationship between their ideas and Winfried Hacker's action-regulation theory. In Chapter 3, Hacker focuses on *task* as the central concept for the analysis of action. Action is task performance, which involves the pursuit and achievement of goals or aims. People relate to the world and other people by acting; action is a relational construct (cf. von Cranach's idea of action as bidirectional adaptation).

Hacker underlines the relational nature of action by arguing that task performance profoundly influences personality development. This apparent leap (from task to personality) is understandable when the notion of task is extended from the short-term tasks designed to produce observable action in the laboratory to long-term complex tasks, experienced by actors as "charges" that have to be interpreted and specified into particular, concrete aims before action can proceed. Such long-term tasks as obtaining a degree, building a house, or controlling an automated industrial process are indeed likely to have an effect on the actor's personality. Similarly, and this is Hacker's particular interest, the evaluation, analysis, and design of such tasks by experts for other people to perform will affect personality development of all the parties involved.

Psychologists can set up task performances to permit the study of action, or they can study naturally occurring actions; the problem is to identify the tasks that are involved in the action. This is necessary in order to understand the action being performed and the psychological processes underlying its generation. The actor, too, must define the task requirements and formulate intentions before he or she can act. Hacker elaborates the psychological aspects of such formulations.

Action is considered in general, and then action in work and learning contexts is treated more specifically. In general, Hacker embeds action firmly in its social context, stressing the necessity of understanding the context in order to understand the action. Moreover, actions themselves are social processes, not only by virtue of co-operation and division of labour, but through the anticipation and manifestation of social evaluation of the results of action. Social evaluation includes self-evaluation, which affects the self-concept (and, thus, personality), and has an important influence on the regulation of action processes by leading to the development of an individual action style. This in turn involves mental rehearsal and planning, and ways of reducing interference during performance. Further, self-evaluation of action—that is, of one's task performance—both depends on and generates levels of aspiration.

Action research, however, is fraught with dangers and difficulties. One is the use of reductional action concepts. These neglect one or more of the defining characteristics of action Hacker has detailed above. Structural reductions over-emphasise formal structural aspects and neglect specific contents. Individual reductions neglect social characteristics: "Social characteristics are . . . simply attached to the actions and are referred to as interactions," thus engendering interactional reductions. Cognitive reductions ignore motivational (and emotional) aspects, thereby neglecting the essential basis for the analysis of action—its goal-directedness. Four levels of action research are distinguishable, ranging from abstract to concrete.

Like von Cranach, Hacker considers access to the cognitions associated with action to be a problem of great importance. Although there is no easy answer to the problem of access, one cannot avoid seeking those cognitions. He then comments on models of action organisation, noting that there is a superfluity of block diagrams and verbal descriptions, both lacking empirical support. However, information-processing studies have yielded valuable insights about the organisation of action and, on the action level, two important sets of structural concepts have proved useful, not just for analytic purposes but also for job design.

First, complete actions have a cyclic structure. The processes constituting the cycle are goal-setting, orientation, design or reproduction of action programmes, selection of modes of action, and checking results against those intended. The intended results, the methods for their achievement, and the conditions to be observed have all been found to be mentally represented and established as the indispensable basis of action regulation. Their representations are subject to change, operating as hypotheses à la Piaget.

Second, goals and action programmes are hierarchically organised and sequentially achieved. This is a useful and widely held assumption but difficult to prove empirically. Some support is available, however.

Hacker then emphasises the links between job autonomy and goal-setting, especially as they pertain to intrinsic motivation, and between cognitive anticipations and motivational intentions. He points out that levels of action regulation differ in terms of the conscious mental capacity required, and that there are wide individual differences in action organisation.

The organisation of action and the setting of the goal around which action is organised can be analysed only to the degree that the analytic model includes a clear and usable conception of goal. Hacker carefully elaborates his notions of goal: goals cannot be attributed solely to the actor, the object, or the situation; they are essentially concerned with relations between objects and men. Goals initiate and control actions and serve as comparison standards for action results; they evoke intentions and thereby are chosen or set by the actors and pertain to their intrinsic motivations.

However, it is the characteristics of the task that at least in part influence the choice of performance goals by the actor, and it is important to discover the particular characteristics of tasks that will lead an actor to set high performance goals. Evidence suggests that the basic task characteristic is autonomy. Autonomy involves the possibilities for goal-setting available to the actor (what Hacker calls ''degrees of freedom'', but also might be termed perceived responsibility), and has been found to be related to the perception of the task, to motivation, to performance, and to other parameters. It is especially interesting that Hacker's group found that ''degrees of freedom'' was more important than ''feedback'' (knowledge of performance with respect to a standard) in its effect on intrinsic motivation. Hacker reviews other studies, in addition to his own, that also indicate the importance of autonomy in work contexts. Actions have effects on actors and so the possibilities for action provided by work influence possibilities for personality development.

Hacker's chapter spans the abstract–concrete levels of action in an impressive way. Motivational, cognitive, and performance features of action are analysed in some detail, while those features (personality, emotion, social interaction) that are not elaborated are commented upon and placed in relation to each other and to the other major constructs in a way that makes clear the author's awareness of the inherent complexities of potential integration.

LANTERMANN

In Chapter 4, Lantermann argues that current theories of action tend to neglect the influence of emotion, and that discussions about the relationship between emotional and cognitive processes as part of an action-generating system have tended to focus on which is prior rather than attempting a delineation of their interactive relationships. Lantermann seeks to integrate this view of cognitive and emotional interaction with the idea of the hierarchical and sequential organisation of action. He sees action as contingent on the possibilities demanded by the environment, and on the knowledge and capacities of the person. Like Hacker, Lantermann employs a feedback notion with respect to motivation—intentions are compared with outcomes during the course of action. After offering a description of action processes, Lantermann introduces his model of action control, which comprises two interacting control systems, one emotional and the other cognitive. He argues that the interrelationship between the emotional and the cognitive systems will differ depending on the intensity of emotion.

The model proposed is complex and is presented carefully. Actions are differentiated according to a variety of criteria, which differ from those employed by von Cranach et al. and by Hacker. Lantermann views his descriptive model as a compromise between a general and a detailed account, which is not designed to take account of all components of action control. Furthermore, he argues that in operational terms it is extremely difficult to distinguish cognition and emotion— these are "more analytical categories for a description and explanation of human action". But in agreement with the prior contributors, Lantermann does acknowledge that the social context of action is a crucial feature of action, and the examples he uses for the explication of his model are about social encounters. Since his chapter is addressed to the neglected area of emotion in human action, Lantermann's treatment of social contexts, like that of von Cranach et al., tends to be limited to considerations of social knowledge, primarily as it is manifested in such concepts as role and convention.

DE WAELE

The "site" of emotion, goals, cognitions, and knowledge, and the agent and producer of action is the individual. Most chapters in this volume are concerned with the description and understanding of human action in general, on the assumption that general statements may ultimately be arrived at about the organisation of all human action. In contrast, De Waele's chapter focuses on individual differences in action and on how individuals may be distinguished in terms of their actions.

No account of human action should fail to discuss the notion of personality. Hacker discusses the long-term effects of action on personality, the ways in which tasks and their design operate to change and control individual functioning. De Waele, in complementary fashion, uses task performance as a means of gaining insight into individuals' functioning. First De Waele offers a detailed and critical review of the present state of personality psychology, from the major psychodynamic theories, to "trait" and "dimension" conceptions, to the more recent "interaction" approaches. De Waele emphasises the assessment of personality as the means by which knowledge about personality processes is obtained, and he critically evaluates methods of personality assessment in both academic and diagnostic contexts. In particular, he reviews the problems arising in extant studies of cross-situational consistency and attempts to demonstrate the universality of personality characteristics.

A major problem stems from the separation of the three basic components of the study of personality: namely, the clinical approach, personality research, and systematic assessment. This artificial separation is due to the institutionalisation of psychology, which has led to distortions of the data on which personality studies are based. These distortions are of three sorts: uncritical use of certain linguistic categories, selective preference for particular methods, and an arbitrary narrowing of the field of personality investigation.

De Waele's account recalls the reference by von Cranach et al. to psychologists' naive theories of action (and also to his assertion that action concepts act back on action). Moreover, even if our language and our exchange of meanings as scientists are inextricably bound up with our language as actors in the everyday world, we assume that research data "can speak for themselves". De Waele argues and demonstrates that this simply is not the case. Further, he argues that what personality theorists and assessors have consistently failed to do is to take account of, to observe and measure, what people actually *do*, that is, human action; nor do they take account of individual biographies in a systematic way (except in individual clinical assessments).

De Waele is not offering action psychology a view of personality and the individual that will amplify a theory of human action in a direct way. Indeed, he sees a psychology-of-action emphasis as a source of resolution of the personality-psychology problems he has described. He expects that "action-analysis can give us a new direct, undistorted access to persons". As he says, the connections between action psychology and the biographical approach are less obvious; they rest on understanding the goal-directedness of human action and in taking account of long-term life goals and aims, similar to Hacker's concept of "charges". This is very much in line with von Cranach's assessment of long-term perspectives as very important, and Hacker's view of the power of autonomy and the degrees of freedom for action offered by specific tasks and by task systems (e.g., in industrial production processes) to affect personality development profoundly. Of course, long-term goals may be difficult to ascertain, although De Waele and his group appear to have had some success over the last few years.

De Waele proceeds to describe his method of Problem and Conflict Situations (PCSs), which he construes as simulations of real life situations where the goal to be achieved is specified and sub-problems have to be solved. The method involves detailed observations of action processes and of the experience of them, and of the social interactions with investigators, together with a detailed interview and subsequent self-confrontation interview (using a videotape of the person's prior PCS performance; see von Cranach). Two particular problem situations are discussed and five examples of the use of their technique are offered. The examples include PCS performances and interpretations in terms of the life biographies of the persons involved.

In summary, De Waele describes means by which interpretations of action of particular individuals can be afforded by a kind of role-taking exercise on the part of partially informed observers, who are required to predict actor's action-choices at specific choice points in the problem-solving process. This is an extremely rich source of information about actor, observer, and action and interpretation processes, and it places the psychology of action and personality psychology in a complementary and mutually facilitative relationship to each other.

CANTER

In his contribution (Chapter 6), Canter also argues that a closer relationship between his own field (environmental psychology) and action psychology would be productive for both fields. Action psychology focuses on sequences of activity that are always and necessarily situated; Canter's interest is in the situations (environmental settings) in which action occurs. Action, Canter argues, can only be understood by reference to the physical context, and the meanings assigned to it, in which the action is performed.

Canter distinguishes the action-psychology approach from that of behaviour-oriented social and environmental psychology, and emphasises three processes that he sees as fundamental to effective social action. These are goal-orientedness, the ways in which people ascribe meanings to physical surroundings and their own and others' actions, and the structuring of situations by reference to social rules and shared definitions. The integration of these three processes by their relationship to the physical context also allows some understanding of how the individual relates to the social world. The relationships between the processes maintain the consistency of patterns of action to be found in any one location.

In discussing the research of his group, Canter expresses a view similar to that of De Waele in that he emphasises the crucial role of research design in limiting what can be discovered, as well as in permitting access to knowledge. Substantively, he contends that people's attributions of intention on the basis of action lead to the association of intentions and goals with locations as well as with dispositions, thereby extending our understanding of attributional processes. The research of his group indicates a body of shared (consensual) definitions of situations couched in terms of who (roles) does what (actions) where (settings), which Canter interprets as reflecting a "cognitive ecology". This view is compatible with recent studies by ecological psychologists that emphasise the importance of role and setting in generating patterns of activity and the subjective experience of satisfaction. Canter goes a step further and locates the social mechanisms for controlling roles (satisfaction apart) in the rule systems associated with roles, especially rules pertaining to spatial behaviour.

EISER

Meanings and interpretations have been regarded as a central feature of action by the authors whose chapters have been summarised so far, and they are the prime focus of Eiser's chapter (7) on social judgements and social action. Von Cranach, Lantermann, and Canter see the individual's stock of social and ecological knowledge as based on consensus, as conventional, and as a necessary store for reference processes by which stored information can be compared to present input. Hacker is somewhat disturbed by the potential "social reductionism" inherent in leaning too heavily on such ideas as role, rules, convention, and so on, with a neglect of the creative, interactional, and improvisational aspects of social action where the actor is not a passive interpreter but a decision-making performer. De Waele is concerned about the influence of implicit personality theories and both lay and institutionalised attribution practices on personality psychologists. Eiser addresses a complementary problem: the fact that the majority of research endeavours concerned with people's ways of interpreting social situations, people, and events have been concerned just with the interpretations as such, and not with interpretations as precursors to, or essential parts of, ongoing action and interaction processes. In his chapter, he demonstrates the links that interpretational processes afford between action psychology and a variety of areas in conventional social psychology.

Eiser reviews work involving attribution theory, expectancy value models, and script and schemata concepts. The communalities between these latter two concepts and the notion of social representation endorsed by von Cranach are especially obvious. Scripts and schemata concepts "explicitly deal with behaviour as an end point through the notion of action rules [and] such work reaffirms the significance of the social judgmental processes of categorization, comparison, selective attention, and evaluation. The simplificatory nature of such processes is vital to a theory of action".

Eiser also addresses some more general issues concerning action psychology. The other authors have implied that action theory is the antithesis of behaviourism, but Eiser points out that, if one is concerned with purposive human action, how can we know what action is purposive and what is not? Eiser then discusses the methodological and interpretive problems involving levels of certainty about the truth-values of objective as opposed to lay attributions.

A further general point concerns moving from discussions of people's interpretations as observers to people's decisions and claims on the basis of their expectancies and evaluations *during* the action process. His discussion of this issue is pertinent to the reliance of von Cranach et al., and others, on the ''confrontation'' and ''loud soliloquy'' procedures for revealing action-related cognitions.

Eiser argues that the concepts of scripts and schemata come closest to satisfying requirements of analyses of social judgement that relate directly to action:

> scripts may be considered essentially as the schemata people hold of sequences of events that occur over time in given situations, in particular sequences of *behavioural* events. As such, they produce a basis for organising our knowledge of action rules and of the appropriateness of given actions in given contexts. . . . [A] theory of how we think about social events and behavioural sequences cannot be content free but must be . . . about . . . our *understanding* of classes of events and situations of which we have had experience . . . much, if not most, of such knowledge is *routine,* in the sense that we are unlikely to be aware that we are using it unless something unexpected happens that makes us re-examine our expectations. (Chapter 7, p. 201)

Having reviewed these potential contributions to our understanding of judgement processes in social action from the research in social cognition, Eiser considers what would be gained by focusing on action and subsequently making inferences about social cognition processes. The problems from this point of view involve the multiplicity of contexts in which action takes place, the relatively automatic unattended-to nature of much of the cognitive processing occurring during social action, and the difficulty of establishing the authenticity of self-reports about motives and decision processes.

The problem of access to the action-related experience and cognitions of actors has been raised and discussed by most authors in the volume. With, perhaps, the exception of De Waele, most of the authors expect such accounts to provide access to cognitive and emotional processes and to contain references to stored social knowledge about roles, rules, and social representations. What is not sought explicitly, and what so far has not received adequate conceptual attention, are the social processes by which such knowledge is achieved, and the means by which people establish its relevance to their individual and joint actions while acting. The next two chapters address this problem, from rather different standpoints.

BRENNER

Brenner's Chapter (8) focuses on action in a particular social context—specifically, the research interview. The research interview has several features that make it especially suitable for Brenner's aim of analysing the situated action processes in a particular and repeatable situation. First, it is a situation that is clearly defined in terms of the actions expected of, and appropriate for, the participants. In role terms, the rights and obligations of interviewer and interviewee are for the most part clearly and conventionally understood. Further, one participant, the interviewer, is (often literally) following a script, and has usually been trained not only to perform her role but also to help the interviewee perform his role correctly. An impressive amount of research data has been accumulated about the interview situation and the actions performed within it, including information about the effects of physical location, situational definition and action (cf. Canter, Chapter 6, this volume), and it also is one for which explicit recording of action is a natural part. Moreover, despite its apparent scripted nature, it is a situation for which there is considerable room for manoeuvre, what Hacker refers to as degrees of freedom. For both participants, the encounter may aptly be regarded as performance of a task, and the goals to some degree are explicated. So, in contrast to many social encounters, the research interview is a relatively open social situation.

It is also a research context, and as such provides the opportunity to achieve some "metamethodological" understanding of one of the more common means by which social scientists gather their empirical data. In this volume, research-interview situations have been employed by von Cranach and De Waele, and have generated many of the research findings alluded to by other authors (especially Canter). An enhanced understanding of this data-collection method would facilitate evaluation of the data it generates, and permit improvement of the measurement procedure itself.

The action-psychological assumptions involved in the research are first presented: action is goal-directed and people's actions express lines of action towards objects and other people in keeping with their goals; as Hacker (Chapter 3, this volume) suggests, action is a relational construct. Second, action requires knowledge of general and specific kinds. Here the idea of script (cf. Eiser, Chapter 7, this volume) is referred to. Action also relies on adequate skill for effective performance, both interpretive (information processing) and motor (expressive and instrumental) skill. Use of feedback systems also is important.

The last two assumptions are closely interrelated, and Brenner presents examples from detailed research-interview action analyses. Action is social, and social action is situated. Chapter 8 confronts these assumptions in a manner not attempted in earlier chapters. Brenner uses the theoretical model developed by McCall and Simmons (1966) to conceptualise the definition of the situation and the negotiation of social and personal identities. This model is interesting in that, apart from being developed from symbolic interactionist conceptions of self and situation (notably those of Mead and Goffman), it also depends on ideas about the mutual and asymmetric contingency of social action (Thibaut & Kelley, 1959). This is important for the psychology of action point of view in that it places goal and goal achievement firmly in the social arena.

On the other hand, the "lines of action" concept that Brenner uses is not exchange theoretical in origin; its analysis for social psychological purposes derives from Turner's classic papers (1956, 1962) on role-taking. Nevertheless, the idea that individual goals are not only contingently achieved but are also (possibly) contingently and probabilistically conceptualised by actors, and perhaps are conceptualised in action rather than motivational terms, is of great importance. The contingency concept is evident but not thoroughly exploited in von Cranach's theory, and the allied notions of autonomy and degrees of freedom are important for Hacker's argument. In Brenner's analysis of the research interview as situated social action, action-steps, presented as illustrative examples, derive from a detailed action-by-action contingency analysis.

The problems of access to the experience of interviewer and interviewee for elucidation of their experiences while acting are commented upon, and von Cranach's use of the self-confrontation interview is discussed.

The McCall and Simmons model introduced for the purposes of action analysis in Chapter 8 brings with it many attendant notions about social interaction that are highly compatible and in some cases are identical to assumptions and themes of the earlier chapters. For example, in delineating the cognitive processes of imputation (role attribution) and improvisation (design and planning of action), McCall and Simmons refer to Bruner's (1958) concept-formation work involving a hypothesis-testing view of cognitive processes. Such a view is in accord with the selective attention function of schemata outlined by Eiser, and with Hacker's ideas of cognitive representations as subject to change with experience. This hypothesis-testing view is implicit in several of the other chapters as well.

In addition, as a cognitive stance, these ideas fit the general idea of role-taking, but as Turner suggests, role-taking is also role-making. Attributions and inferences are inevitably expressed in the performance of action; thus the individual is actively testing hypotheses rather than being merely an observer, a recipient of incoming information. This is in crucial distinction to methodological approaches that allow individual subjects of research to be essentially inactive judges; when acting as well as interpreting, the actor is not doing two things at one time but is doing something altogether different from either passively judging or mindlessly reacting.

Even in the circumscribed interview situation, reliance for goal achievement for both parties cannot rest on shared knowledge of the rules, the social representations, and so on. Some cases of the research interview may well constitute rule-following routines, but there are many examples of what Brenner calls rule-breaking in which corrective action is necessary. For the most part these are handled effectively and often in novel ways that reflect the involvement of identities on both participants' parts (see also the complexities indicated in De Waele's interpretation of his subjects' problem-solving attempts). This strongly suggests that the degree of automaticity in social action, such as it may be, is not of the same depth or quality as the automaticities involved in the motor actions of walking.

KENDON

As noted earlier in this chapter, Kendon's contribution constitutes a social psychological theory of human action. Furthermore, it focuses on goal-directed action, but the goals are not central to the action— although they are crucial. That is, the kind of goal to which his analysis pertains is not the avowed purpose for which the participants are interacting; instead, it is the goal of establishing, maintaining, and regulating a shared frame of reference among the participants in an encounter. Such a goal must underlie the actions of participants in interchanges, but it ordinarily is not the focus of the interchange. Kendon refers to the processes of achieving, testing, and using the common but temporary reference framework as *frame attunement,* and his chapter explores in some detail how such attunement operates.

The distinction between *attentional tracks* is crucial for an understanding of frame attunement. Some of the action is relevant to the main line of business of the interaction, and participants attend to it accordingly. The substantive content of an episode of gossip, for example, would be part of the main line. However, there also is a *directional track,* which contains signs that help to regulate the main activity but are not part of its content. A qualifying facial expression is an example. In addition, there is a *disattend track* such as scratching, smoking, posture shifts, and so on. The participants do respond to the actions in the disattend track, since they play an important part in the negotiation of a shared frame of reference regarding what the interchange will be about. But the disattend and directional tracks are treated by participants as background rather than main track, so that they ordinarily are seen as incidental to whatever "official" act the person is engaged in. Nevertheless, they are seen (or heard).

The incidental activities by which participants co-operatively achieve and attune the shared frame include spatial and orientational positioning, postural adjustments, gaze direction, rhythm (especially the attainment of synchrony), and so on. For the most part, as Kendon notes, the regulatory functions of these activities are highly conventionalized and therefore may vary across cultures and across settings. But he also stresses that the regulatory functions must be served for comprehensible human interaction to occur. Kendon's chapter is an important complement to the other action-psychology chapters in this volume in that it elucidates the non-focal background activity upon which the focal actions described in the other chapters are dependent for their own continuations. Although focal activities vary from one interaction to another, frame attunement must be achieved and maintained in all—and it is accomplished through the action regulators that Kendon discusses.

GINSBURG

The final chapter selectively assesses the current status of human action research and speculates about its future as a paradigm, especially in the context of social psychology in the United States. Ginsburg notes several trends in contemporary social psychological and developmental research that are compatible with an action perspective, particularly because of their emphasis on processes. These include the work on self-presentation and impression management, recent reconceptualizations of attribution processes, certain rule-oriented conceptualizations of moral development, the growing interest in discourse processes, and developmental psycholinguistic research. The meta-theoretical implications of these trends are discussed from an action perspective as well, and it is suggested that they will lead to a reduced reliance on linear, causal explanatory models.

The chapter also reviews a variety of problems inherent in the action approach, some of which are resolvable and some of which probably are not. One problem concerns research design and potentially serious threats to both internal and external validity. Other problems are conceptual, such as the absence of a definition of meaning despite its openly avowed importance in virtually every chapter of the volume. But in general, the prognosis that Ginsburg sees for the psychology of action is a good one, even to the degree of viewing it as part of a vanguard of a new paradigm.

References

Bruner, J. S. (1958). Social psychology and perception. In *Readings in Social Psychology.* (E. E. Marcoby, T. M. Newcomb, & E. L. Hartley, eds.) 3rd edition. pp. 85–94. Holt, Rinehart & Winston: New York.

Heider, F. (1958). *The Psychology of Interpersonal Relations.* Wiley: New York.

Hinde, R. A., & Stevenson, J. G. (1969). Goals and response control. In *Development and Evolution of Behaviour.* (L. R. Aronson, E. Tobach, J. S. Rosenblatt, & D. S. Lehrman, eds.), Vol. 1. Freeman: San Francisco.

McCall, G. J., & Simmons, J. L. (1966). *Identities and Interactions.* Free Press: New York.

Osgood, C. E. (1953). *Method and Theory in Experimental Psychology.* Oxford University Press: New York.

Thibaut, J. W., & Kelley, H. H. (1959). *The Social Psychology of Groups.* Wiley: New York.

Turner, R. H. (1956). Role-taking, role standpoint and reference-group behaviour. *American Journal of Sociology, 61,* 316–328.

Turner, R. H. (1962). Role-taking: process versus conformity. In *Human Behaviour and Social Processes.* (A. M. Rose ed.). pp. 20–40. Houghton Mifflin: Boston.

2

The Organisation of Goal-Directed Action: A Research Report*

Mario von Cranach, Elfie Mächler, and Vera Steiner

The Bernese Research Project

When we began research on the organisation of goal-directed action,[1] two students intended to write a thesis about child interaction (Mueller & Kuehne, 1974). This soon became a project sponsored by The Swiss National Foundation (SNF). The first version of our theory was developed, and subsequently more students became involved. To date, 15 theses on various levels, from "Vorarbeit" to doctoral dissertation, have been produced, and nearly as many are under way. Our SNF research project group (especially U. Kalbermatten) has been the nucleus, but a second SNF project (with Thommen & Ammann) also has been established.

Initially, the scientific climate of academic Western psychology was unfavourable to our approach; we were considered "out of order" even by colleagues in our own institute, and the first author often had to conduct a kind of psychotherapy with his students to strengthen their spirits. So we decided not to publish until we could justify our claims by reference to a greater volume of research findings.

In the meantime, the climate has changed, and action psychology is in vogue, at least in German-speaking countries. Several reports on our research have been published or are in print (von Cranach et al., 1980, 1982; von Cranach, 1982; von Cranach and Kalbermatten, 1982a, 1982b; Kalbermatten and von Cranach, 1981, 1982). In this essay we aim to give a concise overview of the present state of the whole project. More thorough discussions are given in the above-mentioned

---

*The research reported in this article has been sponsored by the Swiss National Foundation. The report depicts the state of affairs at the end of 1982.

[1]Throughout this chapter, we use the term *action* exclusively in the sense of goal-directed action (to be defined below), in contrast to the more general term *behaviour*.

19

sources. First our theory, which is quite complicated, is presented, then the studies related to its various propositions are reported, finally some future prospects are discussed.

Basic Features of a Theory of Concrete Goal-Directed Action[2]

TOPIC AND SCOPE OF THE THEORY

This theory aims at the description and explanation of the organisation of concrete goal-directed action in its normal social environment, and within the constraints of its specific cultural context. A *concrete action* is an action that aims to induce change in the environment by use of manifest behaviour, in contrast to *abstract* (or mental) action, like problem solving, aiming at cognitive achievements. Concrete action is *interactive* when goals or means include interaction with other persons. In our research, we have restricted ourselves to concrete (interactive) action directed towards nearby goals, because its course can be better observed. The term *organisation* refers to the interdependence of patterns of manifest behaviour, cognition, and social meaning, as far as these are action-related, and to the order within these realms.

We hold that in research of this kind, structural description and functional analysis should constitute the first step, and causal analysis only a later step, and that only a wide-ranging theoretical framework makes a functionally valid description possible. Thus our theory is designed as a basis for a comprehensive and coherent description of ongoing action processes. It is meant to constitute a frame for more detailed explanatory theories.

HISTORICAL ROOTS

There are numerous sources in philosophy, sociology, linguistics, and ethology that have influenced our way of thinking. Here, we restrict ourselves to psychology. We concentrate on three main lines of thought that are represented and combined in our theory.

A first and very influential source of action theory is Naive Psychology. Here we have to distinguish between two topics: (1) the common way of thinking about action in everyday life, and its scientific

---

[2]We should like to state that most of the essential ideas that this theory contains are not original, but have already been stated by other authors, sometimes long ago; what is new to an extent, is their combination. For reasons of space, it is not always possible to refer to all the sources.

exploration, as it has been developed in the original work of Heider (1968) and, (2) in a more detailed and sophisticated form, by Laucken (1974). Based on (unsystematic) exploration and phenomenal experience, these authors have presented convincing arguments that lay people in their everyday life make use of psychological explanations that contain, as their core, a well-elaborated theory of action, comprising many important constructs also used in scientific theory: goal, equifinality, decision, resolution, habit, volition, motivation, emotion, and so on. But only in a very limited area, namely *attribution,* have some of Heider's ideas about this topic elicited empirical research, and only recently has the nature of his Naive Psychology been acknowledged as a prototype of action theory. Scientists, however, are Naive Psychologists too, and there are many reasons to assume that it is their shared view, based on commonsense psychology, that has led so many action theorists in different disciplines, from analytic philosophy to Marxist psychology of activity, to use similar concepts.

From the considerations of Naive Psychology, it is not far to the idea of a *retro-action* of concepts about action on the organisation of action itself, as it forms one of the core concepts of symbolic interactionism and phenomenological sociology. A very general formulation (which constitutes, in fact, the basis of our own work) could read: in action, manifest behaviour is governed by cognitions, which in turn are of a social origin. Thus, action is based in society. Obviously, theories of Naive Psychology in general, and also modern attribution theory, should benefit from fitting into this framework. Beyond this principle, modern proponents of this proposition (Goffman, 1961, 1963, 1969; Harré, 1972, 1974; Harré & Secord, 1972) have stressed the related idea that action is essentially rule-governed. The concepts of social convention, rule, and norm have been incorporated into our theory. Similar considerations apply to the concept of knowledge (Luckmann, 1982).

Another research direction, "action-regulation theory", has developed in industrial psychology (Hacker, 1978, and Chapter 3, this volume; Volpert, 1974, 1980), from an integration of viewpoints from Marxist psychology of activity (e.g., Leontjew, 1977; Rubinstein, 1977; Tomaszewski, 1978) and ideas developed in the context of systems theory, computer science, and problem solving (Miller et al., 1960). This theoretical framework constitutes perhaps the most advanced branch of action theory and is backed by a considerable amount of empirical research in general psychology and in industrial psychology. Among its most important propositions are those of the guidance of actions by mental representations (which, in their details, partly correspond to the concepts proposed by Naive Psychology); those about the sequential and hierarchical organisation of behaviour, and the correspondence of degrees of consciousness to levels of regulation; and the importance of regulation by feedback circles. On the other hand, and in contradiction to some of its claims, the scope of action-regulation theory seems to be more or less restricted to individual functioning, and the agent remains nonsocial to a degree. Most of the important assumptions of this approach can be found in our theory, too, although sometimes differently accentuated.

Finally, we should like to point to recent developments of modern cognitive psychology (Aebli, 1980, 1981; Doerner, 1976), namely problem solving and artificial intelligence, where concepts very similar to ours have been developed, with the important difference that they refer to internal (abstract) rather than overt (concrete) action.

STRUCTURE OF THE THEORY

Our theory contains basic postulates, definitions, and empirical sentences. Like any psychological theory, this one is based on a variety of presumptions; most of these have been derived from the literature of psychology and its neighbouring sciences, but they are influenced by our general views about the true nature of human existence in culture. These assumptions are not directly empirically relevant, but form the basis of empirical statements (operationable definitions and testable hypotheses). Because these assumptions deviate, at least partly, from common beliefs of Western psychology, it seems all the more necessary to make them explicit. We formulate them as postulates, since their detailed justification would demand a book of its own.

On this basis, we have derived the empirical part of our theory, which contains both definitions and hypotheses. Because in the present phase of our research the emphasis is on description, the former class has been more fully elaborated; as far as possible, we have tried to include only concepts that we can in fact translate into operations. On the other hand, only some of the possible hypotheses have been actually formulated.

We start our explication from a basic theorem:

Basic action theorem

In goal-directed action (in the context of acts), *manifest behaviour* is governed by (partly) *conscious cognitions* that in turn are (partly) of a *social origin,* so that society (partly) creates and controls the individual's action by controlling his or her cognitions, while the individual, by means of his or her acts, brings societal patterns into existence.

Our theory therefore contains three classes of concepts, referring to manifest behaviour (Class I), conscious cognition (Class II), and social meaning (Class III), as depicted in Figure 1. Each class contains many single concepts; these are interrelated by conceptual and empirical links (Figure 2). To give examples[3]: The *plan* (II) is defined as an anticipatory representation of certain characteristics of the actions' execution, and is thus conceptually linked to the *course of action* (I). If a *node* (I) in the *course of action* (I) receives *attention* (II), a *decision* (II) becomes necessary, which should slow down *manifest behaviour on the operational level* (I) (this is an empirical hypothesis).

Finally, our theory presupposes certain assumptions that are not directly the subject of action theory, but belong to two neighbouring theoretical realms. The first of these is a body of theoretical assumptions about the structure and function of the actor's cognitive system, re-

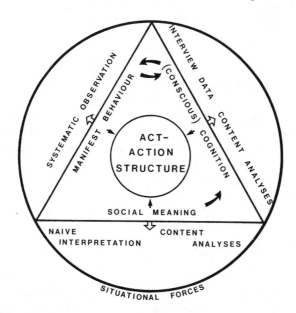

Figure 1.   The triangle of concepts in goal-directed action (GDA). Inside the triangle, the major classes of concepts of GDA theory are depicted; arrows indicate the investigated streams of influence. (Note that the arrow from conscious cognition to social meaning has been omitted; although this feedback certainly exists, it is not part of our theory and research.) Manifest behaviour, conscious cognition, and social meaning in their interaction produce the individual act–action structure. Outside the triangle we have noted the methods related to the particular concept classes. The whole system is embedded in the influences of the given situation, as indicated by a circle.

[3]In this article, we do not treat all theoretical topics in all their detail. The reader is therefore referred to earlier versions of the theory (von Cranach, 1980, 1982). Roman numerals in brackets refer to concept classes.

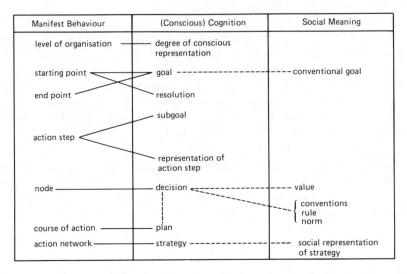

Manifest Behaviour	(Conscious) Cognition	Social Meaning
level of organisation ———	degree of conscious representation	
starting point	goal ——————————	——— conventional goal
end point	resolution	
	subgoal	
action step		
	representation of action step	
node ———	decision ◄————————	——— value
		conventions rule norm
course of action ———	plan	
action network———	strategy ————————	——— social representation of strategy

Figure 2.   Examples of interrelations of concepts in a theory of ordinary interactive action. Solid lines, conceptual relations; dashed lines, empirical relations. (From Hacker et al., 1982, p. 56; reprinted with permission of North-Holland Publishers.)

ferring in particular to the cognitive structures of self, values, and attitudes and their interrelations (von Cranach, 1976, unpublished). The second realm concerns the nature of social representations and their role in the organisation of individual action; this problem is being investigated in two other projects.[4]

Selected Topics of Our Action Theory

DEFINITION OF ACT AND ACTION

The term *act* refers to a (socially defined) unit of action that is characterized by an *action-goal*. Acts occur in socially defined situations[5]; they structure the stream of behaviour into meaningful patterns (Harré, 1972).

[4]A joint French–Swiss research project: "Représentations sociales et organisation de l'action orientée vers un but"; projet de recherche au Laboratoire Européen de Psychologie Sociale, Paris; sous la direction de Mario von Cranach et Serge Moscovici, avec la collaboration de Verena Aebischer et Beat Thommen; and "Handlungskontrolle durch soziale Repräsentationen", NSF project by Mario von Cranach, Beat Thommen, and Rolf Ammann.

[5]The term *socially defined* is meant to indicate that, in society or one of its subunits, there is agreement about the meaning of the situation, which is based on general acknowledgement of its social function. This of course also represents a case of a social representation.

The term *goal-directed action* (or *action* in short) refers to an actor's consciously goal-directed, planned, and intended behaviour, which is socially directed and controlled. The distinction between act and action is important, because it helps us to avoid many conceptual (and consequently empirical) difficulties.

Some of the terms in these definitions have to be further explicated:

An *actor* is a person who is (to a degree) conscious of himself and autonomous, and is held responsible for his behaviour by society. A *goal* is the imagined state aspired to as the outcome of an action. A *plan* is the design of an action, consisting of the anticipatory mental representations of its execution. A behaviour is *intended* if it is voluntarily executed by the actor. An action-related cognition is *conscious* if the actor is subjectively aware of it. *Social control* (internal and external) is assumed to operate through the actors' (conscious) cognition.

Action is thus construed as a behaviour qualified by six mental characteristics. Although these are indispensable parts of the concept, their configurations, and particularly their variations in degree of distinctiveness, intensity, and specific qualities, are already an object of empirical research. In a given case, a behaviour might be qualified as an action if one or even more of he characteristics cannot be traced in the records while all the others are clearly given. Although most of these characteristics are elaborated in particular parts of the theory, some further remarks may be useful here: including the given definitions of goal and plan, our concept of action implies that cognition (which means "information processing") directs behaviour. The term *intended behaviour* introduces volition as an additional requirement. Thus it is assumed that processes of specific activation of energy and force must be added to information processing; in addition to goals and plans, resolutions (execution commands)[6] and continuous efforts are necessary. It is further stated that these processes, to a degree, are consciously monitored, so that the actor is aware of them and can report about them—an idea that presupposes more detailed assumptions about the function of conscious cognition in relation to action, and about attention-directing devices. Finally, our assumption about the operation of social control through individual cognitive control specifies our general assumption that human action is basically social. But it also constitutes an instance of another principle, namely the hierarchical order of steering and control mechanisms, which presupposes a systems view of human action in society.

---

[6]It is interesting to note that the topic of stop commands, which are of a similar nature, has not been treated in the literature.

BIDIRECTIONAL ADAPTATION[7]

Bidirectional adaptation is an essential presumption about the basic functions of action, which influences many of the theory's statements: in order to survive, any system operates under two constraints, those imposed by its environment and those originating from its own internal needs. As to action, we propose:

The function of action is bidirectional adaptation: *outward-directed adaptation* meets the necessities of the actor's relations to his environment, *inward-directed adaptation* considers the actor's own cognitive structure and needs.

We assume that outward- and inward-directed adaptation operate jointly.

TWO-DIMENSIONAL (SEQUENTIAL-HIERARCHICAL) ORGANISATION OF BEHAVIOUR IN ACTION[8]

With Harré, we have distinguished between action and act. The term *action* refers to goal-directed behaviour in general; *acts* are socially meaningful units of action. This important aspect of action structure fits into the more general concept of the two-dimensional organisation of action, which we find in many other action theories, today most explicitly in action-regulation theory (see, e.g., Hacker, 1978, and Chapter 3 in this volume; Volpert, 1982). In short, we state:

---

[7]Note that the term *adaptation* is used here in an active and positive sense, as in biology: it refers to the organisms' constant and active striving to cope with the challenges of given conditions, and does not constitute an instance of weakness (as in some sociologists' uses of the term).

[8]Actually, we are now considering a third dimension, that of *complexity*. It refers to the fact that very often the actor *simultaneously* performs several acts or action steps. Let us begin with the observation that, as a rule, on lower levels of organisation various sequential units (action steps or operations) run off at the same time. During the execution of an act, the actor will simultaneously move his or her head, hands, and feet, and even speak. By closer investigation, we may find that also on higher levels the actor may simultaneously pursue different goals and thus perform simultaneous acts, like skillfully piloting a car through the dense evening traffic while convincing his companion of the dangers of pollution. Thus, simultaneous and consecutive lower level units can serve the one same goal and also different goals. Consequently, we must distinguish between *multiple action,* where simultaneous action steps serve the same goal, and *parallel action,* where several acts are simultaneously pursued. Theoretically, these cases force us to deal with questions of information overload and management (Kaminski, 1973; Fuhrer, 1982, 1983). Methodologically, problems of the allocation of action steps to different acts, and of the establishment of order and coherence in a very general sense, may result. In this essay, no further reference is made to these recent developments.

Action is organised along two dimensions: sequence and hierarchy.

In this statement, *sequence* refers to the temporal pattern of behaviour units on a given level of organisation (simultaneous occurrence included). *Hierarchy* refers to patterns of super- and subordination: higher-order units tend to differ from lower-order ones by extension, inclusiveness (a higher-order unit is related to several lower-order ones), quality, and function (Figure 3). For the sake of simplicity, elements of a similar hierarchical position and function can be conceived as

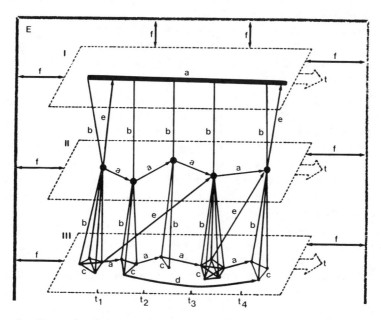

Figure 3.   Dynamic relations between hierarchical levels of organization (LO). (From von Cranach & Harré, 1982, p. 124.)
I, II, III = the three levels of organization.
$t, t_1, \ldots, t_4$ = time.
E = environment (broken line).
a, b, c, d, e, f = different kinds of dynamic relations.

    a = Arrows within a LO in time direction: *sequential* organisation.
    b = Lines between LOs: the dynamic of these lines flows in both directions as *steering* (downwards) and *regulation* (upwards).
    c = Lines between simultaneous units of a LO: for example, of LO III simultaneous movements.
    d = Arrows between units of the same LO that do not stand in a direct sequence (later consequence).
    e = Arrows between LOs and units of LOs that do not stand in direct sequence (later influence on a higher LO).
    f = Arrows between LOs and the environment interaction between all LOs and the environment (at any moment).

located on qualitatively different levels of organisation (or regulation), which are assumed to be interrelated by specific mechanisms of feed-forward and feedback. This general principle is further elaborated in the following assumptions:

Hierarchical organisation

Action is organised and controlled on qualitatively different, inter-connected levels, which may be further structured into hierarchical orders. Higher levels of organisation are mostly organised by choice of supergoals and goals, plans and strategies, and are to a higher degree cognitively and voluntarily steered ("cognitive steering"). Lower levels of organisation are mostly organised by specific mech-anisms (learned skills, motor habits, fixed-action patterns, and taxes in the ethological sense, etc.), and are to a greater degree subcon-sciously and involuntarily steered ("subconscious self-regulation").

Complex actions show manifold nested structures. We emphasize some of the levels thus formed as organisation levels; these are cases where common qualities are exposed over a variety of sequential units. Dif-ferent levels of organisation are consequently qualitatively different. But not each hierarchical level constitutes a "level of organisation"; instead, on each level of organisation, further hierarchical structures can be distinguished. In this regard, our theory differs from other hi-erarchical–sequential models.[9] Different actions can expose different numbers and kinds of organisation levels, and they do so as a rule, just because the flow of action-steering information may be differently structured according to type, task, and history of the given action. So, in contrast to our former view, we no longer hold with a general tax-onomy of organisation levels.

Sequential organisation

In its temporal sequence, action is organised at its various levels into connected segments. Earlier segments determine the later ones and are executed in their service.

---

[9]In earlier versions of our theory (von Cranach et al., 1980, 1982; von Cranach, 1982) we have assumed the existence of three principle levels of organisation: (1) a goal level, on which behaviour is structured into acts through the cognitive determi-nation of socially defined goals; (2) a strategic level on which each act's course of action is structured into sequences of action steps by "cognitive steering"; and (3) an op-erational level on which action steps are organised in their details by means of self-regulation. This assumption has been useful in some of our empirical research; we have however come to the conviction that it constitutes a specific case rather than depicting a general structure.

On its various levels of organisation, the course of action can be described in terms that can easily be transformed into operational definitions: the concepts of starting point, end point, action step, node, characters of node, and network. Let us give examples: Action steps are the smallest units of the course of action on a given level. They are delimited by nodes. At a node, different possible action steps branch off. The various possible courses of action between the same starting and end points constitute a network of pathways. Besides these specific sequential structures, qualitative characteristics of behaviour flow (speed, force, etc.) can be observed. A final remark: it is important to note that the model of two-dimensional (sequential–hierarchical) organisation of manifest behaviour in action reflects the presumed properties of action-steering information processing that is also two-dimensionally organised and operates in sequences of nested feedforward and feedback processes. This constitutes the ''cognitive'' nature of action. If this proposition is not accepted, the model is reduced to a set of unrelated levels of analysis.

COGNITIVE STEERING AND CONTROL[10]

As stated in our basic action theorem, we assume:

Cognitions direct and control action.[11]

In this and the following considerations, the term *cognition* refers to higher-order information processing. Our theory deals with two problems that arise in this context: the structure of cognitive steering processes and the action-specific function and emergence of conscious cognitions. For practical reasons, let us first introduce a classification of action-related cognitions.

Classification of Action-Related Cognitions

Let us begin with a definition:

Action-related cognitions refer, in content and form, to a given action and the related environmental circumstances.

[10]The following definitions and assumptions refer to adult actors in command of their fully developed cognitive abilities. (This concerns especially our operational definition of reflected consciousness; consciousness of course appears in different forms.) If applied to other actors—for example, small children or animals (insofar as these *act* in our sense)—our formulations must be newly examined and modified.

[11]Of course, we do not mean that all cognitions steer actions, nor that all manifest behaviour in action is steered and controlled by cognitions as higher-order information processing.

We classify action-related cognitions according to their function, their temporal relationship to the action, and their degree of conscious representation. The classes that we have thus formed should be systematically linked to patterns of behavioural organisation. Our definition of an action-related cognition demands a functional relationship between a cognition and a given action. If a cognition accompanies an action but does not relate consequentially to it, then, even if it relates to another action or actions in general, it is not considered "action-related" in the present sense.

Classification according to function

Motivation-related cognitions start, stop, facilitate, or inhibit action.
Action-steering cognitions determine the direction of action.
Action-monitoring cognitions survey and control the execution of action.
Action-evaluating cognitions examine the accomplishment of action and its results.

This classification is neither unequivocal nor exclusive. Most cognitions possess their main point, but cross sections and intermediate cases are possible. Thus, decisions serve mainly an action-steering function, while resolutions are primarily action-energizing, but mixed cases are frequent. Reflected emotions serve steering functions in a general sense, but are also motivation related. This is a weak spot: the relationship between steering and energising functions is as yet theoretically unclear (see Hacker et al., 1982). Action-evaluating cognitions, unless they induce a correction, do not influence the accomplished action and its results, but they form a part of its cognitive Gestalt and may influence further actions.

Classification according to temporal relationship

We distinguish between *action execution preceding, accompanying,* and *following* cognitions.

Functionally different cognitions may also differ in their temporal characteristics. Action-monitoring cognitions must be action accompanying; action-evaluating ones must be action following. Energising and action-steering cognitions must be action preceding, but no close temporal relationship between these cognitions and the action is required: it is its very independence from time and space that makes human cognition so uniquely apt for the organisation of action.

Classification according to conscious representation

Action related cognitions differ according to their conscious representation. *Conscious cognitions* are those of which the actor is aware and about which he can report. *Subconscious cognitions* are on the fringe of consciousness, so that the actor is dimly aware of them; they can easily become conscious, just as conscious cognitions can easily become subconscious. Such transitions can occur repeatedly. In regard of their temporal aspect, we can distinguish between preconscious and post-conscious subconscious cognitions. *Nonconscious cognitions* are cognitive processes to which the actor has no access; he cannot report on them but they can be (partly) inferred from their behavioural effects. *Unconscious cognitions* are those that have been repressed from consciousness by defense mechanisms (in the psychoanalytic sense). *Optionally conscious cognitions* can become conscious in relation to the action; *obligatory conscious* cognitions must become so.

This relatively simple classification considers variations in the obvious quality of conscious representation (compare Hilgard, 1980), to which we attribute functional significance. Most important for our theory are the phenomenally represented conscious cognitions, which can in principle be translated into verbal reports, and also the subconscious cognitions. The content of nonconscious cognitions is mostly inferred from the conscious ones. This class, the most comprehensive one, also comprises those cognitions that have been or will become conscious. Unconscious cognitions, in the sense of psychoanalytic theory, cannot yet be treated within the framework of our theory. Finally we have introduced the useful notions of optionally and obligatory conscious cognitions (in the sense of Hacker's [1978] terms *bewusstseinsfähig* and *bewusstseinspflichtig*). In our definitions, these terms refer to the requirement that an action-related cognition should at least once become conscious: *obligatory* therefore does not mean *always* conscious.

Conscious Representation and Attention Processes

In our theory and methodology we emphasise conscious cognition. Here we find ourselves in marked contrast to many cognitive psychologists who tend to neglect conscious representations for theoretical and methodological reasons.[12] These arguments led us to develop a theory that elaborates the properties of action-related conscious representations, specifies mechanisms that are involved in the transition from unconscious to conscious, predicts when an action-related cog-

---

[12]Here, we find the well-known epiphenomenalistic position, but also the view that conscious representation and report are arbitrary selections of ongoing cognitive processes and therefore unsuitable for scientific study. As an example of the latter position, see Neisser (1974, p. 238).

nition should become conscious, and allows a test of these predictions in empirical investigations (von Cranach, 1983). Here, an outline of its general features must be sufficient.

We begin with the assumption that many complex information-processing and acting systems incorporate one or several self-monitoring subsystems, which extract and present important information about the system's own state. Man has at his disposal several such systems, like pain, emotions, and conscious cognitive representations. All of these produce representations, since they select information about neurophysiological processes and translate (encode) it into another qualitatively different form, namely phenomenal experience. Furthermore, we assume that this subjectively experienced information, due in each case to its specific quality, forms a basis for further particular cognitive processes and actions. This is an important point: we understand these phenomenal experiences as functional links in an information-processing chain and not as mere epiphenomena; and it is just on their phenomenal qualities that we think their functional significance is based.[13]

If an information-processing system (as in the human case) incorporates self-monitoring systems, then these will interact. As a rule, the phylogenetically and ontogenetically older ones should be integrated into the younger ones, as occurs so often in the course of evolution. Thus, emotion in the adult human is nearly always embedded in cognitive processes.

Our theory refers to reflected conscious cognition, the most complex human self-monitoring system, although the term *reflected* is often omitted in our text[14]. Since only a few of the very numerous cognitions that can be inferred from behaviour are ever represented, we assume the operation of attention processes that selectively transform nonconscious into conscious cognitions. So much for our basic assumptions. We shall now formulate more precisely those points of our theory that

[13]Let us illustrate this claim with a simple example from the area of pain. Pain is a phenomenal representation of neurophysiological processes that signal that something in the body is wrong, and to a great extent it is this representation, the feeling of pain, that causes the organism to seek improvement and remedy of the bodily state. Because your purulent tooth hurts, you feel the urgent need to see your dentist; and if the pain vanishes (e.g., by use of anodyne drugs or even a kind of yoga technique), this urge is much diminished although the inflammation may continue.

[14]Reflected conscious cognitions are characteristic for the adult human actor who acts in full command of his or her cognitive abilities. If these ideas are applied to other actors, such as small children or animals, as far as these act in the sense of our theory, they should be reconsidered.

concern the direction of attention. Let us start with the following assumptions, which have a long tradition in psychological thinking:

> Nonconscious or subconscious cognitions become conscious through the operation of attention-processes. Attention is either voluntarily or involuntarily directed at parts of the system of ongoing cognitive processes. It is more often directed to hierarchically superordinated than to subordinated cognitions. The focus of attention is relatively narrow.

Thus attention can, but need not, be a goal-directed activity itself. Considering now these statements in relation to our assumptions about the specific action-related functions of conscious cognitions (namely, to enable the organisation and structuring of acts) in improving the results of difficult actions and to facilitate the organisation of action systems, we derive the following attention theorem:

> The actors' attention is directed towards where it is needed in action or stimulated by salient cues.

This proposition serves as a basis for more specific hypotheses, for example:

> Attention is directed to complex and non-routine rather than to simple and routine actions. It is directed to goals, when they are chosen, changed, abandoned, or reached. It is directed to several different actions or action steps at the same time, if these become related or come into conflict. It is directed to those levels of organisation on which information is needed, decisions are to be taken, or for which other difficulties exist.

Obviously, our attention theorem can be further elaborated. Thus, in one of the following paragraphs we discuss the attention-directing function of emotion. Note, however, that these considerations apply only to action-related cognitions, not necessarily to cognitions in general.

Sequential and Hierarchical Organisation of Action-Related Cognitions

Action-related cognitions are sequentially and hierarchically organised: this is the reason why behaviour in action, as stated above, is also two-dimensionally organised.

Hierarchical Organisation. The essential principles of this organisation have already been described.

Action-related cognitions are organised into meaningful units, which can be resolved into lower-order units; thus, a hierarchical structure is derived. Unit formation is determined by two factors, the establishment of meaningful action sequences and the object of the action. Higher cognitive levels refer more to holistic aspects of the act, lower levels more to the details of execution; their specific character depends on their particular content.

Sequential Organisation.   Action-related cognitions tend to repeat an information-processing sequence, the phases of which are:

1. Information input from perception of the environment or recall from memory.
2. Elaboration of this information, also by use of additional stored information, evaluations, and decisions, until goals and plans have been derived.
3. The execution, including decisions, resolutions, and the application of effort and execution control.
4. The final evaluation of the achieved results.
5. The correction of the evaluated action.

This is the complete sequence. In our data we observe many incomplete sequences. Processes of this general nature tend to be repeated; this happens on the various cognitive levels.

ACTION-ENERGISING PRINCIPLES:
MOTIVATION, VOLITION, AND EMOTION

For several reasons it is necessary to introduce these concepts:

1. In the execution of action, we can distinguish between steering and energising functions. Steering mainly determines the direction of action; energising serves the execution of action by providing action energy.[15] These functions are always necessary, but they become conspicuous where barriers have to be overcome in the beginning and execution of action. Our concepts of goal and plan mainly refer to steering. The concepts of motivation and volition provide tools with which to treat the energising function.

[15]Energy is basically a physical concept; if we want to preserve the essence of this term, and to avoid erroneous connotations, we must recognise that there is no such thing as mental energy. Therefore we speak of energy always in a physiological sense. Physiological processes serve to activate this physiological energy and to allocate it to specific purposes. Therefore, we speak of energising rather than energetic functions.

2. In our theory, goals and goal hierarchies appear somewhat as dei ex machina. It seems necessary to consider at least roughly why people arrive at goals. The concepts of motivation and emotion serve this purpose.
3. Emotions and volitions are conspicuous, experienced partial processes of action; therefore we must describe them and try to understand their functions.

In the following text, we restrict ourselves to the most important statements.

Motivation and Motives

Motivation refers to the generalised concept of the drive to act (action tendency). A *motive* is a motivational process that is tending towards a particular action. Motives arise from innate and acquired needs; they steer and energise action. Steering functions serve to direct, control, and evaluate action; energising functions serve to execute action through provision of action energy. In the motive these two functions are not yet separated. Motives are optionally but not obligatorily conscious and therefore not completely controlled. In the fully developed goal-directed action, steering and energising separate and become separately conscious as goal or plan, and as volition.

Our definition of motivation as drive resulting from need is quite traditional. It is however important to stress that motivation also acts as an energising function, since the latter tends to be neglected in modern cognitive motivation theory (e.g., Heckhausen, 1980). The idea presented by Rubinstein (1946) that these two components are united in "activity" and become separated in the development of action provides an explanation for the separate appearance of goal–plan cognitions and volitional processes in goal-directed action.

Volition

Volition is the process of conscious cognitive activation and allocation of action energy. Volitional processes enable the execution and termination of concrete (or mental) actions, the repression of counter-directed action tendencies, and the control of emotions with which they interact.

This statement contains the essence of our conceptualisation of volition: it is conceived as a cognition that refers to action energy. Since such cognitions will occur where specific difficulties arise, volition is (in accordance with our attention theorem) always conscious. The functions of volitional processes are further specified in the following statements:

Volition in concrete action

Volitional processes set, and keep, concrete action in motion (resolution) and facilitate the overcoming of difficulties (effort) which occur in the course of action, by setting free physiological action energy. Action energy results from metabolism in the form of physiological activity, thus enabling concrete and/or mental action.

Resolution to start action

This is a conscious cognition at the beginning of an action, which overcomes inhibitions, releases action energy, and thus starts the action.

Resolution to change the direction or to terminate the action

This is a conscious cognition that mobilizes the energy needed to change or terminate an ongoing action.

Effort

Effort is a cognition that releases energy for the overcoming of difficulties in the course of action. High intensity of effort serves to overcome specific, well-localised difficulties that need more than the amount of energy already available. This is performed by directing attention to the execution command and exclusion of counter-messages; thus, a maximum of action energy is released that may exceed the threshold of physiological structures. Satiation and fatigue are overcome by maximal use of action-energy reserves.

As the reader will notice, we owe much to William James, whose chapter on the will (1890) has hardly been surpassed. In our statements, we have defined resolution as an execution or stop command. This is necessary for the beginning of action: the goal alone does not suffice, many goals are never executed. Resolution is a volitional process that mobilises the energy necessary to overcome physiological inertia; it presupposes goal and/or plan. The difficulties that necessitate effort do not refer to the directives of action, as in decisional processes, but to energy supply. In effort, energy is finally mobilized by directing attention to action, its goal, plan, and resolution—which gives these cognitions priority over competing cognitions.

Emotion

Emotion is a self-monitoring system that provides the organism with a global, qualitatively coloured awareness of its own state in a specific situation.

Our general remarks about the functions of self-monitoring systems apply also to emotions. A somewhat similar view of emotion has been proposed by Bull (1950). We assume that a distinction must be drawn between emotions that are consciously represented and those that are not. The particular nature of conscious emotion is based in the content and encoding of its information, and in its particular functions.

Emotions provide the actor with two kinds of information:

1. They inform him (or her) that something in the situation and/ or his own action is important for him *(notification of importance)*.
2. They tell the actor about his own general stance (positive or negative, in combination with additional qualitative characteristics) in regard to that event *(notification of stance)*.

In these statements the reader will recognize the influence of Arnold (1960) and Lazarus (1966). From its two contents, two (related) functions of emotion emerge.

Attention-directing function

Corresponding to their notification of importance, emotions direct the actor's attention towards salient eliciting events, which thus become objects of conscious cognitive activity; where no event is salient, searching activities are elicited.

Motivating function

Corresponding to their notification of stance, emotions elicit motivational tendencies, which exert energising and nonspecific directing effects upon action; these can be consciously represented. Energising effects give rise to variation in rigour, persistence or arousal/inhibition, and can be consciously reflected in cognitions of resolutions and effort. Nonspecific directive tendencies codetermine the choice of action goals and subgoals and influence subconscious self-regulation.

From both of these functions, specific hypotheses concerning action-related emotions can be derived, for example:

The evaluation of goal-achievement arouses emotions.

Note that our assumptions about emotion and its functions refer to detailed effects on action regulation and also account for energising (behavioural and consciously represented) phenomena: emotion is related to motivational and volitional processes, and it tends to be integrated into the ongoing cognitive processes. Because this integration is so strong, we do not conceive of an independent action-regulating emotional system (for an alternative viewpoint compare Lantermann, Chapter 4, this volume).

SOCIAL STEERING AND CONTROL

Theories of social influence on the organisation of action must deal with both external control by environmental devices and the execution of influence and power by others, and internal control exercised through internalised cognitive, emotional, and motivational structures (like knowledge, scripts, rules, values, needs, etc.) Here, our focus is internal control by internalised cognitions and corresponding emotional and motivational processes. Corresponding to our basic action theorem, we assume:

Internal social control operates through the actors' cognitions, which in turn steer and control action.

In a first phase of our research, we employed the concept of social convention: the notion that ideas that are shared by many members of a communication community would be the most effective in controlling the individual members' action. Theoretical assumptions and research that pertain to this idea have been presented by von Cranach et al. (1980, 1982) and von Cranach and Valach (1984). More recently, we became convinced that it is not just the agreement between group members that is important, but the organisation of ideas and emotions into more or less coherent systems that serve important societal and individual needs: we adopted the notion of social representation (Moscovici, 1961). In two research projects a theory of action control through social representations has been developed (Thommen et al., 1982; von Cranach & Moscovici, 1983), and empirical research executed.

For the sake of simplicity, let us treat the theoretical assumptions of these two phases separately. This seems justified, since the former can be understood as specific hypotheses within the later, more comprehensive theoretical framework. In our first approach, we began by decomposing the statements given at the beginning of this section into three theorems:

Convention theorem

Members of social communities share certain representations concerning matters of functional importance; these are the *social conventions.*

Attribution theorem

Social conventions influence the actor's *perception, conscious represen-tation,* and *interpretation* of his own and of others' behaviours as well as his definition of situations.

Retroaction theorem

Self-attributions (based on social conventions) act back on the actor's organisation of his own actions.

Our concept of attribution does not exclude direct experience of one's own cognitions (conscious representation), as other attribution theories sometimes seem to do; but we hold that experienced cognitions are interpreted in terms of social conventions.

The three theorems, like our assumptions about cognitions in general, imply assumptions about shared information:

Action-relevant knowledge

Action-related cognitions are based on relevant knowledge. Relevant knowledge comprises all those cognitions that have been acquired and stored in long-term memory before the action, and are related to aspects relevant for the action.

This short statement implies that all aspects of knowledge, including memory functions, are of importance for action theory. *Relevant* is knowledge concerning the actor himself, his partner, the situation, and the act and action.

Aspects of knowledge refer to a general characteristic of action-related cognitions, including social conventions. It is also necessary to consider their specific functions and content. In this respect, we distinguish between two groups of concepts: *conventions, rules* and *norms* refer to the (more extrinsic) impact of societal expectations and pre-scriptions; *values* (and their operation in *attitude processes*) refer to the (more intrinsic) influence of internalised social standards.

Social conventions, rules and norms

Social control by conventions, rules, and norms operates through the actors' cognitive steering and self-regulation. A *convention* is a cog-nition based on concordance in a community. Conventions guide the interpretation of concrete acts by the actor himself, his partners, and observers. A *rule* is a convention that refers to an act or action. Ob-jectively, a rule generates regularity of execution of the act; subjec-tively it generates feelings of obligation in the actor, and consequently evaluations of appropriateness by himself and other members of the community.

A *norm* is a rule considered to be reinforced by sanctions. The degree of correspondence between a goal (or subgoal) and a norm (and, to a minor degree, a rule or a convention) influences the actor's cognitive control and self-regulation.

Our concepts of convention, rule, and norm contain partly shared components and thus constitute a coherent system; we must note that these components are behavioural (e.g., regularity of execution) and cognitive, emotional, and motivational. The second statement is a consequence of our convention theorem; it can be used to define and operationalise many other concepts (e.g., conventional goal). Similarly, our last statement can be decomposed into various hypotheses. For the concept of norm, we consider it sufficient if the possibility of a sanction is seen. Let us now turn to our second group.

Values, action attitudes, and attitude processes

Values (positive and negative) and value objects (positive and negative) influence the choice of action goals; attitude processes mediate between values and actions. A positive *value* is an enduring nonspecific cognition that is highly estimated and aspired to. A positive *value-object* is a positively evaluated environmental object. (Negative value and negative value-object are correspondingly defined). If a goal is anchored in a value, the act can be experienced as serving the realisation of the value (elimination of the negative value). Corresponding statements can be formulated for value-objects. Within an act, an attitude (action attitude)[16] is the elaboration of a preference hierarchy of action steps or courses of action, in relation to a specific object in a specific situation. It constitutes an *attitude process,* which integrates evaluations of objects and situations, and the action-related demands of the situation.

These statements are based on the assumption that values and action attitudes are essential means of inner-directed adaptation. Values are part of the central cognitive structure of the person. They are nonspecific (in contrast to goals) and are qualified by positive or negative tendencies. (What is said about the function of values, also refers, *cum grano salis,* to value objects). Values can serve as general guiding principles for action, since they give rise to goals through the attitude process. In addition to this impact, they also influence the course of action in decisions at nodes. Our concept of action attitude differs in essential

---

[16]We have introduced the term *action attitude* in order to avoid confusion with the traditional attitude concept.

points from traditional attitude concepts that seem to refer rather to judgmental processes without direct action consequences.

In our recent studies, we have developed a more comprehensive framework: a theory of action control through social representations. Let us summarise its most essential ideas: We are departing from the concepts of cognition and knowledge as defined above. We assume that society and its subunits organise their knowledge (the knowledge of their members) about important social and nonsocial matters (e.g., norms, factual or action knowledge) in the form of social representations.

Social representations

  Social representation designates the ordered, abstracted, and typified stock of knowledge of society or one of its subunits. A social representation contains the central representations of its object: values, norms, attitudes, and different kinds of knowledge (e.g., categorical, functional, or action knowledge). It constitutes the super-individual symbolic system; it can be institutionalised and transferred.

Thus social representation is basically a sociological construct.

These collective knowledge systems serve several functions for society:

Functions of social representations

  Social representations delimit one group from others, provide their members with common interpretations of the world, and organise and communicate their actions, which in turn represent materialisations (concretisations) of the social structure.

Individual members of social units integrate these social representations, in the form of individual social representations, into their cognitive systems:

Individual social representations

  Individual social representation designates a social representation of those of its parts a person has integrated into his cognitive system. Interacting with a reference group, the individual adopts parts of its social representations; in this process, the latter are adapted and changed. Corresponding to the degree of change, individual social representations show a more conventional or privatised form: more typified by a high degree of social sharing, or more specific for the individual, with a low degree of social sharing.

Thus, we are studying the sociological construct of social representation as a psychological construct on an individual level. From our definition it becomes obvious that the constructs used in our earlier studies—conventions, rules, norms, and values—can be understood as particular subclasses of individual social representations. Besides individual social representations, the individual commands individual knowledge with little or no social meaning (e.g., personal life experiences). We assume that individual social representations serve several functions:

Functions of individual social representations
Individual social representations define group membership and help the individual to identify with his group; they aid in self-presentation; they form a basis of communication. They enable orientation and the interpretation of social reality. They are essential cognitive means in the organisation, evaluation, and justification of action.

It is this latter function in which we are mainly interested: the steering, control, evaluation, and justification of action. As a general principle, we assume that individual social representations serve as a link between the social representation of the group and individual action, by acting on action-related cognitions.

Further assumptions concern the conceptual and figurative aspects of the encoding of social representations, and the cognitive processes of comparison between the various individual social representations (*dialogue externe* and *dialogue interne*).

Classification of action-relevant knowledge
Individual social representations and individual knowledge constitute the total amount of the action-related knowledge of which the individual has command. Action-related knowledge can be subdivided into the following content classes:

- *Positive and negative values* are enduring non-specific cognitions, which are aspired to or rejected (e.g., beauty or honesty).
- *General knowledge* (e.g., knowledge of fundamental interaction rules) is accessible to every member of society.
- *Knowledge of norms and rules* refers to regulations specific to the general context of activity.
- *Contextual knowledge* (e.g., what the patient knows about psychotherapy) refers to the general context of activity.
- *Situation-specific knowledge* (e.g., knowledge of the patient about the first session) refers to the specific situation within the context in which the act is performed.

- *Personality knowledge* contains general knowledge about the characteristics of human beings and their functioning as interaction partners.

- *Person-specific knowledge* refers to particular action partners, and to the actor himself.

- *Planning and action knowledge* embraces particular knowledge about action organisation, and about goals, strategies and operations of particular acts.

The importance and the particular content of these classes depends on the particular study. This classification is not exhaustive.

Action-Relevant Knowledge and Action

In a model of action organisation (Figure 4)[17] we have depicted our assumptions about the connections between action-relevant knowledge (including individual social representations), information-processing, and manifest behaviour. This model also serves as a basis for the empirical investigation of the processes of internal social control. It is in line with the structure of our theory and our assumptions about the organisation of behaviour and cognition in action. In contrast to other parts of our theory, we do not assume that all these cognitive processes are necessarily consciously represented.

The model contains constructs from three realms, manifest behaviour, information-processing and action-relevant knowledge. Our assumptions about the organisation of manifest behaviour coincide with what has been said in the section on two-dimensional organisation of action. We have renounced further elaboration for the moment. The constructs of information-processing have been sequentially ordered into the three phases of situational orientation, action planning and execution, which can be further subdivided into specific action-related cognitions. Action planning and execution are interrelated by decision processes. The hierarchical aspect is mainly depicted in the system of goals and subgoals that steer the other information processes. Since all these processes are action and situation-related, they are of a relatively short duration.

Action-relevant knowledge, our third realm, contains long-lasting goals, values, and the various knowledge classes already described. These enduring cognitions are to a great extent individual social rep-

---

[17]This model has been developed in a study of interactive action in psychotherapy (Thommen et al., 1982).

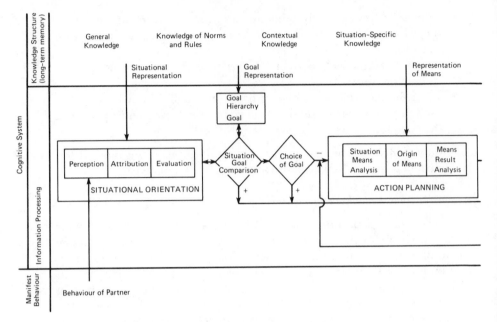

Figure 4.   A model of action organisation and social control.

resentations; like all knowledge they interact with action-related cognitive processes.

Mutual influence of knowledge and action-related cognitions

In the course of action-related cognitive processes, knowledge is actualised to function in the organisation of action; in this process, knowledge itself is stabilised or changed in its content.

Can we describe more closely how knowledge has an impact in the context of action-related cognitions? There are different modes of impact which can be distinguished:

Detailed processes of knowledge impact

In its actualised form, knowledge itself can constitute a particular action-related cognition (e.g., a "script" may be transformed into an action plan).

Knowledge can provide the basis for an action-related cognition (e.g., a perpetual scheme can act as the basis for the perception, recognition or classification of a situation).

Actualised (normally, consciously represented) knowledge can perform a specific role in a specific cognitive process (e.g., a value

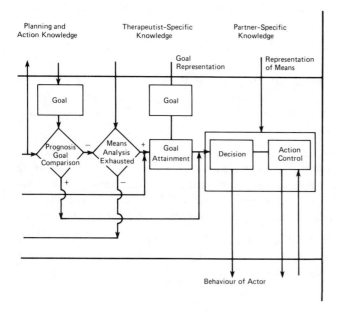

Figure 4.   *continued.*

as a standard in an attitude process, factual knowledge as part of planning or as a criterion in a decision).

The first two of these statements form a continuum; the second two may contain identical knowledge elements. It would seem important to determine how knowledge is actualised. Here, however, we cannot offer more than a very general assumption:

In the course of action, knowledge is evoked, in the form of cognitive processes, by figurative or conceptual properties of the action situation, or of ongoing action-related cognitions.

Next, we have to deal with the action-relevant functions of knowledge. First let us state:

Knowledge functions in all sequences of action organisation and acts on all kinds of action-related cognitions.

Without going into details, we want to emphasize the following instances:

Knowledge serves the functions of recognising and classifying situational cues, selecting goals and plans, choosing between competing alternatives, arriving at resolutions, activating action-related emotions and volitional processes, controlling and evaluating actions, and justifying previously produced action-related cognitions and actions in general.

Finally, maintaining our distinction between more conventionalised and more privatised individual social representations, we have developed hypotheses about the impact of these forms of knowledge on action. To give a few examples:

Conventionalised individual social representations lead to uniformity and interindividual, transsituational similarity of action; they lead to a decrease in conscious representation. In the case of a deviation from a conventionalised individual social representation, the actor experiences conflict that increases conscious information processing.

Privatised individual social representations lead to greater individual variability of action. They demand a higher degree of conscious representation and more substantiation and justification.

INTERACTION

Interactive action is a focal point of our interest. Here we distinguish between interaction in general, communicative acts, and communicative action steps:

Social interaction is the system of two or more actors' behaviours that are characterised by mutual influence. It is structured by the coherence of individual concrete acts and by rules that are specific for interactions and situations. The connection of the interacting partners' individual actions is based on the objective connection of their goal structures, which is reflected in mutual subjective knowledge of action structures, goals and plans. Mutual knowledge of action is based on conventionalised social representations, which refer to goals, plans, and strategies and form a basis for the perception of mutual action steps as characters of nodes.

A *communicative act* is a concrete act with a communicative goal. A communicative action step is directed towards a communicative subgoal. Communicative action steps are co-ordinated by the codes of the communication modalities. Concrete instrumental acts can contain communicative acts or action steps.

The most essential of these assumptions are that the connection of different partners' acts constitutes an important structuring factor of interaction, and that mutual contingency (Jones & Gerard, 1967) is based on mutual perception of action steps at nodes. The importance of various kinds of interactive rules is stressed. Further statements refer to hypotheses concerning the role of social representations in interaction:

> In communicative acts between actors who belong to a group with the same social representation, the conventionalised individual social representation forms the common basis of understanding; it enables meaningful interaction, that is, interaction in which social meaning is produced. In interaction with a partner who shares the social representations of another group, the actor must consider this individual social representation (deviant from his own) in his action organisation. In interaction between group members, privatised individual social representations must be substantiated.

So far we have outlined our theory. It is not simple, although still certainly a simplification of what is really needed. Psychologists who cherish parsimony will not approve of this way of proceeding; but we are convinced that to be useful a theory must not simplify its object too much. And human action in society does not constitute a parsimonious system.

Empirical Investigations

At first, most of our research was performed without a model. We had to adapt existing methods and to develop new ones; and we were primarily interested in finding out whether the factors and relationships that our theory assumed could be detected at all. These studies were mostly concentrated on one of the sides of our conceptual triangle and referred only occasionally to relations between several sides. Later, we began a comprehensive study of the total system of action that embraced all the three types of constructs; this study lasted several years and is now nearly finished. In addition, several studies on particular aspects of goal-directed action have been performed; here, we should like to mention studies on the action-related functions of self-talk, on the conscious representation of action-related cognitions, and on the internal social control of action through social representations.

THE ORGANISATION OF MANIFEST BEHAVIOUR

The Fight for the Possession of a Toy

These first studies have already been reported (von Cranach et al., 1982; von Cranach & Kalbermatten, 1982); therefore, we can be brief here. We investigated a particular type of action in the interaction of children in the kindergarten, the fight for the possession of a toy.

Possession fights have characteristics that make them particularly suitable for our investigations: they are not staged but occur frequently without instruction in the children's normal environment, the kindergarten, and they can easily be detected. Possession fights are clearly structured, since the children follow their true goals and only one of them can win; but they are also sufficiently differentiated: the repertoire of our children consists of about 30 different action steps (strategic level); within these, there is also considerable variation (operational level).

Method. In several studies, over 300 possession fights have been videotaped and analysed, some in great detail. Although the various investigations used slightly different observation systems, they all followed the same basic methodology, which was directly derived from our theory: on account of their bidirectional organisation, the acts were studied by aid of *nested observation systems* (see Kalbermatten & von Cranach, 1982). These investigate behaviour as organised on levels that expose the characteristics of hierarchical dissolution and qualitative differences. Thus the theoretical levels of organisation that we assumed at the beginning of the study find their correspondence in the operational levels of analysis in the method. On each level of analysis, observation units are differently defined due to qualitative level differences (Figure 5); consequently, the units are also differently validated. In our specific case we worked on three levels of analysis: a goal level, a functional level, and a structural level.

On the *goal level,* we defined the specific act of the possession fight, using three characteristics:

1. Two actors (children) claim possession of the same object.
2. These claims occur simultaneously (temporal overlap).
3. At least one of the actors wants to exclude the other from the use of the object.

This is a social definition, based on common social knowledge, which allowed for a reliable determination of the fight (95–100% interobserver agreement). It was validated by proving its social nature: a group of naive judges successfully performed the discrimination without knowing our definition.

On the *functional level* the course of action was structured into action steps functionally defined in their essential parts. These could be reliably discriminated. "Functional definition" means that an action step is defined with regard to its function for achieving the act's goal; *negative functions* are possible. A functionally defined unit is validated by

	Levels of Organisation	Levels of Analysis ➔	Observation Units
I	ACT LEVEL	GOAL LEVEL ➔	SOCIALLY MEANINGFUL
	conscious representations of goals	goal constructs	molar, "natural" socially defined
II	STRATEGIC LEVEL	FUNCTIONAL LEVEL ➔	FUNCTIONAL
	cognitive steering and control	action step etc.	socially meaningful, "natural" functionally defined
III	OPERATIONAL LEVEL	STRUCTURAL LEVEL ➔	STRUCTURAL
	subconscious self-regulation	elements of action steps	molecular, physically and structurally defined

Figure 5. The interrelation between (theoretical) levels of organisation, levels of analysis, and observational units in the hierarchical model. (From von Cranach & Harré, 1982, p. 128; reprinted with permission of Cambridge University Press.)

empirical proof of the function. Thus, the function of the action step "nonverbal threat" was conceived of as preventing fighting by its antecedent symbolic announcement; the empirical investigation showed that the courses of action that contain "nonverbal threat" in fact contain less fighting and were much shorter in general. The reliability of these functional categories is usually quite high. Our observation systems contained about 30 nonverbal (e.g., "approach", "withdraw", "grasp-take away", "fight", etc.) and verbal categories (e.g., "beg", "claim", "verbal threat", "order", etc.).

On the *structural level,* the single-action steps were described in their spatial and temporal details. Our categories on this level contained body-movements and -positions, temporal descriptions, spatial relations, orientations, etc. They tended to be rather comprehensive (many items!) and were different for each action step. The items tended to be physically defined and could be reliably assessed.

Selected Results.   Since we investigated in these studies only one kind of act, the possession fight, questions concerning the distribution of different acts on the goal level were not considered. We searched, however, for general factors that predict the outcome of the possession fight (a variable at the goal level). The combined results from four related studies (Gugler, 1976; Indermuehle, 1983; Kalbermatten, 1977; Mueller & Kuehne, 1974) indicate that goal-attainment was alternatively influenced by dominance-hierarchy and possession-norms of the group.

On the strategic level, we investigated several subsamples. For a sample of 62 fights, we classified the repertoire of action steps according to classes of functionality (clearly positive or negative functions;

"multifunctional" action steps, which can serve several functions; action steps of "alternative" function towards another goal; "reactive" action steps). As was to be expected, the distribution of these classes was distinctly related to the outcome of the fight. Next, we assembled the network of pathways in our sample. This network proved to be very complex, although it showed less variation than would be expected by chance. The analysis of the most frequently used pathways again revealed relations to the fight's outcome: the winner's network is different from the loser's. There were also interesting individual differences in the preferred pathways. Gugler (1976) developed a measure of similarity of action courses; he analysed another set of 94 fights and found that individual networks differed significantly if the partner was kept constant.

A richer insight into the dynamics of behaviour organisation in action can be achieved by analysis on all levels, including the operational one. Since these analyses are extremely laborious, we confined ourselves to the analysis of eight action steps (approach, grasp–take away, secure, nonverbal threat, fight "for object", fight "against partner", let go, use of object) with regard to their coherence with important features of the total act, including other action steps, and to the details of their operations (Indermuehle, 1983; Kalbermatten, 1977; Mueller & Kuehne, 1974). The results show consistent and strong relations of the action steps' organisation on the operational level to antecedents and consequences on all other levels; they support our assumptions about inside and outside directed adaptation in the regulation of the behavioural details. Thus, to give two examples: the details of the approach movement (strategic level) are consistently related to the groups' system of possession norms (antecedents, higher level), to the details of the following grasp movement (strategical and operational level), and to the fight's outcome; he who has the better claim and approaches, and who grasps differently, wins. This is a case of regulation by an internal standard (inwards-directed adaptation). The success (goal-level) of the action step "fight for object" is related to the variation, adaptedness, timing, and effort of its (operational level) detailed movements; or, who fights better, wins. This is an instance of regulation by instrumental standards (outwards-directed adaptation). Analyses so far have shown a very differentiated organisation; functionally stronger action steps seem to expose a clearer structure than weaker ones. We slowly get an idea of the processes involved in multilevel organisation of action, but a greater number of descriptive studies seems necessary to complete the picture and to develop models that could be submitted to a more rigorous test.

Preparing a Room for Children's Play

In a more recent study (still in the evaluation phase), we observed how the actors arranged a room for a group of children to play in. The actors were students from a kindergarten teachers' seminar, they worked in pairs or alone. In these studies, we used a more flexible observation system with five to seven hierarchical levels of analysis. This variability takes into account the phenomenon that primarily separated units amalgamate in the development of routine. The comparison of scientific with naive judgement seems to show that agreement between these two groups of data is low on the lower, structurally defined, and high on the higher, socially and functionally defined, levels of analysis. To conclude, we generally believe that our functional approach proves fruitful; it seems to be truly the function that selects the structure. It is highly encouraging to see that our theoretical concepts concerning the details of hierarchical and sequential organisation can in fact be translated into observations. So it is possible to determine reliably the concepts of the "course of action" and to give revealing multilevel descriptions of manifest behaviour in action; descriptions that can include tests of relationships between detailed single variables give a more coherent and convincing picture than we could achieve with other methods. Finally, we conclude that the separate analysis of manifest behaviour is a necessary but incomplete step in the analysis of action. As our theory asserts, the true action structure can only be reconstructed from the joint establishment and combination of behavioural and cognitive data.

CONSCIOUS COGNITION

Functions of Action-Execution Accompanying Cognitions

Conscious action-accompanying cognitions were studied in several situations. In two investigations we studied the inter-action between teachers and students during their normal ongoing courses (Lang, 1979; Morgenthaler, 1979). In another study, Steiner (1980) investigated the cognitions of interacting pairs who were working at assigned tasks like cooking or packing a parcel. All these were exploratory studies in which we developed and tested our methods and tried to achieve preliminary insights into the properties of action-related cognitive processes. In the already-mentioned study on "preparing a room for children to play", the organisation of action-accompanying cognitions to manifest behaviour is systematically investigated. Other ongoing studies concern the role of cognition in sporting activities. As a consequence of the methods used, the scope of all these investigations is restricted to conscious action-accompanying cognitions.

Method. In our studies we wanted the actor to report what he remembered of his conscious cognitions (including perceptions and emotions) during fixed periods of the act; this report was to be evaluated from the viewpoint of our theory. In particular, we developed a scheme that consists of the following steps:

1. The actor performs a meaningful act under conditions as natural as possible.
2. A videofilm of his action is taken (filming should disturb as little as possible).
3. Immediately afterwards, the video is played back to the actor; in a more or less standard interview, he reports about his remembered cognitions.
4. The protocol of the actor's report is analysed for the occurrence of cognitions related to action theory.

Let us now look at steps 3 and 4 in more detail.

Self-Confrontation and Interview. Phenomenal experience shows that, during ongoing action, action-related cognitions are consciously experienced. Cognitive psychologists explain this as an effect of information processing in short-term memory (STM). (Atkinson & Shiffrin, 1971; Ericsson & Simon, 1980; Shallice, 1978). In our interview, we cannot draw from STM, but we can try to make the interval between action and self-confrontation as short as possible. Self-confrontation should lead to increased "self-awareness" (e.g., Wicklund, 1979); anyhow, according to our experience it is a method that tremendously facilitates the recall of action-accompanying cognitions. This advantage may be countered by the disadvantage that, by looking at the ongoing behaviour, the reported action-related cognitions might be over-synchronised with behaviour. We tried to counterbalance this and other errors by our interview techniques. Various procedures were tested. In our last studies we tried the following: the videofilm was shown in fractions of 15 seconds; after each fraction a semi-standardised interview was administered in which the subject reported about content, time of occurrence, and other features of his action-accompanying cognitions. Cross-questions and playbacks were systematically applied to avoid self-attribution (instead of remembering) and misplacing, as far as possible. Studies of the method itself are necessary and under way. A self-confrontation interview concerning an act of 5 minutes' duration may last up to 1 ½ hours and produces 20 pages of transcript.

Content Analysis. Here we followed the assumption that the meaning of verbal statements is always latent and can be ascribed only on the basis of social experience (Lisch & Kriz, 1978).[18] To achieve objectivity, the rules of coding as well as the coders' decisions have to be laid open. This leads to very thorough, nearly ideographic forms of analysis. The code system originally used (Morgenthaler, 1979) contained about 70 carefully defined categories; later systems have been more restrictive. Lang (1979), who performed a test–retest study with 4-month interval, acting as a coder himself, achieved a high correlation. In the course of our research, we became more and more aware of the fact that the actors' reports are inherently hierarchically structured; so we began to develop hierarchical systems of content analysis.

Selected Results. What are the action-accompanying cognitions an actor will report? Our first studies yielded descriptive results that sustain our expectations quite well. Explicit hints to cognitive activity as well as reports of conscious cognitions related to interactions refer to difficulties in the course of action; goals tend to be mentioned in the beginning, in the case of decisions, and in the end phase of action. Behaviour on the operational level especially tends to be mentioned where its execution meets difficulties.

In an experimental study, Ochsenbein (1982) constructed an "action parcours", a mechanical construction task in which difficulties were hidden at various levels of the act (e.g., a screw needed for the construction had no thread). 88% of the predicted difficulties were mentioned in the self-confrontation interview, making up for a third of the utterances. Another third concerned non-predicted difficulties, the last third other action-related cognitions. Only about 3% of the utterances did not refer to the ongoing action. This result confirms our expectation that conscious action-accompanying cognitions are predictable processes and not unruly concomitants of action.

Within this expected concentration on problematic issues, we do find, however, that all the concepts that we have defined in our theory are in fact represented in our data: they partly reveal further substructures and divisions we did not expect. Some of the concepts, like goals or cognitions of action steps, seem to be unitary, lower-level action-

---

[18]This is in contrast to the classical method of content analysis that is maintained to analyse the *manifest* content (e.g., Berelson, 1952).

related cognitions; others, like plans, strategies, and decisions, constitute higher-level superordinated cognitive processes composed of the former units.[19] As to the assumed flow of information, the emphasis of reports seems to rest on input (e.g., perception of environmental events and own preceding behaviour) and information processing (e.g., plans, evaluations, and decisions); output-related information processing mainly concerns the energetic side (resolutions), monitoring, and evaluations. Feedback processes are occasionally reported.

It seems noteworthy that the superordinated cognitive action processes seem to constitute rather ordered, nearly stereotyped sequences. Several of these have been identified (Morgenthaler, 1979); as an example we have reported the typical order of cognitions in decision processes. These correspond to our assumed attitude-processes in "action-attitudes"; they tend to begin with a perception of the actor's own, or the partner's, action steps, proceed with preliminary interpretation trials and considerations of goals or plans, culminate in the evaluation of decision criteria like rules or values, and end with decisions and resolutions. But we can also identify *judgement-attitudes,* which resemble the traditional attitude concept. These are not concerned with the actor's own behaviour, but typically constitute evaluations of other persons' verbal statements and therefore do not immediately lead to consequences (except the decision about whether to articulate them or not).

Thus, in this case, social control operates on the individual level through the impact of values on decisions (attitude processes). Values determine the choice of goals on all levels; goals may also represent social conventions. In the situations so far investigated, explicit rules and norms seem to play a minor role. In some cases, we were able to describe the relations between value conflict, goal conflict, and behaviour conflict.

Our method also proved adequate for describing cognitive patterns of ongoing interactions, so we have collected examples of the development of thought processes in group interaction and of the goal structures of interacting pairs.

"Thinking out loud" is frequently used as a method for the investigation of ongoing conscious cognitions (Klinger, 1978). On the basis of our theory of action, Engeli (1982) investigated the loud soliloquy in a theoretical and empirical study. His subjects had to practise soliloquy for several days before undertaking problem-solving tasks while

---

[19]In our first reports (von Cranach et al., 1980) we erroneously underestimated the latter's frequency and importance, since we had not yet understood their superordinated and composed nature.

talking aloud to themselves in an experimental situation. Their utterances were content-analysed and compared with manifest behaviour; in a post-interview additional information was retrieved. Engeli concludes from his data that the solioquy is not just an epiphenomenon but functions in the service of outward-directed adaptation as a speech act that serves the steering, execution, and control of action. The soliloquy also serves inward-directed adaptation in the context of motivational and emotional processes. Similar to conscious cognition, the soliloquy occurs in the context of difficulties in the course of action it helps to overcome. To sum up, with the aid of our specific methods we arrived at interesting results with high face validity. It seems to be possible to gain insight into the operation of action-related cognitions. Many results confirmed our theoretical expectations, others revealed unexpected and surprising patterns: Action is in fact accompanied by a variety of conscious monitoring, steering and evaluating cognitions. This cognitive activity reveals more complexity but also more systemic order than we expected. The organisation of action might constitute a true function of consciousness. The comparison of these findings with the interpretations of naive observers should reveal the social basis of action.

SOCIAL CONTROL

Naive Interpretations

We investigated social meaning by eliciting and evaluating interpretations of actions by naive observers. In several studies, different episodes were presented. Nuesch (1976) showed her naive observers the interaction of a mother with her 3-year-old child during their joint meal; Grichting and Herrmann (1978) and Eichenberger, Joss, and Moser (1978) used the possession fight in the kindergarten; Valach (1980) and Mächler (1981) studied the arrangement of toys in a kindergarten room. These studies have also been reviewed by Kalbermatten and von Cranach (1982).

Methods. In all these studies, the investigators proceeded in two consecutive steps:

1. They showed the naive observers a videofilm of an ongoing action and asked them to interpret what they saw.
2. They analysed these reports for the perceived occurrence of action-related cognitions, following the definitions of our action theory.

Within this general scheme, various different procedures have been used: The presentation of the film could occur in (1) consecutive trials, narrowing down the instruction from mere structuring or description to explicit demand for attribution of action-related cognitions and indication of the behavioural clues used; or (2) in 15-second intervals followed by intensive questioning. Interpretations could be given as verbal reports in interviews or as written questionnaire answers in a group situation. The analysis included forms of content analysis (including hierarchical systems) and comparison with the manifest behaviour; questionnaire data were analysed by multidimensional scaling.

Selected Results. *All* important cognition concepts that our action theory contains are used in attribution; they differ in frequency, but this may largely depend on the general context of activity, and a low frequency does not necessarily mean low importance of a concept. Attributions seem to be directly proportional to the manifest course of action. That means that the quantity of attributions augments the quantity and quality of the manifest course of action, as well as their social meaningfulness and with it the functional action interpretation.

In our studies, among the most frequent concepts are goals, information input and retrieval, emotions, resolutions, and action attempts, and also action steps and actions. "Mere behaviour" is mostly attributed where the observer cannot retrieve enough information to attribute more meaningful concepts. Besides the concepts of a dynamic action-process, we also find concepts that refer to more static personality traits, such as attitudes and dispositions.

In all these concepts attributed interactivity may be reflected. Attribution occurs with varying interobserver agreement; many attributions show very high agreement (up to 100%). It seems that the frequency of these attributional concepts is determined by social conventions within which exists a spectrum of individual attributional tendencies. The attributed concepts are grouped in meaningful clusters (e.g., "beginning" and "end" of action, "cognitive control", and "social control") and are attributed with high reliability (correlation between two independent groups and test–retest correlation with a 6-week interval—both about 0.90).

Goals and related concepts constitute the basis of perceiving and structuring ongoing action; action-goals (goals delimiting acts), which frequently occurred in descriptions, were attributed with high agreement on instruction to search for goals; these were also the goals reported by the actor himself. In our interactive studies, these "conventional" action goals were mainly interactive (antagonistic or co-operative) in nature. Action-goal attribution also seems to occur within the context of perceived goal hierarchies, but in general higher agreement about super-goals is difficult to achieve.

These results refer primarily to the convention-theorem (compare our statements about "social control"), which we consider confirmed *cum grano salis*. They also sustain the attribution theorem, in so far as attribution of conventional cognitions to others is concerned, and they form a pre-condition for the investigation of the retroaction theorem. The importance of the goal-concept is underlined.

Action Control through Social Representations

Social control through social representations was investigated in a first project conducted by Aebischer, von Cranach, Moscovici, and Thommen (von Cranach & Moscovici, 1983). The study proceeded in three steps: first, the social representations of two schools of psychotherapists concerning the nature of psychoneurotic disturbances, the client–therapist relationship, and therapeutic techniques were investigated. Second, the individual social representations of the therapists were studied; and third, the therapists (and the clients) were observed and filmed during therapy, and the therapists' action-accompanying cognitions retrieved. In a post-interview, additional information was obtained. The results confirm our expectations about the action-organising functions of social representations; in fact there are only a few important action-accompanying cognitions unrelated to social representations. Individual social representations and individual knowledge seem to function in a similar way. The actors' specific styles of thought seem to be related to the social representations. Further studies in a similar context are under way.

The Actor: Originator of Acts

Let us finally emphasise an essential point: the actor is the source of the energy and directedness that characterises action, and is not a puppet on the strings of society and situation. Of course, it would be foolish to deny the latters' importance; we conceive of an active person who acts in given situations (including other persons) as a member of society. But the sequence in which we have ordered these terms indicates the importance we wish to assign to them.

Thus, we consider it an essential theorectical assumption that the actor, equipped with his cognitions, emotions, and will, and on the basis of his personal history, constitutes the necessary condition for the emergence of action; a dynamic figure against varying backgrounds, he produces meaningful and coherent sequences of acts. Other conditions, like situational dimensions, scripts, rules, and so forth are always present, important, and influential, but insufficient if they stand alone. Therefore, and perhaps in contrast to other opinions, we hold that:

> It is not the situation that produces acts, but *the actor within a situation* (the environment of his emotions, motives, cognitions, and behaviour). Rules, scripts, and grammars do not produce acts (not even in the specific case of the ritual, which is not the subject of our theory) but exert influences on their structure by operating through the actors' cognitions. Computer analogies are misleading if they do not include the client and the operator as parts of the acting (or problem-solving) system.[20]

But although we see people, like other organisms, as primarily active and not reactive, we should not like to construct a false dichotomy: any action must contain reaction to the environment, else it would lose its adaptedness; any adapted movement is at one and the same time an activity of the organism and a reaction to the environment. The ideas we have stressed in this final paragraph are meant as a theoretical antidote against the traditional fallacies of an exaggerated environmentalism, and the modern temptations of information-processing technology. Our research praxis should allow for the true description of the interplay of all factors.

Acknowledgments

We are grateful to Vincent Brunner, Beat Gugler, Katrin Indermuehle, Urs Kalbermatten, and Ladislav Valach, co-workers in the SNF project, and to the students and candidates, whose names are cited in this essay. Without their ideas and efforts, this research would not have been possible.

References

Aebischer, V., and Thommen, B. (1983). *Représentations Sociales et Organisation de l'Action orientée vers un But.* (Rapport de la DGRST). Laboratoire Eruopéen de Psychologie Sociale, Maison des Sciences de l'Homme: Paris.

[20]The script "how to buy a shirt" provides only an incomplete frame, to be filled by strategic and operational planning; and it remains without effect if the actor does not want to buy a shirt. Similarly, grammar does not determine whether something is said and what is said, and only very incompletely how it is said.

Aebli, H. (1980). *Denken: Das Ordnen des Tuns.* I: *Kognitive Aspekte der Handlungstheorie.* Klett-Cotta Verlag: Stuttgart.

Aebli, H. (1981). *Denken: Das Ordnen des Tuns.* II: *Denkprozesse.* Klett-Cotta Verlag: Stuttgart.

Arnold, M. B. (1960). *Emotion and Personality.* Columbia University Press: New York.

Atkinson, R. C., and Shiffrin, R. M. (1971). The control of short-term memory. *Scientific American, 225,* 82–90.

Berelson, B. (1952). *Content Analysis in Communication Research.* The Free Press: Glencoe, Illinois.

Bull, N. (1950). The attitude theory of emotion. *Nervous and Mental Disease Monographs,* Nr. *81.*

Cranach, M. von. (1982). The psychological study of goal-directed action: Basic issues. In *The Analysis of Action: Recent Theoretical and Empirical Advances.* (Mario von Cranach & Rom Harré, eds.). Cambridge University Press: Cambridge.

Cranach, M. von. (1983). Über die bewusste Repräsentation handlungsbezogener Kognitionen. In *Kognition und Handeln.* (L. Montada, K. Reusser, & G. Steiner, eds.). Klett-Cotta Verlag: Stuttgart.

Cranach, M. von, and Harré, R. *The Analysis of Action: Recent Theoretical and Empirical Advances.* Cambridge University Press: Cambridge.

Cranach, M. von, and Kalbermatten, U. (1982a). Ordinary interactive action: Theory, methods and some empirical findings. In *The Analysis of Action: Recent Theoretical and Empirical Advances.* (Mario von Cranach & Rom Harré, eds.). Cambridge University Press: Cambridge.

Cranach, M. von, and Kalbermatten, U. (1982b). Ordinary goal-directed action in social interaction. In *Cognitive and Motivational Aspects of Action.* (W. Hacker, W. Volpert, & M. von Cranach, eds.). North-Holland Publishers: Amsterdam, pp. 52–66.

Cranach, M. von, Kalbermatten, U., Indermuehle, K., and Gugler, B. (1980). *Zielgerichtetes Handeln.* Hans Huber Verlag: Bern. (English version: *Goal-Directed Action.* Academic Press: London [1982].)

Cranach, M. von, and Valach, L. (1984). The social dimension of goal-directed action. In *The Social Dimension.* (H. Tajfel, ed.). Cambridge University Press: Cambridge.

Dörner, D. (1976). *Das Problemlösen als Informationsverarbeitung.* Kohlhammer: Stuttgart.

Dörner, D., Kreuzig, H. W., Reither, F., & Staendel, T. (Eds.) (1983). *Lohhausen. Vom Umgang mit Unbestimmtheit und Komplexität.* Hans Huber Verlag: Stuttgart.

Eichenberger, E., Joss, Chr., & Moser, Chr. (1978). *Der Urteilsprozess in der Zielattribution.* Unpublished dissertation. Psychologisches Institut der Universität Bern: Bern.

Engeli, M. (1982). *Das handlungsbegleitende laute Selbstgespräch.* Unpublished dissertation. Philosophisch-historische Fakultät der Universität Bern: Bern.

Ericsson, K. A., & Simon, H. A. (1980). Verbal reports as data. *Psychological Review, 87,* No. 3, pp. 215–251.

Fuhrer, U. (1982). Defiziente und sub-optimale Strategien des Handelns im Umgang mit hoher Aktivitätskomplexität. In *Psychologische Beiträge,* Band 24, 1982, S. 583–600.

Fuhrer, U. (1983). *Mehrfachhandeln in dynamischen Umfeldern.* Hogrefe Verlag: Göttingen.

Goffman, E. (1961). *Encounters.* Penguin Books: Harmondsworth.

Goffman, E. (1963). *Behaviour in Public Places.* The Free Press: New York.

Goffman, E. (1969). *The Presentation of Self in Everyday Life.* Allen Lane: London.

Grichting, Chr., & Herrmann, M. (1978). *Der Attributionsprozess von Handlungszielen.* Unveröffentlichte Vorarbeit. Psychologisches Institut der Universität Bern: Bern.

Gugler, B. (1976). *Zur Erfassung und sequentiellen Analyse des Streitgeschelens bie Vorschulkindern.* Unpublished dissertation. Psychologisches Institut der Universität Bern: Bern.

Hacker, W. (1973/1978). *Allgemeine Arbeits- und Ingenieurpsychologie.* Deutscher Verlag der Wissenschaften, Berlin. Hans Huber Verlag: Bern.

Hacker, W., Volpert, W., & von Cranach, M. (Eds.) (1982). *Cognitive and Motivational Aspects of Action.* VEB, Deutscher Verlag der Wissenschaften: Berlin. North-Holland Publishers: Amsterdam.

Harré, R. (1972). The analysis of episodes. In *The Context of Social Psychology.* (J. Israel & H. Tajfel, eds.). Academic Press: London.

Harré, R. (1974). Some remarks on "rule" as a scientific concept. In *Understanding Other Persons.* (Th. Mischel, ed.). Blackwell: Oxford.

Harré, R., & Secord, P. F. (1972). *The Explanation of Social Behaviour.* Blackwell: Oxford.

Heckhausen, H. (1980). *Motivation und Handeln.* Springer Verlag: Berlin.

Heider, F. (1958). *The Psychology of Interpersonal Relations.* Wiley: New York.

Hilgard, E. R. (1980). Consciousness in contemporary psychology. *Annual Review of Psychology, 31,* 1-26.

Indermuehle, K. (1983). *Motorische Abläufe, Ziele und Strategien—Versuch einer Verhaltensanalyse auf drei hierarchisch geordneten Niveaus.* Unveröffentlichte Diplomarbeit. Psychologisches Institut der Universität Bern: Bern.

James, W. (1890). *Principles of Psychology.* Holt: New York.

Jones, E. E., & Gerard, H. B. (1967). *Foundations of Social Psychology.* Wiley: New York.

Kalbermatten, U. (1977). *Handlung: Theorie–Methode–Ergebnisse.* Unpublished dissertation. Psychologisches Institut der Universität Bern: Bern.

Kalbermatten, U., & Cranach, M. von (1982). Attribution of action-related cognitions. Paper to the XXII International Psychological Congress, Leipzig. In Brandstätter, H., Hiebsch, H., Kelley, H. H., & Petrowski, A. W. (Eds.). VEB, Deutscher Verlag Wissenschaften: Berlin.

Kaminski, G. (1973). Bewegungshandlungen als Bewältigung von Mehrfachaufgaben. *Sportwissenschaft, 3,* 233-250.

Klinger, E. (1978). Modes of normal conscious flow. In *The Stream of Consciousness.* (K. S. Pope, & J. L. Singer, eds.). Plenum Press: New York. pp. 226-258.

Lang, J. (1979). *Gruppenarbeit in der Schule analysiert mit der Theorie konkreter Handlungen.* Unveröffentlichte Diplomarbeit. Psychologisches Institut der Universität Bern: Bern.

Laucken, U. (1974). *Naive Verhaltenstheorie.* Klett-Cotta Verlag: Stuttgart.

Lazarus, R. S. (1966). *Psychological Stress and the Coping Process.* McGraw Hill: New York.

Leontjew, A. N. (1977). *Tätigkeit, Bewusstsein, Persönlichkeit.* Klett-Cotta Verlag: Stuttgart.

Lisch, R., & Kriz, J. (1978). *Grundlagen und Modelle der Inhaltsanalyse.* Rowohlt: Reinbeck.

Luckmann, Th. (1982). Individual action and social knowledge. In *The Analysis of Action: Recent Theoretical and Empirical Advances.* (Mario von Cranach & Rom Harré, eds.). Cambridge University Press: Cambridge.

Mächler, E. (1981). *Analyseansatz zur Fremdattribution einer interaktiven Handlung.* Unveröffentlichte Lizentiatsarbeit. Psychologisches Institut der Universität Bern: Bern.

Miller, G. A., Galanter, E., & Pribram, K. H. (1960). *Plans and the Structure of Behavior.* Holt: New York.

Morgenthaler, Chr. (1979). *Zur subjektiven Perspektive handelnder Personen.* Unpublished dissertation. Psychologisches Institut der Universität Bern: Bern.

Moscovici, S. (1961). *La Psychanalyse, Son Image et Son Public.* Presses Universitaires de France: Paris.

Mueller, H., & Kuehne, K. (1974). *Zur Analyse interaktiver Episoden.* Unveröffentlichte Lizentiatsarbeit. Psychologisches Institut der Universität Bern: Bern.

Neisser, U. (1974). *Cognitive Psychology.* Appleton-Century-Crofts: New York.

Nuesch, F. (1976). *Wahrnehmung von Zielstrukturen bei einer Mutter-Kind-Interaktion.* Unveröffentlichte Lizentiatsarbeit. Psychologisches Institut der Universität Bern: Bern.

Ochsenbein, G. (1982). *Aufmerksamkeitsprozesse in ziel-gerichteten Handlungen.* Unveröffentlichte Lizentiatsarbeit. Psychologisches Institut der Universität Bern: Bern.

Rubinstein, S. L. (1946/1977). *Grundlagen der Allgemeinen Psychologie.* VEB, Volk und Wissen, Berlin. 7 Auflage 1977.

Shallice, T. (1978). Dominant action system: an information-processing approach to consciousness. In *The Stream of Consciousness.* (K. S. Pope, & J. L. Singer, eds.). Plenum Press: New York.

Steiner, V. (1980). *Zielstrukturen in konkreten interaktiven Handlungen.* Unveröffentlichte Lizentiatsarbeit. Psychologisches Institut der Universität Bern: Bern.

Thommen, B., Ammann, R., & Cranach, M. von. (1982). Handlungsorganisation durch soziale Repräsentationen. *Forschungsbericht aus dem Psychologischen Institut der Universität Bern,* Nr. 6.

Tomaszewski, T. (1978). *Tätigkeit und Bewusstsein. Beiträge zur Einführung in die polnische Tätigkeitspsychologie.* Beltz Verlag: Weinheim.

Valach, L. (1980). *Untersuchung zur Reliabilität der Attribution ausgewählter handlungstheoretischer Konstrukte.* Unveröffentlichte Lizentiatsarbeit. Psychologisches Institut der Universität Bern: Bern.

Volpert, W. (1974). *Handlungsstrukturanalyse als Beitrag zur Qualifikationsforschung.* Pahl Rugenstein: Köln.

Volpert, W. (1980). *Beiträge zur psychologischen Handlungstheorie.* Hans Huber Verlag: Bern.

Volpert, W. (1982). The model of hierarchical-sequential organization of action. In *Cognitive and Motivational Aspects of Action.* (W. Hacker, W. Volpert, & M. von Cranach, eds.). Holland Publishers: Amsterdam.

Wicklund, R. A. (1979). Die Aktualisierung von Selbstkonzepten in Handlungsvollzügen. In *Selbstkonzeptforschung.* (F. Sigrun-Heide, ed.). pp. 153–169. Klett-Cotta Verlag: Stuttgart.

3

On Some Fundamentals of Action Regulation*

Winfried Hacker

Goal-Directed Action as a Relational Category

Actions are processes by means of which people realise their relations to objects, to each other, and to the world about them. Psychologists study individual actions by investigating the performance of concrete tasks. The ways in which actions are evaluated and designed, as a developmental condition of personality, may be viewed as a central concern of psychology.

TASK AS THE CENTRAL CATEGORY

The central category of psychological considerations of action is the *charge* (i.e., the general aim, responsibility, demand, from the actor's point of view), or its interpretation or redefinition as a task, since decisive determinations of the regulation and organisation of actions are achieved by means of the "objective logics" (Rubinstein, 1958) of the task content. Task performance effects changes in the environment; as four-digit relations (Miller, 1971; Rubinstein, 1958), tasks define:

- which changes are realised,
- in which object,
- under which conditions (by which means and ways), and
- by whom.

"Long-term tasks which organise and determine human life for many years", therefore, "are an important component of personality" (Tomaszewski, 1981, p. 21).

The amorphous set of internal and external demands experienced

*On the occasion of the centenary of Walter Blumenfeld's birthday.

63

by the actor that constitute the charge (or "self-set task") have to be reformulated, redefined, in terms of more precise intentions as precursors to action. The redefinition of charges comprises several psychological aspects that concern (Hackman, 1970):

- the degree of comprehension of the demands involved or the demands to be derived; and
- the appraisal of the comprehended demands in relation to the level of aspiration, the needs and personal values, of the actor, and also of his (more or less accurate) assessments of his potential success in performance.

For action performance, the subjective appraisal of the following relations is crucial:

- the relation between perceived demands and own abilities,
- the relation between expected effort and expected utility together with its instrumentality (in the sense of Vroom, 1964),
- the degree of motivation to cope with these demands, and
- the actual abilities available for achievement.

In general, activities differ, first of all in terms of the tasks involved, since these provide the content peculiar to the actions. Further differences arise from the mode of realisation, which can be "impulsively" or volitionally goal-directed, for example, or the kind of realising operations used, which will depend on the degree of skill. Since such actions involve (conscious) transformation of global aims (charges) into more specific tasks, they share some distinctive characteristics.

ACTION AS A RELATIONAL CATEGORY

First, we construe the concept of action as implying a five-figure system in which the following features are interrelated:

- processes of influence and alteration, involving changes in information or energy; directed toward
- objects whose objective laws[1] have implications for, and will exert influence on, any effort to achieve alterations in them;
- direction toward anticipated results;
- performance by certain means and under certain context conditions; and

[1]These inherent laws of the objects to which action is directed have to be widely comprehended. In tasks involving dialogue, for example, they can mean regularities of the partner's or the opponent's behaviour.

- actors with abilities in, and with attitudes to, the activities which, in turn, will influence themselves and others.

Concepts of action that do not meet this five-figure relation, or that will reduce it, are not commensurate with the nature of action.[2]

Restricted to working and learning activities, this relation system allows us to specify the following characteristics:

- Actions in work will create or change objects with respect to the division of labour.
- Actions are goal-directed, anticipated, and volitionally regulated; these characteristics depend on the (at least partial) mediation of the satisfaction of needs by wages.
- The changes that can be achieved are subject to laws of the object itself and to the methods and means available to the actors.
- The goal-directed changes are also determined by the preconditions, qualifications, needs, and intentions of the actors.
- Via needs and intentions, action is interrelated with socially determined individual systems of values.
- Reactively, the performance of actions will change people. The development of actions and the development of personality are interrelated. The possibility of analysing one's own actions and of critically assessing them makes a decisive contribution to self-development.
- In any case, actions are social processes. This holds even for the case of individual performance, where no cooperation with others is involved. In work and learning contexts, this social aspect derives from the division and combination of labour and from the social evaluation of the results that are produced for other people, mostly in paid employment. This social evaluation is anticipated by the worker and thus will contribute decisively to task regulation.

To begin with, the above-mentioned evaluation of one's own actions is discussed in detail, given its importance for the development of personality; the major characteristic of goal setting is dealt with in the section on "Goals as the Decisive Regulation Instance".

The importance of the critical assessment of one's own actions should not be restricted to its influence on the self-concept of the individual. Rather, there are important task-regulating processes arising from such

[2]Recently, the description of this relational structure with the case grammar (Fillmore, 1968) has been thoroughly discussed (Aebli, 1980).

critical self-analysis. These may lead to the development of a critical and rational action *style* of a person. This style involves

- acting according to intentions with a conscious effort to insulate oneself from impinging influences (e.g., from disturbances),
- mental rehearsal of modes of action prior to practical performances, or
- planning, as the mental pre-design of a future reality.

Finally, a particular level of aspiration will result from the workers' self-consciousness regarding their own actions and the respective conditions of performance. This is valid, for example, with respect to the possibilities of the individual being responsible for achieving a relatively complete end-result that will demonstrate his personal efficiency, or with respect to the possibilities of performing actions of manifest importance to other people.

These aspirations or needs for a definite level of action content can contribute to conscious self-development by means of actions being systematically designed or selected according to their developmental potential. This assertation is supported by evidence from labour-turn-over studies.

REDUCTIONAL ACTION CONCEPTS

Neglect of any one of the characteristics outlined above will reduce the variety of real instances of action that can be analysed or evaluated, and such reductions would not provide an adequate basis for the design of actions. There are different forms of reduction, for example:

- *Structural* reductions, which overemphasise the formal and general structural aspects of action, while simultaneously neglecting the specific tasks performed with the respective specific concrete objects.
- *Individual* reductions, which view actions as individual processes and thus neglect their social characteristics. Consequently, these characteristics are outwardly simply attached to the actions and referred to as "interaction". These *interactional* reductions are an inevitable concomitant of individual ones.
- *Cognitive* reductions, which ignore the actually irreducible unit of cognitive and motivational features, inclusive of emotional processes. Consequently, there is neglect of the crucial role of the goal in task regulation and the development of mental processes and, thus, the goals themselves.

Differentiating the *levels* of action research may help us to avoid such reductions (Lompscher, 1979). Actions may be considered on the following nested levels:

- the level of philosophical abstraction as to subject–object relations,
- the psychological level of the relations between activity and personality that will require long-term investigations,
- the level of individual actions as components of activities, and
- the level of information processing and the cognitive processes, which is concerned with the mental and neurophysiological bases of action regulation.

Available knowledge enables some empirically based statements to be made on the level of *actions*. However, there are few methodologically incontestable and substantial findings; these are difficult to obtain, given the lack of conclusive causal links between overt individual actions and enduring characteristics of personality. Links with the information-processing approaches of cognitive psychology are often hypothetical, since this approach mainly involves investigations into elementary processes and ignores their dependence on the task and the interrelationships between mental processes in complete actions.

The theoretical Achilles' heel of the members of the so-called applied psychological disciplines who are actually required to design ''new'' actions and action systems is that, in order to meet societal demands, they are continually forced to transfer between the different levels for which the fundamental disciplines of psychology do not supply the means, while at the same time, they are (legitimately) criticised for dubiously bridging the gaps.

CLASSES OF TASK-DIRECTED MENTAL CATEGORIES

Psychology deals with mental aspects of tasks and the respective actions by which they are achieved. With regard to methodology, three classes of task and action-directed mental categories have been distinguished by von Cranach et al. (1982):

- Mental processes and representations causing and guiding action by means of orientation and regulation. They are real conditions and causes of definite forms of task realisation.
- Mental processes and representations accompanying actions that occur during action, while not, however, guiding it.

- Mental processes and representations explaining, attributing, and justifying actions simultaneous or subsequent to their performance, though not necessarily matching the actually effective categories of guided or caused actions.

These distinctions are important for at least two reasons: on the one hand, the mental categories that may become conscious and may be reported, the so-called cognitions, are only one element of the action-causing and action-guiding processes, and they do not even encompass all the mental processes that determine result or effort. This does not take account of the fact that goal-directed action is, at least, backed by an intention, that is, the result of the decision to achieve the goal, accompanied by decisions about ways and means. Mental aspects of action-regulation, therefore, will involve *more* than the mental processes and representations that may be reported.

On the other hand, not all the cognitions that occur in connection with tasks are actually involved in guiding action (cf. the discussion of Nisbett & Wilson, 1977). Here, the mental processes concerned with explaining the action, the attributions, must be emphasised. Most often, these processes develop as difficulties in task implementation arise, or in response to calls to explain or justify actions. Often, logically complete explanations of strategies are presented. These, however, depend greatly on knowledge of efficient relations and pertinent standards of values (possibly integrated within complete "naive action theories") as well as being dependent on the self-concept, and thus they need not be the mental processes and representations that actually control action. Consequently, not all the processes and representations reported in connection with actions were necessarily involved in causing or guiding action in a particular task.

Central problems of methods of psychological action analysis result from these relations between report and reality (Bainbridge, 1974; cf. von Cranach et al., 1982; Leplat and Hoc 1980).

Some Problems of Models of Action Organisation

To date, the literature has not been short of block diagrams of action regulation (e.g., Kaminski, 1981), or of verbal descriptions of action organisation (e.g., Tomaszewski, 1981). Attempts at their empirical confirmation or disconfirmation, however, can hardly be found. Thus the dispute will be inefficient, though verbose. Unless speculative treatment of action concepts is limited, a loss in seriousness cannot be avoided.

On the information-processing level, there are important, mostly chronometrical, attempts to identify elementary units (cf. Klix, 1976) and some steps toward taxonomies of cognitive elements have been made (Miller, 1971). Weighing their usefulness in support of action research is a future task.

On the action level, there are two connected classes of structural concepts that in practice prove their worth as heuristics of analysis, evaluation, and job design.

CYCLIC STRUCTURE OF COMPLETE ACTIONS

Within the well-founded and obviously undoubted feedback structure of complete actions, it is appropriate to differentiate the phases of preparation and implementation, and of action-causing and action-guiding mental processes and representations.

A more precise differentiation of constituent processes and of models of action-guiding mental representations of the ongoing procedures is, at least, of practical use. Following Tomaszewski (1964), the following processes may be differentiated:

- Goal-setting; that is, the anticipation of, and intention to, effect a future result by calculating means, ways, effort, and effect with a definite utility or with the appropriate instrumentality. The goals set are action-controlling memory items. Actions derive their subjective meaning from these goals.
- Orientation, particularly in the action-guiding memory representations and in the environment.
- Designing or reproducing action programmes as operations within action-guiding memory representations. These programmes fix the means and ways associated with partial goals.
- Selecting *definite* means and ways from alternatives operating on action-guiding memory representations.
- Checking the implementation in comparison with the intended result—that is, the main goal—with the programmes that were established by the goal-setting and design procedures mentioned. Checking is a feedback version of orientation that lets the cyclic structure of action become obvious.

Broad empirical investigations have contributed to explaining the central role of action-guiding mental representations. These representations include three groups of categories: representations of the *results* to be obtained (i.e., the goals); representations of the *methods of transformation* of the initial state into the target state; and representations of the *conditions* to be observed. These have been established as the indispensible basis of action regulation. Their comparatively stable nature does not exclude that they may also involve representations of *processes*. The so-called up-dating of action-guiding mental processes by means of a newly accepted information will, on the one hand, lead to change in the representation when context-dependent thresholds of discrepancy are overstepped, and, on the other hand, itself depends on the existing representations that are effective as hypotheses (cf. Piaget's [1976] differentiation between assimilation and accommodation). The dependence on the response demanded by the task, the schematic nature, the efficiency as hypotheses, are further characteristics of action-guiding mental representations that are empirically well founded (Hacker, 1980b).

The task dependence of action-guiding mental representations that have been achieved via learning processes must be emphasised. In contrast to the general agreement on the function of the task in action regulation, the problem of how actions are controlled and organised by tasks and how mental regulation is so determined, has received little empirical attention. In our investigations we tried to establish both the fact that, and the mode by which, identical information about task conditions results in qualitatively different mental representations of the intended result and of the ways of transforming the actual into the target state, given different procedures being implemented due to different tasks. These differences in the action-guiding representations come to their greatest possible compatibility with the ongoing operations with regard to structure and coding (Cavallo, 1978, summarised by Hacker, 1980b).

The concept of the cyclic structure of complete actions, therefore, does not mean more than that the processes of goal-setting, orientation, programming, deciding, and checking that interact with the task-dependent and task-controlling mental representations are feedback units open to task modification and other external information. Steps of change performed as a result of intention, therefore, are not only rehearsed in anticipation but are also fed back as to course and result and compared with the stored intention. This simple old concept on the one hand integrates the seemingly isolated mental processes and, on the other hand, integrates individual actions into the total flow of activity. This is an important advantage of an action-related analysis of mental processes (Mandl et al., 1980).

HIERARCHIC-SEQUENTIAL AND HETERARCHIC ORGANIZATION

Hierarchic structure is concerned with the above-mentioned integration of individual actions and activities into more complex ones. The basic idea is rather simple. Goals are organised in such a way that the superior and more general ones will contain the minor and more special ones. This hierarchy of goals corresponds with a hierarchy of action programmes. The minor goals and programmes can be derived from the major ones by means of differentiation. With limited capacity, on the one hand, consciousness is thus kept free for generalisation. On the other hand, the parts of activity delegated to subordinate regulation processes are realised by means of well-proven stored minor or step goals and programmes with low effort.

Because processing from superior goals to more differentiated minor goals likewise entails a sequence in time, a sequential as well as a hierarchic structure will result: superior goals and programmes necessarily have a greater anticipation span than subordinate ones.

On the one hand, this concept of a hierarchical-sequential organisation is logically conclusive, heuristically productive, and well proven for generating relations between action analysis and cognitive and motivational psychology. So far, a more efficient concept has not come to light. On the other hand, its empirical validation has proved extraordinarily complicated and has only been implemented unsatisfactorily. One reason for this is that consciousness and verbalisability of ongoing processes are only partially available. Also everyday activities are mostly multiple activities involving two or more goals so that, as a rule, several sequential hierarchically organised processes will intersect each other (Kaminski, 1981; Norman, 1981).

What seems to be valid? Empirical investigations into the planning and processing of actions reveal that people usually do not develop complex and logically complete hierarchies of intentions such as can be generated on paper by means of successive embedding of the so-called TOTE-units. Predominantly, not more than two neighbouring levels are cut out at a time. Processing the hierarchy is achieved at the very moment it is required (Görner, 1968; Hacker, 1977).

Together with some clarifications of the relations between main and subordinate goals, new support and important supplementation has been obtained by the cognitive decomposition of motives. Volpert (1980) thoroughly discussed (i.e., with reference to Raynor, 1974) this motivational interpretation of hierarchic-sequential action regulation. The total sum of instrumentalities of subordinate goals for superior ones is summarised as their valence. Since the result of an action can have instrumentality for different major goals, a new prospect is opened up for the aforementioned intersecting of different hierarchical structures in complex activities (e.g., a job). Psycholinguistic support is available, for example by reference to the linguistics of slips of the tongue (Bierwisch, 1970).

New support for the hierarchic-sequential organisation approach, derived from the analysis of action slips, comes from the study of concepts in cognitive psychology. It associates the motor schema concept (Schmidt, 1975) with intentions and activation processes that can become effective under appropriate conditions. Schemas are a definite kind of stored motor programme. Starting from initial states and required final states, schemas will generate specifications of operation sequences adapted to the relevant conditions, thus warranting high flexibility in the job. Important features are that several different schemas are always simultaneously effective and that superior schemas use subschemes that, in part, process autonomously. The intention is equated to the initiating schema of the highest regulation level: "Any given action sequence must be specified by a rather large ensemble of schemas, organized in a hierarchical control structure" (Norman, 1981, p.4).

This inception of an integration between the cognitive and the motivational approach to action regulation is as yet of only heuristic value, but offers great promise for the psychology of personality.

It seems worthwhile to emphasise the following:

1.   The new approach of linking job autonomy and the required goal-setting activities with their motivating effects allows an understanding that motives and attitudes need not necessarily be personal characteristics existing outside of, and prior to, the activity they will stimulate. An important branch of this way of thinking is an emphasis on intrinsic motivation (cf. section below on "Goals as the Decisive Regulation Instance").

2.   The connection between "cognitive" anticipation of future results and "motivational" intentions within the goal, including a concern with the span of anticipation and planning and their interindividual differences.

3.   The development of a concept of levels of action regulation that differ with respect to the nature and scope of the required conscious mental capacity. Investigations into the relations between job contents and the mental development of adults have demonstrated the utility of the concept of different regulation levels for understanding the consequences of ageing processes.

4. Consistent interindividual differences in action organisation invite investigations into personality differences. Examples of this are the above-mentioned tendencies for individuals to vary in planning and the scope of anticipation, the locus of control, the utilization of job autonomy, as well as the known (from psychopathology) differences in the ability to postpone partial goals and to reactivate them in a systematic order (Luria, 1970).

Taxonomy of Goal-Oriented Actions

The group of goal-oriented volitional actions comprises many kinds of activity that differ from each other with respect to their forms of organisation. Research findings for specific forms of activity can only be generalised to others with caution. Action taxonomies, therefore, are an important concern of psychological research.

Classification according to the following features that specify and supplement each other step by step seems to be useful:

1. Class of *charge or task* (Janes, 1980). Main classes of tasks (which can be further subdivided) include: producing, conveying, or "dialogue activities" (e.g., selling). More general characterisation is possible following the relations between the gaps in the generalised action scheme (for more detail see Aebli, 1980, following Fillmore, 1968).

2. *Subject* of action. Classes of subjects are, for example, people, materials, or kinds of information.

3. *Form of cooperation.* Examples are actions without cooperation or actions in autonomous groups.

4. *Complexity,* as the number and kind of constituent activities that are different in terms of demand. The dimension of action variety is defined by the number and the different types of demands of the constituent activities.

5. *Completeness or incompleteness* of actions. In addition to the overt implementation of the action schema, actions may be distinguished by the presence or absence of more or less autonomous goal-setting as well as programming operations, namely: analyses of goals and conditions of implementation, establishing means and ways, and decisions on means and ways. A taxonomy comprising these aspects has already been proposed (Hacker, 1980a).

6. *Levels of mental regulation.* In close relation to completeness, goal-directed activities can be regulated by unconscious automatic

processes or by mental processes that might, but need not, be consciously controlled, or by mental processes and representations that *are* conscious. These levels can be further differentiated (e.g., Hacker, 1980a, p. 398; Österreich, 1981).

Possibilities for classification according to the ongoing action are also helpful. Actions with, for example, a stepwise approach to the goal via constituent goals or actions with a form of processing that encompasses the goal from varying starting points have to be distinguished.

Goals as the Decisive Regulation Instance

The delimiting designation of goal-directed action already has stressed the goal as the basic characteristic. Goals are a peculiar and fascinating psychological subject: they are images of a reality not yet existing but rather to be created, and thus they link present and future. They are anticipation and intention at one and the same time; this reveals the misorientation entailed by separating cognition from motivation. Goal-setting is a result of individual volitional processes that may, ontogenetically, be explained only by the social division of functions in the adult–child dyad.

Goals can be attributed neither to the person nor to the object nor to the situation alone. Instead they control the concrete connection between object and person in goal-oriented actions.

Goals are action-controlling memory representations of a special kind, as demonstrated by the Zeigarnik effect (Zeigarnik, 1927). Goals have a three-fold function: they initiate actions, they control and organise actions via chains or hierarchies of step goals, and—as a memorised nominal value—they serve as standards with which the actual results of action may be compared via feedback.

The anticipation of the future result of an activity will not become a goal without an intention to achieve this result. In competing anticipations or in complicated realisation conditions, the transformation of an anticipation into an intention will require a resolution. Goals include the motivational and cognitive aspects of the goal-oriented action. Actions are initiated by the stimulus values of the anticipated consequences of the expected results of one's own activities (Heckhausen, 1977). Goal-setting can be extended to a process of evaluating the ways and means marked by step goals, the relation between abilities and demands of performance, as well as the effort required in relation to the results attainable, and to possible redefinitions of the task in view of more acceptable goals.

With regard to the relation between superior goals and step goals, statements from the motivational and cognitive points of view are essentially in agreement: action results that have been anticipated as goals usually do not stand alone. Instead, they bring the actor nearer a superior goal of high value. Value or valence may be understood as the sum of instrumentalities for hierarchically superior goals (Heckhausen, 1980; Lantermann, 1980; Volpert, 1980). A goal can be a step goal on the way to different superior or long-term goals, and can have a respective instrumentality. Goals of a high valence, because they are instrumental for important superior goals, are often emotionally evaluated (Lantermann, 1981).

Consequently, the connections between goals and step goals of the linear-sequential and the hierarchic-sequential kind will determine the organisation of actions to a great extent, since initiating motivational and regulating cognitive processes are operating together in an inseparable mode. Given this decisive influence, the following should be considered: the goals serve to group activity into units or chunks, thus creating the perception of advancing in a series of goals in the approach to a final goal, in contrast to not progressing at all. In addition to this, the reduction of goals to means for attaining superior goals will result in a simpler task structure, as can be shown in the development of skills. Conversely, extending the degrees of freedom for goal-setting will result in the perception of an enriched action content that may lead to more intensive task effort and thus to better achievement. Moreover, the subjective difficulty of goals is positively linearly related to effort and performance. The subjective probability of success and the valences of effort and performance, however, will influence the level of acceptance of an assigned goal, though they will *not* influence effort and performance (Mento et al., 1980). Supporting findings were obtained in studies of the stimulating effect of challenging tasks, which involve the higher goals for performance (Taylor, 1981).

Cancelling or introducing possible goals, therefore, will change the task with regard to challenge or boredom, with regard to so-called intrinsic motivation, to performance, and even to psychophysiological parameters. This relation between autonomy in goal-setting and the perception of the task as well as motivation is considered here in more detail owing to its theoretical and practical importance.

The interesting question is, which characteristics of work and job-related learning tasks will lead the actor to set high performance goals? The background to this question is the well-known fact that goals and their respective motives need not necessarily be available in an advanced form prior to task performance but can also be produced or further developed during performance. Metaphorically speaking, activities do not flatly "consume" their motives, nor do they merely fulfill and delete their goals, but they are able to *create* motives and goals as well.

There are certain preconditions necessary for this to be the case. In three fields, namely:

- in the objective characteristics of the tasks themselves (which is the major concern here),
- in the understanding that characteristics such as these are available (i.e., the identification of the possible challenging tasks for which goals can be set), and
- in the pre-existing needs and attitudes of the person (e.g., the need for control of the situation or the planning tendencies of an individual),

the question about which objective task characteristics affect the setting of performance goals is connected with the intrinsic (as opposed to extrinsic) motivations. Let us consider intrinsically motivating task dimensions.

According to present findings, the relevant basic task dimension is autonomy. A further one is skill complexity or variety. By *autonomy* we understand the totality of possible decisions about different ways of accomplishing self-set or -assigned tasks. The distinctive features of autonomy are the possibility of thoroughly identifying, anticipating, and coping with task demands and performance conditions. The concept of control in the sense used in stress research is involved in this concept of autonomy (Rotter, 1966; Ulich, 1978).

The possibility of developing goals is determined by autonomy. Depending on its degree there may be, for the individual,

- no intentions at all, or
- intentions to be active for a definite period of time,
- intentions with respect to speed,
- intentions with respect to the means to be used or the ways to be pursued, and also
- intentions with respect to the parameters of the results aimed at.

Our group hopes to demonstrate that autonomy and, thus, possible decisions, are the starting points of goal-setting that determine the perception of task, strategies, and performance. In a laboratory study, we tried to distinguish autonomy from skill variety (Table 1). It is clear that, when degrees of freedom for the sequence of operations are given, this autonomy is utilized: intentions are exercised, especially with respect to task content, lower strain is perceived while performance re-

Table 1
Effects of Increased Skill Variety and Autonomy in Continuous Mental Work[a,b]

Consequences	Skill variety		Autonomy	
	Mental routine tasks only	Routine tasks, and problem solving	No freedom in task sequence	Freedom in task sequence
Performance quantity and quality	No significant difference		No significant difference	
Reported volitional effort	—	less (.05)	—	more (.10)
Reported strain	—	less (.05)	—	less (.05)
Perceived progress	No significant difference		No significant difference	
Speed-oriented intentions	—	more (.01)	—	more (.10)
Content-oriented intentions	—	fewer (.10)	—	more (.01)
Subjects modifying task sequence	—	—	—	more (.01)

[a]Modified from Wolff, 1981.
[b]Numbers in parentheses are levels of significance.

mains the same, and there is a tendency for more effort to be made.

Analagous effects have also been found for autonomy, where choice can be exercised in grouping in repetitive tasks (Fritsche, 1981, following Blumenfeld, 1932), as well as for autonomy in individually regulating the pace of work (Troy, 1981).

Irrespective of job autonomy, skill variety also, as shown in Table 1, may have significant positive effects. For example, lower strain was perceived and there were changes in intentions, with increasing skill variety.

Comprehensive field investigations by means of a standardised work analysis method based on these results (Wolff & Wolff, 1980), in more than 100 jobs in the electrotechnical industry, produced similar findings and confirmed the practical importance of these laboratory studies. According to present findings, it is the possible decisions (where autonomy is given) and not those really used that are decisive for task perception and behaviour (Wolff, 1981). Autonomy has also been found to contribute to motivation in learning tasks, but only where that autonomy involves options which have a decisive influence on the ongoing action (Monty, Giller, Savage & Perlmuter, 1979).

As stated above, goal-setting involves interpretations of the task and determinations of means and ways. Furthermore, the use of autonomy for personal goal-setting is often based on calculations of effort and utility as well as of demands and abilities. We investigated such calculation-dependent goal-setting by means of task interpretation in the learning of hierarchically constructed instruction systems, of ill-defined category concepts, and of mathematical functions.

The results of these studies indicate that goal-setting really involves calculations of the relation between effort and abilities that in some degree will influence the strategies for task implementation, but will also partially modify the tasks by redefinition. For instance, in monitoring technological parameters, the required identification of exact numerical data becomes reinterpreted as the estimation of a mere order of magnitude. In addition to the perceived effort, abilities, and attitudes specific to the particular individual, special cognitive style variables and habitual working methods (e.g., planning tendencies) are effective.

Altogether, it is valid to state that autonomy and the variety of demands correlated with it can positively influence satisfaction, monotony, and performance, since they permit a switch to more individually rational solutions. On the other hand, the intrinsically motivating effect of complex task structures, including autonomy and higher demands, is demonstrated if a sufficient individual level of aspiration exists, and the utility of the activity and its results are socially recognised.

Global Dimensions of the Analysis, Evaluation, and Design of Activities

Recently, findings have been accumulating that allow us to consider the relations between task and personality important for the personality aspects of action research. During many years of comprehensive empirical investigation into the development of working and learning motivation, a limited number of crucial dimensions that determine the subjective perception and appraisal of tasks and, thus, performance behaviour, has been identified. This work has found its fruition in the job-characteristic model and the associated method—that is, the Job Diagnosis Survey of Hackman and Oldham (1974)—that has become almost paradigmatic in Anglo-American organisational and social psychology.

The five core job dimensions are skill variety, task identity, task significance, autonomy, in the sense of degrees of freedom for decisions as to job contents and procedures, and feedback on job results. These are conveyed as causal connecting links via the so-called critical states, namely satisfaction, motivation, and performance, and they are modified by the need for self-development.

Verifications by means of factor regression and path analyses (e.g., Schmidt, Schweissfurth, et al., 1981; Schmidt, Kleinbeck et al., 1981), as well as reinvestigations into the effects of the job dimensions predicted by the model, confirm the basic assumptions but demand important modifications. Knowledge of results and, thus, the feedback dimension plays a minimal role. In contrast, perceived responsibility is of crucial importance for intrinsic motivation, job satisfaction, and the elimination of negative effects of jobs, such as perceived fatigue, monotony, or mental saturation. On the basis of comprehensive longitudinal investigations, Karasek (1979) was able to show in the job-strain model that, where autonomy is great, high job demands will have no negative effects (such as fatigue, increased sick-rate, and increased consumption of tranquillizers), while, with restricted autonomy, high demands will cause distinct negative effects. Furthermore, skill variety has a dominant role, similar to that of autonomy. In contrast, evidence for the importance of the role of task identity on satisfaction, motivation, and performance is only suggestive. There are significant intercorrelations between autonomy, variety, and identity.

In a series of quasi-experimental field investigations and experimental laboratory investigations, we studied the effects of autonomy and variety in more detail (Fritsche, 1981; Wolff, 1981). Our main results were

1. Degrees of freedom (or autonomy—choice between alternative procedures) induce the worker to self-setting goals and to dispose actively of the procedures.
2. Degrees of freedom in addition require a minimum variety of demands in order to be perceived as actually useful.
3. Degrees of freedom and variety will change strategies by means of modified goal setting, modified perceived and used controllability of the realisation conditions, and modified sequences of step goals.
4. The effects of variety may be reduced to three components: the change between different demands, the subdivision or chunking of the working time due to this change, and the type of operations alternating with each other.
5. Increased variety does not seem to compensate for reduced autonomy.
6. The effects and modes of effect of the degrees of freedom and of variety are largely independent of personality traits, such as

introversion, rigidity, neuroticism, and test intelligence. In contrast to this, strategies that demand both goal-setting and planning and that require control can actually be generated by adequate job characteristics. These strategies, therefore, are not personal preconditions for the effectiveness of enriched job design. On the contrary, enriched job contents themselves can generate the goals and motives required for their utilization.

7. Degrees of freedom and variety can be generated in job division or combination and in the associated requirements for cooperation.

The importance of the possible classification of jobs according to their completeness introduced above in the section on "Taxonomy of Goal-Oriented Actions" is corroborated by these findings.

Irrespective of important methodological, conceptual, and methodological objections and unresolved problems, this empirically based approach to the analysis of job characteristics is at least encouraging in its potential for the investigation, evaluation, and design of learning and working activities. This holds especially for the differentiated operationalisation of global job dimensions into more precise clusters of characteristics (Hacker et al., 1981; Iwanowa, 1981).

Analysing Jobs in Relation to Objective Job Conditions

The analysis of jobs and of mental processes—representations or traits that regulate the actions constituting jobs and that are developed or degenerated by jobs—must encompass the objective and actual realisation conditions. We have found that the contents and the content-dependent organisation of actions are determined by the "objective logics of the tasks" and their realisation conditions. Actions do not have contents or structures per se. Goal-directed actions and their mental regulation are influenced by several classes of objective conditions, which are

1. The inherent laws of the object of the action, which define the possible and the required activities, and to which these activities must submit. For elucidation, consider the differences between the learning activities involved in, for example, physics versus physical education.

2. The organisational principles of activities, in particular the division or combination of actions among different persons, including

the resulting forms of cooperation. For illustration, consider learning activities in self-organizing small groups as compared with such activities in teacher-controlled classes.

3. The required and available means for the realisation of activities. For example, consider calculation by memory or on paper with calculation on a computer.

It is important to realise that the contents and the complete or incomplete mental structure of activities are, in the first place, a result of this objective determination. Activity structures (e.g., job structures and their mental regulation) are objectively determined in many ways. For instance, activities may be incomplete in different ways:

- due to the rarity of occurrence of an actual job demand, as in monitoring automatic processes;
- due to insufficient cooperation and communication requirements and possibilities;
- due to specialist limitation and, thus, lacking transferability of knowledge, skills, and abilities acquired;
- due to the lack of creative intellectual demands or to the lack of any intellectual demands at all;
- due to the lack of autonomous decision-making requirements ("control"), or even due to the limitations of the action demands on the unconscious sensorimotor execution of tasks prepared, considered, and ordered by other people.

However, because personality traits do develop in the course of activities, they are supposed to be as differentiated and rich or as narrow and poor as the activities through which they develop. Thus, designing task contents and structures will always mean developing personality traits, too, which, in the ideal case, would be self-development via autonomous design of one's own activities. The relations between the scope of demands of professional activities and the improvement or the deterioration of definite cognitive performances, the so-called dequalification, has been demonstrated by, for example, Schleicher (1973).

The contents and structures of tasks have to be analysed not per se or with regard to personal sources only but rather in relation to their determining social and societal skeleton conditions. This is the fundamental object in job design. An obvious example is the way in which the principle of human-centered task design has overcome Taylorist division of labour.

References

Aebli, H. (1980). *Denken; das Ordnen des Tuns.* Bd. 1; *Kognitive Aspekte der Handlungstheorie.* Klett-Cotta: Stuttgart.

Asanger, R., and Weniger, C. (Eds.). (1980). *Handwörterbuch der Psychologie.* Beltz: Weinheim und Basel.

Bainbridge, L. (1974). Analysis of verbal protocols in a process control task. In *The Human Operator in Process Control.* (E. Edwards & F. P. Leeds, eds.). Francis and Taylor: London.

Bierwisch, M. (1970). Fehlerlinguistic. *Linguistic Inquiry, 1,* No. 4.

Blumenfeld, W. (1932). Uber die Fraktonierung der Arbeit und ihre Beziehung zur Theorie der Handlung. Bericht XII. *Kongress der Deutshen Gesellschaft fur Psychologie.* Fischer: Jena.

Cavallo, V. (1978). "Leistungs und beanspruchungsbestimmende Eigenschaften operativer Abbilder." Informationen; Technische Universitat, Dresden 22–16–78.

Cranach, M. von, Kalbermatten, U., Indermuehle, K., and Gugler, B. (1982). *Goal-Directed Action.* Academic Press: London.

Fillmore, C. J. (1968). The case for case. In *Universals in Linguistic Theory.* (E. Bach and R. T. Harms, eds.). Holt: New York.

Friedman, M., and Roseman, R. H. (1959). Association of a specific overt behaviour pattern with blood and cardio-vascular findings. *Journal of The American Medical Association, 169,* pp. 1286ff.

Fritsche, B. (1981). "Arbeitsgliederung-Wirkungen und Wirkungsbedingungen unter Einschluss von Selbstregulationsmoglichkeiten." Diplomarbeit Technische Universitat, Dresden Sektion Arbeitswissenschaften WB Psychologie.

Görner, R. (1968). Vorgestellter und ausgeführter Tatigkeitsvollzug—eine Möglichkeit der Erfassung von Denkverlaufen in der Arbeitstätigkeit. In *Arbeitspsychologie und wissenschaftlich technische Revolution.* (W. Hacker, W. Skell, & W. Straub, eds.). DKW: Berlin.

Hacker, W. (1977). Anforderungsabhängigkeit der Nutzung von hierarchischer Ordnung in Sequenzen. *Zeitschrift fur Psychologie, 185,* No. 1, 1–33.

Hacker, W. (1980a). *Allgemeine Arbeits- und igenieur-psychologie.* DVW: Berlin.

Hacker, W. (1980b). Handlungsregulation; Zur aufgabenabhangigen Struktur handlungsregulierender mentaler Repräsentationen. Kongressbericht XXII. *Internationaler Kongress für Psychologie,* Leipzig, 80–88.

Hacker, W., and Matern, B. (1979). Beschaffenheit und Wirkungsweise mentaler Repräsentationen in der Handlungsregulation. *Zeitschrift fur Psychologie, 187,* No. 2, 141–156.

Hacker, W., Richter, P., et al. (1981). *Tätigkeitsbewertungsverfahren TBS-L.* TU Dresden: Forschungsbericht.

Hackman, J. R. (1970). Task and task performance in research on stress. In *Social and Psychological Factors in Stress.* (J. E. McGrath, ed.). Holt: New York.

Hackman, J. R., and Oldham, G. R. (1974). The Job Diagnosis Survey: An instrument for the diagnosis of jobs and the evaluation of job redesign projects. *Technical Report 4,* Yale University.

Heckhausen, H. (1977) Motivation: Kognitionspsychologische Aufspaltung eines summarischen Konstrukts. *Psychologische Rundschau, 28,* 175–189.

Heckhausen, H. (1980). *Motivation und Handeln.* Springer: Berlin.

Iwanowa, A. (1981). *Validierung eines Tätigkeitsbewertungsverfahrens.* Dissertation Naturwiss-Mathem. Fakultät TU: Dresden.

Janes, A. (1980). Ein Verfahren zur Beschreibung der Verwandtschaft zwischen Tätikeiten. *Vortrag* 26. Kongress der Gesellschaft fur Arbeitswissenschaft, Hamburg.

Kaminski, G. (1981). Überlegungen zur Funktion von Handlungstheorien in der Psychologie. In *Handlungstheorie Interdisziplinar.* Bd. 3, erster Halbband. (H. Lenk, ed.). Fink: München.

Karasek, R. A. (1979). Job demands, job decision latitude and mental strain. *Administrative Science Quarterly, 24,* 85–311.

Klix, F. (1976). Strukturelle und Funktionelle Komponenten des menschlichen Gedächtnisses. In *Psychologische Beiträge zur Analyse kognitiver Prozesse.* (F. Klix, ed.). DVW: Berlin.

König, C. (1980a). Zu einigen methodischen Problemen mehrdimensionaler Untersuchungen der Entwicklung intellektueller Fähigkeiten bei berufstätigen Erwachsenen. *Informationen der Technischen Universität:* Dresden: 22-19-80

König, C. (1980b). Probleme der Planung von Untersuchungen zur Entwicklung intellektueller Fähigkeiten bei berufstätigen Erwachsenen. *Informationen der Technischen Universität:* Dresden.

Kuhl, J. (1980). Action vs. state-orientation; A meta-cognitive moderator of expectancy-value interactions. Internat. Kongress für Psychologie, Leipzig. Kurzfassungsband 2, s.551.

Lantermann, E. D. (1980). *Interaktionen: Person, Situation und Handlung.* Urban und Schwarzenberg: München.

Lantermann, E. D. (1981). Beliefs about feelings toward situations in the context of goal-directed actions. Universitat Kassel, (unveröff. Manuskript).

Lenk. H. (1981). *Handlungstheorien Interdisziplinär.* Bande 1-3. (H. Lenk, ed.). Fink: München.

Leontjew, A. N. (1976). *Bewusstsein, Tätigkeit, Persönlichkeit.* Volk und Wissen: Berlin.

Leplat, J., and Hoc, J. M. (1980). Die Verbalisierung bei der Analyse kognitiver Prozesse. In *Optimierung kognitiver Arbeitsanforderungen.* (s.36–42). (W. Hacker and H. Raum, eds.). Huber: DVW, Bern, Stuttgart und Wien.

Lompscher, H. (1979). Theoretisch-methodologische Probleme der Tätigkeitsanalyse. *Probleme u. Ergebnisse der Psychologie,* No. 68.

Luria, A. R. (1970). *Die höheren kortikalen Funktionen des Menschen und ihre Störungen bei örtlichen Hirnschadigungen.* DVW: Berlin.

Mandl, H., Schnotz, W., and Ballstädt, S.-P. (1980). Learning from text seen from the perspective of action theories. *XXII Internat. Kongress für Psychologie.* Leipzig: LS *8,* Kurzfassungsband 1, s.159.

Mento, A. I., Cartledge, N. D., and Locke, E. A. (1980). Maryland vs Michigan vs Minnesota: Another look at the relationship of expectancy and goal difficulty to task performance. *Organizational Behaviour and Human Performance, 25,* 419–440.

Miller, R. B. (1971). Development of a taxonomy of human performance: design of a systems task vocabulary. *Technical Report 11.* American Institute of Research: Washington.

Monty, R. A., Giller, E. S., Savage, R. E., and Perlmuter C. C. (1979). The freedom to choose is not always so choice. *Journal of Experimental Psychology: Human Learning and Memory, 5,* No. 2, 170–178.

Nisbett, R. E., and Wilson T. D. (1977). Telling more than we can know: Verbal reports on mental processes. *Psychological Review, 84,* No. 3, 231–259.

Norman, D. A. (1981). Categorisation of action slips. *Psychological Review, 88,* No. 1, 1–15.

Österreich, R. (1981). *Handlungsregulation und Kontrolle.* Urban und Schwarzenberg: München.

Piaget, J. (1976). Psychologie der Intelligenz. *Kindler-Taschenbücher:* München.

Raynor, J. O. (1974). Future orientation and the study of achievement motivation. In *Motivation and Achievement.* (J. W. Atkinson and J. O. Raynor, eds.). Winston: Washington.

Rotter, J. B. (1966). Generalized expectancies for internal versus external control of reinforcement. *Psychological Monographs, 80,* No. 609.

Rubinstein, S. L. (1958). *Grundlagen der Allgemeinen Psychologie.* Volk und Wissen: Berlin.

Schleicher, R. (1973). Die Intelligenzleistung Erwachsener in Abhängigkeit vom Niveau beruflicher Tätigkeit. *Probleme u. Ergebnisse der Psychologie, 44,* 25–56.

Schmidt, K.-H., Kleinbeck, U., and Rohmert, W. (1981). Die Wirkung von Merkmalen der Arbeitssituation und Persönlichkeitsvariablen auf die Arbeittszufriedenheit und andere motivationsbezogene Einstellungsvariablen. *Zeitschrift für experiment. und angewandte Psychologie, 28,* No. 3, 465–485.

Schmidt, K.-H., Schweissfurth, W., Kleinbeck, U., and Rutenfranz, J. (1981). Einige arbeitspsychologische Ergebnisse zur Wirkung von Arbeitsinhaltsveränderungen. *Zeitschrift fur Arbeitswissenschaften, 33,* No. 2, 101–107.

Schmidt, R. A. (1975). A schema theory of discrete motor skill learning. *Psychological Review, 4,* 229–261.

Taylor, M. S. (1981). The motivational effects of task challenge: A laboratory investigation. *Journal of Organizational Behaviour and Human Performance, 27,* 255–278.

Tomaszewski, T. (1964). Die Struktur der menschlichen Tätigkeiten. *Psychol. u. Praxis, 8.* Klett-Verlag.

Tomaszewski, T. (1978). *Tätigkeit und Bewusstsein. Beiträge zur Einführung in Die Polnische Tätigkeitspsychologie.* Weinheim und Basel.

Tomaszewski, T. (1981). *Zur Psychologie der Tätigkeit.* (T. Tomaszewski, ed.). DVW: Berlin.

Troy, N. (1981). *Zur Bedeutung der Stresskontrolle: Arbeit unter Zeitdruck.* Dissertation: Eidgenöss. Techn. Hochschule, Zurich (LAB).

Ulich, E. (1978). Entwicklungsmöglichkeiten des Menschen in der Arbeit. *Industrielle Organisation, 47,* 566–568.

Volpert, W. (1975). Der Zusammenhang zwischen Arbeit und Persönlichkeit aus handlungstheoretischer Sicht. In *Arbeit und Persönlichkeit: Berufliche Sozialisation in der arbeitsteiligen Gesellschaft.* (P. Groskurth, ed.). Rowohlt: Hamburg.

Volpert, W. (1980). Das Modell der hierarschisch-sequentiellen Handlungsorganisation. Referat XXII Int. Kongress für Psychologie. In *Cognitive and motivational aspects of goal-directed actions.* (W. Hacker, W. Volpert, & M. von Cranach, eds.). DVW: Berlin.

Vroom, V. H. (1964). *Work and Motivation.* Wiley: New York.

Wendrich, P. (1978a). Reliabilitätskonzeption für Daten aus empirischen Arbeitsuntersuchungen. *Informationen der Technischen Universität,* Dresden: 22-7-78.

Wendrich, P. (1978b). Betrachtung eines Beispiels zu Reliabilitätsproblemen bei Arbeitsanalysedaten. *Informationen der Technischen Universität,* Dresden: 22-10-78.

Wolff, S. (1981). *Zielsetzungsmöglichkeiten als Merkmale progressiver Inhalte der Arbeit.* Dissert. Naturwiss.-Mathemat. Fakult. der TU Dresden.

Wolff, S., and Wolff, T. (1980). *Tätigkeitsbewertungssystem-Kurzform.* VE Kombinat Nachrichtenelektronik: Berlin.

Zeigarnik, B. (1927). Über das Behalten unerledigter Handlungen. *Psycholog. Forschung, 9.*

4

Cognition and Emotion
in the Course of Action

Ernst-D. Lantermann

Introduction

With this contribution, I attempt to formulate assumptions, in a
speculative manner, about the interacting cognitive and emotional processes involved in human actions. My assumptions are based on both
psychological theories of emotion and contemporary psychological theories of action. Before concentrating on my topic, I would like to make
a few remarks about the personal background of this essay's author:
Having studied psychological theories of action for some time (see Lantermann, 1980), I came to the conclusion that whereas an impressive
amount of knowledge has been accumulated and integrated by these
theories on the process of acting rationally, the specification of the *conditions* under which persons act according to a norm of rationality and
goal-directedness has been largely neglected. At this time, psychological theories of action seem to be more in a state of normative setting
than in a state of psychological theory: They consist of—to overstate
this somewhat—rules which, if obeyed, quarantee rational, goal-
directed actions.

With this knowledge I agreed to participate in a seminar with a so-
ciologist, a philosopher, a linguist, and about 15 students from different departments: We chose novels (e.g., *Madame Bovary* and *L'Etranger*)
and tried to understand the action in these novels by assuming that
the protagonists had planned their activities in accordance with the
findings and postulates of various theories of action (e.g., Cranach *et
al.*, 1980; implicit in Laucken, 1974). The results were not very promising. Doubting, driven, sensitive characters—in short, living heroes—
became cool operators, who met the environment squarely, analysed
it; they planned and carried through their actions in terms of cost-
reward considerations. The plots of these novels became business re-

ports; Charles Bovary, for example, turned into an idiot, and L'E-tranger was incomprehensible.

Of course, novels are literary inventions, and theories of action are not instructions as to how to write novels. However, for the reader, the novels become alive and the protagonists' actions are understood. Theories of action claim to explain, to predict, and even to reconstruct human action. Naturally, *understanding* an action does not imply *explaining* an action, that is, retracing it to its determinants. Scepticism spread among the seminar participants when they learned this. If theories of action describe human behaviour as goal-directed, intentional, motivated, and context-dependent, the gap between understanding an action and explaining it according to the theory of action should not be so wide. Besides frequent criticism of details, two major problematic issues were pointed out in the discussions: the lack of a sufficient assessment of emotional processes within the debated theories of action and the lack of concrete statements on the social embedding of human actions. These issues are examined in this chapter.

The limitation of cognitive approaches in explaining human actions without taking emotional processes into account has been apparent in psychological research for some time. The cognitive emphasis in psychology dates back a while; and after the early enthusiasm had faded, emotional processes more and more became constituents of the cognitive approach in explaining human behavior. As a consequence, theories of emotion again became more attractive, links between cognition and emotion came into focus, and, in recent years, corresponding theories have been formulated. To a certain extent one can speak of a cognitive trend in research on emotion, which has been criticised from different perspectives. One cognitive approach in research on emotion that has, in my opinion, been carried too far is Weiner's theory (Weiner, 1974; Weiner et al., 1978): "Cognitions are necessary and sufficient causes of emotion" (Weiner et al., 1978, p. 84) is a central statement of his theory.

Without going into detail, it seems to me that the controversy as to whether emotions are post- or precognitive phenomena is based partly on a misunderstanding. Weiner conceives of emotions—if I understand him correctly— as cognitions which, in turn, contain emotional concepts. One could interpret his work as an empirical foundation for the work of language philosophers (e.g., Alston, 1972; Bedford, 1956) in that these works show the appropriate *usage* of emotional concepts within a defined context of action.

However, processes that are connected with emotion or that occur as a result of an emotion labelling in the further course of action are less the focus of research. I do not want to go as far as Zajonc (1980), who believes that "contemporary cognitive psychology simply ignores affect" (p. 152). Nevertheless, it is evident that if cognitive approaches are set up for the analysis of emotion, they often conceive of emotion in such a way that its properties are lost; emotional processes are represented, then, only as a "cognitive remnant" that can be integrated into cognitive theories without any difficulty. Consequenly, these theories restrict their analyses to the "cold" aspects of emotional processes and neglect the "hot" aspects (see Abelson, 1973; Zajonc, 1980). However, this type of analysis of emotion is not a necessary characteristic of cognitive approaches. The influence of emotion on processes of memory and perception is a traditional subject of psychology. Bower (1981) and Bower and Cohen (1982) present a theory of emotional influences on memory and thinking performance without reducing emotions to cold evaluative judgements. Mandler (1975, 1981), also goes far beyond the approaches previously outlined. On reading the works of Mandler or Zajonc, it seems apparent that the fiery debate about whether emotions are pre- or postcognitive is partly due to the changing definition of cognition.

Mandler differentiates structural information and information about the characteristics of individual components of a given situation or stimulus. Zajonc distinguishes *Diskriminanda* and *Praeferenda* in that they are different attributes of one stimulus. Notwithstanding the differences in their theories, both Mandler and Zajonc postulate that before the inducement of emotional processes, certain information-processing operations must have taken place resulting in identification of specific stimulus aspects. These processes differ from other cognitive processes in that, among other aspects, they are not governed by the voluntary control of the perceiver but instead occur automatically. According to Mandler, other cognitive processes similar to those postulated in Weiner's theory fix the internal quality of emotional processes. The question of whether emotions are post- or precognitive seems to arise from diverging interpretations rather than from empirically distinguishable alternatives.

Both types of information processing, that which occurs automatically and results in the first global emotional evaluation of a situation and that which is more voluntarily controlled and leads to a specification and modification of the first global evaluation, are presented as interacting processes in Lazarus' theory (Lazarus, 1975; Lazarus & Launier, 1978; Lazarus et al., 1980). Appraisal and reappraisal differ from one another in that appraisal represents a global evaluation (often occurring without any extra effort) of a situation according to the categories of "irrelevant", "pleasant", and "unpleasant", whereas "reappraisal" is an evaluation of personal coping possibilities within a situation, resulting in a specific emotion.

Along with these more cognitive-oriented theories, theories of emotion that describe emotions as syndromes of processes with physiological, expressive, and subjective aspects of experience have become more appealing in recent years. Central to these approaches is a functional-adaptive conceptualisation of emotion that derives from an evolutionary point of view. Emotional processes are not an epiphenomenon of cognitive processes, but rather the mentioned aspects of these processes form emotion syndromes with specific purposes or survival functions. According to Plutchik (1980), an emotion is a chain of events that begins with the occurrence of a stimulus. The stimulus is cognized with the result of a specific feeling state. This leads to the activation of the corresponding behaviour that has specific survival consequences for the organism (be it human or animal).

No matter how favourable a biological–phylogenetic orientation for many problems appears, I doubt that it is useful for describing and understanding emotional processes in ongoing human actions. In many of the text's passages the influence of an "ecological" wrong inference suggests itself, because the change from the phylogenetic level to the ontogenetic or even actual level is made too fast and without any additional assumptions.

Averill's (1980) theory proceeds on the basis of totally different premises. He defines emotion as "a transitory social role (a socially constituted syndrome) that includes an individual's appraisal of the situation and that is integrated as a passion rather than as an action" (p. 312). The emotional syndrome consists of a number of components (such as cognitive appraisal, physiological activation or arousal, motor expression, motivational tendencies, and subjective feeling state), which are loosely connected with one another but are "bundled" by the specific social role that the actor in a social situation plays. A transitory social role consists of various aspects, such as the perception of the situation and its imperative content, the emotional reaction to a situation, and the potential action in a situation. In this way, emotions are called a socially constituted syndrome, and various emotions are constituted by their social context. Their functions are primarily socially regulative.

The other aspect of Averill's theory is that emotions are usually interpreted as passions rather than actions. That conception is common to most theories of human emotion.

Even if the various theories of emotion differ in many assumptions and features, they do possess essential similarities. Among other things, they postulate the following:

1. Cognitive and emotional processes interact closely with one another and conjointly organize human behaviour.
2. Emotions signal a specific state of the relationship between people and their environment.
3. Emotional processes are only partially governed by voluntary control.

The present study links up with these postulates. Other arguments from theories of action are also included, especially the common assumption, represented by numerous approaches, that human actions are organized in a hierarchical–sequential manner. It seems profitable to include some perspectives from theories of action in the discussion of the problem of emotion.

If Mandler (according to Gallistel, 1980, p. xii) claims that modern cognitive psychology lacks primarily a theory of action, then this is even more so the case for the psychology of emotion. Although at present there is no satisfactory theory of action, some postulates that occur in many different theories of action can be applied to analyze emotional and cognitive processes in the course of action.

In particular, studies from the German-speaking world dealing with theories of stress (Dörner et al., 1983; Krenauer & Schönpflug, 1980; Schönpflug, 1979; Schulz, 1979) and studies in self-attention and behavioural control (Carver & Scheier, 1981) show how this can be achieved. These approaches assume that human actions are organized hierarchically, and they propose hypotheses about links between cognitive and emotional processes.

This study outlines a theory of interactions between cognitive and emotional processes in terms of how human actions are organized and directed, but it introduces a heuristic model, which contains general assumptions about emotional and cognitive processes and their interaction during the control of a course of action. Subsequently, I illustrate my general assumptions with a few examples. The main focus remains, however, on assumptions about the concrete interacting influences of cognitive and emotional processes in the context of hierarchical–sequentially organized action: under what conditions do emotional processes intervene in the control of the course of action in such a manner as to determine cognitive operations, and in what manner do cognitive control processes determine emotional processes?

In the first section of this study, a few general characteristics of human actions are described in so far as they are relevant to the given topic; then the general model is presented, and cognitive and emotional control are defined in this context. Finally, hypothetical forms of interaction between cognitive and emotional processes in the course of action are presented on the basis of the model.

Characteristics of Human Actions

In this section are presented the characteristics of actions in as much as they are of importance to contemporary theories of action and comply with the argument. I am referring to Gallistel (1980), Cranach et al. (1980), Eckensberger and Emminghaus (1982), Hacker (1973), Kaminski (1981), Lantermann (1980), and Miller et al., (1960).

The environment and the person are interrelated. Action always presupposes a specific environment and, simultaneously that the person has specific skills, abilities, and prior knowledge. Actions are either restricted, facilitated, made possible, or suggested, depending on the current person–environment constellation because not every conceivable action can feasibly be carried out by every person in all possible environments.

Actions begin when the actor is confronted with the present state in his or her relationship to the environment, which does not satisfy his or her expectations and which does not appear optimal to him or her. Therefore, actions are defined, for the present, as intended transformations of an unsatisfactory initial situation into a preferable and anticipated goal situation with the help of appropriate behavioural patterns.

In this sense, acting requires of the actor knowledge of the external (environmental) and internal (personal) conditions that are the presuppositions of a successful completion of a specific action. The actor must also know and have access to behavioural patterns (operations) that are attainable under the given circumstances. In the couse of action, operations are related to the intended events, which direct and regulate the action. These intended events are represented in the actor's memory as partially conscious goal anticipations or standards that remain available as goal values and are compared with events occurring in the course of action. The standard's function is to regulate control during action, in that observed discrepancies between the action's outcome and standard indicate action's present achievement. The actor connects the standards with the values or valences of the stimuli from whose structure the impulse regulation (see Hacker, 1973) or the degree of motivation (Heckhausen, 1980) result.

The course of action is characterized by a specific chronological order that has to be adhered to, more or less, in order to reach the goal. Certain interim gains have to be achieved so that other interim and higher level goals also can be reached. Organization and control of actions are carried out on hierarchically structured levels. These levels complete one another and their regulatory functions differ from one another. At higher levels the *choices* of goals, plans and strategies are represented and controlled; at lower levels the *organization* and control of the action's course take place.

Actions consist of a preparation, an execution, and a completion phase, which are closely entwined. In the preparation phase, one analyses the conditions necessary for an action to take place, one searches for goals and subgoals, and one selects appropriate operations. In the execution phase, the actor controls and applies the intended and planned actions. Subsequently, in the completion phase, he or she evaluates the completed actions; this includes the evaluation of the goals and the course taken. This final analysis leads to a build-up of expectations for future actions.

This description of the structure and process of an action is used here as a conceptual frame into which specific links between cognitive and emotional processes occurring during the action are integrated.

A General Model for Action Control

The central feature of the model outlined in this section is the concept "action control". This concept generally summarizes those cognitive and emotional events that enable the actor to influence events through his or her activities—or non-activities—so that a desired goal situation can be achieved (see, e.g., Bandura, 1971; Kuhl, 1982; Österreich, 1981).

This model postulates two action control systems: an emotional and a cognitive system that interact with each other during the course of action and simultaneously take part in action control. Further components of the models (such as input, transaction schema, and output) are also introduced. First, the relationship between the components is exemplified; subsequently, the individual components of the model are explained in detail.

RELATIONSHIP BETWEEN COMPONENTS

Imagine a tourist who, after a long trip, reaches his destination in the evening. He is standing in the market square of a strange town and wants to decide where he would like to have dinner in order to satisfy his appetite. Everything is strange and new: the language, the town, the mentality of the people. Being a seafood lover, he decides, after some hesitation, to visit the only seafood restaurant in town. He opens the door of the restaurant—and freezes. The room is long and narrow. It is packed with men in ragged clothes. Men are standing in a triple row in front of the bar, which fades into the darkness of the long room. The men, obviously surprised, turn around and look at him and do not make a move to let him get by. What should he do? The tourist still assumes that he has entered a seafood restaurant; that much of the language he knows. Besides that, he is very hungry and in the mood for a nice fish dinner. He looks for a place to sit down. After a while, he finds a table at the back of the room. So he was not mistaken; this is a seafood restaurant. He feels extremely uncomfortable with all these men staring at him, and he is beset with anxiety and fear. Finally, he pulls himself together by examining the ridiculousness of his feelings and walks straight to the table and sits down. A waiter hurries to take his order. Relieved, he leans back in his chair and looks forward to his dinner.

The description of this situation contains most of the model's components (see Figure 1). The hungry tourist who is expecting his fish dinner is sitting in a room that is apparently a seafood restaurant. Translated in terms of our model, the actor is in a specific person-environment constellation. He perceives the individual aspects of the situation (according to our model, the actor transforms parts of the situation into input standards), which he connects to a specific transaction schema by finally identifying the room as a seafood restaurant. He is hungry, he is in the mood for a fish dinner, and he finds himself in a seafood restaurant. But he is uncomfortable.

He knows that he is in the restaurant of his choice and also knows what he has to do to satisfy his appetite. When he has overcome his anxiety, he decides to walk to the table (the transaction schema becomes the input standard for the cognitive and emotional control system). His walking over and sitting down is the integrated output of the two control systems. His behavior is a signal to the waiter to go to the table, which in turn causes the tourist to order. Through the course of familiar activities, he changes his behavior and feels more comfortable.

The relationship(s) among the components of the model depicted in Figure 1 can be summarized in the following way: The actor is in a specific person–environment constellation. The constellation perceived by the actor is the input (1) for the control system. The actor compares the perceived constellation with acquired transaction schemata (2); then

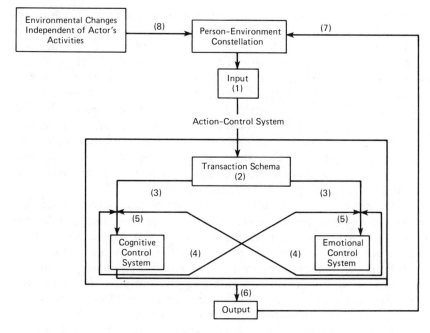

Figure 1. The action-control model. Numbers are explained in the text.

one or more suitable schemata are activated. The components of the activated scheme become input standards for the cognitive and emotional control system (3). The results of both systems can be conveyed to one another (4), but the results can also become the starting point for further activities within the same system (5). The results of both control systems become output standards or are integrated as organized sequences of action (6). This output changes the person–environment constellation (7). These changes, which are either induced by the actor or occur independently (8) can become once again input standards for the control system.

INPUT

A concrete person–environment constellation is considered an input for the action control system. We have outlined this constellation within the model as a present relationship pattern between supply and demands of the environment and demands or possible actions of the person. This relationship pattern is subject to constant changes; person and environment interact with one another in that changes of the environment produce changes in the person and vice versa. Person and environment are in a constant *state of transaction*.

The characteristics of the transaction state that are the input standards of the action control system have to be described independently of the actor's conceptions and interpretations. Environment characteristics (such as temperature, light intensity, room size, number of persons, but also the *demand structure* of the situation, social rules and conventions, etc.) and person characteristics (such as age, intelligence, motive structure, abilities) can be potential input standards for the action control system if they are described and categorized independently of the actor's perspective. If not, these characteristics are more the *results* of the system than input standards.

A momentary constellation between person and environment demands and options—an actual transaction state—can now be explained at various levels of organization or control according to the conceptualisation of human actions as hierarchically organized activities. Different contents relevant to the action, regulation, or control processes, as well as various person and environment characteristics, are assigned to these levels. The characteristics are described at that organization level with which they are conceptually related.

In our example, at a higher organization level, such person and environment characteristics can be found that relate to the actions' goal. The primary goal of the tourist is to satisfy his appetite by eating fish. The goal to eat fish is assigned to the goal level in the action's organization. This assignment, independent of the actor's perspective, is only possible under the naive observer's (or researching psychologist's) assumption that the tourist always prefers a seafood restaurant to any other restaurant when he is extremely hungry; in other words, only if we presuppose a predominant and trans-situational motive or goal structure on the actor's part.

The restaurant the tourist visits is a seafood restaurant. It invites or summons him to satisfy his goal to eat a fish dinner. The present transaction state of the tourist and the restaurant can be described as a congruent or harmonious relationship between personal goals or demands and the environment's option. Since the tourist has no knowledge of the foreign country, it is assumed that he knows only to a certain extent the social rules, conventions, and distribution of roles that are applied in this local restaurant, so instead, he assumes that the rules, norms, and conventions of *his* country apply to this country. However, it is a custom in this fictitious foreign country that when anyone looking like a typical tourist enters a tavern, this person is stared at in order to get him to buy drinks for the house before he is allowed to go to one of the tables. This the traveller does not know. He misinterprets the situation and is confused.

These aforementioned aspects are represented at the subordinate levels of the goal level. The transaction state can be described as a special relationship between those social rules, norms, and distribution of roles that obtain in a situation and those that the actor assumes valid and that guarantee his reaching his goal according to his previous knowledge. In our case, we find a lack of agreement between situational rules, norms, the distribution of roles, and personal knowledge of hypotheses about these rules.

Transaction states at different levels can be described in the same manner. The assignment of an environment or a person component to a specific organization level is generally determined by its postulated function within the examined course of action.

Argyle, Furnham, and Graham (1981) developed a schema for analyzing social situations that is congruent with the present point of view. What these authors suggest for social situations can be transferred to the analysis of person characteristics. Person–environment–transaction states can be analyzed on various hierarchically ordered levels. Which components, and which level of a transaction, cue the present actions and action control processes depends upon the actor's interpretation of the person–environment transaction, which is determined by the chosen transaction schema in a situation.

TRANSACTION SCHEMA

The present state of the person–environment transaction becomes, to that degree, input standard for the control system to which it is perceived and processed by the actor. This interpretation process is produced by a comparison between knowledge represented in memory and the relevant information about the present person–environment transaction. This knowledge, I assume, contains declarative, procedural and emotional components and is organized in the form of transaction schemata. Transaction schemata instance my conception of representations of person–environment transactions in memory. These include both correct, accomplishable actions as well as their consequences and representations of emotional processes that are associated with the occurrence of a specific class of person–environment transactions.

With the concept of the transaction schema, we follow a tradition

which was already present in the early work of Piaget (1926) and Bartlett (1932). In further discussion of schema, I refer to approaches of a
specific type of schema, for example, the "script" in Schank and Abelson's (1977) and Abelson's (1981) sense, in the context of Lang's (1979)
"bio-informational theory of emotional imagery" and Leventhal's
(1980) theory of emotion.

Schemata are objects, processes, and the like, represented in memory which, if they are activated, set off an evaluation process: Incoming information is tested for its compatibility with the activated schema.
In a case of incompatability, the schema is rejected and a new one is
activated. Schemata can tolerate a certain amount of incompatability,
that is, they are open to information that is not yet contained in them.
These gaps can be filled by other schemata, in that several schemata
form a hierarchical structure. The superordinate schemata are in general more universal than their subordinates. Directed by expectation,
they control the subordinate schemata and, in turn, receive feedback
from them. Consequently, an activation of a schema hierarchy includes
top-down and bottom-up processes (see, e.g., Abelson, 1981, p. 178).

In order to activate a schema, not all components of a transaction
have to be tested to see whether or not they are presented in the schema.
Schemata contain central and peripheral components because they are
hierarchically structured. The activation of one central component is
sufficient to trigger the complete schema. Its activation serves not only
as an interpretation of the transaction but also as a control of the action: Schemata also contain instructions for actions (see Abelson, 1981).

Assumptions about emotional components of a schema are missing
in the approaches mentioned. Lang's (1979) and Leventhal's (1980)
theories deal with this aspect. Bower and Cohen (1982) extended the
network theory of memory to include emotional components. One assumption mentioned in these theories is especially important: Even
emotions can be stored in the form of schemata. Emotions are, according to Leventhal and Lang, generalized emotional experiences.
They possess a specific structure in which situational aspects and auto-
nomic, expressive, and instrumental reactions, as well as emotional
experiences, are connected with one another. The activation of an
emotional schema leads to activation of emotional processes that are
represented in the emotional schema. So I postulate that a transaction
schema contains not only knowledge about personal and situational
conditions of action, possibilities for actions, and limitations, but also
about emotional experiences, which are connected with the knowledge
of actions.

In the following, I restrict my attention to those emotions that correspond, in my opinion, to action control. It is not the goal of this study to offer a general contribution to the psychology of emotion but rather to clarify the interrelation of cognitive and emotional processes in action control; therefore, numerous emotions (such as sadness and love) are not considered. However, a number of theories and empirical results (e.g., Lazarus & Launier, 1978; Schwarzer, 1981; Mandler, 1975; Eckensberger & Emminghaus, 1982) suggest that often those aspects of person–environment transaction that reflect the degree of possibilities for action control cause emotions.

After these rather abstract comments about transaction schema, I return to the seafood lover. The activation of a transaction schema is assumed as he enters the tavern. The tourist still assumes that, according to his standards, he has entered a normal restaurant, which means that he has activated a transaction schema that features, among other components, the following: This is the kind of seafood restaurant *I am used to,* with set tables, hasty waiters, a glass case close to the door where you can choose the kind of fish you like, the low voices of the guests. . . . I am looking forward to an extensive dinner, I am going to take my time; soon I will choose a table, sit down and order.

His presently activated transaction schema contains knowledge of the properties of such a restaurant and of the pleasure he usually experiences in such situations. Furthermore, he knows what to do in such a place to satisfy his needs.

The tourist, however, is seriously confused at first. His hypotheses and expectations about this tavern are not confirmed. Instead he finds loitering men who stare at him, no table in sight, much noise, and increasing discomfort. If he had not been so determined to have his seafood dinner, he probably would have turned around immediately (he would have rejected the activated transaction schema and, *consequently,* would have drawn behavioral conclusions). But the tourist keeps on thinking that he is in a seafood restaurant and, therefore, looks for verifications. Indeed, he discovered a few set tables after a while (he adheres to the presently activated transaction schema).

Maybe he also considers the following: Well, I am in a strange country; maybe it is the custom here that tavern and restaurant are in one room; well, you learn something new every day. He has integrated a subordinate schema, "tavern," into the superordinate schema, "I have a great appetite for a fish dinner and I am in a seafood restaurant". Both schemata form the new, hierarchically organized transaction schema whose activation enables the tourist to organize his behavior in this situation in order to receive his fish dinner (to achieve his goal). However, this activation produces specific emotional processes in the tourist (first, discomfort; then, relief and anticipated joy). Like all comparisons, this is a lame one; but I hope it has served to clarify my notion of a transaction schema.

As in the description of an actual transaction *state*, I assume the possibility of a hierarchical structure in the description of the transaction *schema*. Knowledge and emotional experiences that concern the possibilities of action control are hierarchically organized in a transaction schema. At higher levels, personal goals or standards—as far as the actor is conscious of them—are compared to options or obstacles which—in the actor's opinion—exist in the situation, in order that these goals may be achieved. At lower levels, knowledge corresponds to relations of perceived environment and person components that are helpful or constructive in controlling actions directed to achieve goals already set.

In the previous paragraph, I postulate that emotional processes closely correspond with the present action control and hypotheses about it. According to this assumption, I suppose that various emotional experiences can be represented at the different levels of the transaction schema. In this way, the relationship between personal goals and, in the actor's opinion, attainable goals is connected with specific emotional experiences. (The tourist associates with his knowledge—being in a seafood restaurant and having a great appetite—pure joy).

At another level of the transaction schema which, for example, represents the knowledge of what to do in order to achieve a certain goal and the knowledge of restricted possibilities for actions, there are, among other things, the emotional experiences represented. (The tourist may not be able to understand the menu and may fear ordering the wrong dish. This situation might be associated with an unpleasant feeling like apprehension.)

In general, I assume that once the action control level and its corresponding level of the transaction schema are activated, different emotional processes can be initiated. As the tourist activates the goal to eat fish he is happy; as he considers how to achieve this goal, he experiences discomfort. The following section system focusses on these assumptions in detail.

THE ACTION CONTROL SYSTEM

According to my model, person–environment transaction states are interpreted by the actor in that he compares present information from the environment and information about his own person with accessible knowledge about past experiences. By this process, the transaction schema is activated and functions later as the "frame of interpretation". The results of this interpretation process (of which the actor is often unaware; see below) become standards for future action control processes leading finally to further activities that include observable behavior.

As indicated in the description of the model, I distinguish between two control systems whose interaction determines the action control of an actor: I explain first the emotional, then the cognitive control system.

The Emotional Control System

Two groups of properties characterise this control system: specific process features and specific contents. Essential for my description of the emotional control system is the assumption that emotional control processes operate largely beyond the self-control processes of the actor. They start and flow without any extra effort; they are inevitable (see Averill, 1980; Leventhal, 1980; Peters, 1970; Simon, 1967; Zajonc, 1980).

Emotional processes differ in their intensity of degree of arousal. I assume that the more intensely the emotional control processes flow, the stronger their influence on the whole control process. In the following two sections, I specify these assumptions. Physiological measures can be taken to assess the degree of arousal, but, in my opinion, psychological process indices are more important. I assume that arousal of the emotional control system is perceived, in that one feels pushed into specific operations or one is aware of physiological changes in oneself that are more or less beyond voluntary control. To what extent these feelings of being forced to do something and of losing self-control correspond systematically to physiological data has, at present, not been fully investigated. However, the works of Thayer (1967, 1970) can be interpreted, in my opinion, as follows: Verbal statements on the degree of the activation or on the degree of the experienced loss of control correspond well to a combination of various physiological measures.

Besides these process characteristics, the emotional control system is describable by its *contents*. The contents are emotional experiences of a specific *quality*. These emotional experiences can be understood as holistic and inescapable signals of present, past, or future degrees of action control within a specific person–environment transaction state. According to the intensity of the emotional processes and their substantial quality, various cognitive operations and behaviours are initiated (as to the various activities of the cognitive control system, see

the following section). The activity of the emotional system consists of
the processing of the emotional part of the transaction schema. This
processing leads to specific emotional processes of different intensities,
to a development of specific emotional experiences, and to an initiation
of further activities in the cognitive control system.

With regard to action control, the emotional control system has several functions:

1. It selects components of an experienced person–environment
   transaction.
2. It produces irrevocable holistic signals that inform the actor
   about the extent to which discrepancy between the actualized
   standards and a present situation exists and about the extent to
   which the actor is able to control this discrepancy (see Simon,
   1967; Carver & Scheier, 1981).
3. It leads over to various cognitive control processes depending
   on the quality and intensity of the emotional processes and
   thereby limits the range of accessible cognitive and behavioural
   operations.

The Cognitive Control System

In my assumption that human actions are hierarchically and sequentially organized, a number of cognitive control processes are included that regulate actions or sequences of action. My general
description of cognitive control processes is based on action-regulation
theories (see Miller et al., 1960; Hacker, 1973; Österreich, 1981;
Powers, 1973; Carver & Scheier, 1981; and Gallistel, 1980). In Hacker's (1973, p. 113) "comparison–change feedback unit", two action
control functions are differentiated. One is an anticipating plan—a
program—of the succeeding operations that are realized through a sequence of recording steps. The other is the realization process that is
continuously matched with the anticipating plan (besides the step-for-
step control of interim results and interim goals).

Cognitive action control starts with the development of the action
plan and persists with the continuous control in the course of actions.
Input standards of the cognitive control system are the components of
the actual person–environment transaction as they are interpreted by
the actor according to his or her activated transaction schema. The
action plan connects several hierarchically structured "*chunks* of knowl-

edge'' and, on this basis, organizes actions in their chronological sequence.

If actions are transformations of (undesired) initial situations into preferable and anticipated goal situations, then cognitive processes that enable the actor to perceive deviations from the goal standard have to be applied. Furthermore, events perceived in a person–environment transaction are tested with respect to their potential influence on achieving the actions' goals or standards. This testing presupposes that superordinate goals or standards are divided into subgoals or substandards. Goals and subgoals then have to be ordered acccording to their planned execution: A schedule for the execution of subgoals has to be developed. This requires knowledge of the relationship among goals and subgoals. After the chronological order of the execution of subgoals has been determined, operations have to be selected that influence events connected with a standard discrepancy in the desired way and that simultaneously suppress undesired side effects.

In summary, it may be said that an action plan contains procedures that determine the goal or standard and that divide goals into subgoals and specify a chronological order of the goals' execution, as well as a development of behaviours appropriate to gain the particular subgoals.

In an actual flow of action, the cognitive control generally consists of (1) perceiving the course and interim results of an action; (2) comparing the action with the planned course and the intended interim results; (3) initiating, in cases of cognitive discrepancies, correction procedures; and (4) again controlling their realization. In the case of an unexpected discrepancy (i.e., one that is not considered in the action plan), the actor initiates cognitive processes in order to generate alternative actions that are adequate for the plan, considering the expected effect of the event. If these processes do not generate adequate actions, the actor initates further superordinate processing operations that lead to an activation of goals or standards at higher levels and, consequently, to new subordinate processing operations.

So cognitive processes have two general functions with respect to action control:

1. They help the actor develop action plans in a situation in which goals of actions or standards are determined and ordered chronologically and in which appropriate operations for approaching goals or achieving standards are contained.
2. They control presently occurring actions in such a way that the actor compares their progress with the plan progress and, in the

case of an unexpected discrepancy, attempts to initiate an appropriate control mechanism.

Interdependencies

A few of the conceivable relationships among the two control systems, mentioned previously, are explained in detail.

Cognitive and emotional control processes interact again and again with one another in the course of action. Once again, and for the last time, I refer to the tourist example: As he entered the restaurant, he was confronted with a situation that was strange to him, a situation that he could not link with prior experience. After a misinterpretation of certain parts of the situation (e.g., the men who stared at him), he reacted with discomfort and later with a degree of anxiety. Or, in the prosaic terms of the model: The perceived events led to (as input standards for the cognitive control system) the experience of insufficient control in the situation. This experience (as a result of the cognitive control system's activity) led to a higher state of arousal in the emotional control system and to the development of the emotional signal 'anxiety'. This signal induced further cognitive activities on the actor's part which, despite the perceived action barriers producing discomfort (staring men blocking his way, the darkness of the room) were aimed at goal achievement (choosing a table where he could enjoy his seafood dinner).

After the tourist discovers the tables at the far end of the room and experiences his appetite, he interprets the situation as a more familiar one, as a situation in which he knows how to act and what to do in order to satisfy his appetite. This new interpretation leads to a feeling of relief and relaxation.

Both the cognitive interpretation of the room as an atypical seafood restaurant and the feeling of relief cause the traveller finally to become active and to head for a table. Results of the cognitive control processes become input standards for the emotional control system and vice versa; at the end of a control process, the results of both systems are integrated into organized behavioural sequences whose completion is achieved by cognitive and emotional control processes. If the tourist, however, had felt not a *degree* of anxiety but rather is "consumed" by anxiety, then the story would probably have taken a different course. He probably would have left the restaurant immediately and gone to the snackbar next door to get a slice of pizza, unless the event had totally spoiled his appetite.

I postulate that the reciprocal relationship between the two control systems can take various forms according to the degree of arousal in the emotional control system. At a high level of arousal, cognitive processes that Dörner et al. (1983, p. 591) designate as "emergency reactions of the cognitive system" can occur. Their purpose is to achieve a preparedness for fast and general reactions. Cognitive processes that are accompanied by a high level of arousal in the emotional control system are no longer aimed at achieving a concrete goal but rather serve the purpose of an arousal reduction by giving the actor a "breather" and thereby producing new possibilities for goal-directed actions.

I mention another conceivable relationship between the two systems: Since the input standards for the two systems are not necessarily compatible, there may be conflict; the actor may, for example, experience rage, a feeling enforcing a behaviour that is directed to an event, a person, or a situation in order to eliminate the supposed cause of rage; simultaneously the actor sees no possibility (resulting from cognitive control activity) to take action in the situation. This is a case of contradicting control results.

This kind of contradiction can be resolved in various ways according to the degree of arousal of the emotional system. At a high degree of arousal, the emotional control system dominates further control processes (the actor behaves according to his degree of rage); at a low degree of arousal, compromise solutions are sought (i.e., the actor signals the environment that he is in a state of rage, without showing aggressive activities). In this way, both control systems influence each other. The cognitive control system influences the arousal and the contents of the emotional control system, and emotional control processes influence—according to the degree of arousal and varying in extent—the direction and the quality of cognitive control processes.

OUTPUT

In the general presentation of the model, I introduced more-or-less organized action sequences resulting from action control. Actions, as output standards of the two control systems, can be classified and categorized in several ways. I restrict myself to presentation of general aspects by which actions can be described in terms of our model.

Actions can be distinquished from one another by the *goals or standards* they are directed to. Goals or standards can be organized at different *levels* simultaneously, they can include different *substantial* qualities (goals and subgoals differ in their contents). This is the first category, which leads to a distinction between the different output standards of action control. A second category, which is closely related to the first, concerns the *organizational complexity* of action sequences. A single action can be the result of the action control (especially if the standard to which the action is directed is organized at a lower level) or the result of highly structured action sequences (if these sequences aim at goals or standards at a high organization level). Another categorization aspect, which again is closely related to the first category, is the *locus of the desired goal,* that is, whether actions are directed to changing the environment or the person. In this sense, Lazarus et al. (1980) distinguish between two kinds of coping: problem solving and emotion regulation. In a similar manner, Janis and Mann (1977) differentiate between the various forms of problem solving. The purpose of problem-solving ("instrumental") activities is to optimize person–environment constellations by changing the environment components. Activities regulating emotions influence emotions and, thereby, the person components in a transaction. For example, a goal of activities regulating emotions is an interruption of a proceeding action sequence. This interruption enables the actor to have an emotional "fill up" for a fresh and active start (Schwarzer, 1981, p. 79).

The emotional control system restricts—according to its degree of activation—in various proportions, the margin of freedom of the cognitive control system. It limits the range of potential cognitions that influence cognitive operations, and it regulates the choice of cognitive operations, as well as the quality of their execution. In contrast, the type and quality of emotional control processes is determined, to a certain extent, by cognitive activities.

The cognitive system carries the main control activities; that is, every action control is a cognitive activity. The cognitive processes during action control are "covered" by emotional processes. These emotional processes determine the orientation or direction and range in which cognitive activities can spread. In this way, they contribute—according to their degree of activation—to an assessment of the specific form of action control. In this way, emotional processes form the background for the cognitive activities.

In the following section, I illustrate these assumptions with an example of control processes. The example is of an actor who perceives an event while completing an action. The event is connected with an unexpected (not contained in the plan) and undesired discrepancy toward a standard or goal at a lower organization level.

Control Processes at a Medium Level of Arousal

Elsewhere in this chapter, I point out that different levels of arousal in the emotional control system correlate with different forms of action control. At a high level of arousal, the emotional control system dominates the selection of control activities; at a low level of arousal, both systems contribute in the same manner in determining the control operations. In this section, I describe—in a speculative manner—two forms of interaction between the two control systems that can occur at a medium level of arousal; in the subsequent section, several control processes at a high level of arousal are illustrated.

Peter is obsessed with the idea of becoming a musician. He has practised the guitar for several hours a day for over a year; in his opinion he has reached a level of performance that fits him to join the music scene of the town. One evening while eating, Peter notices that Paul is sitting at a table next to him. Paul is the unchallenged leader of the musicians' group, and Peter knows that there is no way to get around Paul. Just as Peter has made up his mind to address Paul, a woman enters the restaurant. Paul looks at her; she notices him and comes running toward him. They embrace each other. Then she sits down at Paul's table. Peter is perplexed, a little annoyed even, and emotionally irritated. Just before achieving his goal, this had to happen!

I assume that Peter had a medium level of arousal. I mention elsewhere that the level of arousal in the emotional control system relates to the degree of losing control, that is, the experience of being forced to do something. A low level of arousal is accompanied by a voluntary exhaustion of all necessary cognitive operations for action control; however, a medium level of arousal impedes an optimal action control for the actor. At a high level of arousal, initially intended goals have to be neglected in favour of attempts to master the high degree of arousal (see previous section).

Peter is fairly irritated as he has to watch how the woman endangers his plan. What should be done? First, Peter considers whether he should wait for a better occasion to address Paul. Since he meets Paul very rarely, the situation is urgent. Peter finds himself in a situation he has already experienced several times: He makes up his mind to do something and another person blocks his plan. Normally, he reacts angrily or even furiously and then tries to "neutralize" the other person. Slowly, Peter becomes angry with the woman; after all she is the one who made it impossible to establish the long-desired contact with Paul.

The feeling that occurs when a plan is blocked by an intervening event from the environment is rage. To simplify matters, I distinguish, for the case of undesired increasing discrepancy (here, the woman impeding the goal of contact with Paul), between two feelings (see Eckensberger & Emminghaus, 1980; Weiner et al., 1978; Lantermann, 1980).

Rage

The achievement of a goal is blocked by events from the environment (attribution of external causes), but the actor still sees an opportunity of reaching the goal through his actions.

Anxiety

The achievement of a goal is threatened by events from the environment, and the actor does not see any way of reaching the goal through his actions.

Peter becomes angry (in the following section, I assume, however, that he became anxious). In this situation, it is quite likely that Peter's further actions are organized and controlled in a pattern of circularity; while under the influence of anxiety, the actor would be likely to introduce more skips in the process of action control.

CIRCULARITY

Peter holds on to his plan. He waits until the two have greeted each other, then he looks at Paul and nods his head as Paul turns away from the woman for a second. Yet nothing happens. Obviously, Paul is more interested in the woman than in anything else. Unable to think of anything that could be helpful in this situation, Peter starts talking in a loud voice to the man at the table next to him. The topic of this conversation is "the possessive woman". Although he still cannot detect a chance to establish contact with Paul, he tries again and again to communicate with him; and in the process, he becomes more and more excited and furious. Other guests in the restaurant notice this and become slightly amused at his behaviour. Finally, Peter pulls himself together, walks over to the table next to him, interrupts the intimate conversation between the woman and Paul by addressing the woman: "Excuse me, but I simply have to talk to Paul." Paul looks at him and starts talking to him.

I now tell the story in terms of the model. The actor (Peter) finds himself in a person–environment constellation that he associates with a specific transaction schema. The activation of a transaction schema leads to an activation of specific knowledge about the characteristics of the situation, the person, and the potential goal-directed actions. Moreover, certain emotional processes are initiated. The approaching woman is interpreted by the actor as an event that leads to an increasing goal discrepancy and impedes the completion of actions adequate to his plan. The perceived increase in goal discrepancy leads to a higher state of arousal in the emotional control system. Further results of the cognitive control system (high priority) lead to a greater increase of arousal until a medium level is reached. Simultaneously, the actor attributes the cause of the blocking of his action to the environment (the woman). The results of the cognitive control system level leads to a production of the emotional signal, rage. This is supported by emotions produced by the activated transaction schema.

The feeling of rage triggers further cognitive control processes (such as a deficient analysis of the situation as a whole; maintaining the initially chosen hypothesis, namely, that the cause of the blocking of the action is the woman; the decision to hold on to the once-chosen goal and to complete corresponding actions). The activities of the two control systems result in the actor completing his planned actions. The actor relates the result of these actions to the initial goal and again records the goal discrepancy. This discrepancy leads to an increase of the level of arousal in the emotional control system (greater and greater rage), and the actor again tries to maintain his first cognitive assessment of the situation and to approach this goal through his own actions.

In this way, circularity is a special form of action control. Circularity characterizes a process of control which returns over and over again to its starting point: Once a goal is chosen, it is maintained; similar analyses of the person–environment constellation are carried out; despite the absence of success, actions that aim at the same goal are completed again and again. This process is largely determined by the activities of the emotional control system, that is, a medium level of arousal prevents the actor from escaping from the already initiated cognitive sequence of operations; however, the produced emotional contents determine the direction of these operations. Circular control processes have not only negative effects but also positive functions in that they relieve the actor—at least for some time— of further demands from the action; in this way, they allow the actor a "breather" that gives him a chance to optimize his possibilities of control.

SKIPS

In an alternative version of the story, I assume that Peter felt threatened rather than furious when the woman entered. What turn does the story take now? Peter finds himself in a situation he knows: He has made up his mind to do something, but another person blocks his plan. He knows that he often reacts with a high degree of arousal and with a feeling of threat or anxiety. He becomes anxious, imagining that he might not achieve his planned goal and afraid of the resulting negative consequences. In this case, anxiety signals an external threat with which the actor cannot cope in an adequate way.

Peter experiences anxiety as he watches the intimate greeting between Paul and the woman. He stares at them without thinking of how to improve the situation. Instead, he remembers how important it is for his career as a musician to establish contact with Paul. One year of intensive practice seems wasted. The woman is spoiling everything completely. More thoughts come to his mind: What else can he do? He has no job; his parents are urging him to stand on his own feet; and so on. But these thoughts frighten him even more. He pulls himself together and tries to think of what he can do in this situation in order to make contact with Paul. But nothing comes to mind. Again he becomes anxious and starts thinking of his general situation, his general ineptitudes, and so forth. Again he forces himself to find some possibility for action, but in vain. He becomes so excited that he finally jumps up and leaves the restaurant without paying the waiter.

I now return to the model. The actor finds himself in a person–environment constellation that leads to the activation of a corresponding schema in himself, and, thereby, to the activation of specific knowledge about the situation and about himself, as well as to an initiation of specific emotional processes. Realizing that the goal is blocked by the occurrence of an event in the environment (the woman) and realizing his lack of ability to act in this situation, the level of arousal in the emotional control system increases and the emotional signal 'anxiety' arises, supported by emotional processes that were induced by the activation of the transaction schema.

This is communicated to the cognitive control system, resulting in an initiation of further cognitive control processes in the actor (deficient analysis of the situation as a whole, maintained hypothesis that the woman is the cause of the goal's blocking, consideration of further options in the course of action without success, etc.). Furthermore, these cognitive processes contribute to the goal discrepancy with further goals or standards represented at a higher organization level. At these higher levels, goals are organized that concern one's own self (important personal goals, norms, standards).

To a great extent, these cognitive processes operate automatically because in a state of medium or high arousal of the emotional system, the results of the activities and the processes of this system advise or direct the cognitive control system in its activities (see the section on the general model). The activation of higher level goals and the interpretation of concrete events (the arrival of the woman), as well as the blocking of these goals, lead to an increase in the intensity of anxiety. The degree of arousal does not yet exceed the medium level, so the actor makes a great effort to try to find goal-adequate actions. He returns to the starting point, analyses the situation in the same manner, and returns to the conclusion that he is unable to act and that the situation is highly important for the achievement of his goal. Again, goals of a higher level are activated and options for the course of action are considered, until the level of arousal in the emotional control system has reached a high level. At this moment, the actor gives up trying to act according to his goal and selects a behaviour that is aimed at reducing arousal (he leaves the restaurant).

In this way, another form of interaction between the emotional and the cognitive control system is described. Skips that reflect a special control process at a medium level of arousal, are in general characterized as follows: The actor activates, during the processing of a goal, additional higher level goals *and then*, without any further cognitive activity, returns to the previously considered standard or goal *and then*, again, tries to reduce the perceived goal discrepancy through his own actions. The actor skips over—forced by the activity of the emotional control system—the steps of the analysis during the action's control that would have been necessary for a successful handling of the situation through his own actions.

Control Processes at a High Level of Arousal

Skips and circularities are forms of action control that remain goal-oriented even if they do not exhaust all options. They are directed towards a change in the person–environment transaction in order that the actor's planned goal may be approached. Until the end, Peter did not give up his goal of establishing contact with Paul; he tried again and again, despite adverse circumstances, to reach the goal. At the end of the second version of the story, he left the restaurant in a hurry. He could not stand it any longer: He became more and more excited and anxious, and his thoughts became more aggressive and uncontrolled. He had to leave because he could not bear the situation and his excitement and anxiety. Let up follow him a little farther. He runs into the street, almost failing to notice a parked bicycle, keeps on running and "gets it off his chest". Little by little he gains some relief. Anxiety eases and thoughts are under control again. Peter realizes that he has been running around like a madman. Involuntarily, he slows down and finally stops. He feels slightly embarrassed and continues to blaming himself. Then he considers what to do. Should he return to the restaurant? Would he make a fool of himself by doing so? Excuses for his sudden disappearance could be found very easily; for example he remembered an urgent call he had to make. So he turns around, walks back to the restaurant, and forces himself to enter, relaxed and whistling. He walks straight up to Paul, who still sits at the table and is a little bored. Then he starts to talk.

What happened in terms of the model? The two control systems forced each other upwards. Cognitive processes were executed imprecisely and imperfectly and led to unfavourable results that initiated the emotional process control system, which signalled increasing anxiety to the actor. Finally, the arousal exceeded the medium level. The actor was highly aroused and very anxious. This state resulted in further control processes that concerned the arousal itself. The instrumental control of goals was temporarily replaced by processes regulating emotions. According to Dörner (Dörner et al., 1983), "emergency reaction of the cognitive system" took place. In this context, it would be more precise to say that an emergency reaction of the control system as a whole took place. The actor tried to control his emotions by avoiding the demands of a situation he could not cope with. Peter escaped. After the successful regulation of emotions (reducing the arousal to a lower level) the actor began again to perform instrumental goal-directed actions. He oriented his further behaviour according to the original goal.

Control processes at a high level of arousal are, in general, characterized as being directed towards the successful regulation of emotional processes resulting in more favourable conditions for goal-directed actions.

Despite their assumed spontaneity and naturalness, actions regulating emotions remain context related. The activated transaction schema contains, as I explained previously, emotional aspects, which are connected with cognitive knowledge or knowledge about the present person–environment transaction. According to the perceived state of this person–environment, various options to act are initiated. The emo-

tional state of anxiety leads, according to the situation, to specific be-
haviour(s) that are *equifinal* in that they support the actor in reducing
his anxiety, at least for some time. Averill (1980) presents a theory of
emotion that includes assumptions about actions occurring at a high
level of arousal (with a high level of *involvement*). Under these circumstances, the actor is constrained by his social role within the person-
environment transaction and organizes his behaviour correspondingly.
This assumption is similar to the one mentioned above, in that actions
regulating emotions that are likely to occur at a high level of arousal
in the emotional control system are context bound.

   With these remarks, I conclude the description of the model. The
model accounts for only some components of action control. Cognitive–emotional processes, such as "new versus familiar" and "simple
versus complex", that are connected with the assessment of a concrete
event (see Berlyne, 1960; especially Mandler, 1975, 1981) have to be
neglected. According to the type of problem, different kinds of analytic
decomposition of the control of action becomes necessary. In this presentation of the model, I have attempted a compromise between a general and a detailed description.

Concluding Remarks

   I have utilized existing concepts from various fields of psychology
for the development of a general model of action control. Everything
discussed would remain vague if it were impossible to derive concrete
research programs from the model. However, this is exactly what I am
doing. In the near future, I hope to acquire and present more concrete
information about the process of action control. At this stage, I simply
emphasize a few aspects of the model.

   First, the examples I have used are limited to negative emotions (rage
and anxiety), but this does not restrict the potential applicability of the
model. In my opinion, not only losing or threatening action control
but also having or regaining it can be explained by this model; and,
thus, the interaction of *positive* emotions and further components of this
model can be explained. For example, the unexpected experience of
having control that is accompanied by the emotional signal "joy" can
lead to skips in the same way anxiety does, which may result in inadequate or omitted goal-directed actions. When joy occurs unex-
pectedly, the situation is often not analysed in detail, because joy is
associated with the feeling of "having made it", of being able to manage the situation or personal demands without any extra strain.

To summarize briefly, the central aspects of the model of action control are as follows. Human actions are directed and controlled, not only by cognitive, but also by emotional processes that are closely intertwined with one another. The control takes place at various distinctive levels of the organization of actions. Emotional and cognitive control interact in the course of action in many ways. Cognitive operations influence emotional processes and their quality. Emotional processes—according to their intensity—force cognitive operations and certain behaviour(s) upon the actor.

Cognition and emotion cannot be distinguished clearly from each other in their observable influence on the course of actions: They are more analytical categories for a description and explanation of human actions. Control processes can always be considered from an emotional or cognitive perspective, and it would be very difficult to classify events as purely cognitive or emotional. To this extent this model remains somewhat arbitrary because it distinguishes two systems of action control whose function leads to results in which both aspects melt together. Nevertheless, this distinction seems appropriate, and should remain so, for the description of human action. Many theories of human action—some even more recent than the one discussed in this chapter—give me cause for optimism on this point.

References

Abelson, R. P. (1973). Structural analysis of belief systems. In *Computer Models of Thought and Language*. (R. C. Schank & K. M. Colby, eds.). Freeman: San Francisco.

Abelson, R. P. (1981). Psychological status of the script concept. *American Psychologist, 36*, 715–729.

Alston, W. P. (1972). *Emotion and feeling*. In *Encyclopedia of Philosophy*. (P. Edwards, ed.). Macmillan: New York. pp. 479–493.

Argyle, M., Furnham, A., & Graham, J. A. (1981). *Social situations*. Cambridge University Press: Cambridge.

Averill, J. R. (1980). A constructivist view of emotion. In *Emotion: Theory, Research and Experience*. (Vol. 1). (R. Plutchik & H. Kellerman, eds.). Academic Press: New York.

Bandura, A. (1971). Self-efficacy: Toward a unifying theory of behavioural change. *Psychological Review, 84*, 191–215.

Bartlett, F. C. (1932). *Remembering*. Cambridge University Press: London.

Bedford, E. (1957). Emotions. *Aristotelian Society Proceedings 57*, 281–304.

Berlyne, D. E. (1960). *Conflict, arousal and curiosity*. McGraw Hill: New York.

Bower, G. H. (1981). Mood and memory. *American Psychologist, 36*, 129–148.

Bower, G. H., & Cohen, R. R. (1982). *Emotional influences in memory and thinking: Data and theory*. Paper presented at the 17th Annual Carnegie Symposium on Cognition.

Carver, Ch., & Scheier, M. F. (1981). *Attention and Self-Regulation: A Control Theory Approach to Human Behaviour.* Springer-Verlag: New York, Berlin.

Cranach, M. von, Kalbermatten, U., Indermühle, K., & Gugler, B. (1980). *Zielgerichtetes Handeln.* Bern: Huber.

Dörner, D., Kreuzig, H. W., Reither, F., & Staendel, T. (1983). *Lohhausen. Von Umgang mit Unbestimmtheit und Komplexitat: Ein Forschungsbericht.* Bamberg.

Eckensberger, L. H., & Emminghaus, W. B. (1982). Aggression und Moral. In *Aggression, Naturwissenschaftliche und Kulturwissenschaftliche Perspektiven der Aggressionsforschung.* (R. Hilke and W. Kempf, eds.). Huber: Bern. pp. 208–280.

Gallistel, C. R. (1980). *The Organisation of Action: A New Synthesis.* Lawrence Erlbaum: Hillsdale, N.J.

Hacker, W. (1973). *Allgemeine Arbeits- und Ingenieur-psychologie.* Deutscher Verlag der Wissenschaften: Berlin.

Heckhausen, H. (1980). *Motivation und Handeln.* Springer-Verlag: Berlin, New York.

Janis, I. L., & Mann, L. (1977). *Decision Making.* Free Press of Glencoe: New York.

Kaminski, G. (1981). Überlegungen zur Funktion von Handlungstheorien in der Psychologie. In *Handlungstheorien interdisziplinär III.* 1. Halbband. (Lenk. H., ed.). W. Fink Verlag: München.

Krenauer, M., and Schönpflug, W. (1980). Regulation und Fehlregulation im Verhalten III: Zielsetzung und Ursachenbeschreibung unter Belastung. *Psychologische Beiträge 22,* 414–431.

Kuhl, J. (1982). The expectancy-value approach to the theory of social motivation: Elaborations, extensions, critique. In *Expectations and action.* (N. T. Feather, ed.). Erlbaum: Hillsdale, N.J. pp. 125–160.

Lang, P. J. (1979). A bio-informational theory of emotional imagery. *Psychophysiology, 16,* 495–512.

Lantermann, E. D. (1980). *Interaktionen—Person, Situation und Handlung.* Urban & Schwarzenberg: München, Baltimore.

Laucken, U. (1974). *Naive Verhaltenstheorie.* Klett: Stuttgart.

Lazarus, R. S., & Launier, R. (1978). Stress-related transactions between person and environment. In *Perspectives in Interactional Psychology.* (L. A. Pervin & M. Lewis, eds.). Plenum Press: New York.

Lazarus, R. S., Kanner, A. D., & Folkman, S. (1980). Emotions: A cognitive–phenomenological analysis. In *Emotion Theory, Research, and Experience.* Vol. 1. (R. Plutchik & H. Kellerman, eds.). Academic Press: New York.

Leventhal, H. (1980). Toward a comprehensive theory of emotion. In *Advances in Experimental Social Psychology.* Vol. 13. (L. Berkowitz, ed.). Academic Press: New York.

Mandler, G. (1975). *Mind and Emotion.* Wiley: New York.

Mandler, G. (1982). *The structure of value: Accounting for taste.* Paper presented at the 17th Annual Carnegie Symposium on Cognition, Erlbaum: Hillsdale, N.J.

Miller, G. A., Galanter, E., & Pribam, K. H. (1960). *Plans and the structure of behaviour.* Holt: New York (bei Klett, Stuttgart, 1973).

Österreich, R., (1981). *Handlungsregulation und Kontrolle.* Urban & Schwarzenberg: München, Baltimore.

Peters, R. S. (1970). The education of the emotions. In *Feelings and Emotion: The Loyola Symposium* (M. B. Arnold, ed.). Academic Press: New York.

Piaget, J. (1926). *The Language and Thought of the Child.* Harcourt, Brace: New York.

Plutchik, R. (1980). A general psychoevolutionary theory of emotion. In *Emotion: Theory, research and experience.* (Vol. 1) (R. Plutchik & H. Kellerman, eds.) Academic Press: New York. pp. 3–34.

Powers, W. T. (1973). Feedback: Beyond behaviourism. *Science, 1979,* 351-356. (Vol. 1) (R. Plutchik & H. Kellerman, eds.). Academic Press: New Schank, R. C., & Abelson, R. P. (1977). *Scripts, Plans, Goals, and Understanding.* Erlbaum: Hillsdale, N.J.

Schönpflug, W. (1979). Regulation und Fehlregulation im Verhalten: I. Verhaltensstruktur, Effizienz und Belastung—theoretische Grundlagen eines Untersuchungsprogram ms. *Psychologische Beitrage, 21,* 174-203.

Schulz, P. (1979). Regulation und Fehlregulation im Verhalten. II: Stress durch Fehlregulation. *Psychologische Beiträge, 21,* 597-621.

Schwarzer, R. (1981). *Stress, Angst und Hilflosigkeit.* Kohlhammer: Stuttgart.

Simon, H. A. (1967). Motivational and emotional controls of cognition. *Psychological Review, 74,* 29-39.

Thayer, R. E. (1967). Measurement of activation through self-report. *Psychological Reports, 20,* 663-678.

Thayer, R. E. (1970). Activation states as assessed by verbal report and four psychophysiological variables. *Psychophysiology, 7,* 86-94.

Weiner, B. (ed.) (1974). *Achievement, Motivation and Attribution Theory.* General Learning Press: Morristown, N.J.

Weiner, B., Russell, D., & Lerman, D. (1978). Affective consequences of causal ascription. In *New Directions in Attribution Research.* Vol. 2. (J. H. Harvey, W. Ickes, & R. F. Kidd, eds.). Erlbaum: Hillsdale, N.J.

Zajonc, R. B. (1980). Feeling and thinking. Preferences need no inferences. *American Psychologist, 35,* 151-175.

5

The Significance of Action Psychology for Personality Research and Assessment

J. P. de Waele

Present-Day Problems of Personality Psychology

Since the 1950s, it has become evident that the term "crisis" is no longer adequate to describe the state that characterizes present-day personality psychology. The difficulties besetting the whole field, once thought to be essentially of a methodological nature, have been discovered to have profound institutional roots. If one defines the field of personality psychology as the study of whole single persons, and if theory construction, systematic scientific research, and diagnostic assessment are considered to be the three pillars on which it rests as an intellectual enterprise, then no extended investigations are needed to discover that there exist only very few institutions whose activities involve a conjunction of theorizing, research, and assessment aimed at the knowledge of whole single persons. Instead, a chronic dispersal of efforts has eventually made of personality psychology an underdeveloped field, the specificity and the legitimacy of which has been questioned by psychologists to whom the concept of "person" is apparently devoid of meaning.

The clinical setting, where the weight of therapeutic requirements is difficult to reconcile with research interests, is no longer the source of the kind of grand speculations that helped to define personality psychology as a distinct field of investigation. True, Freudian, Jungian, Adlerian, and other conceptualizations of psychotherapeutic origin lacked the kind of methodological sophistication that we in the last years of the twentieth century consider ourselves entitled to require from theoretical formulations. It can also be argued that much of what once passed for theory among the founding fathers of personality psychology was, in fact, the ethnocentric naturalization of culturally determined normative conceptions destined to define the normal or fully functioning person (Rogers, 1961) and thus to legitimize therapeutic endeavours. Still, clinical work and psychotherapeutic practice retain the unequalled advantage of being based on long and repeated interactions between patient and clinician. This intensive aspect of the professional's practice constitutes its unassailable strength.

When, through the research performed mainly by G. W. Allport, K. Lewin, and H. A. Murray, personality psychology became academically salonfahig, it achieved scientific recognition by lending itself to conceptual analysis and to empirical verification. However, the costs it had to bear for achieving academic status were high. Personality psychology became a technique-centered discipline based on data, gathered according to the rules of extensive designs, the personal relevance of which could never be ascertained. The heavy statistical artillery that was called to the rescue never made up for the inaccessibility of what was to remain the exclusive hunting ground of the clinician. At most, it made available a set of highly sophisticated mathematical techniques that were to inspire a host of more or less systematized researches on various dimensions of personality. While inspired theorists either went on working within a totalizing framework, as did Cattell (1946), or attempted to provide their basic dimensions with neurophysiological foundations, as did Eysenck, too many others discovered the pre-established harmony existing between methodological positivism and the bureaucratization of research. Indeed, the academic institutions, whose functioning is characterized by the bureaucratization of funding and research and its implied publication imperatives, make of personology, defined as the study of whole single persons, a totally unrewarding undertaking since every basic norm of sound personology runs counter to institutionally defined scientific success. This has led to the investigation of isolated dimensions of personality, especially since the early 1950s, including authoritarianism, response style, approval, anxiety, achievement, field dependence, dogmatism, Machiavellianism, state and trait anxiety, affiliation, power, locus of control, trust, repression-sensitization, sensation seeking, and so on. A tremendous investment of time, money, and personnel resulted in the elaboration of what I call very limited monothematic theories, which were and still are of very little help in understanding individual persons. Thus, Carlson (1971) could justifiably ask: ''Where is the Person in Personality Psychology?''

Of course, arguments can be adduced for organizing the whole research enterprise in personality psychology on the model of an analytical approach, but then one would at least hope that the efforts made would lead to stable results. There, however, are most disappointing. For example, Edwards and Abbott (1973) found 106 studies that could be classified as examples of theory-testing research. Nineteen involved the Extraversion scale, 39 involved the Locus of Control scale, 14 involved the Manifest Anxiety Scale and 34 involved the Repression-Sensitization scale. As Table 5.1 demonstrates, the outcome of these studies can only be considered as a severe blow to the whole approach: In general, the hypothesis was as frequently not confirmed as confirmed (about 40% for each).

As to methods, the research on the 18 dimensions considered by Edwards and Abbott was often conducted essentially by questionnaire. This was so even though three major reviews, covering a total of 702 investigations and conducted 20 years earlier, had already raised grave doubts about the adequacy of questionnaires as a basic technique in personality research and assessment (Ellis, 1946; Ghiselli & Barthol, 1953; Windle, 1952).

The most recent fad in personality psychology is interactional personality psychology (Endler & Magnusson, 1976; Magnusson & Endler, 1977; Pervin & Lewis, 1978). Its avowed purpose is to analyze person-by-situation interactions, and it is purported to represent a new beginning based on a direct approach of whole single persons coping with concrete situations. Alas, a cursory review of the literature shows that the essential method used is the questionnaire and that, to most authors, the concept of interaction is identical with the one used in analysis of variance.

Neither in the field of systematically organized assessment nor in the field of psychodiagnostic techniques have developments since the early 1950s been very promising. The great success scored with projective

Table 1

Outcomes in Percentage of Hypothesis-Testing Studies Using Personality Scales[a]

	Extra-version ($N = 19$)	Locus of control ($N = 39$)	Manifest anxiety ($N = 14$)	Repression–sensitization ($N = 34$)	All four scales ($N = 106$)
Outcome:					
Hypothesis confirmed	47	49	29	29	40
Hypothesis not confirmed	42	36	42	53	43
?	11	15	29	18	17

[a]Adapted from Edwards and Abbot, 1973, Table 1.

techniques after the Second World War has stimulated many critical and validational studies. One conclusion that clearly emerges from this voluminous literature is that there exists a marked disproportion between the amount of research generated and the disappointing results obtained. Although one may very often entertain serious doubts about the adequacy of the methods by means of which the validity of projective techniques has been studied, on the whole, one is faced with the inescapable conclusion that projective techniques have not come up to the high expectations placed in them. Yet, one of the most irritating problems confronting psychodiagnostics is the glaring contradiction existing between the results of research reports and the claims made by practitioners concerning the value of projective techniques. As the practitioners persistently invoke their accumulated personal experience, there must be something wrong either with practitioners or with researchers or with both. But to whatever alternatives one's preferences may go, a critical situation has emerged since the early 1950s to which a solution must urgently be found. It is to the solution of this puzzling problem that Chapman and Chapman (1969), as well as Starr and Katkin (1969), have made decisive contributions by their work on erroneous psychodiagnostic judgements engendered by the existence of illusory correlations. Using the Draw-a-Person Test, the Rorschach Test, and incomplete sentences, they have convincingly demonstrated that when naive persons are confronted with projective test data that have been randomly paired with contrived symptom statements about the subjects who produced them, they "rediscover" the same relationships between test characteristics and symptoms as clinicians report on the basis of clinical practice, although these relationships were absent in the material. A question arises, then, as to whether these illusory correlations are reflections of implicit personality theories and are generated by processes that underlie person perception.

In fact, the way out of the distressing dilemma confronting clinical psychology would then seem to consist in treating current diagnostic practices based on projective techniques as special, rather sophisticated cases of person perception. Those practices could then become the object of further investigations but could no longer be considered as a privileged, primary source of objective and reliable knowledge.

To all this must be added the heated controversy that was generated by Meehl's (1954) monograph, "Clinical versus Statistical Prediction." Although one often had the impression that old scores were paid off between academicians and professionals, the discussion had a sobering effect on the exhorbitant claims of clinicians. Besides labouring the obvious, that is, that a clinician can hardly compete with a regression equation, it also demonstrated that relatively few diagnostic situations and instruments were meeting the requirements of actuarial prediction. The scope of the discussion was broadened by the distinction introduced by Sawyer (1966) between *mode of data collection,* which can be judgemental, mechanical, or either or both, and *mode of data combination,* which can be either clinical or statistical, thus yielding eight possibilities instead of the two from which Meehl started. It appeared (1) that the best method is the one that combines judgemental and mechanical inputs and statistical combinations, and (2) that the clinician may be able to contribute most, not by direct prediction, but by generating, in objective form, judgements to be combined mechanically.

Still, the whole discussion did not come to an end in any satisfactory way. Because it took place within the narrow framework of neopositivistic philosophy of science equating explanation with prediction, too many basic issues were left untouched. Moreover, the logic of clinical activity was not adequately represented because of the lack of an explicitly defined idiographic methodology. Thus, essential aspects of psychodiagnostics were simply left out of the picture.

Systematically organized assessment of individuals has fared just as badly as the psychodiagnostic techniques. The publication of Murray's (1938) "Exploration in Personality" raised great hopes. It looked as if teamwork based on the application and comparison of different techniques, together with the elaboration of a differentiated conceptualization embodied in a standard terminology, would open the way for a systematic science of the individual person. For some mysterious reason however, the Harvard Psychological Clinic never followed up those initial steps. Murray's influence is certainly still to be felt in most areas of personality psychology, but the first "explorations in personality" have apparently never been continued.

"The Assessment of Men," (1948) contained many of Murray's ideas about personality assessment, but it was the result of applied military assessment done for the Office of Strategic Services (O.S.S.) Assessment Staff. Its main objective was to select those people who would be most apt to fulfil O.S.S. assignments in foreign countries. The war assignments were extremely diverse and the absence of proper criteria and evaluations made it an almost impossible task to study the predictive validity of the procedures used.

A few years before Murray published his "Explorations in Personality", Max Simoneit (1943), a pupil of N. Ach, who is known for his work on determining tendency in thought, had been put in charge by the German High Command of the Wehrpsychologie, a military organization comprising a large number of stations where officers and specialists were to be assessed and selected. Many of his ingenious procedures and ideas about military assessment were adopted by the Americans and later by the British, who took them as models. Simoneit's data were destroyed, and, therefore, the high claims made for his methods have never been substantiated. The experience of the British has been presented very summarily and only global statistical evaluations are available.

In 1951, Kelly and Fiske published their report, "The Prediction of Performance in Clincial Psychology", based on a large-scale assessment program directed at the evaluation of the procedures used to select clinical psychologists. The immediate results were most disappointing. Predictor-criterion intercorrelations in no case accounted for more than 10% of the criterion variance, and significant correlations found in one sample disappeared in the next one. A follow-up study initiated in 1957 (Kelly & Goldberg, 1959) demonstrated that only half of the initial sample–knowing what they now knew–would ever again choose clinical psychology as a professional specialization.

The study of the Menninger selection program of psychiatrists, planned by K. A. Menninger, R. P. Knight, and D. Rapaport (Holt and Luborsky, 1958), yielded only a small amount of useful information in relation to the extraordinary expenditure of time and effort, as in the preceding case. The vast research program undertaken by the Institute of Personality Assessment and Research (IPAR) on the effectiveness of Air Force Officers (1958) was a complete failure. Neither contributed to the reputation and prestige of systematically organized assessment programs. The disrepute into which systematic assessment gradually fell during the fifties is clearly expressed in McNemar's (1952) verdict on the Kelly and Fiske research:

> In summary, the major prediction of our time fell far short of expectations. Its fall involved tripping over the criterion problem despite the recent experiences of wartime psychologists with this old stumbling block. With its feet enmeshed in a web of uncritically selected tests, and its head over-burdened with clinical intuitions, it never attained equilibrium, but landed prostrate in a field already strewn with efforts noble and otherwise. Its collapse might have been forestalled by the injection of fruitful new ideas, but such ideas are indeed hard to come by.

However, a more ominous sign of the decline of personality assessment and psychodiagnostics is to be found in the reduction of the space devoted to these topics in the *Annual Reviews of Psychology* since 1950. From 1950 until 1959, a chapter dealing with assessment or psychodiagnostics was published each year. Then one had to wait for five years (1964) for the next one. Six years elapsed (1970) before the subject of "Theory and Techniques of Personality Measurement" was taken up again. Three years later (1973) the next review was published, then not again until 1980 and 1983.

The reasons for this evaluation are not difficult to diagnose. Systematic personality assessment can only be organized by institutions that have powerful financial means at their disposal and that make use of assessment procedures as a pragmatic implementation of their policies. This entails several consequences that run counter to the objectives of the personologist. First, the motivations of the individuals being examined frequently are incongruent with those of the organization, and, rather than being induced to collaborate with the latter, they in fact get involved in a game-like situation with the whole enterprise of assessment. Second, the investigators are only the producers of information and have little direct influence on the decisions; they tend to be involved only to a limited extent in their diagnostic activities because they have more important professional interests to defend with respect to their employers. Thus, little room is left for scientific endeavours, and usually only "established" knowledge is used. This often leads to improvised choices and hazardous selections of tests that depend to a large extent on what the test market has to offer at the moment. The reason that systematic assessment studies have so often stumbled on the criterion problem is that the criterion problem can be solved neither by decree nor by improvisation.

Indeed, the definition of criteria destined to evaluate the efficiency of predictions requires a good deal of preliminary research work. Detailed job analyses and work-sample analyses, intensive study of individuals considered to be representatives of the best and of the worst performers of the task, analyses of the way both kinds of persons are described and judged, and analyses of the personal relationships they establish and their co-workers and supervisors are all needed if criteria are to be formulated and if appropriate predictive techniques are to be selected. However, these self-evident requirements are of a much too clinical nature to fit in with the extensive predictive paradigm which underlies systematic assessment. In fact, the establishment of valuable criteria requires an approach that is antithetical to the applied science model favored by organizations. Still, if the criterion problem is dealt with in the way we have sketched, predictive efficiency can reach surprisingly high levels, as demonstrated by the insufficiently known and never replicated study of Stern, Stein, and Bloom (1956).

The deterioration of the clinical psychotherapeutic approach, of personality research, and of systematic assessment has had disastrous consequences for personality psychology. They can easily be summarized by contrasting each pair of constituents with the remaining third. Clinical work and the research activities lack the global diagnostic approach that is necessary for proper, systematic assessment. The clinical approach and systematic assessment are devoid of the scientific aims and methods of personality research; and personality research and assessment have in common the absence of the intensive individual contacts that are specific to the clinical approach. The consequences as a whole amount to the virtual disappearance of the scientific, intensive study of whole persons—a process that can be traced to the beginning of the 1960s.

The centrifugal movement that has separated the three basic components of personology from each other is due to the different forms taken by the institutionalization of psychology. Thus, the eclipse of personology is to a large extent an artifact of institutionalisation. At the same time, parallel developments led to systematic distortions of the data on which personality studies were based. These distortions can be grouped into three categories: The first involves the uncritical use of certain linguistic categories; the second includes distortions due to methods; and the third results from an arbitrary narrowing of the field of personality investigation.

LANGUAGE AS A POSSIBLE SOURCE OF ARTIFACTS

Carr and Kingsbury (1938) drew attention to the language-induced abstraction process that may be held responsible for conceptualizations of personality devoid of sufficient empirical support. They distinguished the verbal, the adverbial, the adjectival, and the substantival modes of expressing personality characteristics; and they pointed out that moving from one descriptive mode to another carries with it implied changes in the conceptualization of personality, changes that take place without explicit justification. In the verbal mode of expression, a person acting in a situation is conceptually presupposed. By moving to the adverbial mode ('Arnold acts aggressively'), abstraction is made of the situation. Behaviour is abstracted when the adjectival mode is used ('Arnold is aggressive'). In its turn, the substantival mode substitutes abstract entities (e.g., anxiety, dominance) for the person (aggressiveness). Ultimately one is left with concepts that become the foundation of so-called trait-theory, while the person, its behaviour, and its contexts have disappeared in the process. It is the same omnipresent language-induced abstraction process that may be held responsible for the construction and attribution of artificial behaviour consistencies and the belief in the existence of universal personality traits.

The same distortion has blinded psychologists to the fact that cross-situational consistency of personality characteristics, on one hand, and their possible universality, on the other, require different approaches. Assessment of the nature and consistency of a personality characteristic requires a detailed description of the characteristic as displayed by the person and of the situational and personal contexts in which the display occurs. This has to be carried out on an *intra-individual* basis. In other words, this first stage requires the study of individual persons. Whether a given characteristic appears in different situations, and what the nature and the range of these situations are, also requires an intra-individual approach, because generality across situations means that each person must be studied singly in different situations. This may eventually lead to the discovery of second-order characteristics, certain individuals being generalizers to a larger extent than others. However, the universality of certain personality characteristics can be studied only through *inter-individual* variation, and it presupposes that the proper analyses of identification and cross-situational generality have been carried out. Needless to say, few researches in personality psychology have ever followed this pattern; investigators have taken for granted precisely what is problematic.

However, formal distortions resulting from the imposition of grammatical forms are not the only kind of selective construals of linguistic origin. The research results accumulated by Norman (1963, 1967), D'Andrade (1965), Tupes and Christal (1958, 1961), and Hakel (1969) have demonstrated that ratings made on trait names lead consistently to the emergence of five distinct orthogonal factors: extroversion, agreeableness, dependability, emotional stability, and culture. Each factor can be defined by four bipolar scales, as in the following list of traits:

1. Extroversion
   a. Talkative versus silent
   b. Frank, open versus secretive
   c. Adventurous versus cautious
   d. Sociable versus reclusive
2. Agreeableness
   a. Good-natured versus irritable
   b. Not jealous versus jealous
   c. Mild, gentle versus headstrong
   d. Cooperative versus negativistic

3. Conscientiousness
   a. Fussy, tidy versus careless
   b. Responsible versus undependable
   c. Scrupulous versus unscrupulous
   d. Perserving versus quitting, fickle
4. Emotional Stability
   a. Poised versus nervous, tense
   b. Calm versus anxious
   c. Composed versus excitable
   d. Not hypochondriacal versus hypochondriacal
5. Culture
   a. Artistically sensitive versus insensitive
   b. Intellectual versus unreflective, narrow
   c. Polished, refined versus crude, boorish
   d. Imaginative versus simple, direct

Thus, it seemed that five independent factors represented the "natural language" of personality ratings. These factors were found to possess a high degree of internal stability, since the study of similarity of meaning ratings (D'Andrade, 1965) and the analysis of probability of cooccurrence (Hakel, 1969) yielded the same five factors.

Obviously, a certain degree of internal structuring of a set of rating scales is a necessary condition for the same ratings to be applied to an external object of judgment. But, as Pasini and Norman (1966) have shown, there are situations in which trait-attribution reflects nothing but the semantic relationships of the terms employed. When they asked subjects who were complete strangers to each other to rate one another "as they would imagine one another to be", the same five factors emerged. In Muliak's (1964) study where stereotyped persons like suburban housewife, mental patient, and Air Force General were to be rated, the same basic structure emerged. Quite obviously, these results throw great doubt upon the external validity of the five basic personality trait factors. In fact the trait names used were chosen from among the 4054 trait names assembled by Allport and Odbert (1936), which were first reduced to 171 terms by Cattell (1946), then, by means of cluster analysis to 35 bipolar rating scales, until finally, Norman (1963) retained 20 ratings from Cattell's list.

If one takes into account the results of the aforementioned investigations, the inescapable conclusion seems to be that the five basic trait factors that were repeatedly and reliably identified express the semantic structure of the language used in decribing persons, but this does not prove that they reflect object characteristics of the individuals being rated. True, it has been shown by Norman and Goldberg (1966) that inter-rater agreement increases from .45 to .70 when ratings are made about individuals known for a period of one to three years as compared with unknown persons. This suggests that the system of five trait factors possesses some external validity, but that validity derives from the experience stored up in the language and not from critical and disciplined observations. Moreover, even if the language actually contains a basic taxonomy of personality traits, there still remains the task of investigating the generating mechanisms underlying their referents. At any rate, grammatical form and semantic structure combine their masking and filtering effects to induce conceptualizations that foster the illusion of knowledge about personality characteristics.

MISREPRESENTATION DUE TO METHODOLOGICAL FALLACIES

A problem that chronically besets personality research and psychodiagnosis is the accumulation of divergent or contradictory results. One of the possible sources of inconsistency, variously called ''method specificity'' or ''method variance'', has often been invoked. Its importance is stressed by Campbell and Fiske (1959) who, by analyzing correlations among personality measures reported in the literature, found that much of their common variance was attributable to similarity between the methods employed. Conversely, Becker (1960) found that factors obtained from different sources, such as questionnaires and behaviour ratings, are not matched closely enough to justify their existence as independent from the media through which they are obtained. This state of affairs led Campbell and Fiske to advocate the use of multitrait–multimethod matrices. Although relatively little research had been conducted along these lines, on the basis of the few examples these authors found in the literature, they conclude that the typical case shows an excessive amount of method variance, usually exceeding the amount of trait variance.

Of course, one can only be grateful to Campbell and Fiske for having uncovered the widespread mistake consisting in believing, without proof, that personality variables could be considered as invariant with respect to the technical medium through which they are investigated. However, one cannot help feeling exasperated by the fact that such discoveries have still to be made in the field of personality research. In fact, the inconsistencies resulting from method variance can only appear if researchers and diagnosticians neglect the process through which the assignment of a value to a personality variable is generated in the course of the application of a given method.

Indeed, a common aspect of the usual assessment and research techniques that time and again needs to be stressed is their one-sided reliance on final results of behaviour processes as fundamental data. The advantage of the exclusive use of *Leistungsbegriffe* (achievement concepts) is clear since they facilitate the quantitative treatment of data. However, a great deal is lost by this kind of abstraction, namely, the most compelling aspect of all personality-relevant behaviour: the action processes through which the personality is expressed. That the same final effects can be reached by different processes and, conversely, that different final effects may have the same origin, has often been noted but rarely taken into account. On the whole, personality assessment seems to have been inspired by the words of Thurstone who wrote, "If critics were consistent who point out that identical test scores do not necessarily measure the same mental processes, they should also object that two men have identical incomes for one of them earns, while the other one steals" (1947).

Our point is that psychologists interested in personality—and also, all morally responsible persons—should indeed object and be consistent in the way Thurstone urges them to be. By doing so, they would also discover that the neglect of action processes as such also leads them to neglect the existence of expressive phenomena, which are inseparable from them and which belong to the fundamental data that psychology is interested in. Besides, learning to distinguish between process and product would also teach them that the fallacy of method specificity is heir to a more basic fallacy that is already committed when one single method is applied with complete disregard for the variety of processes that lead to the final result.

In fact, the blindness of many researchers in the field of personality concerning the product–process distinction seems to be a case of what Black (1952) so aptly calls the "product process" fallacy. In personality psychology, this fallacy derives its importance from the fact that it is precisely at the point where knowledge about process shows gaps that we see language-induced abstractions insidiously creeping in to fill them.

ARBITRARY NARROWING OF THE FIELD

The overwhelming bulk of personality research and of systematic assessment is centered on the analysis of short diachronic time-slices of behaviour in situations on which various degrees of environmental constraints are imposed. As long as the investigator is exclusively interested in well-defined units of behaviour of an essentially instrumental character, the limited time-extension and the simplification of the situation can be justified. However, as soon as motivations, emotional expression, goal-setting, and meaning-attributions, which are essential to personality psychology, are involved, other factors take on paramount importance: The subject's time-perspective, the biographical situation of his or her actions, their relationship to his or her everyday activities, and the hierarchy of goals to which they are subordinated. In other words, the definition, analysis, and interpretation of personality data inevitably issues into problems pertaining to the life trajectory of which they are a segment. Moreover, the diagnostic assessment of individual persons is impossible without a minimal reconstruction of their biographies, if only for the self-evident reason that the problem, whether clinical or predictive, that the investigation is called to solve is anchored in their past histories. Although a renewal of interest in life-span psychology has manifested itself since 1975, it is a curious fact that neither scientific researchers nor clinicians nor psychodiagnosticians have devoted much attention to the study of life trajectories, or, to quote the title of Ch. Buhler's (1933) famous but little-read book, to "Der menschliche Lebenslauf als psychologisches Problem". Contrasting with the comparative neglect of developmental and longitudinal aspects of personality, Potkay (1974), after reviewing more than 30 studies dealing with the role of personal history data as a source of information in clinical judgment and related contexts, produced clear evidence of the fact that personal history data are at least equally, if not more, effective than projective and objective test sources of information for purposes of personality description and prediction.

True, biographical studies require too much time to be academically rewarding. The questions they can answer and the kind of knowledge they yield do not fit in with the unilateral paradigm of nomothetic science. It is also a well-established fact that researchers and psychodiagnosticians simply do not have the time demanded by the reconstruction and analysis of life histories. But it is equally remarkable that the founding fathers of modern psychotherapy in particular, and the clinicians in general, have produced very few intensive studies of individual persons. Brody (1970), who made a special study of Freud's case load, shows that the published 12 major cases (cases that are at least several pages in length) include some details of the patient's life circumstances and are used in a theoretical discussion. The remaining minor cases comprise 113 patients to whom only passing reference is made. The cases edited in various collections like Greenwald's *Great Cases in Psychoanalysis* (1979) or Paul's (1979) review of personal documents demonstrate clearly that Freud was a relatively prolific writer of detailed case studies. A survey that we conducted on the publications of 213 authors considered to be experts in the field of personality from the beginning of the twentieth century to the present showed that only 17% ever published case material of a biographical nature.

This clearly indicates the existence of an unsolved problem which, in our opinion, is not difficult to identify but which, for reasons of space, cannot be discussed here: the absence of a systematically developed idiographic methodology which, far from excluding the nomothetic approach, would supplement the insufficiencies of the latter (see de Waele & Harré, 1979).

After these long but indispensable preliminaries, we can finally state our thesis that the much needed reconstruction of personality psychology can only be worked out within the framework of an action psychology.

To make our argument fully cogent, we should elucidate the role played by act–action processes in the heuristic theoretical model of personality with which we are working. Since we cannot discuss the difficult problems related to the concepts of person and personality here, we must restrict our claims to the solutions on action psychology can bring to the three kinds of misconstructions we have attempted to define. Furthermore we shall attempt to show by means of concrete illustrations how an action psychology can contribute to a renewal of personality research and assessment.

If the essential contribution action psychology has to make to personality psychology is taken to mean that the study of individual whole persons has to start with the description, analysis, and interpretation of act–action processes, then it follows that action analysis can give us a new, direct, undistorted access to persons. Linguistic artifacts of the kind we have analyzed can thus be avoided because, instead of starting—like Allport and Odbert (1936) and Cattel (1946)—from a semantic inventory of personality characteristics contained in the language, we begin by detailed, quasi-ethological observations of action processes as they manifest themselves in the behaviour and expression of individuals coping with concrete situations. Consistency, generality versus specificity, and universality versus individuality of personality characteristics are empirical problems that can be solved only by detailed analyses of well-identified action processes and of the conditions under which they appear or by which they are elicited. Of course, language cannot be ignored; on the contrary, a heightened consciousness of semantic fields and factors and of grammatical modes is required to control the way in which descriptions are formulated. But what a given term can possibly mean must be established on the basis of the empirical observation of action processes.

As to the product–process fallacy, it is obvious that there is no better antidote against it than an action-centered approach where the distinction between act and action (cf. Harré and Secord, 1972; von Cranach et al., 1980) makes the occurrence of the fallacy impossible. It is also clear that an action psychology approach to personality through the analysis of individual characteristics as they appear in and through goal-directed act–action processes must of necessity elaborate its conceptualizations, primarily on an intra-individual basis, and favour intensive designs over extensive ones.

The connections between action psychology and the biographical approach are less obvious. The interesting remarks contained in Lazarsfeld's (1970) article, "Some Historical Notes on the Empirical Study of Action", may help to delineate the convergences. As he indicates, there are at least two approaches to the psychology of action. One takes as its starting point the goals pursued by individuals. But to analyze their content, their successive emergence and their hierarchical structure, one has to take a developmental view. This is what K. Buhler and Ch. Buhler (1933) did in their pioneer studies on children and adults. But one can also start with the dynamics of intention, and as Lewin (1935) did, study the effects of interruption, substitution, satiation, and frustration of action of relatively short duration. These approaches actually are complementary because goal setting presupposes intention, and intentions are aimed at goals. The link between both approaches is constituted by cycles of activities of variable periodicity that mediate between micro-action processes and those more macroscopic developments oriented by the life-goals defining the biographical trajectory.

Lest this should sound too programmatic, we now consider the methods that we have used to implement an action psychology approach to personality research and assessment. During recent years, we have made use of what has been called problem and conflict situations (PCSs). These PCSs can be applied individually or in groups. For the purpose of the present discussion, we concentrate on the individual PCSs.

In order to prevent misunderstandings, PCSs first have to be contrasted with an assessment technique with which they are easily confused, that is, the so-called situation test.

Situation tests are defined and discussed by several authors in slightly different ways (Anastasi, 1961; Cronbach, 1964, English & English, 1958, Flanagan, 1954; Kleinmuntz, 1967; Krech & Crutchfield, 1959), but the common core of the definitions is that situation tests are characterized by being approximations, or simulations, of real life situations. In addition, Flanagan adds another defining property when he notes that the complexity of the situation makes it difficult for the persons tested to know that actions or aspects of actions are being scored; and Kleinmuntz underlines the fact that the conditions under which the behavior of the subjects is being observed are usually stressful. Moreover, according to this author, one of the aims of situation tests is not only to conceal from the subjects which behaviour variables are being observed and scored, but occasionally to trap subjects into performing in specific ways.

The fundamental differences between situation tests and PCSs are the following:

1.   PCSs are not to be judged by any kind of psychometric criteria, for they are not tests. It may be very interesting to note that the psychologists of the O.S.S. Assessment Staff who were working with situation tests achieved rather high reliabilities in their ratings and that the reliability coefficients obtained by Greenwood and McNamara (1967) were also high, but the objective of PCSs is not to create the opportunity to make ratings. This would only repeat the product–process fallacy on the basis of process data.

2.   PCSs are completely foreign to the exclusive performance and prediction-oriented applications of current situation tests. If comparisons, predictions, and extrapolations are to be formulated, they have to be made not on the basis of global judgmental interpretations or of predefined response units, but on the basis of interpretations suggested by the analysis of the observed action processes.

3.   PCSs are in no way intended to be replicas or simulations of real tasks. The realism of PCSs, though not to be rejected, is not one of their essential attributes. To admit with Murray (1938) as a matter of principle that "a given subject will respond to similar environmental situations in a similar manner" is to take for granted a state of affairs that is a matter of empirical investigation. The same goes for the realism of a problem situation, defined as a situation test or otherwise. The investigator's view that a situation is realistic does not, ipso facto, warrant the realism of a subject's behaviour.

To give a positive characterization of PCSs, the two dimensions used by Willems and Raush (1969) to locate various techniques provide a useful framework. The first dimension describes the degree of the investigator's influence upon, or manipulation of, antecedent conditions of the behaviour studied. The second dimension describes the degree to which units are imposed by the investigator upon the behaviour studied. With fieldwork being considered medium and with naturalistic investigation being considered low on both dimensions, psychometric testing and classical experimental designs would be regarded as high on both dimensions. There are still other combinations that are not considered here, though PCSs can be described as being medium in the degree of manipulation of antecedent conditions while being low on the degree of impositions of units. When confronting a person with PCSs, the investigator defines, by means of the instructions, only the necessary conditions of the situation. The others are, as it were, filled in by the subject's interpretative construction of the situation. It is indeed essential to the method of PCSs that the observed person have the opportunity to structure gradually the problem situation in which he or she has been placed.

The emergence of active or reactive attitudes, such as suspiciousness of the investigator's intent, various modes of responsiveness to the demand characteristics of the task, or evaluation apprehension, belong to the kind of fundamental data the method of PCSs is destined to elicit, even though they might be considered to be the source of disturbing artifacts when other methods of assessment are used. Also, the fact that every research experiment or assessment procedure is a social situation with its proper characteristics, conflicts, and evolution should be fully acknowledged and used as an additional resource. However, as the observations and recordings are concentrated on action and expression processes with their verbal accompaniments, it is indispensable that the lowest degree of unit imposition on the ensuing behaviour should prevail.

Previous research by Gottschaldt (1956) and his collaborators, as well as our own findings, demonstrate that the richest and most revealing data are obtained when the initial conditions are so defined that they develop into one or more temporary conflict situations. It is when the individual whose personality is being investigated has to come to terms with a conflict of growing intensity that the unfolding processes take on their most fascinating individual qualities. Thus, it is not only essential that the problem situations lead to either soluble or insoluble conflicts but also that the task and the means at the disposal of the subject for its execution be such that as much as possible of the action and expression processes may be directly observed and recorded.

A few words should be added concerning the staging of the PCSs. Great care must be taken to enrich the action field appropriately. This means that the environmental background against which various means–end structures can emerge as figures must have a carefully organized content destined to favour the appearance of a great variety of meaning attributions, restructurings of the situation, and adaptive and defensive moves. For example, it is quite obvious that if no perceptible substream is provided for them, no substitute actions will ever appear. It is for this reason that it may be important that the specific task used in a PCS be embedded in the context of familiar objects and of some kind of daily life environment.

In short, an optimal individual PCS is a single global task requiring for its completion the solution of a few sub-problems. The nature of the problems, the materials used and the whole setup of the problem field should be such as to allow the most detailed observation and recording of the action and expression processes as well as of the social interactions with the investigators. After the application of a PCS, there should be ample opportunity for the investigators to interview the subject and elicit his or her accounts of the course taken by the whole problem situation as he or she experienced it. What the subject remembers and is able to reconstruct should eventually be supplemented by the description and interpretations given when he or she is confronted with the video-recording of his or her behaviour. Used in this way, PCSs are closely related to the new strategies for personality research advocated by Fiske (1978).

Two Problem-and-Conflict Situations

Among the various individual or group PCSs that meet the criteria we have summarized, two techniques are of outstanding interest because of their capacity to elicit highly individualized action and expression processes. They are (1) the Saugstad problem (Saugstad & Raaheim, 1957), which was used in studies on problem solving, and (2) the flower problem used by Dembo (1926) in her well-known dissertation inspired by K. Lewin: "Der Arger als dynamisches Problem"

Both are, in fact, practical Kohler-type problems but specially devised for human beings. Both involve the discovery of an instrumental detour action under highly artificial circumstances. However, in both cases, the nature of the problem is such that excellent conditions are provided for the detailed observation of problem-solving behaviour, effects of frustration, action and expression dynamics, and also for interactions with the investigators. It should be underscored that the visible presence of observers (optimally, two or three) is never considered a cumbersome artifact, but one of the essential components of the situation. This is also the reason why interactions between subject and observers are not at all avoided. There are, however, important differences between the two PCSs that make interesting comparisons possible, especially if the PCSs are applied in a well-defined sequence: first the Saugstad and then the Dembo.

The Saugstad PCS presents the subjects with a problem that is solvable in several ways although one solution is a particularly efficient one. Actually, two sub-problems must be successively solved. The material put at the disposal of the subjects and the setup of the situation offer diverse action possibilities, among which the manufacture of various primitive instruments is the most conspicuous. In other words, in the Saugstad-PCS, there is always something to be done.

In the Dembo PCS, however, action possibilities are not only reduced, but three different solutions must be given to the same problem. Consequently, the discrepancy between action possibilities and solution is somewhat exacerbated. Furthermore, the problem situation becomes almost exclusively a conflict situation when the subject is induced to look for a non-existent solution.

After both PCSs, a detailed focused interview takes place. Its aim is to clarify the episodes and to reveal the subject's perspective on the setting, the task, and the critical incidents it involved.

In order to give the reader a precise representation of the problem and conflict situations we have often used, a description of both the Saugstad PCS and the Dembo PCS follows, as well as the outline of the focused interview.

The Saugstad Problem. In the Saugstad problem (Figure 1), the subject is given the task of transferring a handful of marbles from a container (1) on a grating (2) in front of which there is a wooden frame (3), to an empty container (4) placed just in front of a small box. Container (4) should not be moved. The subject should perform this task while remaining at a distance of approximately 3 m, behind a line indicated by wooden slats. This line, which should not be crossed, delimits two zones: a zone in which the subject can move freely and a zone that he or she is not allowed to enter.

The following materials, which may be used to solve the problem, are lying in a wooden box on a table: a ball of string, a hammer, cotton, a pair of pincers, nails, a few pieces of brass wire, a spoon, a comb, a pulley, a knife, a screw driver, a pair of scissors, used-up bobbins, keys, a small coat hanger, clamps, bolts, rubber bands, a little box with paper clips, and drawing pins. The subject also has at his or her disposal a pile of papers, located on the table, and a chair.

There is no time limit, and the subject is free to do whatever she or

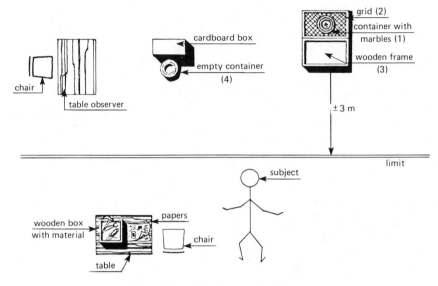

Figure 1.   The Saugstad problem.

he likes. If additional questions are asked, answers are given in the sense that the subject is free to decide what will or may happen. The subject is asked to inform the observers of the things he or she thinks about so that they can follow what's happening. The observer intervenes when he or she thinks it to be necessary (e.g., to make the subject formulate his or her difficulties, to set the subject off again, or to assist him or her, if necessary). Although all possible solutions are accepted, there is an ideal solution: With the pieces of brass wire, (or with the nails, which should then be folded) the subject has to construct a 3-dimensional hook, which he or she fixes to a string. With this instrument, the container with the marbles is pulled up to the subject. Obviously, many variations on this technique are possible. Afterwards, the subject has to construct a cylinder with the papers, the paper clips, and the rubber bands. Having made one end of this cylinder rest on the brim of the container, he or she can then roll the marbles through it. Other solutions are also possible, but to be efficient, they require considerable skill in manipulating the material available.

   The Dembo Problem. For the Dembo problem (Figure 2), the subject is placed in a square, delineated by wooden slats, which he or she is not allowed to leave. A chair is put in this area. Along two sides of the square, 14 wooden rings are lying on the floor. In front of the subject, at a certain distance from the square, there is a table on which a flower in a container is put. At the subject's back, also outside the square but

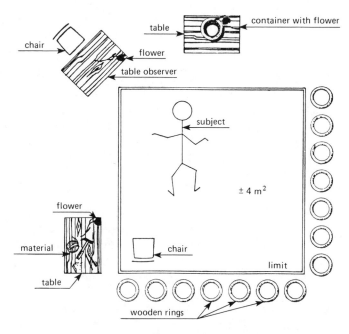

Figure 2.   The Dembo problem.

within easy reach, there is another table on which other material is put (a hammer, a metal cover, a pencil, three sheets of paper, a *Playboy* magazine, and a publicity booklet on flowers) and on which a flower also is lying. On the experimenter's table, there is a third flower, also within reach of the subject.

The subject is given the task of taking the flower from the container on the table in three different ways while keeping both feet inside the delineated zone. The material on the table can be used but should not be damaged. This means that the magazines must remain intact. Furthermore, the subject is asked, if possible, to inform the observers of what he or she is thinking about while attempting to solve the problem. The task is constructed such that the subject is asked to find three different solutions to a problem, whereas only two solutions are possible. One solution consists in bridging the distance by means of one's own body, for instance, by leaning on one arm outside the square but keeping both feet inside and taking the flower with the other hand. The other solution consists in using a point of support (e.g., the chair) to bridge the distance. Generally, these two solutions are found easily. All other suggested and carried out solutions are rejected as mere variations on the two other solutions and as not being fundamentally different from the two accepted solutions.

The observer puts an end to the task when he or she has the impression that the subject's repertoire is exhausted and/or when the situation is becoming too frustrating for the subject.

Focused Interview. Two observers, who are visibly present, make a written record of all aspects of the subject's behaviour, expressions, and utterances. They are helped by other observers hidden behind one-way mirrors. Besides, the whole situation is recorded by means of three cameras in order to supplement the observer's notes when the final maximally detailed protocol is elaborated.

The focused interview to which the subjects are submitted is summarized below, with a detailed outline presented in Appendix 1.

1. Personal evaluation of achieved results (satisfaction, time estimate, comparison with others, implications of performance).
2. Condition and situation of subject before test (physical, psychological, preparation).
3. General attitude towards test (before, during; interpretation of test).
4. Goals and aspirations (time and quality goals and expectations, goal changes, effects of goals on actions).
5. Affective and cognitive processes revealed during test (mood evolution; attentiveness pattern; approach through reasoning, inspiration, trial and error; fixations, confusions, blocking of thought, heightened clarity or productivity).
6. Thought and action tendencies elicited by task or situation (avoidance attempts, aggressive tendencies, compulsions).
7. Interactions with observers (sensitivity to social situation, role taking, voiced attributions, situated social comparisons).
8. Comparisons with other situations.

The answers given by the subjects during the intensive focused interview are important resources for the interpretation of PCS performances and, ultimately, for the use of the PCS action data as a basis for a person description of the subject.

Interpretations of the Observations Made on Five Individuals

To demonstrate the possibilities inherent in the description and interpretation of detailed protocols of the action and expression processes elicited by individual problem and conflict situations, we have chosen five cases, one of which (J. T.) was a young murderer who was submitted to intensive personality investigations at the Penitentiary

Orientation Center. Both V. R. and A. M. were male psychology students, age 21. H. C., a male, age 30, was a teacher and a student of educational psychology; and V. D. I. was a female, age 21. As the full protocols, including the interviews amount to an average of fifty typewritten pages, lack of available space makes it impossible to publish them in extenso in this article. The protocols for J. T., V. R., and V. D. I. follow; those for the other two can be found in Appendix II.

We have tried to construct a hypothetical interpretation of the individualized aspects of their action processes by keeping as closely as possible to the observational as well as to the interview date. Although we cannot make our theoretical frame of reference fully explicit here (see de Waele & Harré, 1979), the importance of a few basic concepts should be pointed out.

First, there is the definition of the situation proper to the subject who is being investigated. This may be a unique inprovisation but usually reflects a more basic and relatively permanent way of situating oneself in the world. Correlated with the definition of a situation is the role-rule model—either standardized and routinized or creatively invented—which the individual follows in his dealings with the social environment. These dealings may be conducted (1) as an agent that is as a "worker" producing things by acting on them, or (2) as an actor, that is, as a partner in social and interpersonal relationships. Whether as an actor or as an agent, the individual who follows a given role-rule model not only enacts a given—possibly fugitive—role and performs intentional activities according to rules, but he or she has also to keep up a self-presentation, or persona, which enables him or her to define his or her identity to an intelligible way through the possibilities of expressive display it offers.

The interpretative scheme adopted in reading the basic protocols consists in trying at each moment to ask and to answer the following questions: What is he trying to do? What does he believe to be the most appropriate means of reaching his goals? How does he act and express himself? To what extent does he—by means of an appropriate self-presentation—produce an intelligible identity for himself and others as agent and as actor?

CASE 1: J. T. (MALE, AGE 25)

The Saugstad PCS (91 min)

From beginning to end, J. T. avoids getting personally involved in the task. He displays a strategy that enables him to play for safety and to keep the stakes as low as possible. Each of his actions and utterances can be understood as being guided by a role-rule model, as well as a self-presentation, the various components of which can be readily discriminated and repeatedly noted in the protocol.

First, he does not take the task seriously, acts in a casual, offhand way, and through his numerous commentaries and questions, conveys the idea that to him the test is not much more than a game. By keeping his aspirations low and by considering the task as not being a serious one, he seeks to avoid failure as well as critical evaluation.

Second, he does a great deal of talking, which is obviously directed at the observers but most of which takes the form of thinking aloud in a pseudo-egocentric way. This talk and his expressive display are aimed at creating and sustaining an agreeable, somewhat playful relationship with the observers. Besides, through his commentaries and remarks, he tries to involve them as participants in his performance. It is indeed essential to him to keep control of the whole situation. He keeps the meaning of whatever he does under control by a running stream of more or less humorous commentaries. He also takes the initiative of making ironical remarks and of laughing at moments he deems appropriate. His self-presentation is clearly that of an inconspicuous easy-going, unproblematic young man, ready to help the investigators to do their work.

Third, his pseudo-egocentric thinking aloud is partially intended as the communication of the meaning of his actions. Instead of accepting the status of a person being observed in a problem-solving situation, who inevitably gives off information concerning personal action cum expression processes, he instead attempts, through the attribution of supposedly shared meanings, to dictate, as it were, his own protocol to the observers. As he later acknowledges in the interview, some of his attempts at solving the problem, for example, the exploration of the material at the beginning of the test and the building of a bridge between the slats and the container, were executed only for the purpose of giving the observers something to describe. Thus, trying to please the observers while controlling the impression made and, at the same time, hoping to hit upon a workable solution appears to be the complex intended meaning of the bridge episode.

The mediocre level of activation manifested by J. T. is not an independent aspect of the role-rule model he manifests during the examination. It is but another feature of it. Keeping a self-imposed relaxed attitude is to him another way of avoiding any form of intense task involvement. He even keeps in check possibilities of achieving part-solutions, either by refraining from putting a hunch into action or by postponing its execution (e.g., the use of the string, which must first be disentangled; the transfer of the marbles by means of a roll of papers). J. T. persistently prefers to keep some distance between him and what he experiences as the social pressure exerted by the investigators to get him involved in the requirements of the task and prefers to wait and see whether some other personally less exacting solution, less demanding in efforts and risks, does not emerge.

As a consequence of the strategy implied in the role–rule model he follows, J. T. can hardly avoid drifting into a double-avoidant conflict. On one hand, he avoids involvement in the task; but on the other hand, he also wants to avoid failure. Thus, to the objective difficulties residing in the task are added those stemming from J. T.'s personal strategy: to find the easiest solution requiring the least self-involvement. Eventually—as he states in the interview— the result he has achieved is perceived by him as a rather ambiguous one; he locates it somewhere between success and failure. Although he claims to have found a solution, he does not consider it to be a very interesting one, because of its clumsiness.

As appears very clearly in the observation protocol, J. T.'s problem solving is characterized by a low degree of systematic planning. Especially his exploration of the available material—which is also intended to give the investigators something to observe—is too superficial to yield any valuable clues. He proceeds by successive steps with little anticipation of consequences and of further steps to be taken. By sticking to obviously inefficient methods of solution, the succession of his attempts has all the characteristics of a quasi-blind perserveration. He also remains fixated on untested presuppositions, for example, that the distance between the slats and the container is too great to be bridged by a cylinder and that the available papers cannot be used to manufacture one. In the interview, he attributes his particular way of coping with a problem to his laziness, which makes him stick to apparently easy solutions. He also avows a dislike of having to think seriously. He prefers to start doing something and to wait for insights to emerge from his trials.

Througout this PCS, he never intensely concentrates on the task. His attention is rather diffusely distributed, and he readily admits to being easily distracted by truant thoughts and external events. The low cognitive level at which he performs (in spite of an IQ of 148) is apparently a consequence of the role-rule model that underlies his approach to the task, as well as his relationship with the observers, and by means of which he endeavours to have it all his own way.

From the interview, it is known that under any circumstances he hates being looked at while acting. Defining the situation as a game which is to be played in an atmosphere of self-created pleasant social interactions indeed provides a solution to his double problem: to protect himself against self-involvement and to neutralize the observational work done by the investigators. In the interview he acknowledges that the role-rule model which can be inferred from his present performance quite generally structures his endeavours to bend problem situations to his own hand. But he objects to a formulation which would entail that he deliberately tries to deceive people and negotiates a modified one, devoid of any such morally objectionable implication. Having achieved that piece of self-insight he goes on reflecting that he hasn't always acted in this way in the past, e.g. - when he was still at school.

The Dembo PCS (66 min)

In spite of the similarities existing between the Saugstad PCS and the Dembo PCS, J. T.'s behaviour shows some striking changes that can only be accounted for by his personal definition of the problem situation.

At the beginning, J. T. shows himself somewhat less involved in this PCS than in the former one. As soon as he feels unable to make much progress, he gradually loses whatever interest he had in the task. In fact, he spends more than 1 hour (66 minutes) looking for possible starting points of solutions. But throughout this time, he does not try out a single solution. Although he does not proceed in a very systematic way, he keeps exploring the field in order to discover some action possibility. He talks much less than formerly and now addresses himself directly to the observers. His remarks show that he is at a complete loss to find available means to tackle the problem.

In the course of time his interest in the task diminishes, but signs of the tension persist as evidenced by the numerous *Verlegenheitsbewegungen* which can be observed. Several episodes of *Aus-dem-Felde-gehen* occur, and—according to the interview—he is carried away from the task several times by short states of daydreaming about personal topics. As he reveals later on, some of his doings and sayings had no other purpose than to check whether the observers were still noting everything about him.

At first sight, this PCS ends in complete failure, with J. T. not having been able to find the two very simple solutions to the problem. At least that is how "testers" or students of problem solving would treat the matter. However, J. T.'s utterances and the information yielded by the interview make it possible to qualify and to explain this rather surprising failure.

To put it in a nutshell, J. T. fails, because the Dembo PCS is such that he cannot cope with it by patterning his problem-solving behaviour after the role-rule model that guided him in the former PCS. That model requires (1) a number of action possibilities that could be actualized in a game-like fashion, and (2) some form of protection against the danger of being observed. However, those requirements cannot be met in the Dembo PCS. The relatively unstructured character of the task and the nature of the material impose narrow limits on the activities that can be executed. Furthermore, the two acceptable solutions involve the use of the subject's body and, therefore, would expose him to the observers. It is for both of these reasons that J. T. apparently fails to find the two solutions to the Dembo PCS.

In fact, he has found one solution, but he expresses it only in a substitutive way by drawing a sketch of it on a piece of paper (use of the chair as a point of support while reaching for the flower). From the interview, we learn that he even imagined a second one, that is, trying to reach for the flower while lying on his back. But he executes none of these imagined solutions because he considers them to be impracticable. Moreover, he fears that the uncertainty of their outcomes may possibly involve some danger and such physical exertion as to make him a defenceless object of ridicule for the observers. He considers solutions necessitating the use of one's body to be too circus-like, and while he declares himself ready to try them out, he admits he is afraid of being misjudged as being a clown. It is also interesting to note that his fears concerning the dangers involved in making use of the chair seem to have induced in him a gross distortion of his estimation of the distance between the slats and the flower.

Obviously, the function of the role-rule model that he generally follows is to give him control of the situations in which he has to act. If the conditions for the application of this model are not given, he simply cannot act adequately—and this is exactly what has happened in the Dembo PCS.

CASE 2: V. R. (MALE, AGE 21)

The Saugstad PCS (50 min)

V. R. is visibly impressed by the external aspects of the problem situation and by the instructions given to him, and from the outset, he shows clear signs of tension. The additional information he asks for demonstrates his uncertainty and his desire to conform to the definition of the problem. The only question he asks later on is whether he is allowed to use an object (a hammer). During the interview following the PCS, he remembers that as soon as he was told what the problem was about, he thought that it was either insoluble or that it would be too difficult for him.

V. R. works steadily and economically, avoiding unnecessary manipulations. Toward the end of the task, however, when he is coming close to the final goal, he speeds up his actions, becomes more tense, behaves somewhat less carefully, and is slightly disturbed by a few minor frustrations resulting from difficulties with the material.

Although the cognitive plan that guides his solution of the problem is almost identical to the one contained in the ideal protocol, he does not frame it as a whole. Instead, he discovers it in successive steps. Whereas he experiences no difficulties in discovering the solution of the problem, he has a lot of trouble with its material execution. Several times he has to start over again before reaching a satisfactory result.

As evidenced by the expressions punctuating the progress of his work and the temporary setbacks he has to face, he seems sensitive to momentary successes and failures but does not let them interfere with the successive phases of his actions. Because of the strict self-control he exerts on his expressions, they show little variety and are considerably stereotyped (72% of his observable expressive behaviour [57 items] are distributed over three expressions: frowning, 16%; chewing his cheek, 21%; smiling, 35%).

This expressive control is only a partial aspect of what is, in fact, the most characteristic feature of his whole performance, that is, the great variety of the repeated control operations he performs. One can summarize them as follows:

1. Repeated reviews of the overall situation;
2. anticipative control of the conditions under which he is about to perform an action sequence;
3. control of the selected materials as to their suitability;
4. manual and/or visual control of products and testing of the latter by simulation;
5. checking for possible reactions of the observers.

When he has completed the task successfully, he waits for about a minute and then, without having been asked to do so, dismounts his construction, unrolls the paper cylinders, and puts everything back in its original place.

From the interview, it appears that V. R. was quite concerned about doing his best to find the solution to the problem. Therefore, he is only moderately satisfied with his performance. He criticizes himself for having done superfluous things like driving a nail into a wooden block. Although he considers his solution an obvious one, he is not quite sure whether there are not better and more sophisticated ones. According to him, the aim of the Saugstad PCS is to study a person's capacity to act in a controlled way, as well as his reactions to frustration like giving up and asking for help. This problem situation, he believes, could also be used to observe the social influence exerted by continous observation.

As to his own performance, he believes that he has succeeded in keeping himself under control. There is no doubt, although in the past he used to act too impulsively—and sometimes still does—that V. R. can be considered to act in an overcontrolled way. This can be seen as the consequence of his following a role-rule model involving the comparison of any action and its consequences with a standard of comparison and its eventual correction. The function of this role-rule model is to compensate the anxiety generated by the anticipation of conflicting possibilities inherent in action situations. It can be hypothesized that the compulsive adherence to standards of perfection has its origin in some source of pressure for social conformity.

His interpretation of the aim of the Saugstad PCS is a direct reflection of his personal role-rule model. The fact that he was able to follow it almost to perfection may be held responsible for his remaining unaware of his underlying lack of self-confidence. The only thing he is still conscious of is his former impulsiveness.

The Dembo PCS (80 min)

The application of the Dembo PCS involves an unforeseen complication resulting from the fact that V. R. has, quite accidentally, been informed during a lecture that in this problem situation subjects were induced to look for three solutions, whereas in fact only two were possible.

When entering the situation, he puts up a smile that immediately alerts the observers to the fact that he may be familiar with the Dembo PCS. However, this does not prevent him from starting to look for the first two solutions.

From the outset, clearly noticeable changes occur in V. R.'s behaviour. One general formula covers them all: Doubts and hesitations take the place of control.

While looking for the first and second solutions he repeatedly hesitates over whether or not to act. The same indecisiveness appears in the way he musters the available material. It also takes him quite a time before he brings himself to ask the observers a question: Each time he signals that a question is coming and then only after taking a run does he formulate it. Meanwhile, he offers to the observers a real festival of *Verlegenheitsbewegungen*. As to the second solution, when he at last discovers it (after 24 min), he is not at all sure that what he has found is an acceptable solution, and he has to be told so by the observers before believing it.

When the crucial moment to start looking for the nonexistent third solution has come, he tells the observers that he knows there is no such thing. But the way he does it is quite typical of his persistent doubts and hesitations. Looking worried, he tells the observers, in a low, hardly audible voice, that he knows there is no third solution. But, when one of the observers, putting on a poker face, tells him that he does not understand what he means by "no third solution", he no longer presses the point, and, yielding to social pressure, begins to search for the third solution. This time, just as in most interactions with the observers, he appears very self-conscious.

He shyly looks at the floor while talking, and several times his face reddens. In the interview he states that in his contacts with strangers, he is very anxious not too lose face by acting stupidly. To him, eating in front of people who look intently at him, crossing a dance-floor, or the mere idea of having to act in a play is an ordeal. The essential point is that in situations that are considered to generate social anxiety, he simply is not sure what is the most appropriate thing to do.

His search for the third solution does not last long. Soon he wants to stop it because he is again convinced that there is no third solution. But he hesitates to tell the observers that he would like to put an end to the examination. When he is told that he should go on searching, he says he is sorry not to reach any result. Gradually, he drifts out of the situation. He momentarily relates a few details to the problem, but, again, he leaves the field. As the observers treat him as if he were still looking for the third solution, he makes what to him must sound like an audacious remark about "feeling like a prisoner in jail". Although he definitely wants to stop working on the task, he indecisively waits for more than three quarters of an hour before accepting gratefully the observer's suggestion to put an end to the examination.

Although he still makes considerable efforts at self-control, he behaves much more restlessly than in the previous PCS. Also, his repertoire of *Verlegenheitsbewegungen* has increased notably.

In the interview, he attributes to the Dembo PCS the same aim as the Saugstad PCS: to investigate impulse control, perseverance, and the social influence exerted by observation. Once more his definition of the PCSs meaning mirrors his own concerns. His final judgment about the Dembo PCS is that it is the most stupid one he knows of. Besides, he considers that being observed while being unable to do anything was a most disturbing experience.

Given the substitution of persistent doubts and indecision for a variety of control operations in a problem situation where action possibilities are restructured, it is tempting to hypothesize that both are nothing but the expression, under different conditions, of an identical cognitive structure characterized by permanent internal conflicts. Before acting, he perceives and conceives problem situations as containing conflicting action potentialities of equal weight. Hence his indecisiveness. After an action course has been chosen, the internal conflict of his cognitive structures reappears under the form of potential discrepancies between goals and means. Hence all the control operations he performs during the execution of a task.

In the first case, situations defined as inherently conflictual are handled by a role-rule model that leads him to avoid the judgments implied in being the object of social perception by others. Given a state of indecision resulting from a balance between conflicting forces, he is, indeed, extremely sensitive to approval and disapproval because little is needed to turn the scale towards one side or the other. Being thus very susceptible to influence, he can only resist it by conscious self-control.

In the second case, a modified role-rule model, still including self-control, but additionally involving strict adherence to socially desirable standards of excellence, induces him to act as a perfectionist and, at the same time, solves his problems both as an agent and a social actor.

CASE 3: V. D. I. (FEMALE, AGE 21)

The Saugstad PCS (94 min)

During the first minutes, V. D. I. explores the material and the problem situation very thoroughly. She ties a string around a wooden block and after a few attempts, manages to draw the frame near to her. At this point, her easily observable, ordered behaviour ends and is replaced until the end of PCS by uninterrupted sequences of actions which, as time goes by, lose their goal-directedness. There are moments when one has the impression that she is on the verge of pure chaos. In fact, purposiveness and a certain temporal hierarchy of successive acts are undoubtedly present, but this protocol is so complicated that it calls for special study. Its essential features are closely related to each other but must, for clarity's sake, be considered separately. They are the following:

1. Through a lack of anticipation of the results of her actions, V. D. I., instead of solving sub-problems, creates new problems as a consequence of most of her actions. These new problems lead to new difficulties with which she will have to cope. Sub-goals substitute themselves for goals and sub-sub-goals for sub-goals in such a way that in the end, the original problem is completely transformed and eventually leads to a global ersatz solution.

2. Parallel to this process, V. D. I., on six occasions, makes proposals to relax and to modify the rules under which she is trying to solve the problem. In fact, she attempts to substitute an easier, more expeditious version of each problem for the one she is confronted with.

3. Simultaneously, V. D. I.'s behaviour is characterized by the accompaniment of an unceasing stream of uninhibited verbal and non-verbal expressions.

What follows is an illustration of the way her actions lead to an ever more complicated nesting of sub-problems.

V. D. I. tries to bring the grating nearer by throwing a block tied to a string, but in doing so, she upsets the container filled with marbles, which roll away in all directions. Once she has the grating, she throws it at the marbles in order to recover them, but now she upsets the second (empty) container. Going on with throwing the grating, she hits the second container once more, and makes it roll farther away. Now she throws her wooden block at the second container, but the string slips from her fingers beyond reach. She has to manufacture a new instrument to get hold of the second container, and, after some efforts, she finally lays hands on it.

Rather impulsively, she pushes the second container back into its original position. It is just beyond reach when she changes her mind: In order to solve the main problem, she wants to fill the second container with marbles before putting it back in its initial location. Now she attempts to get it back by means of an elaborate procedure: She throws the grating on top of the container, and then she fishes for the grating by throwing a wooden block tied to a string. Having finally achieved her ersatz solution she once more pushes back the container filled with marbles but does it so brusquely that she overturns the container and spills the marbles all over the forbidden zone. Making use of her wooden-block-plus-string device, she retrieves the marbles one by one. In the same way, she recovers the second container. While throwing the wooden block at the last marbles, it gets stuck under the table. Once more she has to manufacture a new instrument (a ruler tied to a string) to recover the wooden block plus string.

After having filled the second container with marbles, she adds a few objects to it in order to make it more stable. Then she pushes the container into its former position by means of the grating and the frame, only to discover that she has not solved the problem at all. In fact, she has completely lost sight of the initial problem. Still she makes a plea to have her ersatz solution accepted because it wasn't her fault that the container was so often upset.

While V. D. I.'s awkward attempts at solving the problem lead to an intricate succession of new problems, she asks a number of suggestive questions, all of which are intended to modify the instructions and to substitute new and easier tasks for those that were initially to be executed. For example, she asks whether she needs the lost marbles. In order not to have to recover a container, she would like to substitute the first one for the second one. Later on, she asks permission to penetrate into the forbidden zone, either by creeping on all fours or by walking on papers. Finally, she asks if she has to put all the marbles in the container or if she is allowed to stop as soon as she feels satisfied with her work. From the interview data, it appears that she also performed a few fugitive imaginary substitutions. At one moment, she imagined the forbidden zone to be a swamp. At another moment, when making use of the block and the string, she thought she was angling.

These verbally formulated suggestions are part of an almost continuous stream of verbal utterances. V. D. I. is, in fact, talking all the time: Either she thinks aloud or she speaks to the material and makes all kinds of anticipating and accompanying commentaries. Actually, she verbalizes everything she does and when she appears to be silent, she is still silently talking to herself.

The vicissitudes of her activity are punctuated by a rich diversity of exclamations and of facial expressions. Often she mimics vocally and expressively the results of the actions she is attempting to perform. Each effort is accompanied by grimaces and followed by deep sighs. If she meets an unexpected difficulty, she either compresses her lips, sucks her lips, or whistles. To major obstacles, she reacts by cursing or by slapping her thighs. Apart from their diversity, the most striking feature of this expressive flurry is that it is completely uninhibited.

The fact that she is of small stature, round faced with hardly differentiated childish features certainly favours her impersonation of a schoolgirl (rather than a mother of a child, which she is), who, in a spontaneous and pleasant mood and with a moving good grace, fulfils her task. There are some rare moments that clearly suggest that she consciously monitors a well-defined persona; for example, when reflecting, she keeps a finger in her mouth, and when expressing surprise, she rolls her eyes. But most of the time, her performance looks perfectly routinized.

V. D. I.'s impressive display of impulsiveness can hardly be likened to an overflowing euphoric hyperactivity. She manifests no excess of activation. It is rather the regulation of her actions that is wrong. Her distant goals are vague, and she only seems able to pursue short-range objectives. But, besides acting within a very limited perspective, she never anticipates the possible consequences of her actions. Acting on the spur of the moment, she easily gets into trouble. To this she reacts by some further impulsive action so that she eventually gets caught in a vicious circle of self-maintaining impulsiveness. There is also an all-or-nothing quality to the actions she performs and the expressions she displays. Being apparently unable to exert a graded control over her actions and expressions, she either acts and expresses herself without inhibition or does not do anything at all.

Furthermore, one cannot help thinking that the perceptual schemata of her present environment are not adequately integrated in the cognitive maps of her world and its possibilities and that, consequently, the maps of possibilities only insufficiently direct her explorations and actions. It is also tempting to suppose that her unceasing verbal activity, which only duplicates or follows her actions, hampers the elaboration of mental plans and prevents their realization as effective operations. This hypothesis that attributes V. D. I.'s difficulties to defective interiorization and exteriorization processes could, of course, only be substantiated by further investigations.

Be that as it may, V. D. I.'s attempts at solving the problem end up with the attainment of a substitute goal, which she reaches after having drifted away from the original one as a result of her accumulated failures. Her naive belief that a substitute solution will be accepted, together with her protest that it wasn't her fault if things did not turn out as expected, is completely in keeping with the childish persona she has displayed during this PCS. It once more brings to the fore the egocentric wishful character of her performance, which she attempted to recast into a self-defined task several times.

V. D. I. tells the interviewer that she is quite satisfied with the result obtained. Even if she had put only one marble in the container, she would have considered it a success because it is her personal interpretation of her performance that really matters.

She thinks she has sometimes cheated a bit by not respecting very strictly the limits of the forbidden zone. She also has some doubts about the adequacy of her solution, but she finds some solace in the idea that she was not the only one to have acted that way. She admits being very clumsy and to have very often been criticized by her husband for the stupid things her awkwardness has made her do.

V. D. I. also mentions that at moments, she felt very aggressive and would very much have liked to throw an object or to drop it on the floor. However, she kept herself under control, as she usally does in the presence of other people, with the exception of her brother. Towards him she feels no obligation to control herself. As a consequence, they have already fought with knives. She is quite ready to describe herself as impulsive, and she adds that, in her case, the Dutch expression "to be so excited as to run up the walls" is literally true. At least once, she ran up a wall with both feet and landed on the floor. Talking without interruption is something she does to counter the oppressive feeling she experiences when she finds herself amidst a zone of silence. It is from her husband, who always needs much noise around himself, that she claims to have learned to avoid silence. In fact, she would have found the task much more pleasant if there had been some music in the room.

With the exception of some interesting anecdotal information, the interview does not reveal anything that would make us revise our interpretation of her problem-solving behaviour.

The Dembo PCS (48 min)

From the beginning, one is struck by the fact that V. D. I. interprets the Dembo PCS as being nothing but a special case of the former one. At least she acts as if it were sufficient to transfer the solutions that were adequate to the Saugstad PCS in order to find the solution of the Dembo PCS.

She starts by fitting a weekly inside a few rings and tries to reach the flower by means of this cylinder. Then she throws rings at the flower in order to make it fall on the floor. Finally, she manages to put a ring around the container and, while sitting on the chair, to pull the container nearer and to take it with her hands. When she is told that the container shouldn't be moved, she looks very surprised. As she explicitly tells the observers, she was convinced that just like in the former PCS she would have to pull the container towards her, take the flower, and then push the container back to its original position.

She is obsessed by the rings but does not know how to make use of them. Suddenly noticing the little notebook, she performs a beautiful substitutive action by writing a note to the observers in which she asks them to bring her the flower. As this solution is not accepted, she repeats her former strategy of sitting on the chair and pulling the flower towards her. She is quite convinced that she has found a second solution. One of the observers has to explain to her that she has already made that attempt and that it had not been accepted because she moved the container. Apparently, she has forgotten everything about it.

In a very short time, her attitude changes completely. It is clear that she does not want to go on working on the problem. She looks tense and somewhat angry at the flower and at the observers. Without intending to take the flower, she throws a few rings at it as a substitutive discharge of the increasing tension that she manifests visibly by a more rigid attitude.

For the third time, she makes the attempt at solving the problem that has already been rejected, and when told once again that it cannot be counted as a solution, she decides to stop and give up all further attempts. She stands in front of the observers with her arms crossed and her lips compressed and defiantly looks them straight in the eyes. After a few moments, she protests against being kept in the problem situation and threatens to start reading the *Playboy* magazine, which she does rather nervously for several minutes. When she is again prodded into action, she explains that she has found one solution and that she is quite satisfied with it. Again she looks defiantly at the observers, ready for a trial of gaze-strength and announces that, being extremely stubborn, she is not going to give in. She will leave and go home.

On the whole, V. D. I. is much quieter than in the former PCS. She acts less, talks less, and displays a smaller variety of expressions. Still her visible behaviour is not qualitatively different from that she exhibited previously. In the interview, she criticizes the material for not offering enough action possibilities. And, indeed, all the time she proceeds by short, disconnected and impulsive attempts. However, to understand how she has acted in this PCS, it is necessary to know what happened on the evening when she came home after having been observed in the Saugstad PCS. Indeed, when she told her husband about it, he immediately found the efficient solution and ridiculed her for not having hit upon the idea of manufacturing a cylinder by means of rolls of paper. Consequently, when she was to undergo a second PCS, she was still impressed by the simplicity of the solution that her husband had found so quickly but, at the same time, was quite convinced that she would be utterly unable to solve the new problem. When she twice reproduces impulsively an inadequate solution, she reacts to her failures by resorting to substitutive actions, and the third time, she becomes just as impulsively negativistic as she had formerly been.

Impulsiveness, lack of goal analysis and of planning are here once more quite conspicuous. However, the ease with which she assimilates the Dembo PCS to the Saugstad PCS and the readiness with which she acts substitutively suggest the existence in V. D. I. of a markedly defective integration of cognitive processes with action sequences.

V. D. I. additionally tells the interviewer that she is worried about the aggressive stubbornness she has shown toward the observers. She feels sorry for one of the observers whom she likes very much and explains that, although she felt compelled to assume a sulking attitude, she attempted to moderate her aggressive stubbornness in order not to present herself in contradictory ways: "She [the observer] must have thought I was some kind of a gentle pussy-cat, and now I had to act quite differently." This is undoubtedly a confirmation of our interpretation about her self-presentation in the Saugstad PCS and, at the same time, an illustration of the kind of conflict she is drawn into by her impulsive stubborness.

Conclusions

The use of the detailed, process-oriented assessment procedures described in the preceding, leads us to several conclusions that bear upon the misconstructions noted previously (pp. 121–125) as being common in the field. But in addition, it is clear that a full understanding of any pattern of concrete actions requires an integration of the study of action and the study of personality. These matters are described briefly as follows.

1. A first conclusion that can be drawn from the analysis of the action and expression processes manifested by our subjects, as well as from their accounts, is that, in situations characterized as medium in the degree of manipulation of antecedent conditions and low on the degree of imposition of units, the study of action processes and the study of basic personality characteristics are inseparable.

Only short behavioural sequences interpreted by means of achievement concepts yield seemingly impersonal data. But as soon as more extended, hierarchically organized action sequences are considered, various aspects of the agent's individuality are repeatedly displayed. Personality and task performance can only be artifically separated when investigation is concentrated on end results judged by comparison with an external criterion. However, if analysis is focused on the ongoing action process, personality characteristics appear as immanent constituents of the performance. In other words, when process analysis is made the central concern, it becomes obvious that the display of personality characteristics and the execution of the task are welded together in one single performance. Thus, from out point of view, action psychology and personality psychology not only complement each other, but they are also mutually necessary. Action processes cannot be investigated without a study of the agent's personality, and, reciprocally, the analysis of action processes is essential to personality research and assessment.

2. With the method advocated here, misconstructions resulting from the uncritical use of linguistic categories can be avoided if the investigators keep closely to the original protocol and mould their terminology on the observational data having, if needs be, recourse to paraphrases and neologisms to remedy the defects of the current psychological vocabulary. An essential task must indeed still be fulfilled by action psychology, that is, the elaboration of a detailed analytical taxonomy of human action. Only then shall we be able to introduce differentiations that presently are sometimes difficult to make. Take, for instance, A. M. (Appendix 2) and V. D. I., both of whom a trait theorist would rate high on the traits of impulsiveness and extraversion. However, if one goes over the written protocol and the video-recording, it is quite clear that A. M. is a euphoric hypomanic whose impulsiveness manifests itself by an overflow of activation, whereas V. D. I.'s impulsiveness seems to result from a defective cognitive steering of her actions. Are these two phenotypical expressions of the same genotypical impulsivity or do these two action modalities differ on the genotypical level? This is exactly the kind of question we must learn to formulate and attempt to answer instead of subsuming them under illdefined labels.

3. Being completely process centered, the PCSs and the observable coping operations they elicit hardly induce investigators to commit the product–process fallacy. But, the more refined the analyses of observed action processes and the better they fit with interview data, the more acutely the problem of comparing different action processes exhibited by the same subject confronted with different tasks arises. For instance, our subject V. R. behaves in such a way that, on the basis of the Saugstad PCS protocol, we describe him as exerting a high degree of control on the objects he manufacturers as well as on his own behaviour and expressions. However, when confronted with the Dembo PCS, an abundance of hesitations and vacillations apparently substitutes itself for his former attempts at controlling each phase of his actions. How are these two kinds of action processes to be compared? Do they have the same origin? That is, Do they depend on some identical generating mechanism or are they alternative ways of coping with what V. R. perceives as conflict situations?

To provide definite answers to such questions, more has to be known about the ways in which the same individual adapts to the varying requirements of situated tasks. In other words, the close relationship existing between action psychology and personality psychology calls not only for comparisons between action processes manifested by different individuals in the same PCS, but also for the analysis of the various action structures that a single individual exhibits in different PCSs. Quite obviously, it is at this juncture that new perspectives emerge, which may lead to an integration of the psychology of situations with action and personality psychology.

4.   The new approach to personality research and assessment is an essentially open method that is opposed to any arbitrary narrowing of its scope. Collective or individual PCSs—however artificially contrived they may look—are social situations involving social interactions and self-presentations. Confrontation with protocols and video-recordings followed by focused account eliciting interviews contribute to a gradual extension to the interpretative perspective to everyday interactions and eventually to biographically situated experiences. An interesting method that enables investigators to integrate the interpretation of PCS protocols and the associated interviews with present and post biographical material consists in summarizing them in such a way that the subject can be induced to perform successive sorts on them in order to yield a Kelly matrix that can then be analyzed in the usual way.

5.   One of the most pressing problems raised by the analysis and interpretation of PCSs concerns the consistency of the observed action and expression patterns. In order to solve it, two different but convergent approaches can be used. The first is based on the use of homogeneous sources, and the second on the use of heterogeneous sources of information. By homogeneous sources we mean other individual or group PCSs involving different task requirements, whereas members of the family, friends, the others having direct personal acquaintance with the person are considered to be heterogeneous sources of information.

After having given several action modalities observed in a PCS in a multiple-choice format, judges having at their disposl either homogenous or heterogeneous information are asked (1) to choose from among a set of alternatives the one actually exhibited by the person submitted to the PCS, (2) to justify explicitly the choice made, and (3) in case the first choice was wrong, to make a second choice and also to justify it.

In order to evaluate the meanings attributed by the judges to the wrong as well as to the correct alternatives, all of them are previously rated along a number of dimensions (e.g., social desirability) by a group of independent judges.

The design underlying the comparisons by means of this method differ considerably from the usual designs used in consistency studies. In fact, a double comparison is made. On one hand, when the observations and interpretations resulting from a PCS applied to a person are compared with the predictions made by family members of that person who knew him or her by direct acquaintance, the observed behaviour constitutes the criterion for their choices. On the other hand, the observers of the person engaged in a PCS, while extracting from the protocols characteristic action modalities on which the correct action modalities are based, have also elaborated an interpretation of the individual's personality. In this part of the design, it is the accounts given by family members as justification of their choices that constitute the criterion for the observers' interpretations. This design with the two criteria involved in the double comparison may be represented as in Figure 3.

This promising design also has the advantage that it allows a close integration of personality assessment and person-perception.

6.   It is also clear that our descriptions and analyses of the action and expression processes elicited by PCSs are still quite crude. Progress is needed in the recording and transcription of action sequences. But, although much can be expected from the use of sophisticated technical devices, an essential task must still be fulfilled, for which no apparatus is available: i.e. the elaboration of a detailed analytical taxonomy of human action. This is an urgent and immense task which must be accomplished together with the conditional-genetic analysis of action processes. It is also a sine qua non for the further development of the PCSs method, without which research could degenerate into a new form of observational impressionism.

Take for instance our subject V. R. who behaves in such a way that, on the basis of our protocol, we describe him as exerting a high degree of control on the products he manufactures, as well as on his own behaviour and expressions: are these two kinds of control, two phenotypical expressions of the same genotype, or are these two different and possibly independent kinds of "control"? And what about V. R.'s hesitations and vacillations which, in the Dembo-PCS, apparently replace his former control? Do they have the same origin, i. e. do they depend on the same generating mechanism, or are they alternative ways of coping with what V. R. perceives as conflict situations?

Let us now compare A. M. and V. D. I. whom we may be tempted to label as "impusive": is V. D. I.'s "impulsiveness" of the same natural kind as A. M.'s "impulsiveness"? A trait-theorist using rating-scales would hardly be troubled by this question and would probably rate both as high in the trait impulsiveness and attribute to both a high

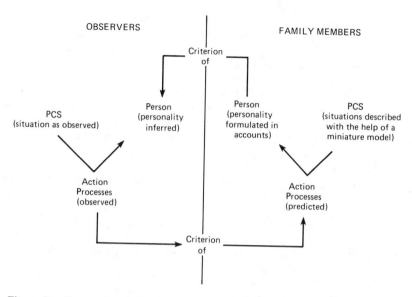

Figure 3.   Comparisons of predictions made by observers and family members.

degree of extraversion. We, on the contrary, have great doubts. Indeed A. M. is an euphoric hypomanic whose "impulsiveness" may best be described by making use of the metaphor of an "overflow" of activation energy, whereas V. D. I.'s "impulsiveness" seems to result from defective cognitive steering of her actions.

These are the kinds of questions I think we must learn to formulate and attempt to answer. As far as I can see, the diagnostic use of PCSs of various kinds may contribute to a renovation of the description and analysis of individual personality characteristics and contribute to a new conception of personality assessment. But it will also be a rich source of questions to which only the systematic analysis of action and expression processes will be able to provide an answer.

Appendix 1: Outline of the Focused Interview

  I. Personal evaluation of achieved results
    A. Satisfaction with the achievement
       1. Degree of success or failure
       2. Reasons for appreciation
       3. Possibilities of improvement
       4. Grading of the achievement on a 10 point scale
       5. Maximum within the subject's reach.
    B. Estimate of the time elapsed

    C. Comparison with other person's achievements
    D. Influence exerted by the achievement and by the method
       1. Consequences of the obtained result for future examinations
       2. Conclusions or lessons drawn by the subject from the investigation
  II. Condition and situation of the subject before the test
    A. General physical and psychological condition on the day of the test (good vs. bad day; relaxed vs. tense; tiredness vs. fitness)
    B. Particular worries or specific events that may have had an influence on the results
    C. Preparation for the test
       1. Expected versus unexpected; in possession of preliminary information or not
       2. Preconceived ideas or prejudice
    D. Influence of the environment (rooms, waiting period)
 III. General attitude towards the test
    A. First thoughts when being given the instructions or at the sight of the material
    B. Attitude towards the test
       1. Interesting, attractive
       2. Agreement between kind of task and subject's preferences or abilities
    C. Change of attitude during the test (different phases and reasons for changes)
    D. Meaning and purpose of the test
       1. General or main purpose of the test
       2. Reason for putting the subject through the test
       3. Solvability of the task
       4. Representativeness of the test situation with relation to real situations
  IV. Goals and aspirations
    A. Level of aspiration (qua time needed, correctness, approach and impression on the examiner[s]); subjective probability of success at the beginning of the task
    B. Possible changes of goal or of emphasis in the course of the test, and their causes
    C. Hidden or subordinate goals that the subject has set for himself or herself
    D. Ultimate goal set by the subject
    E. Influence of goals set on the actions performed.
    F. Substitutive goals: the wish to realize something other than what was asked for in the instructions or to achieve better in another test and so forth
   V. Affective and cognitive processes emerging during the test
    A. Evolution of the mood and the affective state of mind during the test
       1. Nature of the changes, their causes, their moment of origin
       2. Control of affective reactions (at crucial moments)

    3. Tension and fatigue
    4. Level of concentration and perseverance
 B. Thematic relief of the test
    1. Concentration of attention and its drifting away during the test
       Crucial moments or *Aha-Erlebnisse* (which? when?)
       Starting all over again
       Making a new start for certain parts
    2. Reactions to partial successes or failures
    3. Moments of intense involvement with the task
 C. Methods applied
    1. Constant or partial attempts at systematic and analytic reasoning; procedures of analyses (which? when?)
    2. Trial and error or attempts with a more specific purpose in mind, emanating from past experience, functional or material relations
    3. Attitude of passive expectation; role of inspiration; waiting for a flash of inspiration that would bring the subject insights enabling him or her to make up for lost time
    4. Attempts to guess the solution by looking for indications, such as traces left by or on the material or wear and tear
 D. Interruptions and changes of the stream of thoughts
    1. Fixation on certain hypotheses or attempts; wrong suppositions made concerning certain components of the task
    2. Periods of confusion and of cognitive disorganization; efforts to overcome these episodes
    3. Blocking and inhibition: periods of thoughtlessness; impression of turning around in a circle; inability to look at the problem from a different angle
    4. Impression of heightened clarity of thought; accelerated trains of thought; quick and incoherent succession of ideas
    5. Ideas that come and go at the moment when they should be applied
VI. Tendencies mobilized by the task and by the situation
 A. Thoughts strange to the test and even to the situation; their transient or compulsive nature; control of these thoughts
 B. Felt impulse to do and say things connected or not with the task; motives of their suppression
 C. Tendencies related to the task.
    1. *Aus-dem-Felde-gehen*; intention to quit or stop; view of the possible consequences; motives preventing the subject from giving up
    2. Momentary inclination to do something in order to dismiss the test from one's mind
    3. Wish to have never accepted the task or, on the contrary, satisfaction at having participated in the test
    4. Wish never to think back to the situation or be put again in a similar situation; wish that no other test would follow
    5. Aggressive tendencies toward the material; causes, why and how suppressed

6. Comparison with previous tests, with similar situations, or with affective reactions when doing other tests or in other situations
7. Comparison with other individuals subjected to a similar test (with whom? results of the comparison?)
8. Active attempts to conceive the situation in a way different from reality

VII. Interactions with the observer(s)
    A. Sensitivity towards the social situation
        1. Stimulating or inhibiting effect of the observer's presence
        2. Wish that the observer would put an end to the test or be absent for a moment; comparison of the performance with and without an observer present
        3. Thoughts ascribed to the observer at certain moments
        4. Attitude attibuted to the observer by the subject (e.g., ironical, hostile, cooperative, understanding, friendly, protective)
        5. Attitude towards possible help or towards the help really given by the observer
        6. Wish that certain persons would be present during the test; imaginary representation of the reactions of those persons; persons whose presence is best avoided during the test; reasons
        7. Aggressive feelings towards the observers (e.g., wish to observe them in similar situations or to put them to the test by asking various questions)
    B. Reactions to various aspects of the social situation.
        1. Interpretation of and reactions to the keeping of a protocol
        2. Role of time; importance attributed to the use of the chronometer
        3. Attempts to read the notes of the observer or to get to know what he or she writes down
        4. Comparison of the work done by the observer with the work done by the subject
        5. Reactions to announcement of the result and to the observer's remarks and critical observations

VIII. Comparisons with other situations
    A. Other psychological investigations
    B. Real life situations

Appendix 2: Summaries of Two PCS Interpretative Protocols

CASE 4: A. M. (MALE, AGE 21)
The Saugstad PCS (32 min)

From the outset, A. M.'s self-presentation is all self-assertiveness. Neither the nature of the task nor the presence of the observers affects him in the least. As soon as he has received the instructions, he dashes forward to use the slats in order to reach the container filled with marbles. The objection made by one of the observers does not upset him, and he immediately goes on looking for another solution, maintaining the same high level of activity with which he started. Equally characteristic of his style of acting is his rough handling of the material. Instead of disentangling a piece of string from the ball, he first breaks off two pieces and then ties them together. In order to empty the material box, he bluntly turns it over and a few moments later, he throws this fairly heavy box in the direction of the grating with the results that he upsets the container with the marbles.

His exploration of the material is minimal. Still he takes a spoon in his hands in order to have a closer look at it, but he bends it so brusquely that he breaks it. Meanwhile, no particular mimic or pantomimic expression is to be observed. Always acting in quick tempo, he tries a nail, a hook, and pincers together with a piece of string and without hesitation throws it at the container. He does not even notice the fact that the pincers, flying off the string, land on the floor a considerable distance away.

Considering that there is only one possibility left to him, he throws, four times in succession, a handful of marbles at the second container and only once a single marble. After little more than a quarter of an hour has elapsed, and although only a single marble has eventually landed in the container, he consideres his task completed and is ready to stop.

After some prodding by one of the observers, he admits that there may exist two other solutions, which he formulates rather vaguely, adding however that they are not worthwhile trying because it would take too much time to implement them.

Still he agrees to have another try. He starts again throwing the marbles at the container, but this time he has placed the grating and the frame around the container so as to be able to recover them. This time he throws the marbles one by one, but he does it so violently that in two throws, he completely destroys the container.

Although this incident has exerted no visible influence on him, he can no longer be moved to try some other solution and, paying no further attention to the observers, he puts an end to the task by clearing everything away.

To interview A. M. is not an easy task. Many questions—even the simplest—must be repeated or rephrased because he doesn't understand them the first time. Questions about his thought processes or imaginative performances are answered only with great difficulty. His answers are mostly vague and evasive and often contradictory. The same questions repeated a short time later elicit different or contradictory answers. As the syntax of his speech is very defective, it is difficult to understand him. Rarely does he finish a sentence. Instead, he interrupts himself, starts another sentence, gets lost in it because he prematurely attempts to qualify what he has just said, then tries to retrieve a former line of thought, without seemingly being aware of it, and ends up in complete confusion. The following is an example of his confused thinking: He is satisfied with his performance, and grading it on a 10-point scale, he awards himself a 7 for speed of decision. His interpretation of the aim of the task is that it enables observers to judge a person's speed of decision and action. His own goal was to get, in the shortest time, as many marbles as possible in the container. When the moment comes when he should grade himself on the self-chosen dimension of speed of execution, he has already forgotten his initial intention. Instead, he explains that he should have imposed on himself a time limit of 10 min. Then, as he "reasons", he would have earned a 10, which "combined with his former 7" would finally yield 8.5. Somewhat later, he rates his performance by the number of marbles he has been able to throw into the container, that is "one on 10 or 15".

Among the intelligible things he says, the following are worth mentioning. He admits to having been criticized in the past for acting overhastily. There also was a time when he had too many hobbies. That his handling of the material could be interpreted as aggressiveness comes as a complete surprise to him. He thought it was obvious that the damage done was nothing but the consequence of his speedy way of acting. Besides, he feels confident that anybody trying to solve the problem would have broken the container. The breaking of the spoon is an exception for which he feels sorry: He should have noticed that it could not be bent completely. Eventually, he considers that he can best be described as "impulsive but with a great deal of self-control".

His astonishing way of attempting to solve the second part of the Saugstad PCS is the only episode on which his accounts shed new light. In fact, as he did not immediately find the link—as he puts it—between the marbles and the empty container, rather than losing time looking for an adequate solution, he opted for the quickest solution and started throwing handfuls of marbles at the container. Thus, this action apparently owes its unexpectedness to its emergence as an impulsive substitute action.

When A. M. is told about the existence of a much more efficient solution involving the construction of a cylinder from rolls of paper, it is clear that this solution had never crossed his mind. But he immediately rejects this solution: It would have taken too much time and

the task was not interesting enough to justify such an effort. To quote
an expression he uses repeatedly: "It is only an isolated activity which
does not contribute to a whole".

A. M.'s role-rule model, as it can be hypothesized on the basis of
his behaviour in this PCS, is completely tailored to his high level of
activation and, rather than efficiently controlling his level of activation, at the very most it canalizes it in socially meaningful ways. First,
it consists of an assertive self-presentation concealing his impulsiveness
under the mask of boldness. Keeping up this self-image to others and
to himself is no mean task since his hyperactivity also results in a much
less than optimal level of flexibility and differentiation of the cognitive
structures determining his level of performance and his verbal utterances. However, he manages to reconcile both by imposing definitions
derived from egocentric interests on situations in which he is called to
prove himself. Thus, it becomes possible for him to discount failures
and criticisms by qualifying them as extraneous to his personal frame
of reference. Testifying to the immaturity of his role-rule model is the
fact that, while providing him with rationalized outlets for his hyperactivity, it is only after the event that he is able to account for outcomes. Another aspect of A. M.'s role-rule model that underscores its
immaturity is that it is primarily centered around the expresive display
of his self-presentation and involves him only secondarily as an agent.
This may explain his insensitivity to failure.

The Dembo PCS (91 min)

The way he enters the problem situation and starts looking for the
three solutions is quite similar to the one he adopted in the former
PCS. After trying two solutions involving gross physical effort like
moving tables, he discovers the two accepted solutions in a very short
time. Given the elementary character of the first solutions, he seems
very challenged by the idea of discovering a third one—which to him
cannot possibly be an obvious one.

For one hour and a half, he pours out an unceasing stream of 18
different attempts at solving the problem, each of which he tries out
several times before giving up and switching over to the next one. His
handling of the material is quite similar to that exhibited in the former
PCS. A magazine is kicked about, a notebook is thrown on the floor,
the wooden rings are noisily knocked against each other. Taking up
the hammer, he swings it, with ample gestures, over his head. Some
of his attempts are acrobatic and not without danger. For example, he
puts both feet behind the front slat, and, flexing his knees, he swings

himself forward in order to land, arms flexed, with both hands on the edge of the table. He also attempts to get the flower by throwing wooden rings at it. As he throws them much too violently, he inevitably breaks the container.

He moves about a great deal and takes a great number of positions that follow quickly upon each other. After 71 min of uninterrupted goal-oriented activity, he gradually gives up. He does not know how to put an end to the PCS. On one hand, he refuses to make any further trials, but on the other hand, he leaves the field only psychologically by starting to read a weekly. After 20 minutes, he spontaneously starts to clear away the whole set up.

Among the numerous attempts he successively makes, there are a number of repetitions or quasi-identical trials involving only minor variations of the same basic pattern. Other proposed solutions are more original, as when he manufactures an instrument composed of a hammer and the stem of another artificial flower in order to increase the reach of his arm and pick the flower up from the container. There are also his more violent attempts consisting of throwing wooden rings or balls of paper, in which he clearly acts out a considerable degree of pent-up aggression.

Although he is producing an unceasing sequence of attempted solutions, there are, between repetitions of the same attempt, pauses during which he does not act. But quite characteristically, these episodes are spent exclusively in preparing the next attempt. In fact, he never stops to reflect about the problem as a whole. He never recapitulates his attempts or analyzes the conditions under which he must act. In spite of the successive refusals he has to meet with, he never stops to consider what the definable characteristics of an acceptable solution might be. Therefore, he is unable to conceptualize the task adequately. To him, a third solution, is simply a different solution, but he has never taken the time to reflect on what the difference should consist of.

Thus, notwithstanding his productivity, his performance remains at a low level. As he does not keep track of his various attempts, his hyperactivity several times threatens to degenerate into blind perseveration.

In the second interview, A. M.'s answers are just as confused as in the first one, and contradictions abound. He is satisfied with the result achieved because, as he remarks, to find two out of three possible solutions is a 66% success. But somewhat later, he also states, that like with the former PCS, he has failed. In fact, according to his standards of success and speed, he should have found the third solution in 20 min. He first defines the Dembo PCS as a "frustration test" and later adds: "In order to get me frustrated, you would have to go much further". At another moment, he states that the Dembo PCS tests the capacity of a person to refuse resolutely to go on with a task when he is fed up with it. This is somewhat clarified by his statement that he has successively pursued two goals: first, to find the three solutions, and second, to find a way to put an end to the whole situation. The task itself he considers to be only trivial, and he reproaches himself for not having stopped much earlier.

As to the container he has broken again, he gives three different versions of this episode: (1) He considered breaking the container as a possible solution to the problem while telling himself, "I shall try to inflict on the child as little pain as possible", (2) he did not intend to break the container, and, when it happened, he was not at all upset because he thought that the observers had plenty of them in reserve; (3) he never behaved aggressively towards the material and has always done his best to prevent the destruction of the container, "but . . . if it must happen . . . if there exists no other possibility . . . ." On the whole, he is completely unaware of the way he has handled the material.

He is surprised to hear that there is no third solution and labels this information as the "happy end" of the whole task. His most interesting statement is to the effect that he persisted so long looking for a third solution becuase he feared making the same mistake as before (Saugstad PCS) when he overlooked a solution. While reporting this, he mixes up both PCSs and speaks about the third solution to the first PCS.

Obviously, to A. M., the Dembo PCS—especially after having been confronted with the Saugstad-PCS—is a kind of trap into which he falls headlong by transferring impulsively what he believes to have learnt previously. His behaviour is guided by the same role-rule model. However, certain aspects of it stand out more clearly.

CASE 5: H. C. (MALE, AGE 30)

The Saugstad PCS (19 min)

From the first moment, H. C. shows maximal involvement in the task and even anticipates an incompletely worded instruction. His exploration of the available material is systematic, and he also takes a detailed view of the spatial relations proper to the problem situation. He asks additional questions that are intended to make the instructions as precise as possible.

After having thought it all over, he starts working on the first part of the problem, which he solves in a few minutes. Through a sudden insight, he discovers the function of the papers and starts making rolls of paper and fitting them into a cylinder.

He concentrates fully on the task. Its execution, including the brief checks to which he submits his work, progresses very smoothly. He anticipates the problem posed by the bending of the cylinder and solves it by using the frame as a support. Before dropping all the marbles through the cylinder, he tests the cylinder and then, with a broad smile, gets them all into the empty container.

With the exception of a few minor details, his performance approximates remarkably well the structure of the ideal protocol.

The interview makes clear that he was very anxious to do his utmost best. After some short initial doubts, he was convinced that he would solve the problem and then aspired to nothing less than perfection. He also adds that he wanted to finish the whole task as quickly as possible because he had planned to end the evening by going to the movies.

He considers the task itself to belong to the kind of games he likes to play because it does not involve the sort of shoddy work he particularly dislikes. What is essential to him is that the instructions and the initial conditions should be stated clearly so as to enable him to plan the solution. He remembers having participated in a group problem-solving test called "the ideal town", which he disliked because no definition was given of what was meant by "ideal". He admits that he is a passionate planner and that, given the opportunity, he tries to elaborate long-range plans. His preference goes to creative activities. He thinks he has invented a new apparatus to cut Isomo (plastic) plates and intends to present it at an inventor's exhibition.

His performance on the Saugstad PCS is of such a high level that his behaviour as a social actor is likely to go unnoticed. From the moment he enters the room, he deals with all the social aspects of the situation with great ease. He comes in smiling puts his things away, and greets everybody. He is well dressed, with taste and discretion. His speech is perfect and sometimes approximates written language, although he makes no visible efforts at speaking correctly. With all the flexibility and smoothness of manners he displays, H. C. is anything but a more or less passive opportunist. On the contrary, his calm assurance and his straightforward, goal-directed way of acting conveys a high degree of self-assertivenss. But he displays it in such a way that it does not evoke any resistance and is accepted as natural and almost self-evident.

He tells the interviewer that the presence of observers, far from disturbing him, exerts a rather stimulating influence on him—and, indeed, while manufacturing his cylinder, he started working with his back towards the observers. But he quickly noticed that they could not see what he was doing, so he immediately turned himself towards them to make his work visible.

The role-rule model followed by H. C. presupposes the existence of some basic abilities that he undoubtedly possesses. It is one that can be summarized very briefly: skillful self-assertion as an agent, as well as an actor.

The Dembo PCS (73 min)

He starts this PCS roughly in the same way as he did the first. He quickly imagines a solution and attempts to draw the table nearer by making use of the hammer. When one of the observers indicates that moving the table is not allowed, he is taken aback and remarks that he was not told so. A long series of questions follows about what he is allowed to do and what objects are available, and finally, he sums up the observers' answers by asking ironically: "What am I allowed to do?"

Suddenly, he puts the chair between the slats and the table, leans on it with one hand and with the other one takes the flower out of the vase by means of a ring he has put around the extremity of a hammer. He waits and apparently believes that he has completed the task. To his surprise, he is told that he still has to look for two additional ways of solving the same problem. This instruction is the starting point of a number of discussions with one of the observers about the exact meaning of the terms used in the instructions. The situation gradually grows more tense and culminates in a conflict to which an end is put by terminating the PCS.

A first discussion takes place after H. C. has thrown a ring at the flower and picks it up from the floor where it has fallen. One of the observers calls it an unacceptable solution because it consists in merely shifting the problem but not in solving it. There then ensues a discussion about the meaning of "shifting" or "displacement" and about what makes one solution different from another one. In order not to give anything away, the observer remains vague and in doing so exposes himself to H. C.'s criticism; H. C. is in a good position to find fault with the instructions he is given but feels unable to make any progress beyond the series of actions he has already performed. In fact, H. C. believes that finding different solutions consists in finding different ways to take the flower out of the vase while leaning in the same way on the same chair. The criticism of one of the observers is obviously directed at the fact that a real difference in the solution method concerns the support used to bridge the distance between the slats and the table.

While both go on discussing at cross purposes, a rather tense situation is generated. The observer rebukes H. C. curtly while H. C. alternates serious objections with ironical remarks and occasionally looks him in the eyes. At the height of this episode of conflict, H. C. asks the observers in a neutral tone of voice, "Are you perhaps waiting until I get angry?" At last, H. C. decides to stop searching and firmly resists any prodding from the observer. He lights a cigarette, reads a few pages from a weekly, and thereby shows that he has left the problem situation for good. Although remaining quite polite and keeping himself under perfect control, he repeatedly walks towards the observers' table and looks at them with a domineering and defiant—almost provocative—attitude until one of the observers, after a last refusal, tells him that it is all finished and that he is free to leave—which he does after having greeted both observers.

During the interview, H. C. is not at all worried about his poor performance. In fact, he is still mainly interested in the meaning to be given to different solutions. He still maintains that the only significant differences that could be introduced involve some device functioning as a continuation of the hand. He is also convinced that the reason the observer never gave precise instructions was in order to be able to reject all his suggestions by invoking some non-explicitly mentioned condition. The second part of the PCS, that is—as he defines it—the part that begins from the moment he refuses to go on looking for a solution, he defines as a frustration test destined to assess his tolerance of frustration. That he started smoking a cigarette is, according to H. C., to be interpreted as the emergence of a change in mood. He also admits having asked himself questions like, "Am I really so stupid that I can't find the solution?" At another time he had felt the easily controlled urge to ask one of the observers with whom he is familiar whether *he* had been able to find three different solutions. Still, he claims to have experienced a level of tension that might have induced some emotional misfiring on his part, or even a real conflict with the observers.

What has still to be explained is why in this Dembo PCS there is so little to recall his brillant performance in the Saugstad PCS. As he himself explains, the former PCS had induced a very definite self-confident success orientation, which he carried over into the Dembo PCS. Although from the outset, he did not like the kind of instructions he received, he easily found a first solution and executed it as if at the same time he was successfully completing—*pars pro toto*—the whole task.

Even during the interview, when his attention is drawn to the problem of finding a proper support, he does not find the solution. When he is told that it only consists in putting one's knees outside the square, he still does not believe it, because he takes it as self-evident that the distance between front slat and table is too great to be bridged in this easy way. Not only does he need a demonstration, but he has to be induced to try it by himself before he can believe it.

Further interview data make it relatively easy to explain his blindness to a second solution. It is obvious that, according to his success orientation and his high level of aspiration, he expected that the second solution would be something difficult requiring a special act of insight. But there was another obstacle of a different origin that was preventing him from discovering the nearly obvious. Indeed, to execute that solution he would have had to get on his knees and that—like any other solution involving a direct contact with the floor— was completely excluded because it was unthinkable that he should risk spoiling his suit.

Considering all the evidence available, it seems that the reasons for his partial failure in the Dembo PCS can be traced to those that made for his success in the Saugstad PCS.

H. C. certainly still handled the social aspects of the situation with great ease, and in his discussions with one of the observers, he even managed to almost gain advantage over her and to tell her what to do. However, his highly developed social skills did not prevent him from becoming a victim of his self-presentation: the suit he was wearing and which is an essential aspect of his self-presentation, constituted an insurmountable obstacle to the discovery of an extremely simple solution.

His avowed passion for elaborating plans starting from clearly defined premises and conditions also failed him because his high aspirations made him look for sophisticated solutions, whereas nothing of the sort was required. Another conclusion concerning the cognitive aspects of the role-rule model that was inferred from his former performance is that they have to be considered as rigidly limited to some specific situations since confronting H. C. with the Dembo PCS was sufficient to induce their partial breakdown.

References

Allport, C. W., & Odbert, H. S. (1936). Trait-names: a psycholexical study. *Psychological Monographs, 47*(1, Whole No. 211).

Anastasi, A. (1961). *Psychological Testing*, 2nd ed. Macmillan: New York.

Becker, W. C. (1960). The Matching of Behaviour-Rating and Questionnaire Personality Factors. *Psychological Bulletin 57*, 201-212.

Black, M. (1952). *Critical Thinking*. 2nd ed. Prentice Hall: Englewood Cliffs, N.J.

Brody, B. (1970). Freuds Caseload. *Psychotherapy: Theory, Research and Practice, 7*, 8-12.

Buhler, Ch. (1933). *Der Menschlichen Lebenslauf als Psychologisches Problem*. S Hiegel: Wien.

Campbell, D. T., & Fiske, D. W. (1959). Convergent and discriminant validation by the multitrait–multimethod matrix. *Psychological Bulletin, 56*, 81-105.

Carlson, R. (1971). Where is the person in personality psychology. *Psychological Bulletin, 75*(3), 203-214.

Carr, H. A., & Kingsbury, F. A. (1938). The concept of traits. *Psychological Review, 45*, 497-524.

Cattell, R. B. (1946). *The Description and Measurement of Personality*. World Books: Yonkers-on-Hudson.

Chapman, J. J., & Chapman, J. P. (1969). Illusory correlations as an obstacle to the use of valid psychodiagnostic signs. *Journal of Abnormal Psychology, 74*, 271-280.

Cronbach, L. W. (1964). *Essentials of Psychological Testing*. Harper and Row: London.

D'Andrade, R. G. (1965). Trait psychology and componential analysis. *American Anthropologist, 67*, 215-228.

Dembo, T. (1926). Der Arger als Dynamisches Problem. *Psychologische Forschung*, 1-140.

De Waele, J.-P., & Harré, R. (1979). Autobiography as a Psychological Method. In *Emerging Strategies in Social Psychological Research*. (G. P. Ginsburg, ed.). Wiley: Chichester. pp. 177-224.

Edwards, A. L., & Abbott, R. D. (1973). Measurement of personality traits: Theory and techniques. *Annual Review of Psychology*.

Ellis, A. (1946). The validity of personality questionnaires. *Psychology Bulletin, 43*, 385-440.

Endler, N. S., & Magnusson, D. (Eds.). (1976). *Interactional Psychology and Personality*. Hemisphere Pub. Co.: Washington and London.

English, H. B., & English, A. C. (1958). *A Comprehensive Dictionary of Psychological and Psychoanalytical Terms*. Longman Green: New York.

Fiske, D. W. (1960). The situational test as a method for studying drug effects. In *Drugs and Behaviour*. (L. Uhr & J. G. Miller, eds.). John Wiley and Sons: New York.

Fiske, D. W. (1978). *Strategies for Personality Research*. Jossey-Bass: New York.

Flanagan, J. C. (1954). Some considerations in the development of situation tests. *American Psychological Association Personnel Psychology, 7*, 461-464.

Ghiselli, E. E., & Barthol, G. (1953). *Journal of Applied Psychology, 37*, 18-20.

Gottschaldt, K. (1956). Handlung und Ansdnick. In "Der Psychologie der Personlichkeit." *Revista di Psychologia Annol*, Fascicolo *IV*, 161-175.

Greenwald, H. (ed.) (1979). *Great Cases in Psychoanalysis*. Jason Armeon, Inc.: New York.

Greenwood, J. P., & McNamara, W. J. (1967). Interrater reliability in situational tests. *Journal of Applied Psychology, 37*, 18-20.

Hakel, (1969). Significance of implicit personality theories for personality research and theory. *Proceedings of the 77th Convention of the American Psychological Association*. pp. 403-404.

Harré, R., & Secord, P. (1972). *The Explanation of Social Behaviour*. Blackwell: Oxford.

Holt, R. R., & Luborsky, L. (1958). *Personality Patterns of Psychiatrists: Vol. 1: A Study of Methods for Selecting Residents.* Basic Books: New York.

Holt, R. R., & Luborsky, L. (1958). *Personality Patterns of Psychiatrists: Vol. 2: Supplementary and Supporting Data.* Menninger Foundation, Topeka: Kansas.

Kelly, E. L., & Fiske, D. W. (1951). *The Prediction of Performance in Clinical Psychology.* University of Michigan Press: Ann Arbor.

Kelly, E. L., & Goldberg, (1959). Correlates of later performance and specialization in psychology. *Psychological Monographs, 73*(12, Whole No. 482).

Kleinmuntz, B. (1967). *Personality Measurement.* Dorsey: Homewood, Ill.

Krech, D., & Crutchfield, R. S. (1959). *Elements of Psychology.* A. Knopf: New York.

Lazarsfeld, P. (1970). *Philosophie des Sciences Sociales.* Gallimard, Paris.

Lewin, K. (1935). *A dynamic theory of personality.* McGraw-Hill: New York.

Magnussen, D., & Endler, N. D. (Eds.). (1977). *Personality at the Cross-Roads: Current Issues in Interactional Psychology.* Lawrence Earlbaum: Hillside, N.J.

McNemar, Q. (1952). Review of the Kelly-Fiske study. *Journal of Abnormal Social Psychology, 47,* 857–860.

Meehl, P. E. (1954). *Clinical Versus Statistical Prediction.* University of Minnesota Press: Minneapolis.

Muliak, S. A. (1964). Are personality factors rater's conceptual factors. *Journal of Consulting Psychology, 28,* 506–511.

Murray, H. A. (1948). *Exploration in Personality.* Oxford University Press: New York.

Norman, W. T. (1963). Toward an adequate taxonomy of personality attributes: Replicated factor structure in peer nomination personality ratings. *Journal of Abnormal and Social Psychology, 66,* 574–583.

Norman, W. T. (1967). 2,800 personality trait descriptors: Normative operating characteristics for a university population. (Available from author, Department of Psychology, University of Michigan, Ann Arbor.)

Norman, W. T., & Goldberg, L. R. (1966). Rates, ratees and randomness in personality structure. *Journal of Personality and Social Psychology, 4,* 681–691.

Office of Strategic Services Assessment Staff. (1948). *Assessment of Men.* Rinehart: New York.

Pasini, F. T., & Norman, W. T. (1966). A universal conception of personality structure. *Journal of Personality and Social Psychology, 4,* 44–98.

Pervin, L. A., & Lewis, M. (eds.) (1978). *Perspectives in Interactional Psychology.* Plenum Press: New York and London.

Potkay, Ch. (1974). The role of personal history data in clinical judgement. *Journal of Personality and Social Psychology, 4,* 44–49.

Rogers, C. R. (1961). *On becoming a person.* Houghton Mifflin: Boston.

Saugstad, P., & Raaheim, K. (1957). Problem-solving and availability of functions. *Acta Psychologica, 13,* 263–278.

Simoneit, M. (1943). *Grundriss der Charakterologischen Diagnostik.* Teubner: Berlin-Leipzig.

Starr, B. J., & Katkin, E. (1969). The clinician as an aberrant actuary: Illusory correlation and the incomplete sentences blank. *Journal of Abnormal Psychology, 74,* 670–75.

Stern, C. G., Stein, M. I., & Bloom, B. S. (1956). *Methods in Personality Assessment.* Free Press Glencoe: Illinois.

Thurstone, L. (1947). *Multiple Factor Analysis.* University of Chicago Press: Chicago.

Tupes, E. C., & Christal, R. E. (1958). *Stability of Personality Trait Rating Factor Obtained under Diverse Conditions.* USAF WADC Tech. Note, 1958, No. 58–61. United States Air Force: Washington, D.C.

Tupes, E. C., & Christal, R. E. (1961). *Recurrent Personality Factors Based on Trait Ratings.* USAF ASD Techn. Rep. No. 61–97. United States Air Force: Washington, D.C.

von Cranach, M., Kalbermatten, U., Indermuhler, K., & Gugler, B. (1980). *Zielgerichtetes Handeln.* Hans Huber: Bern.

Willems, E. P., & Raush, H. L. (Eds.). (1969). *Naturalistic Viewpoints in Psychological Research.* Holt, Rinehart and Winston: New York.

Windle, C. (1952). Psychological tests in psychopath's prognosis. *Psychological Bulletin, 49,* 451–482.

6

Intention, Meaning, and Structure: Social Action in Its Physical Context

David Canter

Actions and Behaviour

One of the advantages of focussing on the term *action* rather than the term *behaviour* is that a clear distinction is implied between the conventional laboratory-based, psychological study of responses and motor movements (what has usually been termed behaviour) and the study of *situated sequences of human activity* (what I take to be the starting point for the study of *social action*). The great value of providing this distinction is that it enables psychologists to embrace the fact that what people do occurs within a specifiable context. It is no longer necessary to focus on the limited behaviours of an isolated organism or to develop a stilted social psychology based upon the rudimentary exchange of stimuli and responses between individuals. Instead the focus of psychological attention can legitimately be human activities and experiences within their natural settings.

From this perspective the study of social action can be seen as a development which is very much part of a widely ranging evolution of social psychology. This evolution in which American authors such as Ginsburg (1979) have joined, can be seen occurring in Britain through the work of Argyle and his associates (Argyle et al., 1981), as well as through U.S. psychologists in collaboration with Polish (e.g., Nowakowska, 1981) and Soviet psychologists (Wertsch, 1981). The studies in Switzerland by von Cranach (and Harré 1982) and his German colleagues, such as those contributing to the present volume, also serve to show how international are the changes sweeping through social psychology. All these authors and others have written at some length about the value of exploring the meanings of naturally occurring purposive human actions and the importance of elaborating the psychological significance of the situations in which those actions occur.

DISCOVERY STRATEGIES
IN THE PSYCHOLOGY OF ACTION

Because of the complexity of the interrelated issues that emerge once the decision is made to take human action as the focus of study, it is understandable that different psychologists typically choose to focus on different aspects of the full range of important issues. Some focus on the significance of human agency (Harré, 1979); others on the consequences of actions as sequences of events over time (Forgas, 1979). Yet others focus on definitions of the contexts (or situations) within which actions occur (Cantor, 1981). However, any integration of human action must recognise that all the different components of actions interrelate with each other.

Environmental Links

One group of researchers within psychology that has always been faced with the problem of understanding human actions in their naturally occurring contexts is environmental psychologists (cf. Canter and Craik, 1981; Russell and Ward, 1982). Their focus has been on the role of the physical environment in human activities and experience. Even when using laboratory-based experimental procedures, they have needed to keep clearly in view the representativeness of their conditions, regarding them as simulations rather than merely as interesting stimuli to be presented under controlled conditions. The majority of environmental psychologists have deliberately eschewed the problems of validating simulations by operating within such existing settings as hospitals, schools, offices, and recreation areas. It might therefore be expected that the developments in social psychology, that are also taking it out of the laboratory to explore the context of human actions, would provide the basis for building bridges between these two closely related branches of psychology. This possibility and the progress being made in this bridge-building activity has been discussed at length elsewhere (Canter, 1980). The present chapter, as a consequence, focuses on those processes that are integral to social action by virtue of their physical contexts. In other words, we are asking what can be learned about social action by considering directly the physical context in which it occurs.

In the present chapter then, my intentions are (1) to discuss the role that the physical environment plays in the organisation and development of social actions, and (2) to illustrate that even when the physical-environmental aspect of social actions is the focus of attention, the other nonphysical components of human activities must still be integrated into any account of the role of the physical context.

Before moving on to consider directly the way in which the physical environment plays its roles, it is of value to emphasise three processes that are fundamental to effective social action. It is the recognition of the existence of these processes which makes it possible to understand the role of the physical surroundings.

ORIENTATION TO GOALS

The purposive, active, goal-oriented nature of human activity serves to emphasise that in any exploration of what people are doing, it is important to understand why (from their points of view) they are doing it. This involves the recognition that people are in any given place for some purpose; and as von Cranach and Harré (1982) argue at some length, that they are able to draw upon some conscious awareness of what their goals are. The conscious, purposive nature of human action thus directs us to the individual's active utilisation of his surroundings. The physical surroundings can be seen, in this light, as one of the tools available to a person for use in personal or social activities as that person deems appropriate.

THE ASSIGNMENT OF MEANING

The understanding that any given individual assigns to the significance of his or her actions (their meaning) is a fundamental process. All the psychologists referred to above have recognised this. But it is an especially fruitful starting point for considering the role of the physical surroundings, because over the last ten years or so those professional groups responsible for physical surroundings have been prepared to discuss the meanings that those surroundings might have (see the review by Groat, 1982). Thus there is a possibility now, as there was not when architects did not accept that their buildings held meanings, to explore the way in which the meaning of our physical surroundings contributes to, or detracts from, the meaning of the actions we perform in those surroundings.

THE STRUCTURING OF SITUATIONS

Human action is noted, now, for happening in a particular situation. In order for this to be possible, those situations require a structure. This structure exists both as a set of social rules, and as a set of conceptualisations held by the participants in those situations, about what actions occur where. A situation inevitably has a physical locus and physical properties. It is, as a consequence, no large step to claim that the meanings and reasons for actions can be understood and seen to derive in part, at least, from the physical properties of the situations in which they occur.

The Physical Context as Process Integration

The three processes of intention, meaning, and structure cannot be separated from each other in their consequences for human action at anything other than a logical level. Indeed it is their relationship to the physical context that gives these processes their integrated form. Furthermore, this is not a coincidental agglomeration of processing; their interrelationship is essential to the human condition.

To understand the integrating and integral roles of the physical surroundings, it is fruitful to recognise that one of the central questions of social psychology is how the individual, with all his or her private, subjective experiences, manages to function within, and to contribute towards, the development of a public, social world. That the actions of individuals are part of a social process is fundamental to the study of social action. Yet how are the individual and the social incorporated within each other? Part of the answer to this question comes from the fact that all individuals interact with a physical world that has a recognised existence independent of their own.

This argument can be taken a stage further by accepting that the three processes summarised above each bear a different relationship to the personal and public perspectives of concern here. The intentions and objectives that a person has in any situation, although influenced by social processes, are essentially within the personal (often private) domain of any particular person. However, the meanings assigned to actions and the places in which they occur, whilst having a personal significance, nonetheless operate by virtue of social codes and frameworks. As is argued in more detail later, it is this assignment of meanings which brings into the social context the personal intentions of any given individual. One consequence of this translation of personal intentions into place meanings is that publicly available structures of place-related activities can then be observed. The observation of what happens where will of course influence a person in what he or she wishes to do, thus completing an important feedback loop for the social control of individual aspirations. Some time ago Canter (1977) outlined a cruder version of the relationships between these three processes, citing them as examples of a self-fulfilling prophecy that maintains the consistency of the patterns of activity found in any given place. The interrelationships implied for these processes is shown schematically in Figure 1.

The schematic relationships in Figure 1 are intended only as a summary of a number of complex processes, most of which have still to be fully understood. For the present chapter they are best seen as a set of

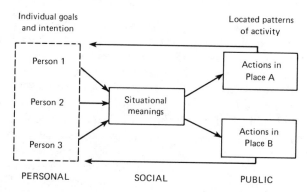

Figure 1. Physical context as integrater of personal intentions and patterns of social action.

interrelated research questions that are now to be explored individually through a consideration of the empirical research.

Environmentally Located Goals

Social psychologists generally have recognised the importance of examining human goals, at least since Kurt Lewin pointed to the existence of ''goals'' in the ''life space'' and Allport wrote about ''becoming''. But it is those who are directly concerned with goal-directed action who have emphasised recently the importance of classifying the goals and intentions significant to people (von Cranach and Harré, 1982).

The environmental perspective on the question of motives and intentions generates a different view of these concerns. It leads to questions such as: Are places distinguishable by the characteristic purposes of their occupants? Is the role of the physical setting a function of the uses that its users wish to make of it? There are many similar questions. What they all have in common is the search for an account of the organisation and structure of the environmentally relevant purposes that people have. Put in other terms, these are questions about the classification of the objectives people have in their use of places. The multi-modal qualities of place-experience attest to the fact that a person's interactions within a place always have a number of related objectives, or referents. The essence of the argument here, which has been presented at length elsewhere (Canter, 1977), is that although the experience of a place can be broken down into components for analysis, the experience itself is unitary. A person, for example, always has a physical and a social existence. Questions may be asked that direct attention to how a place contributes to the physical or social well-being of a person, without implying that the physical and the social are totally distinct systems and especially without assuming that they are orthogonal dimensions.

It is this recognition that the physical and social aspects of experience can be treated as foci of attention, rather than independent domains that must somehow "correlate", that frees a purposive model from the conundra besetting environmental psychologists who follow, even if only implicitly, a stimulus (environment)–response (behaviour) approach. Because these obviously fundamental aspects of place-experience are not seen as orthogonal dimensions, it is not surprising that the research literature, which has been based on factor-analytic and principal-component procedures, has not revealed this fundamental distinction. However, some researchers who have eschewed the factor-analytic approach have revealed nonorthogonal distinctions. For example, in his review of housing satisfaction Rapoport found it of value to classify the components of evaluation under the headings of "social" and "physical". In their overview of approaches to environmental evaluation Friedmann et al., (1978) place as central the study of what they label as (1) "the users" and (2) "the proximate environmental context." In her study of the quality of life of young men, Levy-Leboyer (1982), using correspondence analysis, identified what can be best translated as "needs", which she put under the headings of "full social life" and "environmental comfort".

What also emerges from this literature is that the physical component of human experience of places usually has two identifiable aspects. One relates directly to the spatial component with all its connotations of demarcation and privacy; the other relates to the services and comfort that a place provides. Levy-Leboyer, for example, distinguishes between "environmental comfort" and "secure personal space". The fact that these areas of human physical experience have been dealt with quite independently by researchers, as revealed by the way they are handled in introductory text books (under separate headings), supports the contention that they are important, distinct aspects of place-experience. Yet they are always co-present in any place.

In relation to goal-directed action, the importance of this distinction is that intentions always have physical as well as social referents. Furthermore, in any given situation it is essential for these different varieties of referent to complement one another if the place is to be effectively used. Wanting to perform a particular act implies some knowledge of the physical conditions under which it can occur and the places available for it.

Situationally Located Meanings

Individuals' intentions, then, have social and physical orientations. These both cohere in the effective conduct of actions. Yet, unlike the essentially personal quality of intentions, actions can be observed by others. Thus any consistent pattern of associations between intentions and locations will lead people to identify those locations with particular intentions. It is this which gives places their meanings. Thus situational meanings are goal driven. They depend on an individual's understanding of the relationship between goals and the locations in which those goals can be achieved.

Cognitive Ecology

The rich patterns of knowledge and understanding of who might be found where, doing what, might be called a *cognitive ecology*. This internal representation of an ecology of actions is seen as providing the basis for the meanings situations have. It should therefore be possible to provide empirical clarification of these internal representations. Such clarification would be expected to reveal consistent relationships between the physical form of places, whether they be buildings, parts of buildings, or other natural settings, and the assumed functions of those places. The demonstration of these patterns has drawn heavily upon various methodological developments discussed in detail elsewhere (Canter, 1985). Because of the holistic structure that such methods present, it has been possible to compare very different data bases generated under varying circumstances. It is the consistency of the cognitive structures found in different studies that is so encouraging. Let us consider, as an example, some studies of buildings.

It can be argued that buildings, like rooms in a house, can accommodate some combinations of activities more readily than others. A school may not be expected to house activities associated with blocks of flats, whereas it might be expected that offices and factories be similar to each other. One of the important issues that emerges from this is whether the design of buildings, taken as a whole, represents the range of intended activities usually accommodated, and if the similarities in building form reflect similarities in assumed activities. Do architects make a university look more like an office block than a school because they are referring to a structured relationship between the uses of those places?

One direct way of studying this is to show people pictures of buildings and to ask them what the buildings are and then to derive correlations from the resulting agreements and disagreements. In other words, illustrations that are typically thought to represent similar types of buildings can be placed together in some multidimensional space. Young (1978) has carried out such a study in Britain, with a number of refinements, and complementary yet completely independent studies have been carried out by Groat (1982) in California and Krampen (1979) in Germany. What all these studies reveal is that there is an organised, structured relationship between what buildings look like and the types of activities and institutions that those buildings are expected to house. In effect, these studies show that the physical form of a building can be used to indicate the patterns of activity anticipated within them.

The clearest illustration of how the interpretation of buildings has a coherent structure can be derived from Young's (1978) study in which he asked people to produce drawings which represented each of six typical types of building. He then showed these drawings to another group and asked them to guess which types of building they were. Each of the drawings was thus scored on the basis of the accuracy with which people recognised its creator's intentions, and these scores were used to produce a multidimensional scaling (MDS) configuration (discussed in more detail in Canter, 1985). A qualitative order was found in the MDS space: in effect, a circle from houses to offices to factories to schools to churches and back to houses. Young used only these six building types in his study; the location of such other places as hospitals, shops, traffic terminals, and so on is therefore an open question. But it is noteworthy that, in using the same six building types in Germany, Krampen (1979) produced a very similar structure. The only difference was that schools were closer to offices than factories, presumably indicating something about cross-national differences in attitudes to education.

Some Limiting Antecedents

Having indicated that there is a clear physical component to the psychological processes underlying human actions, it is surprising how long it has taken others to acknowledge such a literally obvious aspect of a setting. So before moving on to see how situational meanings facilitate and interact with patterns of activity in places, it is important to identify the antecedents which have slowed the development of this perspective.

Two antecedents to our present perspective help to explain why this awareness is still so novel. The first is the impact of the notorious Hawthorne Investigations (Roethlisberger and Dickson, 1939). We are still suffering from the popular misconception that these studies showed that the physical surroundings had no effect on performance. A closer examination of that piecemeal set of studies shows that the effective roles of the physical surroundings were in its symbolic properties and the types of social interaction the surroundings facilitated. Changing the lighting levels clearly carried meaning for the relay assembly inspectors, even though those changes did not have the anticipated effect on performance. Furthermore, the isolation of some workers in separate rooms clearly left its mark on the social processes. The acknowledgement of the symbolic role of the physical surroundings and of its consequences for social interaction has only recently occurred, but both of these roles have now been substantiated by a number of separate investigators (see Levy-Leboyer, 1982, for an introductory review).

Another reason why the role of the physical surroundings has not been examined by social psychologists, despite clues from the Hawthorne studies and subsequent research, can be traced to the impact of the second antecedent to our present perspective of ecological psychology. Barker (1978) and his colleagues of the Midwest field station in Oskaloosa set out to study human behaviour in naturally occurring settings. Their work was quite deliberately formulated as an attack on the domination of the laboratory-based Skinnerian approach, especially when used to study human development. The remarkable thing about all the work that emanated from the midwest field station was that it gave no indication of the physical properties of the behaviour settings in which actions happened. Imagine Darwin writing his diaries on the Beagle without saying where he made his observations. What sense could be made of speciation in the Galapagos without knowing that they were islands? Yet it is a parallel limitation that has been imposed on our understanding of human activities.

Ecology and Conceptual Systems

Once the physical context of action reaches the level of the psychologist's awareness, and its potential symbolic and social significance is recognised, then the structure of actions in different settings and their consistencies become topics of research interest. Indeed, the major single contribution to the environmental psychology literature by the New York group of Proshansky and his colleagues (1970), has probably been their adaptation of conventional observational techniques to include the locus of the observation, which they called *behavioural mapping*. The significance of this procedure has been to show quite clearly that the human use of space is not random. Furthermore, the observed patterns do have clear psychological significance, which is consistent across settings.

The way in which the meanings associated with different places readily mirror, and thus presumably enhance, the actions that occur in those places can be illustrated by two published examples.

The first example is drawn from the study by Canter (1974) of wards in a children's hospital. In those wards the nurses' station is in the middle of the ward, on one side of the aisle. Opposite it are four bedded bays. Behind it are preparation and utility rooms. Thus the centre of the ward is definitely the nurses' domain. At the far end from the ward entrance is a day-space/play area in which children were often observed to be on their own. Along the aisle from the entrance are cubicles large enough for a mother to stay with her child.

These modern wards were certainly regarded as a great advance on the earlier Victorian wards. A questionnaire survey showed that nurses and many of the hospitalised children's parents and the doctors expressed great satisfaction with them for their brightness and spaciousness. Nonetheless, the demarcation of domains, even though it was never made explicit, left its mark on the use of the ward and certainly contributed to parents' anxieties about the ward. In effect they were separated from the day-space by a region of nursing space. Behavioural mapping showed that it was very rare for parents to venture through the nurses' domain, or to be found in the day-space. Interviews revealed that parents were concerned about knowing what they could do when on the ward or where they could go. Clearly the design and the cognitive ecology it invoked had not facilitated communication between different groups.

An Obstetric Example

Taking the larger scale of a hospital as a whole, a fascinating study of an obstetrical hospital carried out by Rosengren and Devaults (1963) throws some useful light on some of the more subtle ways in which the physical surroundings reflect and enhance certain activity patterns. Over a four-month period they spent 150 hours observing what went on in "a large lying-in hospital in an eastern metropolitan area" of the United States. They observed all the activities of the service and talked informally with staff in the lounges and work situations, making detailed records as they went along. Their initial concern was simply to record what occurred in the hospital; they found, however, that it was incomplete and of questionable utility to speak of the doctor–nurse relationship without specifying where those two persons interacted. Their observations of the same people in different settings revealed that there was a spatial distribution of types of interaction. In other words, just as animal ecologists have found that different species are to be found in different regions of an area, so Rosengren and DeVaults found that there were distinct regions of the hospital:

> Each region is itself set apart in several ways from the others. This segregation appears to be accomplished not only by space but also by rules of dress, of expected behaviour and of decorum—all of which serve to indicate the dissimilarity of each place, as well as to present an image of the place that might cast both patients and staff into desired roles with respect to one another. (1963, p.443)

Thus, in the context of obstetrics at least, a variety of distinct roles exist for the nurse. In the admitting office, in which no barriers such as doors existed, the staff was friendly and casual, the relationship between the medical and nursing staff being equally informal. By contrast the delivery rooms was clearly under the control of the nurses and consequently the symbols of their office, uniforms, stainless steel, and brilliant lighting were especially apparent.

Examples drawn from many institutions such as hospitals and schools reveal similar results. Even in supposedly open-plan settings different role groups are to be found, characteristically, in different locations. Hospital wards usually have areas where nurses are to be found, and open-plan classrooms have places for the teacher. Such findings are especially interesting when taken together with the conclusions on environmental meanings presented above. In this light the consistent patterns of space use can be seen as reflecting the meanings different places have for their users, which in turn relates to what they see as the primary purposes (or functions) of those places.

Role and Setting

When we put together all the themes above, including the consistent yet multivariate part played by the physical surroundings in social action and the significance of understanding the purpose a person has in those surroundings, questions can be raised about the differences between people in their use and conceptualisations of places. As it turns out the query about individual differences leads to some of the most valuable practical consequences of this approach and also emphasises the concept of role. In this context role can be seen as a major indication of the reason a person has for being in any given place. Thus the pattern of activities in which a person partakes, and the meanings assigned to those places and the activities they house are seen as being a function of what is required of the individual by the social system of which he or she is a part. The intentions a person has for any given setting is, as a consequence, a personal translation by the individual of the goals of the organisation to which they belong.

This view provides an interesting insight into the satisfaction a person has with the design and use of any given place. It suggests that that satisfaction will be a function of the extent to which a person feels able to achieve his or her goals in that place. It follows, therefore, that people performing different roles in any given place will have different patterns of satisfaction with that place. Furthermore, it is precisely this differentiation through the satisfaction which provides the feedback loop to modify goals and intentions in Figure 1.

Roles and Satisfaction

The first empirical question to answer is whether there are, indeed, differences between the satisfactions of people with different roles. Canter (1979) summarises a number of studies which show quite clearly that the pattern of interactions a person has in a place will relate to his or her place-satisfaction (Canter, 1979). One study, for example, illustrates the similarity and differences between different inhabitants of a school who were asked to evaluate that school (Gerngross-Haas, 1982). Her results show with great clarity that the parts of the school to which the individual has access, or the responsibilities he has within the school, distinguish him from others in terms of his evaluation. Indeed, the more difference there is between people in their environmental role the more likely they are to have differing satisfaction with their settings. Thus, Gerngross-Haas was able to order the users of a school building from the headmaster, through technical and teaching staffs to older pupils and then younger pupils, so that the further apart they were from each other in succession the less correlated were their evaluations of the different parts of the school.

What then are the implications of role differences in satisfaction for the structures of activities in different places? One type of answer can be drawn from a study by Canter and Walker (1980). Walker interviewed all the people involved in creating a local authority housing estate. She asked them what their major concerns about the housing estate were. She then examined the similarities and differences between individuals on the basis of their concerns. Some people were concerned with the administration of the building, some with the building fabric itself, and some with it simply as an aspect of the borough's housing requirements. People differed also in terms of how much interaction they had with the actual building. The criteria they applied to the creation of the housing facility were different because of their different types of interaction with the entity being produced. Indeed the whole notion of "housing" meant something different to each role group.

One reason why this type of finding is of such practical significance is that one of the most important role differences with regard to the environment is whether a person is using, managing, or creating that environment. Thus all the indications are that by virtue of their different relationships to their surroundings people will be thinking about and evaluating their environment in different ways. The architect consulting the manager will obtain, in the workers' conceptualisations, a predictably inappropriate account of the role of the building. This poses organisation and management problems for design briefing, which the psychologist is in a unique position to resolve.

Place Rules

It has been argued that the spatial patterning of social action is based on the knowledge of what to do where. This appears to be related to each individual's understanding of his or her role in a given setting. Yet there must be mechanisms for controlling these roles and not allowing personal satisfaction to become the sole feedback mechanism for shaping patterns of activities. The most viable social mechanisms for this are probably the rules associated with roles and, most notably, rules that relate to spatial behaviour.

Of course the use of a role/rule model within the environmental framework owes much to the social psychological literature, in which there is a long and rich history to the study of social rules (Douglas, 1973; Harré and Secord, 1972; e.g., Mischel, 1969). What was not anticipated is the power of this formulation when looking at the use and significance of physical surroundings. Here there is growing empirical evidence about the stability of place rules. This evidence is possibly strongest when social systems are under threat. If an extant role/rule structure is maintained even in those situations, then its power in daily life is given even more credence. Examples of places under environmental threat, most notably houses and other buildings on fire, provide some interesting examples to illustrate these issues (Canter, 1979).

For example, in one major fire, at the Summerland recreation complex, many of the staff left by the fire exit that they normally used for coming into work. They went to no effort to show members of the public out that same way. This reflected the rather distant and uninvolved nature of the relationship they had with the customers who used that place. On the other hand, in the Kentucky Supper Club fire a quite different pattern of relationships between staff and patrons emerged. Here staff in the small private dining rooms showed out people at the tables for whom they were responsible, in some cases leading them out through the kitchens.

In both cases the form of relationships and the use of space existing before the fire were carried through into the disaster itself. In smaller domestic fires an analogous continuation of role differences is found. Men are more likely to search for others or fight the fire, whilst women are more likely to warn others and help them escape.

Conclusions

If there is one central point we have drawn from the new developments in social psychology as they pertain to the study of social action, it is that the person who is the focus of our study is the starting point for our enquiry. It is this person's understanding and aspirations that we need to explore. In taking such a gift from our more social colleagues we offer in return the insight that by providing a physical context to the focus of our study, not only is the complexity of human action more likely to reveal its patterns, but those patterns which do emerge are more likely to have some practical significance for human affairs.

Time, the Forgotten Dimension

Having identified three processes that facilitate an integration of our understanding of the role of the physical surroundings in social action, it is important not to lose from view the one aspect of human action that is rarely considered in studies of the physical surroundings: the temporal quality of those actions. After all, our experience of environments beyond the scale of the room, through buildings to streets and cities, is inevitably temporal. However, one of the weaknesses of much research within the environmental psychology perspective has been the dearth of attention paid to temporal phenomena. This is quite possibly a weakness it has inherited from its forebearers in personality and social psychology, and environmental psychology may benefit from embracing wholeheartedly the social action perspective. The whole notion of action involves the idea of movement and change. It is therefore very probable that as environmental psychologists more fully adopt models of human action, their theories will be more likely to encompass this almost forgotten dimension. Nonetheless, for the moment, the themes that link action to environment are generally concerned with stable structures and existing states, rather than with movement and change.

References

Argyle, M., Furnham, A., and Graham, J. A. (1981). *Social Situations.* Cambridge University: Cambridge.

Barker, R. G. and Associates (1978). *Habitats, Environments and Human Behaviour.* Jossey-Bass: London.

Canter, D. (1977). *The Psychology of Place.* Architectural Press: London.

Canter, D. (1979). Y a-t-il des lois d'interaction environmentales? In *Proceedings of 4th IAAP at Louvain-la-Neuve.* (J. Simon, ed.). University Catholic: Louvain.

Canter, D. (1985). Putting situations in their place. In *Social Behaviour in Context.* (A. Furnham, ed.). Allyn and Bacon: New York.

Canter, D., and Craik, K. H. (1981). Environmental psychology. *Journal of Environmental Psychology, 1,* (1), 1–11.

Canter, D., and Walker, E. (1980). Environmental role and conceptualization of housing. *Journal of Architectural Research, 7,* 30–35.

Cantor, N. (1981). Perceptions of situations: Situation prototypes in person–situation prototypes. In *Toward a Psychology of Situations: An International Perspective.* (D. Magnusson, ed.). Erlbaum: Hillsdale, N. J., pp.229–244.

Douglas, M. (ed.). (1973) *Rules and Meanings.* Penguin: Harmondsworth.

Forgas, J. P. (1979). *Social Episodes: The study of Interaction Routines.* Academic Press: London.

Friedmann, A., Zimring, C., and Zube, E. (1978). *Environmental Design Evaluation.* Plenum: New York.

Gerngross-Haas, G. (1982). Organizational role differences in the evaluation of an experimental school. *International Review of Applied Psychology, 31,* (2), 223–236.

Ginsburg, G. P. (ed.). (1979) Emerging Strategies in Social Psychological Research. Wiley: Chichester.

Groat, L. (1982). Meaning of post-modern architecture: An examination using the Multiple Sorting Task. *Journal of Environmental Psychology, 2,* (1), 3–22.

Harré, R. (1979). *Social Being.* Blackwell: Oxford.

Harré, R., and Secord, P. (1972). *The Explanation of Social Behaviour.* Blackwell: Oxford.

Krampen, M. (1979). *Meaning in the Urban Environment.* Pion: London.

Levy-Leboyer, C. (1982). *Psychology and Environment.* Sage: Beverley Hills.

Mischel, W. (ed.). (1969) *Human Action: Conceptual and Empirical Issues*. Academic Press: London.

Nowakowska, M. (1981). Structure of situation and action: Some remarks on formal theory of action. In *Towards a Psychology of Situations: An interactional perspective*. (D. Magnusson, ed.). Lawrence Erlbaum: Hillsdale N. J.

Proshansky, H. M., Ittelson, W. H., and Rivlin, L. G. (eds.) (1970). *Environmental Psychology: Man and His Physical Setting*. Holt, Rinehart and Winston: New York.

Roethlisberger, F. J., and Dickson, W. J. (1939). *Management and the Worker*. Harvard: Cambridge, Mass.

Rosengren, W. R., and Devaults, S. (1963). The sociology of time and space in an obstetrical hospital. In *The Hospital in Modern Society*. (E. Freidson, ed.). The Free Press of Glencoe: London.

Russell, J. A., and Ward, L. M. (1982) Environmental psychology. *Annual Review of Psychology, 33,* 651–688.

von Cranach, M., and Harré, R. (eds.) (1982). *The Analysis of Action: Recent Theoretical and Empirical Advances*. Cambridge University Press: Cambridge.

Wertsch, J. V. (ed.) (1981). *The Concept of Activity in Soviet Psychology*. M. E. Sharpe: New York.

Young, D. (1978). *The Interpretations of Form: Meanings and ambiguities in Contemporary Architecture*. M.Sc Thesis (unpublished). University of Surrey.

7

Social Cognition and Social Action

J. Richard Eiser

The Role of Theory

The role of theory and social psychological research is more complex than might at first be supposed. There are few examples in our discipline of the kind of archetypical controversy where rival theories contend to account for the same phenomena. One may think, perhaps, of the debate between protagonists of cognitive-dissonance theory and self-perception theory. Even in this context though, it has been argued that the respective theories are conceptually indistinguishable (Greenwald, 1975), or alternatively that they are applicable under somewhat different limiting conditions (Fazio et al., 1977). More commonly, research based on different theoretical approaches has addressed itself to more or less subtly different ranges of phenomena, observed under more or less subtly different conditions.

Theories are selective in the phenomena they seek to explain, and different theories are differentially selective. Thus, implicit in support for a given theory is a judgement of *preference* concerning what are worthwhile problems for study, and also a *categorization* of such problems according to definitions of relatedness, which in turn depend partly on the theory itself. Such selectivity is probably indispensable as a basis for any practicable empirical research. It is not something for which one needs to apologize. Nonetheless, it is not something to which theorists often easily admit, and the reason for this may well be that theorists, like ordinary people, have only limited insight into why some things attract their attention and others do not. Where difficulties arise is often in the context of attempts at generalization of a theory to new paradigms and phenomena. On the one hand, a theory which suggests no possibility of generalization is not a very inviting theory. On the other hand, considerable confusion can result if theorists do not make explicit their own categorizations and the judgements of preference implicit in their approaches to particular phenomena of interest.

The term *action theory* seems to be used to signify, on the one

DISCOVERY STRATEGIES
IN THE PSYCHOLOGY OF ACTION

hand, a rather general approach to the explanation of human behaviour, incorporating notions of purposiveness, goal-directedness, and suck like; and, on the other hand, a number of more specific formulations within this general approach, of which that presented by von Cranach (Chapter 2) is probably the most distinctive example. I should therefore start with a warning to the reader, as well as a confession: I am frankly uncertain how broadly the term *action theory* should be defined. There is a danger of defining it so broadly that almost any contemporary approach in social psychology could be included within its borders. This is obviously unhelpful. On the other hand, greater specificity can only be achieved by choosing the most typical or paradigmatic of the different theories of action, and such a choice may well appear, and ultimately be, arbitrary.

I am therefore assuming that *action theory* refers to a sub-class of theory within contemporary social science that is exemplified by specific formulations such as that of von Cranach. I do not insist that von Cranach's formulation necessarily is typical, but for purposes of this chapter I propose to treat it as such. Where the term *action theory* appears in the singular, therefore, the reader can add, in parentheses, "as presented by von Cranach". I am not attempting directly to compare alternative formulations, nor indeed to present them: that comparison is something that is best made by considering the variety of different chapters in this book.

The approach I am taking in this chapter, then, is not to attempt to discriminate critically between different action theories. My aim is rather to pose the question of whether action theory, as an approach to the explanation of social conduct, which is claimed (at least by some) to have very general applicability, is in fact saying anything that is not also being said by more "mainstream" social psychological theories. Note that I am not asking whether mainstream or action theories are "better". I shall, more simply, summarize a few of these mainstream approaches that relate to the kind of phenomena with which action theories attempt to deal. It could be that some of the criticisms that such evidence implies can be turned into arguments for adopting an action-theory approach. At the same time, it could be that some of these criticisms apply with equal or even greater force to action theory itself.

Relating Cognition to Behaviour

To a large extent, psychology is a victim of its own terminology. We have adopted, and assigned a distinctive status to, a whole range of concepts, such as motives, emotions, drives, attitudes, intentions, cognitions, behaviour, response, and action. We then seek to study these concepts empirically, at which point it becomes much more difficult to insist that we can succeed in observing or measuring any of these in a way that is unambiguously independent of any of the others. At this point there is a real danger of researchers losing sight of the questions they profess to be answering.

The nub of the problem is the very different kind of language we seem to have to use to refer to physical or behavioural events on the one hand, and to mental or cognitive events on the other. There have been a variety of reactions to this problem. Best known, probably, is the radical behaviourist tradition, which treats mentalistic descriptions as irrelevant to an analysis of behaviour (although actors' own reports of their mental states are included as examples of behaviour). I do not deal with this approach directly, although establishing that cognition *is* relevant to an analysis of behaviour is by no means as easy as might be supposed. Another tradition, about which I have more to say, is that which attempts to study cognitive structures and processes 'for their own sake', regardless of their implications for overt behaviour. This tradition has been particularly influential in social psychology, but in many respects, I feel its influence may now be somewhat counterproductive.

In between these opposing traditions a few attempts have been made to deal specifically with the relationships between cognitions and behaviour. Interestingly, much of the initial impetus for such work has come from outside psychology, from economics, and, more recently, computer science and artificial intelligence. Decision making as a field of research is now very much part of psychology, and its implications for social judgement and social action is one of the main themes of this chapter. But in considering this field, a central point must be remembered: it is one thing to model hypothetical decisions or to derive formulae, algorithms, or regression equations, whereby behaviour may be predicted from presumably antecedent cognitive events; it is quite another to establish that such cognitive events were antecedent to the behaviour, or even that they occurred at all. Furthermore, even if the presumed cognitive events did occur, were they in fact either necessary or sufficient conditions for the behaviour, rather than, say a by-product of one's own investigatory procedures? Furthermore, even if they were preconditions of the behaviour, what alternative hypotheses might be generated to account for their relationship to behaviour?

Research has so far only scratched the surface of these problems. It is an area for circumspection, rather than absolutist claims. A model may make statistically reliable predictions and still be incorrect as a proposed explanation of how people arrive at decisions. Writing words in boxes and connecting the boxes by arrows may mean that one is constructing a valid theory; on the other hand, it may not. When the words themselves can be interpreted in many ways, appearances of precision are deceptive. Action theory itself both addresses the general issue of the relationship between cognition and behaviour, and concentrates on certain specific aspects of this relationship (e.g., how action sequences unfold over time) that are not the central focus of this chapter. My concern here is with the broader question of what kind of theoretical approach to social judgement and decision processes is needed to begin to account for relationships between cognition and behaviour, and what kind of evidence about social cognitive processes must any theory of social action take into account. If action theory claims to provide enlightenment in this area, it must also answer a number of possibly simpler questions, which may be set out as follows.

ACTION AS DISTINCT FROM MERE BEHAVIOUR

Much of the rhetoric of action theory conveys the impression that it should be regarded as an antithesis or behaviourism. 'Action', as conceived, for instance, by von Cranach, is purposive and goal-directed rather than merely a behavioural response. This presumably does not mean that all human behaviour is to be redefined as action and interpreted in terms of goals and purposes. If it does not, however, what are the criteria for saying that one piece of behaviour is purposive (i.e., 'action'), but another is not?

AWARENESS OF PURPOSE

If purposiveness is a criterion of action, does this require that an actor must always be aware of the reasons for his or her actions? If one considers the history of such notions from Tolman onwards, the answer is surely 'no'. But if 'no', how is one to interpret the use of self-report measures of goals that seem to assume such awareness? In the context of such methodologies, how is one to establish evidence of such awareness, or decide if self-reported reasons are 'true'?

RECORDING HYPOTHESIZED MENTAL EVENTS

If one is concerned with the cognitive processes that accompany ongoing action, can one record or measure such processes without refocussing the actor's attention so as conceivably to alter the very processes (and actions) one is attempting to study?

CALCULATIONS OF CONSEQUENCES

The notion that action is directed towards the achievement of expected goals implies behavioural decisions made on the basis of some kind of calculation of expected consequences. However, there are a variety of suggestions in the literature about how such decisions are made, not all of which assume rationality in any normative sense. Therefore, need action reflect a ''rational'' weighing-up of the consequences of alternative options (as for instance, I take von Cranach's approach to imply)?

Such questions, however, are questions for this volume as a whole, and not specifically for this chapter. Whatever objections may be raised against action theory, it does at least attempt to relate cognition to action. In comparison, much of the more widely cited research in the field of social cognition seems to make little such explicit attempt, although Carver and Scheier (1982) provide an important recent exception. Let us therefore consider some of the more familiar theories in the field of social cognition to see what prominence any of them give to the issue of the relationship of cognitive states and processes to social action. These theories are described in what seems to me to be very roughly an increasing order of relevance to action. All, however, are deliberately theories of cognitive structures and processes, rather than theories of action.

Balance and Cognitive Consistency

Heider's (1946) theory of cognitive balance is one of the most widely known in social psychology, but its influence on research has been curiously indirect. Compared with the massive literature on attribution theory—the later crystallization of Heider's ideas—relatively few studies have set out to test it directly (although this is obviously not true of later developments of the notion of cognitive consistency and, of course, cognitive dissonance). As for any remotely practical applications, they have mainly been confined to fields such as interpersonal attraction and reactions to interpersonal evaluations.

Yet balance theory is in many ways archetypical of much of cognitive–social psychological theory. The concern of the theory is specifically with the phenomenology of the individual. It purports to describe how individuals perceive social relationships but does not describe such relationships per se. So we are dealing in this theory with how thoughts relate to thoughts, not with how people relate to people.

Also, for a simple theory, it can be quite difficult to explain to students. Part of the reason is that the rules of "psychologic" that Heider proposes can seem so like ordinary "logic" that it may be difficult to see why they are supposed to constitute a new theory at all. But, of course, the principles proposed by Heider are not strictly rational at all. On the contrary, they describe a particular kind of *cognitive bias,* which may be conceptualized as an attempt to achieve the simplest possible evaluative frame of reference. It is important to note, also, that balance, in Heider's sense, is only one of a number of such possible influences on cognitive organisation and may be applicable only under special conditions (e.g., Gollob, 1974).

One way of representing this bias has been suggested by Jaspars (1965), based on an application of Coombs' (1950, 1964) model of preferential choice. According to Coombs, judgements of preference and evaluation depend on (1) the perceived locations of the objects of judgement along one or more underlying attributes and (2) the individual's own *ideal point* along these attributes. Small perceived distances from the ideal point are reflected in more positive evaluations, allowing a geometric mapping of different patterns of preference judgements. Now, when dealing with a Heiderian triad involving a perceiver (P), another person (o), and an object or issue (x), one can usually start from the assumption of a positive self-concept (or at any rate, one needs to do so for Heider's theory to be applicable in its simple form). So, we can (approximately) substitute P for Coombs' ideal point. A positive P-o (or P-x) link then requires that o (or x) be placed near to P; and a negative link, that it be placed further away. Add to this the additional requirement that the distance between o and x should be taken to represent P's perceptions of whether the o-x link is positive or negative, and one has the possibility of what Coombs would call a *preference space.*

What then, is the form of this space? The answer is a fascinating one: for balanced, but not imbalanced structures, the preference space is unidimensional. Imbalanced triads cannot be so represented. This may be seen from Figure 1. The only exception is the triad with three negative relations (which Heider originally considered ambiguous), under the special circumstances where P occupies an intermediate position between o and $x,$ which are represented as at opposite extremes of a given dimension. An example might be that of a political moderate who dislikes extremists of both left and right, but also expects these extremists to dislike one another.

Other evidence that suggests that balance is in fact a bias towards simplicity comes from studies of individual differences in cognitive complexity–simplicity. Press et al. (1969) found that cognitively simple

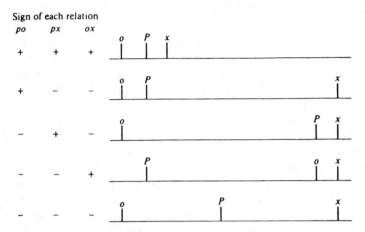

Figure 1.   Representation of triads in a unidimensional preference space. (Reproduced from J. R. Eiser, 1980.)

subjects were quicker at learning balanced than imbalanced structures when presented with a set of like–dislike relationships among groups of four hypothetical persons. Ware and Harvey (1967) found differences between cognitively simple and complex subjects in their preparedness to generalize on the basis of evaluatively consistent or inconsistent information about other people. Also Streufert and Streufert (1978) have related cognitive complexity–simplicity to the kind of information search in which people will engage after receiving consistent or inconsistent information.

So where does this leave us as far as implications for action theory are concerned? The terms in which action theory is formulated often appear rationalistic. So, at first sight, does that of cognitive consistency theory; but this first impression is deceptive. The hypothesis of a tendency towards balance does not in fact assume that we organize our attitudes according to rational rules. Rather, it assumes that we distort our perceptions of the social world in the direction of simpler category systems and more all–or–nothing evaluations. The starting point of this assumption is our need to predict events, but not necessarily our ability to do so accurately. It should be noted that predictions can be made with varying degrees of uncertainty or tolerance of ambiguity. Such tolerance may be a function of both cultural factors and individual differences, for example, in cognitive complexity (Streufert & Streufert, 1978). My point is simply that an individual who conforms closely to the predictions of balance theory is one who shows little tolerance of complexity and ambiguity.

Attribution Theory and Research

The predominant influence in social psychology over the last ten to fifteen years, at least in North America, has been attribution theory. Like balance theory, it owes its origins to the work of Heider (1944, 1958), and many of the same tensions are apparent between concepts of rationality on the one hand and cognitive biases on the other. The purpose of this section is mainly to highlight some of these tensions, rather than to give anything like a representative account of what is by now a vast literature.

The development of Heider's ideas in this field relied to a great extent on the notion of phenomenal causality. Just as it is possible to create illusions of causal influence between physical objects (Heider & Simmel, 1944) so, according to Heider, environmental factors can lead one to infer different kinds of causal relationships between people and objects in one's social environment. Thus, Heider's main preoccupation was with how people attribute causes to events. However, attribution theory has expanded to the point that it has become an umbrella for researchers whose interests are not in perceived causality as such, but rather in questions of perceived intentionality, impressions of personality, moral judgement, and motivation. Although some notion of causality is crucial in all these fields, it is by no means the case that attributions deal with perceptions of causality and little else, as apparently implied, for instance, by Brewer (1977).

Two influential early formulations of attribution theory were those of Jones and Davis (1965) and Kelley (1967). For Jones and Davis, the main question was how people infer the characteristics of actors on the basis of their behaviour. Their assumption was that a perceiver, on observing a person's overt behaviour, will make "certain decisions concerning ability and knowledge which will let him cope with the problem of attributing particular intentions to the actor. The attribution of intentions, in turn, is a necessary step in the assignment of more stable characteristics to the actor" (p. 222). Thus *intentionality* assumes a key role as a "necessary step" in the attribution of personal characteristics. The completely fallacious assumption here is that one can only attribute characteristics to a person on the basis of intentional action. In other words, Jones and Davis write as though no sense can be made of stable individual differences in behaviour unless that behaviour is intended. (How about traits of carelessness, forgetfulness, or compulsiveness?) In broader terms, a trend is set in motion here which, taken to its extreme, implies that theories of social cognition should be concerned only with deliberate, "mindful" decisions and their behavioural consequences. It is for the reader to judge how near different formulations of action theory come to that extreme.

Kelley's (1967, 1971) approach was to propose that perceivers process information about social events by attending to critical features of that information: "distinctiveness," "consensus," and "consistency". These three features are then supposedly processed as though they were three orthogonal factors in an analysis of variance—hence the characterization of this model as the "Kelley cube". This formulation is perhaps the most assertive in its apparent claims about human rationality, and for this reason, there is ambiguity over whether it is essentially a prescriptive or a descriptive model. The trouble with claiming it to be descriptive is that a variety of effects, for example, the lesser influence of consensus than distinctiveness information (McArthur, 1976) cannot be explained by the model itself, but require extraneous notions of the differential salience of different kinds of information. Much of the same applies to evidence of "self-serving biases" and "defensive attributions" (Miller & Ross, 1975; Shaver, 1970), and "actor–observer differences" in the attribution process (Jones & Nisbett, 1971; Storms, 1973). Another example is that of attributions of cooperative or competitive intentions, specifically in the Prisoner's Dilemma game (Kelley & Stahelski, 1970). Here Kelley and Stahelski come close to postulating basic personality differences between "cooperators" and "competitors" to account for the latter's apparent inability to take account of the causal influence of their own behaviour on the other player (but see Miller & Holmes, 1975).

A variety of explanations have been offered for these phenomena, relying to greater or lesser extents on motivational or information-processing concepts. However, the main issue is that of the relative status of these phenomena on the one hand, and the "Kelley cube" on the other. Should these phenomena be seen as exceptions to a general set of rules encapsulated in Kelley's approach? Or should one start from a view that they often reflect more widespread and basic processes, and that it is the "Kelley cube" that describes the more exceptional circumstances? More generally, one might even question whether people make attributions at all in the way hypothesized by Kelley, or at least, if they do, what the limiting conditions are. Jaspars et al. (1983) provide evidence that people do not in fact combine information in the way predicted by Kelley's analysis of variance formulation, but rely instead on more 'commonsense' interpretations even under the somewhat contrived laboratory conditions typical of much of this work. Wong and Weiner (1981), using less restrictive response formats, have shown that people will spontaneously attempt to make attributions for events, but that such attributional search is more likely when the events are negative or unexpected.

Another important distinction between workers in this area is that between those in the tradition of Kelley (1967) and Jones and Davis (1965), who have been mainly concerned with how people explain events which have already occurred, and those who have explored how the attributions people make influence their later behaviour. Kelley and Michela (1980) seem to regard this latter trend as somewhat independent from attribution theory proper and label it as "attributional" research in order to highlight the difference. Most influential within this attributional tradition is the work of Weiner (1970) on achievement motivation and Seligman (1975) on "learned helplessness."

For both Weiner and Seligman, the crucial question is that of how individuals acquire expectancies concerning the contingencies between their own actions and positive or negative outcomes. Seligman seeks to explain depression as a learned response to (mainly) negative events which are uncontrollable or unpredictable (though these terms are not completely synonymous, and there is hence some ambiguity here). Weiner is concerned with how people's explanations for their own success or failure at a task will influence their motivation to attempt similar tasks in the future. The central concept for Weiner is that of *expectancy* of success or failure, which he sees as dependent on previous outcomes and on whether those outcomes are attributable to stable or unstable factors. Success that is attributable to a stable factor (e.g., ability) will lead to a higher expectancy of repeated success than if it is attributable to an unstable factor, such as luck. Similarly, failure which is attributable to a stable factor, such as lack of ability, will lead to a great expectancy of repeated failure than if the attribution is to a less stable factor, such as lack of effort. Note that the issue of internal versus external locus of causality (whether the behaviour is the result of attributes of the actor or of the environment) is somewhat less important for Weiner and is not assumed to influence expectancy. Where internal versus external locus is important, according to Weiner, is in influencing a person's emotional reactions to success or failure. Weiner's views on this matter, however, have developed considerably since the original formulation of his theory. Weiner et al. (1979) have shown that, in achievement-related contexts, specific attributions are associated with specific emotional reactions, and that cognitive and emotional states can be inferred from each other. Internal versus external locus is mainly influential in the context of emotional reactions related to self-esteem. This last finding might be especially relevant to research on learned helplessness and depression, where perhaps low self-esteem is a more distressing problem than reduced feelings of personal control.

Attributional concepts thus can be integrated into theories of the relationships between cognition and social behaviour, but many researchers have been content to take observed behaviour as the starting point and attributions as the end point. The influence of attributions on future behaviour can be shown to be important, but the nature of this influence deserves further study. The implication for action theory seems to be that processes of social cognition need to be conceptualized with behaviour in mind from the onset. Action theory claims to do so, and this may be the main justification for its appeal.

Expectancy-Value Approaches

Some of the most influential attempts to relate attitudes and preferences to behaviour have been based on a common set of assumptions referred to as expectancy-value theory. These assumptions relate to *prescriptive* notions used by economists to define which of a number of alternative options are likely to yield the greatest benefit or the smallest cost. The two crucial variables in such formulations are the *probability* that a given end state will occur if an option is chosen, and the worth of that end state. Strictly speaking, expectancy-value theory applies only when objective measures of both probability and worth are available. If one is dealing with only estimated or perceived probability, one should talk of *subjective* expectancy, and if one is talking about perceived desirability, then the term *utility* is used instead of *value*. With regard to the distinction between utility and value, it should be remembered that the relationship between them is typically nonlinear— for instance, the subjective difference in desirability between a gain of £1,000 and £2,000 is typically seen as greater than that between £101,000 and £102,000.

Expectancy-value theory has come into psychology mainly as the result of work by mathematical psychologists such as Edwards (1954, 1961). A great deal of the relevant research has used laboratory situations in which subjects are required to express their preferences between imaginary gambles. However, less precisely defined applications of similar notions have been influential in many other fields, including, it would seem, action theory. Within social psychology, one of the best-known theories of this type is the Fishbein model of attitudes and behavioural intentions (Fishbein, 1967; Fishbein & Ajzen, 1975). According to this theory, intentions to perform a behaviour are jointly influenced by attitude towards that behaviour, and subjective norms (i.e., what actors feel other people would think of their performing such behaviour). It is proposed that attitudes towards a behaviour are predictable from the *sum* of *evaluative beliefs* concerning the consequences of that behaviour. This is calculated by considering important ("salient") potential consequences of the behaviour, and then, for each consequence, calculating the *product* of measures reflecting perceived desirability (utility) and strength of belief (subjective expectancy) that the consequence will occur. An overall attitude score is then derived by summing these products.

These expectancy-value approaches have been subject to a number of criticisms. The first applies to the choice of which possible consequences may be assumed to influence the overall attitude and hence behavioural intention. Fishbein and Ajzen (1975) say that calculation of their attitude index should be based only on those consequences that are important or salient to the individual, but in practice little attention is paid to the possibility that different individuals may see different consequences as salient. This is especially noteworthy in that such differences in salience may reflect and possibly underly differences in attitude (Eiser, 1971; Eiser & van der Pligt, 1979).

The second objection relates to the meaningfulness of the expectancy-value product term itself. On the one hand it is intuitively plausible that a decision-maker will somehow consider the desirability of possible consequences of alternative courses of action, and also will somehow take account of the perceived likelihood of such consequences. Such notions have applicability across a broad range of psychological phenomena, not the least of which is animal learning (Tarpy, 1982). On the other hand, it is by no means obvious that considerations of desirability and perceived likelihood must be combined in a way that reflects a simple multiplicative function. So what of the evidence?

Across a wide range of situations, overall preferences can be shown to be broadly predictable from the product of expectancy and value measures. However, as has been argued by many researchers, notably Coombs (1975), such research has typically failed to choose situations where one can distinguish the predictions of expectancy-value and alternative theories. For this reason, a favoured research strategy has been to present subjects with choices between alternative hypothetical gambles or risky choices. In this way preference for a particular option can be related to its expected value, and different options can be presented with the same expected value but with the expectancy and value components manipulated independently. Under such conditions, the basic axioms of expectancy-value theory have been shown to be continually violated (Coombs & Huang, 1976).

It is by now clear that individuals do not typically process probabilistic information in the manner required by prescriptive models of the expectancy-value type. Instead, they tend to rely on simplificatory strategies, or rules of thumb, referred to as *heuristics* by Tversky and Kahneman (1974). Nisbett and Ross (1980) have reviewed a great deal of research demonstrating the vulnerability of our statistical reasoning to a variety of biases. However, what is of central importance here is the argument that such biases and heuristics are part of normal adaptive (as well as maladaptive) cognitive processing, and not mere deviations. Any theory relating social cognition to social action must therefore take these into account.

Recently, Kahneman and Tversky (1979) have proposed an alternative to expectancy-value theory as a theory of risky decision-making. This they call *prospect theory*. Among its features are, firstly, that outcomes are assessed not absolutely, but in terms of *changes* from some reference point, which could be one's current state of affairs or any other meaningful standard or comparison level (cf. Thibaut and Kelley, 1959) and, secondly, that subjective probabilities are not considered as simple multipliers. Rather, their influence on choice is represented by means of a weighting function, which expresses the subjective importance attached to the probability of obtaining a particular outcome. This weighting function allows the theory to predict the extra importance attached to certain as opposed to less certain outcomes. Finally, it is assumed that, in multiple-choice decisions, alternatives may be assessed and rejected sequentially in a manner representable in terms of a "decision tree", so that different criteria and frames of reference may be relevant to different stages of the decision process.

Empirical work on this theory is still in its early stages (e.g., Fischhoff, 1983). The general message for action theory, however, is clear: It is one thing to say simply that action reflects the anticipation of certain outcomes or goals, but it is quite another thing to be able to specify precisely the decision processes that relate expectancies and evaluations to choice.

Scripts and Schemata

One of the most exciting developments in social cognition research over the last few years has been work concerned with the general notion of scripts and schemata. It would be misleading to suggest that this field is, or even may necessarily become, a unified one. Nonetheless, what the different strands of research appear to have in common is a preparedness to build models of cognition around questions of how people deal with *familiar* situations and events, such as occur in their everyday lives. This emphasis is compatible with many of the concerns of action theory that relate to the rule-governed and sequential nature of action.

The concept of schema is more general than that of script. Its first use in psychology appears to be Bartlett's (1932) work on memory and recall. Since then it has been taken up by a number of researchers who espouse the view that cognition and information processing is *hypothesis-driven*. What this means is that perceivers rarely confront their experience in total naivety. Rather, information is assimilated according to its goodness of fit with a greater or lesser number of alternative prior assumptions about its probable meaning. Such prior assumptions and hypotheses help fulfil probably the most important requirement of any cognitive system—they allow perceivers to pay selective attention to their experience.

The term *schema* refers specifically to the cognitive representation a person has of some event, object, or process. Schemata may be encoded linguistically or symbolically and may be socially acquired and shared. As such they relate closely to the concept of *représentations sociales* that is used by French social psychologists (e.g., Herzlich, 1973; Moscovici, 1961). Stereotypes concerning members of social and ethnic groups may also be interpreted in terms of schematic processing (e.g., Tajfel, et al., 1964; Taylor et al., 1978).

Of particular importance in the light of the recent hegemony of attribution research is the notion of schemata concerning causal processes. Kelley (1971) explicitly introduced the notion of *causal schemata* into attribution theory. His essay distinguished, among other things, between multiple sufficient, multiple necessary, and compensatory causes, and generally followed the line that different kinds of causal attributions could reflect the operation of different representations of cause–effect relationships. Kelley's approach, however, does not seem to capture quite as well the notion of schemata as representations of more concrete causal processes. For instance, it is reasonable to ask what causal schemata people might have about the working of different social systems, such as political parties, administrative, and governmental hierarchies, labour-management negotiations, university selection, assessment procedures, and so on. Indeed, without insight into such schemata it may be far from easy to explain why individuals interact with such systems in the way they do, why they can feel powerless or influential, justly or unjustly treated, and such like.

Another important set of schemata may relate to people's subjective representations of their own physiology, and of the causal relationships between their own behaviour, environmental influences, health, and disease. Such schemata must clearly be implicated in any decisions people may take to seek treatment or change their lifestyle in the hope of improving their health. The power of such schemata to influence behaviour need not depend on the validity in the sense of support from scientific evidence. Traditional conceptions on the nature of addiction may arguably reflect the adoption of a misleading schema of what it is to be dependent on a drug that can greatly influence the behaviour both of drug-users and of those who try to 'cure' them (Eiser, 1982; Schachter, 1982).

Scripts may be considered essentially as the schemata people hold of sequences of events that occur over time in given situations, in particular of sequences of *behavioural* events. As such, they provide a basis for organizing our knowledge of action rules and of the appropriateness of given actions in given contexts. Schank and Abelson (1977) describe script theory mainly within the context of work on artificial intelligence, and much of the empirical work inspired by this approach has concentrated on topics such as text comprehension and memory (Bower et al., 1979). However, Abelson (1981) has recently emphasized the broader applicability of the script concept to other areas, including social psychology.

The single most important observation by script theorists, from the point of view of social theory, is that a theory of how we think about social events and behavioural sequences cannot be content-free but must be explicitly a theory about our *world-knowledge*, that is, our understanding of classes of events and situations with which we have had experience. A large part of social cognition, in other words, consists of "knowing" what is going on in a situation, and what is going to happen next. What is also important is that much, if not most, of such knowledge is tacit in the sense that we are unlikely to be aware that we are using it unless something unexpected happens which makes us re-examine our expectations.

Situations differ in the extent to which they invoke a dominant script, or set of expectations for any particular role-holder. Behaviour conforming closely to situational expectations is said to be *scripted,* and the implication is that scripted behaviour generally requires less cognitive effort and is more automatic. Corresponding loosely to the distinction

between *scripted* and *unscripted* behaviour is Langer's distinction between 'mindless' and 'mindful' action. In a series of studies, Langer
has shown that many aspects of our behaviour and processing of information are 'mindless' in that we pay little attention to what we are
doing and do not typically engage in analytic comparisons of alternatives (Langer, 1978). One consequence is that people's responses to
requests from another person can be influenced by subtle aspects of
the way such requests are phrased (Langer & Abelson, 1972; Langer
et al., 1978). Also, initial mindless processing of information can restrict the way that information can subsequently be used in behavioural decisions—a process referred to as 'premature cognitive
commitment' by Chanowitz and Langer (1981).

Such research is important for a number of reasons, but particularly,
in the present context, because of its emphasis that much behaviour
and processing of information may be carried on in a somewhat automatic way, with the person paying little deliberate attention to what
is going on. Even if one did not fully accept the claims by Nisbett and
Wilson (1977) concerning our inability to report accurately about our
own mental processes, the clear implication is that cognitive processing
is not synonymous with conscious awareness. Action theory can be
formulated so as to avoid presuming such conscious awareness. Without such a presumption, though, there are methodological problems
in identifying goals and purposes objectively.

Conclusions

Many of the concerns of researchers in the action-theory tradition
are shared by workers in other areas of psychology, and particularly
cognitive social psychology. In this chapter, I have attempted to convey
the flavour of some major areas of theoretically generated research in
social cognition. Surprisingly, much of the research I have described
has had little to say explicitly about the relationship between social
cognition and social action. Some of it has more to say, but perhaps
only with regard to certain kinds of action or behaviour. By comparison, the action-theory approach starts from a consideration of overt
acts and action sequences, and this, one might think, would give it an
advantage in terms of relating cognition to behaviour. The problems,
however, are just as great since most, if not all, naturally occurring
behaviours could reflect the operation of any number of different kinds
of cognitive processes. Observing behaviour over a nonselective range
of situations is not the appropriate strategy for attempting to discrim-

inate between alternative hypotheses about cognitive processes. Action theory is therefore no different from any other theory in social psychology in requiring experimental tests of its hypotheses, regardless of whether these hypotheses are based on naturalistic observations, or tested in the laboratory or elsewhere.

Nor can we simply rely on people's self-reports about their own motives and decision processes. Our culture is one in which justifying, and indeed even just intelligibly explaining, our behaviour requires that we show it to be rational and goal-directed, at least in intention. We have been socialized into a particular view of how we ought to think, and maybe we do think that way, sometimes. Maybe we would even think this way, sometimes, without the influence of our particular cultural socialization. Maybe. The validity of a scientific theory, however, requires more than an appeal to culture-bound assumptions.

Human beings can plan, and their plans can fail. We need to know when and why their plans fail if we are also to know how they can succeed. In this respect the problems of action theory are contained within those of cognitive social psychology as a whole.

References

Abelson, R. P. (1981). Psychological status of the script concept. *American Psychologist*, *36*, 715–729.

Bartlett, F. C. (1932). *Remembering*. Cambridge University Press, Cambridge.

Bower, G., Black, J. R., and Turner, T. (1979). Scripts in text comprehension and memory. *Cognitive Psychology*, *11*, 177–220.

Brewer, M. B. (1977). An information-processing approach to attribution of responsibility. *Journal of Experimental Psychology*, *13*, 58–69.

Carver, C. S., and Scheier, M. F. (1982). Control theory: A useful conceptual framework for personality-social, clinical, and health psychology. *Psychological Bulletin*, *92*, 111–135.

Chanowitz, B., and Langer, E. (1981). Premature cognitive commitment. *Journal of Personality and Social Psychology*, *41*, 1051–1063.

Coombs, C. H. (1950). Psychological scaling without a unit of measurement. *Psychological Review*, *57*, 145–158.

Coombs, C. H. (1964) *A theory of data*. Wiley: New York.

Coombs, C. H. (1975). Portfolio theory and the measurement of risk. In *Human Judgment and Decision Processes*. (M. F. Kaplan & S. Schwartz, eds.). Academic Press: New York.

Coombs, C. H., and Huang, L. C. (1976). Tests of the betweenness property of expected utility. *Journal of Mathematical Psychology*, *13*, 323–337.

Edwards, W. (1954). The theory of decision making. *Psychological Bulletin*, *51*, 380–417.

Edwards, W. (1961). Behavioral decision theory. *Annual Review of Psychology*, 473–498.

Eiser, J. R. (1971). Categorization, cognitive consistency, and the concept of dimensional salience. *European Journal of Social Psychology, 1,* 435–454.

Eiser, J. R. (1980). *Cognitive social psychology: A guidebook to theory and research.* McGraw-Hill: London.

Eiser, J. R. (1982). Addiction as attribution: Cognitive processes in giving up smoking. In *Social Psychology and Behavioral Medicine.* (J. R. Eiser, ed.). Wiley: Chichester.

Eiser, J. R., and van der Pligt, J. (1979). Beliefs and values in the nuclear debate. *Journal of Applied Social Psychology, 9,* 524–536.

Fazio, R. H., Zanna, M. P., and Cooper, J. (1977). Dissonance and self-perception: An integrative view of each theory's proper domain of application. *Journal of Experimental Social Psychology, 13,* 464–479.

Fischhoff, B. (1983). Predicting frames. *Journal of Experimental Psychology: Learning, Memory and Cognition, 9,* 103–116.

Fishbein, M. (1967). Attitude and the prediction of behavior. In *Readings in Attitude Theory and Measurement.* (M. Fishbein, ed.). Wiley: New York.

Fishbein, M., and Ajzen, I. (1975). *Belief, Attitude, Intention and Behavior: An Introduction to Theory and Research.* Addison-Wesley: Reading, Mass.

Gollob, H. F. (1974). The subject–verb–object approach to social cognition. *Psychological Review, 81,* 286–321.

Greenwald, A. G. (1975). On the inconclusiveness of "crucial" cognitive tests of dissonance versus self-perception theories. *Journal of Experimental Social Psychology, 11,* 490–499.

Heider, F. (1946). Attitudes and cognitive organization. *Journal of Psychology, 21,* 107–112.

Heider, F. (1958). *The Psychology of Interpersonal Relations.* Wiley: New York.

Heider, F., and Simmel, M. (1944). An experimental study of apparent behavior. *American Journal of Psychology, 57,* 243–249.

Herzlich, C. (1973). *Health and Illness: A Social-Psychological Analysis.* Academic Press: London.

Jaspars, J. M. F. (1965). *On Social Perception.* Unpublished Ph.D. Thesis. University of Leiden.

Jaspars, J., Hewstone, M., and Fincham, F. (1983). The state of the art. In *Attribution Theory: Essays and Experiments.* (J. Jaspars, F. Fincham, & M. Hewstone, eds.). Academic Press: London.

Jones, E. E., and Davis, K. E. (1965). From acts to dispositions: The attribution process in personal perception. In *Advances in Experimental Social Psychology.* (L. Berkowitz, ed.). Vol. 2. Academic Press: New York.

Jones, E. E., and Nisbett, R. E. (1971). The actor and observer: Divergent perceptions of the causes of behavior. In *Attribution: Perceiving the Causes of Behavior.* (E. E. Jones, D. E. Kanouse, H. H. Kelley, R. E. Nisbett, S. Valins, & B. Weiner, eds.). General Learning Press: Morristown, N. J.

Kahneman, D., and Tversky, A. (1979) Prospect theory. *Econometrica, 47,* 263–292.

Kelley, H. H. (1967). Attribution theory in social psychology, In *Nebraska Symposium on Motivation.* (D. Levine, ed.). *15,* 192–238.

Kelley, H. H. (1971). Causal schemata and the attribution process. In *Attribution: Perceiving the Causes of Behavior.* (E. E. Jones, D. E. Kanouse, H. H. Kelley, R. E. Nisbett, S. Valins, & B. Weiner, eds.). General Learning Press: Morristown, N.J.

Kelley, H. H., and Michela, J. L. (1980). Attribution theory and research. *Annual Review of Psychology, 31,* 457–501.

Kelley, H. H., and Stahelski, A. J. (1970). Social interaction basis of cooperators' and competitors' beliefs about others. *Journal of Personality and Social Psychology, 16,* 66–91.

Langer, E. J. (1978). Rethinking the role of thought in social interaction. In *New Directions in Attribution Research.* (J. H. Harvey, W. J. Ickes, & R. F. Kidd, eds.). Vol. 2. Erlbaum: Hillsdale, N.J.

Langer, E. J., and Abelson, R. P. (1972). The semantics of asking a favor: How to succeed in getting help without really dying. *Journal of Personality and Social Psychology, 24,* 26–32.

Langer, E., Blank, A., and Chanowitz, B. (1978). The mindlessness of ostensibly thoughtful action: The role of "placebic" information on interpersonal interaction. *Journal of Personality and Social Psychology, 36,* 635–642.

McArthur, L. Z. (1976). The lesser influence of consensus than distinctiveness information on causal attributions: A test of the person–thing hypothesis. *Journal of Personality and Social Psychology, 33,* 733–742.

Miller, D. T., and Holmes, J. G. (1975). The role of situational restrictiveness on self-fulfilling prophecies: A theoretical and empirical extension of Kelley and Stahelski's Triangle Hypothesis. *Journal of Personality and Social Psychology, 31,* 661–673.

Miller, D. T., and Ross, M. (1975). Self-serving biases in the attribution of causality: Fact or fiction? *Psychological Bulletin, 82,* 213–225.

Moscovici, S. (1961). La psychanalyse, son image et son public. *Etude sur la répresentation Sociale de la Psychanalyse.* Presses Universitaires de France: Paris.

Nisbett, R. E., and Ross, L. (1980). *Human Inference: Strategies and Shortcomings of Social Judgment.* Prentice-Hall: Englewood Cliffs, N.J.

Nisbett, R. E., and Wilson, T. D. (1977). Telling more than we can know: Verbal reports on mental processes. *Psychological Review, 84,* 231–259.

Press, A. N., Crockett, W. H., and Rosenkrantz, P. S. (1969). Cognitive complexity and the learning of balanced and unbalanced social structures. *Journal of Personality, 37,* 541–553.

Schachter, S. (1982). Recidivism and self-cure of smoking and obesity. *American Psychologist, 37,* 436–444.

Schank, R. C., and Abelson, N. P. (1977). *Scripts, Plans, Goals and Understanding: An Inquiry into Human Knowledge Structures.* Erlbaum: Hillsdale, N.J.

Seligman, M. E. P. (1975). *Helplessness.* Freeman: San Francisco.

Shaver, K. G. (1970). Defensive attribution: Effects of severity and relevance on the responsibility assigned for an accident. *Journal of Personality and Social Psychology, 14,* 101–113.

Storms, M. D. (1973). Videotape and the attribution process: Reversing actors' and observers' points of view. *Journal of Personality and Social Psychology, 27,* 165–175.

Streufert, S., and Streufert, S. C. (1978). *Behavior in the Complex Environment.* Winston: Washington, D. C.

Tajfel, H., Sheikh, A. A., and Gardner, R. C. (1964). Content of stereotypes and the inference of similarity between members of stereotyped groups. *Acta Psychologica, 22,* 191–201.

Tarpy, R. M. (1982). *Principles of Animal Learning and Motivation.* Scott Foresman: Glenview, Ill.

Taylor, S. E., Fiske, S. T., Etcoff, N. L., and Ruderman, A. J. (1978). Categorical and contextual bases of person memory and stereotyping. *Journal of Personality and Social Psychology, 36,* 778–793.

Thibaut, J. W., and Kelley, H. H. (1959). *The Social Psychology of Groups.* Wiley: New York.

Tversky, A., and Kahneman, D. (1974). Judgment under uncertainty: Heuristics and biases. *Science, 185,* 1124–1131.

Ware, R., and Harvey, O. J. (1967). A cognitive determinant of impression formation. *Journal of Personality and Social Psychology, 5,* 38–44.

Weiner, B. (1970). New conceptions in the study of achievement motivation. In *Progress in Experimental Personality Research.* (B. Maher, ed.). Vol. 5. Academic Press: New York.

Weiner, B., Russell, D., and Lerman, D. (1979). The cognition–emotion process in achievement-related contexts. *Journal of Personality and Social Psychology, 37,* 1211–1220.

Wong, P. T. P., and Weiner, B. (1981). When people ask "why" questions, and the heuristics of attributional search. *Journal of Personality and Social Psychology, 40,* 650–663.

8

The Analysis of Situated Social Action: The Case of the Research Interview

Michael Brenner

Introductory Remarks

This essay is directed toward understanding and conceptualising socially reactive data-collection situations as problems in the psychology of action (see Brenner, 1981). The research described here derives from an interest in the psychological functioning of persons while they participate in research contacts (like interviews and experiments). Furthermore, detailed insight into the psychological organisation of data-collection encounters should permit refinement of the psychological means needed for adequate measurement, for example, by means of the development of more effective interviewing techniques and interviewer training procedures. After an outline of some of the action-psychological assumptions involved in the research has been presented, some ways in which the research interview can be regarded as situated social action are considered.

Action-Psychological Assumptions

ACTION IS GOAL-DIRECTED

The person externalises lines of action towards objects and other people in keeping with his goals. The person develops goals actively or reactively, that is, freely, on his own account, or in response to internal or external influences or pressures. Active goal development is captured in statements such as, ''He acts because he wants to do it'', ''He has intended to do it for some time'', ''He has chosen to do it''. Reactive goal development is expressed in statements such as, ''He wants

DISCOVERY STRATEGIES
IN THE PSYCHOLOGY OF ACTION

to do it because he is angry'', ''He does it because he knows circumstances will not permit any alternative line of action'', ''He does it because his friend has asked him to''.

Whatever the origin of goals, once a goal is cognised by the person, it directs action towards anticipated outcomes. This is the reason for the equifinality of action (Heider, 1958, p.108). That is, as long as the goal is cognised, the person will select and try one or more lines of action until the goal is attained. This implies that goals, besides directing action, also energise action through ''the arousal of tension upon the activation of the goal, which continues to exist until either the goal has been reached or it has been deactivated in some manner'' (Staub, 1978, p. 91).

Thus, the construct *goal* is perhaps best used to denote motivation; it ''implies a preference for certain outcomes or end states, or an aversion for certain outcomes and the desire to avoid them. It also implies a striving toward or away from these outcomes'' (Staub, 1978, p. 90). It should be noted that the pursuit of goals is not always successful, due to environmental constraints and the actions of others, for example. Therefore, even in a brief encounter, lines of action may be shifting as goals develop, are revised, or vanish.

ACTION REQUIRES KNOWLEDGE

Effective action is impossible when a person is unable to select a line of action likely to be appropriate for the particular situation within which a goal is pursued. Furthermore, situational knowledge is also required for the effective selection of goals here-and-now. When hungry, for example, it is important to know that, having entered a restaurant, the waitress will get you the meal you have asked for; to ask her for the same dish on a bus would be ''odd'' and the action would be ineffective.

There seem to be two kinds of knowledge, general and specific, which persons bring to bear in their here-and-now selection of goals and lines of action. ''General knowledge enables a person to understand and interpret another person's actions simply because the other person is a human being with certain standard needs who lives in a world which has certain standard methods of getting those needs fulfilled'' (Schank & Abelson, 1977, p.37). Again, when hungry, once a restaurant has been selected, there is no need to worry how one gets a meal, nor does the waitress need to wonder why the customer placed an order.

General knowledge enables us to experience our social world as ''native'', but we still need specific knowledge, which Schank and Abelson

(1977, Chapter 3) call "scripts", in order to interpret action and participate in action with ease. "Such specific knowledge exists in detail for every mentally competent person in the world with respect to every standard situation that he has been in many times" (Schank & Abelson, 1977, p.38). When acting in a standard situation, use of the appropriate script allows us to do less information-processing and problem-solving than if less specific knowledge were available. For example, if we know the "restaurant script" we do not need to ask why we can order only from the menu and why we have to pay for our meal. Given that "a script is a predetermined, stereotyped sequence of actions that defines a well-known situation" (Schank & Abelson, 1977, p.41), it is clear that scripts cannot handle totally novel situations. In these instances, action becomes ineffective, if not impossible.

ACTION REQUIRES SKILL

Given goals and knowledge, effective action relies, first and foremost, on the person's adequate motor performance, that is, on the person's behavioural capacity to express the action as intended. The relevance of motor skills for effective action is most apparent when considering examples such as "driving a car" or "playing the piano". However, the adequate motor performance of social behaviour is similarly important. Argyle and Trower (1979, p.116) give an example of skilled goal-directed action:

> He sizes up the situation, reads the social signals, and decides on a line of action. From his repertoire of skills he chooses one which he thinks will have the desired effect; to dominate, persuade, seduce or provoke. Having acted, he will watch the effect, and act accordingly, perhaps changing his tactic, deploying another skill.

It is clear from this example that it is not only the person's skilled motor performance that makes his action effective; he is also perceptually skilled, that is, adept at "the coding of, and giving coherence to, the multitudinous sensory data that pour in through the sense organs, and in linking these data to material stored in memory to give them context in both space and time" (Welford, 1976, p.12). Furthermore, the person's intellectual skill, his "ability to decide what should be done in particular circumstances" (Welford, 1976, p.12), is also well developed, as perception may lead him to change his tactic.

So far the fundamental person characteristics of action, goals, knowledge, and skills have been discussed. Notice that these characteristics provide the necessary and sufficient conditions for a person's action, that is, if one characteristic is absent, action is impossible. The person's action system is modelled in Figure 1.

ACTION IS SOCIAL

Action is social action when the person orients his action towards others besides himself. Action is social in the sense that we act, to a great extent, for others as well as for ourselves. Others make a difference to us when we act; we are influenced by their presence, as they are by ours. As Blumer (1953, p.194) has pointed out:

> Taking another person into account means being aware of him, identifying him in some way, making some judgement or appraisal of him, identifying the meaning of his action, trying to find out what he has on his mind or trying to figure out what he intends to do.

Given that social action is action influenced by others, it is best understood in terms of social interaction. That is, encounters cannot "be viewed simply as a result of two independent units simultaneously unwinding their self-determined lines of action. The action of one unit is

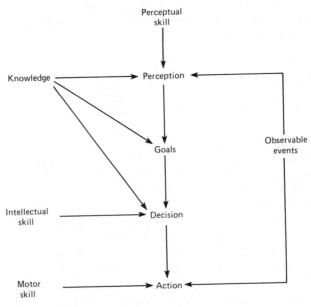

Figure 1. The person's action system.

dependent upon the action of the other, and *vice versa*" (McCall & Simmons, 1966, pp.48–49). The interactional character of social action affects, in particular, the ways in which persons pursue, and can pursue, goals. As Charon (1979, p.127) has written,

> the actor does something *meant* to *stand for* something to others. . . . Social action tells other people what we are, what we were, and what we are about to do. It tells others our ideas, our perspectives, our wants, our motives, our intentions, our morals, our background, our strengths, our identity.

In illustration of the issue, consider instances of social action where at least one participant cognises more than one goal at a time. Argyle (1980, p.73) gives the following example:

> P wants to persuade Q to do something which Q does not want to do; for example, a husband wants to persuade his wife to go to a certain place for their summer holiday. Each has a second goal—to sustain good relations with the other.

What will P do? Whatever he does it is likely that he will have to revise or abandon one of his goals. How will whatever P does affect Q? The general approach to P's dilemma that may be taken here is to understand the psychological processes involved in the interaction in terms of Kurt Lewin's field theory (for a summary, see Shaw & Costanzo, 1970, Chapter 5). According to field theory, any action is the resultant of forces within the person, forces that may exert pressures in different directions, and that may interact or conflict with each other. The constellation of such forces at any given time constitutes the psychological field of the person, and his action becomes understandable in terms of the properties of that field.

Returning to P, we know that his psychological field is minimally made up of two goals that exert pressures for action in different directions. Given the goal conflict that P experiences, he can do two things. He can decide to act on the basis of the psychological field existing here-and-now and pursue the goal that exerts the strongest pressure for action. This has the consequence that one goal is abandoned. A further consequence would be his wife's frustration when P starts trying to persuade her. Alternatively, P can decide to revise his psychological field, for example, by revising his holiday goal so that it becomes congruent with his second goal. Interpersonal influence in social action where a participant cognises more than one goal affects, therefore, the person's psychological field, as when P, knowing that his wife wants to sustain good relations with him, decides to drop his initial holiday goal. Notice further that whatever P does, it will affect Q's psychological field. For example, when P starts to persuade Q to do something she does not want to do, she may revise her goal of sustaining good relations. The action system involving two persons in social action, each cognising more than one goal, is given in Figure 2.

Let me give another example of social action where at least one participant cognises more than one goal at a time, namely an introductory negotiation of a research interview. Consider Mrs. Brown, whose doorbell has just been rung by an interviewer from Opinion Research Centre. When the interviewer has introduced himself and has asked Mrs. Brown to give an interview about her voting intentions, she has set up a particular kind of social action, the prospect of interviewer-respondent interaction in which Mrs. Brown must now decide to accept or to refuse to participate. What forces are likely to be operating in her psychological field that will determine her initial response to the interviewer's request?

Given Mrs. Brown's refusal, the interviewer's goal, to conduct the interview here-and-now, has been frustrated. She has now three options for action. She can abandon her goal; she can revise it, to try to make an appointment with Mrs. Brown for the interview to take place at a more convenient time; and, following in fact the standard procedure used in survey research, she can intensify her efforts in influencing Mrs. Brown to accept the respondent role. Having decided to intensify her efforts, she explains in detail the content, purpose, and

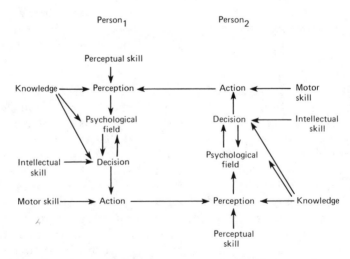

Figure 2.   The action system of two persons, each cognising more than one goal.

Acceptance	Action	Refusal
To obtain relief from boredom.	"I'm afraid I don't have time for an interview now because I have to get a cake in the oven."	Not to invite a stranger inside
To satisfy curiosity as to what the interview is like.		To get on with housework
		Not to reveal information to strangers
To help the interviewer.		

procedure of the interviewing. She stresses the confidentiality of the information gathered, points out that Mrs. Brown is a member of a carefully preselected sample of respondents and offers assurance that the interview will not take longer than an hour, among other things. The interviewer's actions result in changes in Mrs. Brown's psychological field with the effect that she decides to participate in the interview.

The assumption that action is regulated by, and reflected in, persons' psychological fields is useful, if only heuristically, given the various problems of measuring action-related cognitions, since it facilitates a realistic view of goal-directed action. As social action is interaction, persons have to fit their own actions to the actions of others, which are also goal-directed. In addition, persons may have to decide, sometimes on affective grounds, which goals, out of a set of currently cognised goals, to pursue. There may not only be problems of goal selection; in particular, there is the continuous problem of bargaining between participants about which goals to pursue in interaction, that is, jointly, co-operatively. This really means that we, as participants, have to be prepared, as McCall and Simmons (1966, p.136) have put it, to "modify our own lines of action on the basis of what we perceive alter's implications to be with respect to our manifest and latent plans of action." This process of interpersonal influence, I hypothesise, is continuously reflected cognitively in persons' psychological fields, and the continuous changes in persons' psychological fields necessitate continuous modifications in the choices of goals and the appropriate lines of action. It is the interactional character of goal-directed social action

Acceptance	Action	Refusal
To obtain relief from bordeom.	"Come in."	To get on with housework.
To help the interviewer.		
To support the purpose of the research.		
To become a respondent.		

that gives it its complex form, as Charon (1979, p.131) has pointed
out:

> I determine a line of action, act overtly. The other (alter) acts overtly toward
> me, and I interpret what that act means (represents) in light of my own act. I
> alter my line of action slightly or to a great extent. The other must do the same
> in acting toward me. The conceptualisation of actors constantly shifting what
> they do in relation to what others do is a highly complex view of the human
> being. We must interpret the other, and we must communicate to the other,
> and the other, in turn, must alter his or her direction accordingly. This is a
> constant, never-ending process.

SOCIAL ACTION IS SITUATED

Social action can be viewed as a mutual influence process between
persons. That is, persons, by taking lines of action, communicate to
each other which goals they are pursuing. In this way they define for
each other which situation it is in which the encounter is placed, or
should be placed, as far as they are concerned. Consider in this respect
the above example of an introductory phase of a research interview.
For Mrs. Brown, given the constellation of her psychological field at
the time of initial contact with the interviewer, her definition of her
situation was derived from the goal she was pursuing, to get on with
the housework. For the interviewer, entering the presence of Mrs.
Brown, the situation was "the introductory phase of the interview",
apparent in the line of action that she took. That is, she defined Mrs.
Brown not as a housewife but as a prospective respondent. What happened in the bargaining between Mrs. Brown and the interviewer was
not only that Mrs. Brown's psychological field was transformed by the
interviewer's action, but that she dropped her initial definition of her
situation and accepted the interviewer's definition, namely, to be about
to have an interview.

It is important to emphasise that the "definition of the situation" is
a purely cognitive process. That is, the assumption that social situations can influence action per se, in any external sense, is mistaken.
Situations are real only to the extent to which persons define, on their
own grounds, which situation it is that is involved in their relationship.
(Interestingly, a relationship can involve two situations, when ego and
alter attribute to it two different definitions). William and Dorothy Thomas (1928, p.572) captured the cognitive process by which
situations become real: "If men define situations as real, they are real
in their consequences." We do not respond to situations, but act vis-
à-vis realities as we define them. As Charon (1979, p.136) has put it:

If I see a situation as threatening, then I will act accordingly, even if people in that situation did not mean to appear threatening. If I define school as hard or good or silly, then I will act toward school in that manner, no matter if others feel as I do and no matter if it is in reality harder, better, sillier than other schools. Our realities are our definitions of situations.

Furthermore, the situational consensus that persons may have achieved at the onset of a relationship does not mean total agreement about which situation it is precisely that will unfold during interaction. Although an interpersonal definition of the situation established a platform on which to base the encounter, as expressed in the division of roles between participants, the future of the relationship is to some degree ambiguous and unstructured. Thus, strictly speaking, "the definition of the situation is a process" (Waller, 1970, p.162). Participants have to monitor continuously the degrees to which the initial "working agreement" (McCall & Simmons, 1966, p.127) still stands. If the definition of the situation is threatened, and if it matters, it must be renegotiated to enable the effective pursuit of the goals that initially gave rise to a situational definition.

Social situations have a characteristic social structure. This is made up of interlocking social positions, roles, which enable the performance of actions in meaningful relationship to other actions. The notion of the role of interviewer, for example, is impossible to define without reference to the reciprocal role of respondent. Central to the concept of role as a relational construct is expectation. Once participants have defined their roles, they then anticipate that they will act in particular kinds of ways. For example, in interviewing, it is the interviewer who asks the questions, not the respondent, and both participants expect this.

The concept of role helps to account for the general social structure of a relationship, but is not in itself sufficient to explain the considerable variation in persons' performances when comparing interactions involving the same role relationships, such as research interviews. Thus, in line with individual differences in defining a situation of a given kind, it is more appropriate to assume that role performances are informal. The expectations operating in the interaction are formed as part of the development of a *particular* relationship; they are defined by participants and may be subject to a continuous process of redefinition, as may be the situation as a whole. Once a pattern of expectations has been established between participants, the cognitive processing of the other persons becomes simpler, as Lalljee et al. (1976, p.30) have pointed out:

Rather than judging each new act of his partner as a novel and unanticipatable event, he judges it as maintaining or deviating from an already established pattern. As long as our partner behaves in a relatively predictable way, and we, likewise, behave in a coherent and relatively predictable way, the task of understanding particular acts . . . and of deciding . . . what we are going to do . . . becomes much simpler.

SUMMARY OF ASSUMPTIONS

The action-psychology perspective, then, assumes that people's actions are goal-directed and that the actions can be directed toward more than one goal at a time. Furthermore, as the performers of actions people are assumed to be knowledgeable and skillful in their formulation and execution of appropriate, complex sequences of activities. However, action in general is social, and actors are interdependent in their goals, knowledge, skills, and activities. Continuing negotiation and modification of the psychological field of each person is the normal state of affairs in any episode of social action. Finally, social action always and necessarily is situated, but the situation relevant to action is the situation as defined by the actor. The actor's definition of the situation is a process, not a static product, and therefore it is continuously susceptible to revision through negotiation or other aspects of the actor's private and social experiences. As a rule, the parties to an interaction episode produce a temporarily shared working definition of the situation, one that provides the basis for coordinated activity but that may have required considerable revision of personal goals to achieve. This was illustrated by the opening interplay between an interviewer and a potential respondent. The remainder of this chapter uses the action-psychology approach to clarify the processes involved in one of the most commonly used and most potentially reactive research contacts in the social sciences: the personal interview.

The Research Interview as Situated Social Action

The research interview is not after mere information. As Cannell and Kahn (1968, p.530) have put it, "it has to do with that particular quantitative form of information getting called *measurement*. The interview is one part, and a crucial one, in the measurement process as it is conducted in much of social research." Thus, from the researcher's point of view, the only objective of research interviewing is to obtain from respondents valid answers in response to the questions put to them, these answers meeting particular response requirements posed by the questions or the questioning procedures. From an action-psychological point of view, the attainment of measurement adequacy requires from interviewer and respondent, once engaged in interaction, the pursuit of interview-relevant goals, knowledge (not only situational knowledge, but, in the case of the respondent, the accessibility of the required information), and interviewing skills (both of interviewer and respondent).

Given that interviewer and respondent pursue the relevant goals (that is, they wish to accomplish in their interaction a body of knowledge that is, as far as the respondent is concerned, valid and, as far as both are concerned, relevant to the research) and given further that both parties possess the relevant knowledge and that the interviewing skills employed are adequate, one may assume that interviewer–respondent interaction enables measurement. By implication, as has been pointed our earlier, if one of the three components of action—goals, knowledge, skills—is deficient, measurement will be biased. What are the goals, the kinds of knowledge, and the skills that interviewer and respondent should involve in their interaction such that measurement bias be avoided?

Looking at the interviewer first, she must know that validity of answering and, in the case of certain questions, also precision of answering, constitute the main goals in research interviewing. She must also know which actions to take for the adequate pursuit of goals in question–answer sequences. Her actions must not bias the response process. This means that the interviewing must be done nondirectively; she must leave it entirely to the respondent to provide answers to questions. For example, questions must never be asked in a leading manner, as this exerts pressure on the respondent to answer in particular ways ("You haven't experienced any problems in getting information from these staff?", which implies as the "right" answer "No", as against the nondirective, "Do you experience any problems in getting information from these staff?").

In more general terms, the interviewer, in her actions, must maintain a neutral stance; whatever the topic of the conversation, she must not express her personal views about the issues under consideration, as this would amount to an explicit interviewer effect on the respondent that might endanger, as in the case of leading or directive questioning, the validity of the information reported. Impartiality of the interviewer's action vis-à-vis the answers given by the respondent does not, however, imply the desirability of total interviewer neutrality, as sometimes recommended by interview methodologists. "Current research-interviewing-technology assumes the desirability of sterile conditions in the interview situation; neither the interviewer nor the instrument should act in any way upon the situation" (Deutscher, 1972, p.325).

The interviewer's actions, besides being nondirective when it comes to questioning and to clarifying issues, extend to the management of the response process in social terms. By means of socially effective interaction with the respondent (by showing interest in the respondent's participation in the interview, by thanking him from time to time for his effort, for example), she must try to maximise, on the part of the respondent, the motivational forces, the goal, to report adequately. This implies also attempting "to reduce or eliminate the negative forces, the barriers to communication" (Kahn & Cannell, 1957, p.62). That is, the perceptually skilled interviewer will notice respondent problems when faced with certain questions (his inability to recall, to answer adequately, his problems in cognising what is meant by a question, for example), and will volunteer clarification or the repetition of the question.

In order to circumscribe the knowledge that is relevant to interviewer–respondent interaction, methodologists have written out the "Do's and Don'ts of interviewing" (Smith, 1972, pp.59–61); they have also provided guidelines regarding the use of adequate interviewing techniques (see Atkinson, 1972, Chapter 9; *Interviewer's Manual,* 1976, Chapters 3–5). The Do's and Don'ts of interviewing and the guidelines devised in conjunction with them are not by fiat; they are the result of extensive research into the biasing effects of inadequate interviewer, as well as respondent, performance (see Cannell & Kahn, 1968). While knowledge of the Do's and Don'ts, together with the guidelines, provides the interviewer essentially with a set of subgoals that the interviewer must enact before the main goal, valid information reporting, can be attained, this knowledge by itself does not ensure that the interviewer can actually act in a goal-directed manner. To this end, the interviewer must know which particular action to take when a goal is cognised as salient in interviewer–respondent interaction; furthermore, by means of interviewer training, she must have developed the appropriate intellectual and motor skills needed for the effective execution of goal-directed action.

One of the ways in which the researcher can approach these issues is to design, by means of pretesting and in conjunction with the particular questions to be used in the data collection, a repertoire of actions that enables the interviewer to perform adequately. Once the design is complete, the interviewer is then trained, using role-playing of the action repertoire and video-feedback as the main means of skills acquisition. However, before considering the design of interviewer actions, the respondent must be considered.

Once the respondent has agreed to be interviewed his main goal will be, or at least should be, to answer the questions adequately. The interviewer will continuously encourage the respondent in the pursuit of this main goal, but she must be prepared for the respondent to develop, during question–answer sequences, a number of subgoals, some of which may be in conflict with his main goal. The respondent may require the interviewer to repeat an action (a question, a clarification, an instruction, for example); he may request clarification of what is meant by a question or of what is involved in following an instruction; he may refuse to answer. A respondent action that is not always goal-directed, though it conflicts with his main goal, is that he may give inadequate information. (This action is not goal-directed when the respondent assumes that his answer is adequate.) When such respondent actions arise, typically intermitting question–answer sequences, the interviewer must be able to deal with them in such a way that it is likely that in the end her goal, adequate answers, will be accomplished. While requests for repetition are unproblematic, as the interviewer only needs to repeat the appropriate action, handling the other kinds of action can be difficult, if not impossible. When encountering inadequate answers, refusals, and requests for clarification, it is most essential, in order to avoid interviewer bias, that the interviewer can manage to remain nondirective in her actions. For example, she may use nondirective probes (such as, ''Can you tell me more about it?'', ''How do you mean?'') to clarify information she does not understand, or she may emphasise the confidentiality of the data collection with the aim of overcoming a refusal. In all, it is important to notice, given that the respondent can develop subgoals the interviewer cannot always meet effectively, that there is no guarantee in a data collection programme of total success in measurement, from the point of view of interview–respondent interaction.

Another aspect of the respondent's participation in the interview relates to the fact that the definition of the situation as research interview is only compelling for the interviewer. As the respondent cannot be forced, but only influenced, by the interviewer to maintain his initially agreed main goal, he may start defining the encounter in different terms, for example, as an opportunity to talk about issues beyond the subject of the interview. He may also develop the goal of challenging the interviewer as a person, for example, by doubting her competence (see Brenner, 1978a). Such alterations of the definition of the situation may be subtle, that is, difficult for the interviewer to detect. For example, respondents may display "acquiescence", that is, a tendency to agree or disagree with items independent of their content (see Couch & Keniston, 1960); they may feel a "need for social approval", that is, a need "to respond in culturally sanctioned ways" (Crowne & Marlowe, 1964, p.354); they may be influenced by considerations concerning the social desirability of answers (see Phillips, 1973). Finally, it must be noted that there is, at least in principle, nothing to stop the respondent from using any means of action to damage, or destroy, the interview as a measurement situation. As Sudman and Bradburn (1974, p.16) have pointed out:

> The primary demand of the respondent's role is that he answers the interviewer's questions. Answering certain questions will require considerable effort on his part, if the respondent is not sufficiently motivated to perform his role, the whole enterprise falls apart.

Due to the degrees of freedom of the respondent's performance of his role, the interviewer must be prepared to encounter problems and instability in the relationship with the respondent. (This means, by the way, that it is impossible, as well as undesirable, to expect totally standardised research interviews; there must be room for improvisation in interviewer–respondent interaction, though in keeping with the interviewer's main goal of achieving adequate information reporting.) While many kinds of problems can be dealt with successfully by means of the appropriate interviewer actions, it must be acknowledged that the interviewer can only attempt to resolve problems that relate to the interview in terms of content or procedure; she cannot socially control the respondent's overall conduct, as this would amount to a severe interviewer effect on the respondent. Thus, ultimately, adequacy of data collection relies on the respondent's good will to maintain the necessary working consensus, which the interviewer will try to influence positively but cannot entirely create on her own.

SPECIFICATION OF ACTION REPERTOIRE

Given the social and psychological character of measurement in the research interview, clearly, in order to improve measurement adequacy, we have to increase the degrees of control over interviewer–

respondent interaction. One way of doing this, as mentioned above, is to prepare the interviewer in detail for the data collection, that is, to provide her with detailed knowledge about the research interview as a measurement situation—this including, in particular, knowledge about the repertoire of actions necessary to accomplish adequate data collection—and to train her intensively in interviewing skills. In addition, as is discussed below, it also is important to assess the extent to which the response process has been biased.

Central to the first way of increasing control over interviewer–respondent interaction is, as indicated, the design of an adequate repertoire of interviewer actions. When designing such a repertoire we need to consider a number of issues. First of all, questions vary in terms of the form of answers desired. There are two types of questions, closed and open. *Closed* questions require a definite response; *open* questions allow the respondent to answer in his own words. Second, as indicated, question–answer sequences may be complicated by the respondent's request for repetition of an interviewer's action, or for clarification, and by the delivery of inadequate information and refusals. Third, question–answer sequences must be designed in such a way that three sets of subgoals can be fulfilled. The respondent must have sufficient time to comprehend the question and to decide on a line of action (to answer, or to request clarification, for example); the interviewer must be able to assess fully the degree to which an answer is adequate; she must be able to record the answer fully and to establish whether the information is correct.

Three examples of action repertoires for adequate research interviewing may be proposed, beginning with action sequences related to unproblematic closed and open question–answer sequences. I then consider the case of the "half-hearted" refusal. Notice that the action repertoires below offer only a *general* solution to the design of question–answer sequences. Given a particular data collection programme, these suggestions would need refinement and alteration for concrete application.

STRUCTURE OF ACTION INVOLVED IN CLOSED QUESTIONS WITH DEFINITE RESPONSE

This first illustration presents a simple cycle of Interviewer (I) and Respondent (R) interaction using closed-response questions and discretionary, nondirective probes by I.

Action	Subgoal	Example	Main goal
I reads question as worded, slowly and with correct intonation and emphasis	To give R time to understand the question as meant by the researcher	I: "Do you read *regularly* any journals or magazines related to your work?"	
(Pause)	(Where necessary to give R time to provide a response)		
R answers adequately	To answer the question	R: "No"	Obtained
I records the response	To enter the response into the questionnaire		
(I may repeat the response)	(To ensure, if in any doubt, that the answer recorded is correct)	I: "No"	
(R may give feedback)	(To indicate whether the response is correct)	R: "Mm"	
(I may thank R for his cooperation)	(To encourage R in his cooperation)	I: "Fine"	

STRUCTURE OF ACTION INVOLVED IN OPEN QUESTIONS

The following action repertoire illustrates the use of open-ended questions, including procedures by which I maintains I–R coordination.

Action	Subgoal	Example	Main goal
I reads question as worded, slowly and with correct intonation and emphasis	To give R time to understand the question as meant by the researcher	I: "What would you say are the *disadvantages* of living in the Upper Afan?"	
(Pause)	(Where necessary to give R time to provide a response)		

Action	Subgoal	Example	Main goal
R answers adequately, I records the information verbatim immediately	To enter R's information as accurately as possible into the questionnaire	R: "Well you have to catch a bus if you haven't got a car to go from the village that's a disadvantage."	
(I may give feedback)	(To indicate attention)	I: "Mmhm"	
(R may provide more adequate information, I records the information verbatim immediately)	(To enter R's information as accurately as possible into the questionnaire)	R: "The other disadvantage is you've got to work outside because the colliery is now closed."	Obtained
(I may request repetition of previous information)	(To become able to enter R's information as accurately as possible into the questionnaire)	I: "Sorry can you repeat what you've just said?"	
(R repeats previously given information)	(To comply with I's request)	R: "Yes we've got to work outside because the colliery is now closed."	
(I may probe nondirectively for further information)	(To obtain more information)	I: "Are there any other disadvantages?"	
(R provides more adequate information, I records the information verbatim immediately)	(To enter R's information as accurately as possible into the questionnaire)	R: "No I don't think so."	Obtained
I repeats the full answer	To ensure that the information recorded is correct	I: "You said that one disadvantage is that you have to catch a bus if you haven't got a car to go from the village the other disadvantage is that you've got to work outside because the colliery is now closed."	
(R may give feedback)	(To indicate whether the information is correct)	R: "Yes that's it."	
(I may thank R for his cooperation)	(To encourage R in his cooperation)	I: "Thank you."	

THE SPECIAL PROBLEM OF REFUSAL TO ANSWER

Refusals by a respondent to answer a question occur very rarely but can be extremely difficult to deal with. When the respondent firmly refuses to answer, the interviewer must accept the refusal. This is, of course, because the respondent not only has the right to refuse, but it is also impossible to force the respondent to answer. Luckily, most refusals are really "half-hearted" refusals. The respondent raises specific problems that make it impossible for him to answer, but is otherwise cooperative. Thus, the respondent provides a basis for discussing the refusal and moving towards an answer. In negotiating the refusal the interviewer must use nondirective means of problem-solving (repeating the question or instruction, nondirective clarification) in order to avoid any biasing interviewer effect. Another good means of problem-solving is to point out the confidential nature of the data collection, as in this example:

Action	Subgoal	Example	Main goal
I reads question as worded, slowly and with correct intonation and emphasis	To give R time to understand the question as meant by the researcher	I: "Do you experience *any problems* in getting information from *your* staff?"	
R gives half-hearted refusal	To refuse	R: "I don't think I should answer that because I'd be saying things about colleagues".	
I clarifies	To clarify	I: "Well as I said at the start of the interview any answers you provide will be treated in confidence and no individual will be identified in our report".	
R requests "rhetorical" clarification	?	R: "It's in confidence then?"	
I gives feedback	To clarify	I: "Yes".	
R answers adequately	To answer the question	R: "Well yes I do have problems some people are uncooperative" (carries on answering)	Obtained

ASSESSMENT OF BIAS IN I–R INTERACTION

Even when interviewers are trained through specification of the major, common action sequences, it still remains to assess the extent to which the response process has been biased. This is done after the data have been collected. From a methodological point of view, two enquiry strategies offer themselves. One is concerned with the cognitive processes that accompany and regulate interviewer–respondent interaction. Following von Cranach et al. (1980), one particular method of detecting cognitive processes is to confront participants with a record of their actions in the interview and to interview them systematically for cognitions that, they remember, have regulated or accompanied their past actions. Such cognitions can relate to participants' goal states, perceptions of the other participant and of the questions, problems experienced in answering the questions, and affective states. If the reported cognitions were valid, this would enable a cognitive representation of the structure of action involved in research interviews; in particular, any cognitive sources of bias (for example, anxiety arising from threatening questions, social desirability effects, "negativistic" respondent motivation) would show up.

The findings presented by von Cranach et al. (1980, Chapter 8), based on the use of the confrontation interview method in various research contexts, are impressive, but limited exployment of the technique for the study of research interviews, using sacrifice subjects in the laboratory for pretest purposes, has pointed up some problems. The confrontation interview is an interview situation likely to involve the same interpersonal influence processes and degrees of freedom for action for the respondent as any research interview. Thus, clearly, the reporting of cognitions in an interview context will lead to an underreporting, and to some misrepresentation, of the actual cognitive experiences of subjects, due to recall problems, due to fabrication of cognitions, due to, perhaps, "negativistic" subject motivation (the goal of destroying the procedure), due to the interview process itself that, in a sense, artificially but necessarily guides the production of cognitions. In particular, it is presently unclear what effect the interviewer has on subjects' reporting, to what extent, for example, the interviewer by his questioning exerts demand characteristics that compel the subject to reconstruct, or to fabricate, past cognitive experience rather than to remember it and to admit, when necessary, memory failure. Experimental variations in the conditions under which confrontation interviews are conducted are not directly helpful in detecting biasing interviewer effects. Clearly, "variations in the organisation and execution of the self-confrontation interview will lead to variations in the interview material" (translated from von Cranach et al., 1980, p.265); yet, which kind of organisation and execution is least biasing? As there is no way of observing a subject's cognitions, as available to him, directly, "it is not possible to test whether there is a correlation between what someone thinks and what he says he thinks. Therefore, one has to allow for the possibility that there is no correlation between the two" (Bainbridge, 1979, p.411). Thus, in contrast to usual research interviewing where, in principle, verification data may be used to assess the extent of response error, this is impossible in confrontation interviews.

One of the ways of tackling the problem, using test–retest designs or an experimental variation of interviewing styles, would, perhaps, be to investigate in detail the linguistic structure of subjects' reports accomplished under the various experimental conditions. Careful content analyses of the material, as proposed by von Cranach et al. (1980), might help to detect interviewer influences by classifying in detail which linguistic reporting style is contingent upon a preceding interviewing procedure. While a validation of the confrontation interview method would be cumbersome, the strategy to take is straightforward:

> Although there is not necessarily any correlation between verbal data and the behaviour it is supposed to report, this does not necessarily mean that there is never any such correlation and that all verbal data are completely invalid. Instead, if we want to use verbal data we need to know what factors influence the way verbal reports are produced, so that we can minimize the distortions and maximise the validity of the evidence. (Bainbridge, 1979, p.413)

Turning now to the other assessment strategy, this relates to the overt analysis of the interaction stream involved in research interviews. Technically, one of the established ways of performing action analyses of research interviews is to tape-record a sufficiently large sample of interviews by each interviewer. The tapes are then coded, using coding systems sensitive to the particulars of adequate research interviewing practice. This strategy also has obvious limitations. It is as cumbersome to operate as the confrontation interview, since the tape-recording analysis requires, to be sensitive, action-by-action coding, and, to be valid and reliable, the repeated coding of the same material. Furthermore, the categorisation of action, being observer-based, usually involves coding problems. Nevertheless, using sequence analysis methods for representing dynamic structure in the coded material, it is possible to demonstrate with reasonable clarity sources of failure in measurement attributable to observable interviewer–respondent interaction. For example, in one study (Brenner, 1978b) assessing the performances of professional market and social research interviewers involved in a mobility survey, it was found to matter a great deal *how* the questions were asked. In the case of the closed questions used in the survey, significantly altering them led to an increase in initially inadequate responses, while asking them directively gave rise to the opposite effect. If cards showing alternative answers to closed questions were not provided for respondents, inadequate answers were much more likely. On the whole, it was clear that where interviewers were not acting with a sufficient degree of skill, respondents' answers were inadequate; the response process was seriously affected by biasing interviewer effects.

Conclusion

Some of the possible contributions that a particular line of action-psychological reasoning can make to research interviewing practice have been outlined. Measurement in the interview is a psychological process much richer than is conventionally assumed by users of the instrument. This is by no means a novel assertion; for example, Kahn and Cannell have said, "we have emphasized the interview as an interactional process. Consistent with this approach, we have insisted on the importance of both interviewer and respondent as partners in the process and have argued that the interview itself, as the product of their interaction, depends on both of them" (1957, p.64). What is, perhaps, of additional value is the insistence that the longstanding acceptance of the interview as an action phenomenon be taken seriously in the research practice of psychologists, both in terms of investigating (and improving) the interview qua action and using it, sensitively, in the same terms.

References

Argyle, M. (1980). The analysis of social situations. In *The Structure of Action*. (M. Brenner, ed.). Blackwell: Oxford. pp.66–107.
Argyle, M., and Trower, P. (1979). *Person to Person*. Harper and Row: London.
Atkinson, J. (1972). *A Handbook for Interviewers*. HMSO: London.
Bainbridge, L. (1979). Verbal reports as evidence of the process operator's knowledge. *International Journal of Man–Machine Studies, 11,* 411–436.
Blumer, H. (1953). Psychological import of the human group. In *Group Relations at the Crossroads*. Harper and Row: New York. pp.185–202.
Brenner, M. (1978a). *The Social Structure of the Research Interview*. D. Phil Thesis: University of Oxford.
Brenner, M. (1978b). Interviewing: the social phenomenology of a research instrument. In *The Social Contexts of Method*. (M. Brenner et al., eds.). Croom Helm: London.

Brenner, M. (ed.) (1981). *Social Method and Social Life*. Academic Press: London.
Cannell, C. F., and Kahn, R. L. (1968). Interviewing. In *The Handbook of Social Psychology*. 2nd edition, Vol. II. (G. Lindzey & E. Aronson, eds.). Addison-Wesley: Reading, Mass.
Charon, J. M. (1979). *Symbolic Interactionism*. Prentice-Hall: Englewood Cliffs, N. J.
Couch, A., and Keniston, K. (1960). Yeasayers and naysayers: Agreeing response set as a personality variable. *Journal of Abnormal Psychology, 60,* 151–174.
Cranach, M. von, et al. (1980). *Zielgerichtetes Handeln*. Huber: Bern.
Crowne, D., and Marlowe, D. (1964). *The Approval Motive*. Wiley: New York.
Deutscher, I. (1972). Public and private opinions: Situations and multiple realities. In *The Social Contexts of Research*. (S. Z. Nagi and R. G. Corwin, eds.). Wiley: London.
Heider, F. (1958). *The Psychology of Interpersonal Relations*. Wiley: New York.
Interviewers Manual. Institute for Social Research: Ann Arbor, Michigan.
Kahn, R. L., and Cannell, C. F. (1957). *The Dynamics of Interviewing*. Wiley: New York.
Lalljee, M., et al. (1976). *Social Interaction*. The Open University Press: Milton Keynes.
McCall, G. J., and Simmons, J. L. (1966). *Identities and Interactions*. Free Press: New York.
Phillips, D. L. (1973). *Abandoning Method*. Jossey-Bass: London.
Schank, R. C., and Abelson, R. P. (1977). *Scripts, Plans, Goals and Understanding*. Erlbaum: Hillside, N. J.
Shaw, M. E. and Constanzo, P. R. (1970). *Theories of Social Psychology*. McGraw-Hill: New York.
Smith, J. M. (1972). *Interviewing in Market and Social Research*. Routledge and Keegan Paul: London.
Staub, E. (1978). Predicting prosocial behaviour: A model for specifying the nature of personality–situation interaction. In *Perspectives in International Psychology*. (L. A. Pervin & M. Lewis, eds.). Plenum Press: New York.
Sudman, S., and Bradburn, N. M. (1974). *Response Effects in Surveys*. Aldine: Chicago.
Thomas, W., and Thomas, D. (1928). *The Child in America*. Knopf: New York.
Waller, W. (1970). The definition of the situation. In *Social Psychology through Symbolic, Interactionism*. (G. P. Stone & H. A. Farberman, eds.). Xerox College Publishing: Waltham, Massachusetts.
Welford, A. T. (1976). *Skilled Performance*. Scott Foresman: Glenview, Illinois.

9

Behavioural Foundations for the Process of Frame Attunement in Face-to-Face Interaction

Adam Kendon

Introduction

Unlike sticklebacks and herring gulls, at least as they are proverbially understood and, so it would seem, unlike baboons and even chimpanzees, humans are not constrained to respond to each other or to each other's actions in specific ways. For humans, any action of p can be interpreted by another in a wide variety of different ways. By doing X, p is in no position to be sure that q will do Y. Furthermore, p not only cannot be assured that q will respond to a particular action of his in a particular way; he cannot even be sure that q will apprehend his action in the same way in which he himself apprehends it. Yet it is impossible for p to formulate a coherent program of action without some basis for supposing that it will be understood in a given way. To be able to act in the presence of others is to be able to assume that one's acts will be taken in a certain way. Whereas animals never seem to have any doubts, for human interactants there is always the possibility that each participant regards the other, his actions, and the interaction situation in quite different ways. This means that prospective participants are faced with the problem of establishing what each other's interpretative perspectives are. Interaction simply cannot proceed except insofar as participants are able to share at least some assumptions about the situation and each other's intentions in it. Thus we may expect to find that participants in interaction have ways of assuring themselves of how their co-participants are interpreting the situation and ways of communicating with one another about their interpretative prespectives so that a consensus between them may be arrived at and maintained.

DISCOVERY STRATEGIES
IN THE PSYCHOLOGY OF ACTION

The notion that coherent social interaction requires participants to share the same sets of assumptions has been expressed by several different authors in a number of different ways. For example, Garfinkel (1963) argued that coherence in social interaction requires that the participants all share a number of basic assumptions, including the assumption that these assumptions are shared. Such a condition he referred to as 'trust', and he showed, through a series of demonstrations, the confusion, anger, and considerable anxiety that could very quickly be generated if a participant in an interaction acted as if one or more of these basic assumptions did not apply. Goffman (1955, 1957, 1961, 1963, 1974), in his analyses of face-to-face interaction argued in a similar fashion. He distinguished what he referred to as occasions of 'focused interaction': when two or more individuals openly join together to sustain a single common focus of concern as is done, most characteristically, perhaps, in occasions of talk. In such circumstances participants co-operate together to establish and maintain an official or common focus of attention on the topic at hand. Goffman pointed out that in any focussed encounter a particular 'definition of the situation' comes to be shared by the participants, which serves to define what will be considered, for the time being, as irrelevant as well as what is relevant. A *frame* comes to be placed around the actions and utterances of the participants, which both determines the sense in which they are to be taken and serves to define whole ranges of possible acts as irrelevant (as not to be included).

The question we wish to discuss in this essay is how this shared frame, this common interpretative perspective, comes to be established. How do people come to know that they share each other's assumptions? As Garfinkel (1963) put it, 'the constitutive expectancies of a situation' may be applied to different sets of events so that different constitutive orders of events are established. For coherent interaction to ensue, the participants must be agreed upon how these constitutive expectancies are to be applied. The question is, how is this accomplished?

It is seen that p cannot wait to see what q will do in response to anything that he does, because he needs to have some inkling of how q will take any line of action he may offer in order to be in a position to begin a line of action in the first place. Thus communication about interpretative perspectives appears as a kind of prior in interaction. It seems that coherent interaction requires this commonality of interpretative perspective to be established first. Yet, clearly, unless we are to admit the possibility of some sort of direct transmission of interpretative perspectives, the only way that p can know how q is taking the situation and how he will apprehend p's own line of action is by observing what q is doing. He must be able to see how q is behaving in relation to his own behaviour before being able to know what q's interpretations of his actions are likely to be. p is thus in something of a bind. He cannot formulate a line of action unless he knows how q will take it. Yet he cannot know how q will take any line of action he may produce, except by seeing how q is indeed taking his line of action.

Routinisation

The resolution of this paradox is achieved in part through the routinisation of interactional situations and events. Interactional situations are to some extent classifiable into types, and rules of conduct appropriate to each type come to be laid down in advance. Sometimes these rules are made quite explicit, and participants can be taught how to identify the kind of interactional situation they are in and the rules of conduct that apply. One comes to learn 'how to behave' in Church and at afternoon tea, how to ask for a drink in Subunun (Frake, 1964), or how to enter a Yakan house (Frake, 1975). Participants also operate in terms of categorisations of each other. As Goffman has reminded us (Goffman, 1959), participants are able to establish selves for themselves in interaction, because they are able to manage their own appearance and manner according to established conventions that govern the significance of dress ensembles, patterns of conduct, grooming configurations, and the like. In this way, the range of possible interpretative frames a participant may expect to find being employed in a given situation or by the various people he may encounter within it can be considerably narrowed. Nevertheless, when a participant enters an actual encounter, when he comes to be called upon to take action in respect to others with whom he is in current interaction, there still remains considerable room for uncertainty. For example, if I am to offer you a greeting, how do I know that you will receive my salutation as I intend it to be received? If several persons are participating together in a conversation, how can any one participant count upon the continued participation of any of the others? What evidence can any of them provide for their continued participation without actually speaking? And, should any of them speak, how can the speaker know that his intended recipient is ready to receive his utterance, and how do the other participants know for whom the utterance is intended? Or consider the question of how occasions of focussed interaction are brought to a conclusion. In maintaining themselves as participants in a focussed interaction, the participants have negotiated a common per-

spective of relevance for each other's actions. For this to be changed
or to be brought to an end, it is necessary for all of the participants to
agree to the change or termination before it actually occurs. If such an
agreement is not reached, then any action of p's that, from his own
perspective, belongs to a new frame of interpretation, will be interpreted by the other participants in terms of the currently prevailing
frame and, accordingly, will be perceived as irrelevant, inconsistent,
or in some other way disjunctive. For new actions to be perceived and
responded to as meaningful, the frame of interpretation must be
changed first. Thus for changes or terminations to be accomplished in
a well-managed fashion, participants must be able to communicate with
one another about their intentions to change or to terminate before
they actually do so. The question is, how is this accomplished?

Differential Attention in Interaction

The processes by which participants are able to negotiate the *working
consensus* of the interaction depend to an important degree upon the
willingness of participants to allow that only certain aspects of behaviour
count as action. It appears that participants in interaction do not attend to all aspects of each other's behaviour in the same way, and they
do not accord all aspects of it the same significance. A distinction tends
to be drawn in that certain aspects of another's stream of action are
regarded as intentional and vehicles of explicitly intended messages,
and certain other aspects are not regarded in this light. Such a distinction makes it possible for people to embark upon lines of action in
respect to one another, and to observe each other's modes of dealing
with those lines of action without, as it were, officially doing so. By
making this distinction, by regarding only some aspects of behaviour as
intended (explicitly acknowledged action) whereas other aspects are regarded as unofficial, participants make it possible for themselves to
explore one another's interpretative perspectives. They thereby negotiate some measure of agreement before either of them needs to address to the other any explicit action.

Goffman (1974) has drawn attention to this differentiation in the
treatment participants in interaction accord various aspects of each
other's behaviour by his metaphor of *attentional tracks*. He suggests that
in any social encounter there is always an aspect of the activity going
forward that is treated as being within a *main-line* or *story-line track*. A
domain of action is delineated as being relevant to the main business
of the encounter, and it is oriented to as such and dealt with accordingly. Other aspects of activity are not included, but this does not mean

that they have no part to play. Thus Goffman suggested we may also distinguish a *directional track*. Here, in Goffman's words, there is 'a stream of signs which is itself excluded from the content of activity but which serves as a means of regulating it, bounding, articulating and qualifying its various components and phases (Goffman, 1974, p. 210). One may speak, too, of a *disattend track* to which are assigned a whole variety of actions not counted as being part of the interaction at all. Goffman mentioned here, in particular, various 'creature comfort releases'—scratching, postural adjustments, smoking, and so forth—that are, so to speak, allowable deviations from the behavioural discipline to which all participants in a focussed encounter are expected to conform. As Goffman himself made clear, and as a moment's reflection reminds us, it is, of course, not that the actions treated as being in the 'disattend track' are not cognised and responded to by participants. On the contrary, they often play an important part in the very process of negotiating common perspectives that, as we have seen, is an essential part of what makes focussed interaction possible. What I wish to suggest here, however, is that unless this kind of differential–attentional treatment is engaged in, the process of *frame attunement* in interaction would not be possible.

Usually, there is considerable agreement among interactants as to how various aspects of behaviour are to be assigned to these various tracks. One way in which this may be demonstrated very readily is to play the game of 'timmy'' (Kendon, 1978). In this game, one player, who may be called the Challenger, gets another, the Responder, to agree to imitate his actions. The Challenger says 'do as I do' and he then holds up both his hands and, touching each fingertip of the left hand with his right index finger in succession, and saying 'timmy' each time he does so, works his way from little finger to thumb and back again. After he has finished, he then lowers his hands and clasps them together in a resting position. The Responder is then expected to follow the Challenger's instruction to 'do as I do', and what he does is to repeat the timmy performance just described. However, the Responder almost never imitates the resting position of the Challenger's hands. Since the Challenger, without any advance indication to the Responder, has included the resting position of his hands as part of the performance to be imitated, he is always able to maintain that the Responder has failed in his imitation.

This game shows us not only how interactants proceed in terms of the notion that their co-participants share the same set of assumptions as he does; it also shows us how consistent participants are likely to be in what they decide to treat as *background action* and *foreground* or *figure action.* The game works because the Challenger can be secure in his assumptions about what the Responder will include as relevant aspects of his behaviour to be imitated.

The Challenger can rest secure in this assumption, in part, because it appears that some modes of behavioural organisation are almost automatically assigned main-track status, simply by virtue of their nature. Thus it appears that vocalisation and speech are specially oriented to and take a kind of first place in the attentional hierarchy. There is even evidence that suggests that humans are neurologically predisposed from the earliest age to give special attention to human speech (Cutting & Eimas, 1975; Liberman, 1980; Marler, 1980). It also seems probable that certain patterns of organisation of bodily movement are given main-track status simply by virtue of their character. Elsewhere (Kendon, 1978) I have reported a preliminary study in which subjects were asked to report what they had observed of someone's actions after having watched a silent film of a man making a speech to a large gathering. It was found that all observers first reported only those movements that, they maintained, had to do with what the speaker was trying to say. Furthermore there was a very high degree of agreement between subjects as to which aspects of his movements were referred to in this way. Other investigators have reported findings in agreement with this. Freedman and Hoffman (1967), for example, have shown that naive observers can discriminate what they have termed *object focussed movements* (movements of the forelimbs made in conjunction with speech) with a very high degree of reliability.

It must be seen, however, that if we are to understand how such significant acts function in interaction, we must understand how they become relevant for specific other individuals. It will be seen that, to understand what was going on in the timmy game, we need to ask not only about the features of the Challenger's performance that the Responder selects as relevant for imitation, but also how it was that someone came to regard the timmy performance as relevant for him and not for someone else, and how it was that the Challenger came to know that he had the Responder's agreement to play the game. Of course, the Responder might say 'I agree'. But how does the Challenger know when to start? Close observation of timmy games, as of other occasions of interaction, shows that the initiator of significant or main-track action does not begin just anywhere. He begins, characteristically, only when the attention of participants is properly organised. However, how does any one know how the attention of another is organised? In terms of actual patterns of behaviour that occur, how is the necessary alignment of attention accomplished?

The Communication of Attention

An everyday example may allow us to identify some of the main components of this process. Consider a circumstance in which a child who has recently learned how to make a yo-yo perform a number of different tricks seeks to show these off to her father.

Father is sitting in the living room in his comfortable chair, reading the newspaper. His three children are in various parts of the room, all practising with their yo-yos. Now one says, 'Dad, watch all the tricks I can do', and she steps forward to a place somewhat in the middle of the room, stands fully erect, and fully faces Father and looks at him. Father is looking up and looking at Daughter, and Daughter begins to yo-yo. As she begins she looks down at the yo-yo, following its movements. She brings one yo-yo sequence to an end, looks up and then says, 'Now watch' and yo-yos some more, again following the yo-yo with her eyes, not looking directly at Father. She does this several times. The yo-yoing is, thus, divided into segments or bouts, with each bout separately labeled and separated from the next bout by a pause in yo-yoing, during which Daughter looks at Father. After several such bouts of yo-yoing, Daughter again pauses, Father makes a remark and looks down at his paper, and Daughter turns away from him and moves to a different part of the room.

It is to be noted that in this sequence of yo-yo bouts the yo-yoing becomes the focus of a jointly focussed interaction. In doing so, a distinctive spatial location and orientation is taken up. As the performance is announced the child moves to a location that she will occupy for the entire duration of the performance. Once the performance is over, she leaves that location. Within that location, again for the entire duration of the performance, she maintains an orientation of her body such that her front, rather than her back, can be seen by her father. For each bout of yo-yoing she assumes a distinct orientation and posture, and the yo-yoing itself is preceded and succeeded by a distinctive posture and orientation; it is also preceded and succeeded by looking at Father. Further, and this is very important to note, the yo-yoing itself gets underway only when Father has also oriented himself in such a way that he can be seen to be able to see the yo-yoing. If Father is looking at his newspaper, this will be remarked upon, and the yo-yoing will not commence until he is looking at Daughter.

We see, thus, in this example, how an activity such as yo-yoing comes to acquire main-track status in a focussed interaction by virtue of it being provided a locus in both space and time that sharply contrasts with what precedes and succeeds it. What is also crucial in providing the yo-yoing with main-track status, however, is that it should be done within the frame of an *address and its reciprocation*. That is, the behaviour that has been provided a distinct spatial and temporal locus must be oriented to by another, and this orientation must be co-ordinated within the spatial and temporal boundaries of the activity that acquires this status. The actions that give the behaviour that is to be given main-track status its delineation have, thus, an interactional significance as great as the main-track activity itself, for they make possible the 'prior' orientation of the other to them; they make it possible for the other to know when and to what to orient. The yo-yoing does not begin until Father is looking at the child. If he does not look up when she calls out that she is going to do her yo-yo tricks, Daughter may even repeat one of her *framing actions,* such as stepping again to the location she will use for the performance, but this time stamping her feet to provide auditory evidence that she is moving to a new place. Thus what is required for focussed interaction to get underway is that there be (1) aspects of behaviour that serve in the process of providing spatial and temporal locus to the activity of the interaction, and (2) that these aspects of behaviour be different from those aspects constituted as the main-track activity. It is seen, then, that for any analysis of an episode such as this, to focus simply upon the main-track actions of yo–yoing itself and Father's proffered comments at the end would be to miss completely the processes by which the episode is made possible at all.

Spatial-Orientational Positioning

As we have just seen, the yo-yoing episode was demarcated by Daughter entering into and maintaining a particular spatial-orientational arrangement with Father. It appeared that, from her point of view, as long as she was in the spatial-orientational position she used for yo-yoing for Father, she was ready to yo-yo. Thus we can say her intention or plan to perform with her yo-yo for her father was indicated by her maintenance of this spatial-orientational position. This interpretation is borne out by the fact that when Father did not look up, Daughter made her stepping into position audible, by stamping her feet.

The yo-yo episode as a whole was characterised by a sustained spatial-orientational arrangement that was distinctive. Subepisodes within the yo-yo episode were also marked by Daughter assuming repeatedly a particular posture and position for each bout of yo-yoing, alternating with a contrasting posture and position for each interval between bouts.

The establishment and maintenance of spatial-orientational arrangements, it seems, is one way that participants can provide one another
with evidence that they are prepared to sustain a common orientational
perspective. By arranging themselves into a particular spatial-orientational pattern they thereby display each to the other that they are
governed by the same set of general considerations. By co-operating
with one another to sustain a given spatial-orientational arrangement,
they can display a commonality of readiness.

The spatial and orientational position of an individual can provide
information about his interpretative frame or attentional domain in the
following way:

First of all, it has to be recognised that a person's activity is always
located somewhere. Any line of action that a person is pursuing is always carried out in a specific relation to a specific environment. If I
am to write, I will organise myself in relation to environmental features
such as a desk, in such a way that I have access to a little domain within
which I can engage in writing and within which the various items
needed for this line of action are to be found. If I am to watch television, I will organise myself in relation to appropriate environmental
features so that again, a domain is available to me within which there
is free space between myself and the television set. If I am to spend
half an hour in quiet meditation, I will again organise myself in a way
that fits that activity to an appropriate domain of space. At any moment, thus, there is a spatial consequence for any line of activity, and
the individual is continuously re-adjusting himself in relation to his
surrounds as he changes this line of activity. The spatial domain to
which p organises himself to have easy and direct access for a given
line of activity has been referred to as the individual's *transactional segment* (Kendon, 1977). The transactional segment is the space into which
the individual addresses his gaze as he carries out his line of activity,
whatever it may be; it is the space from which he immediately and
readily reaches for whatever objects his current project may require he
manipulate; it is the space immediately in front of him that the individual projects forward and keeps clear if he is moving. In short, it is
the space that the individual seeks to maintain clear for his own purposes.

An individual's transactional segment may be recognised by others
from the position, orientation, and postural organisation of his body.
The body, it will be observed, can be viewed as an organisation of
segments, each one capable of a somewhat different orientation. However, the orientation of some segments sets limits upon the domain of

the environment to which other segments may orient. Further, each of the segments of the body differs in the ease with which its orientation may be changed. Thus there is a kind of descending hierarchy of orientational mobility, from the eyes to the lower body, combined with an ascending hierarchy of orientational limitations, from the lower body upwards. Although the eyes can change very rapidly the direction in which they may point, the domain of the environment over which they may move is limited by the orientation of the head. The orientation of the head, which may be changed almost as easily as the orientation of the eyes, is itself limited by the direction in which the upper body is facing. The direction in which the upper body is facing can also be varied (an individual may twist his upper body to the left or right) but less easily, and it is limited in the changes it can make by the orientation of the lower body. Where a person seats himself, or where he may have planted his feet when standing, provides a frame within which he may then orient his upper body, and this, in turn, provides a frame within which changes in the orientation of the head and eyes may take place.

Changes in orientation of upper body segments, such as the head and eyes are characteristically done within the framework of limits set by the position of the lower body. Changes in the orientation of lower body segments, therefore, have longer term implications for change in attention than changes in the orientation of upper body segments and are seen as having more momentous implications for whatever new environmental domains are to become the concern of the individual.

It is seen, in short, how the hierarchy of priorities and longer and shorter term commitments in the organisation of the individual's attention is directly perceivable by the way in which the various segments of the body are oriented. When this is taken in conjunction with the actual environmental settings in which these organisations occur and with observation of the actual activities in which the individual is engaged, it will be seen that bodily orientation can be a source of quite detailed information about what is relevant for an individual at a given time and therefore what his interpretative frame may be.

Formation Arrangements

When two or more individuals are present, they are able to provide information about the relevance of each for the other according to how they space themselves and how they include or exclude each other in their respective transactional segments. Thus we find that people co-present in a setting tend to organise themselves into spatial patterns of various kinds, co-operating together to maintain them. We may therefore speak of people entering into various kinds of *formations*.

There are many different kinds of formation to be observed. Here I discuss only one type, one that commonly occurs when two or a few individuals enter together into a focussed interaction, such as conversation. This type of formation has been referred to as an F-formation (Kendon, 1977), *facing-formation,* and *face-formation* (see Deutsch, 1977; McDermott & Roth, 1978; Scheflen & Ashcraft, 1976). An F-formation may be said to arise whenever two or more individuals agree to position themselves in such a way that their transactional segments overlap, thereby establishing a space between them to which they have equal access. This space is an area over which all participants exercise control and for whose maintenance and protection from internal and external disturbances all are responsible. Thus whenever two or more individuals are placed close to each other, orienting their bodies in such a way that each of them has an easy, direct, and equal access to every other participant's transactional segment, and agree to maintain such an arrangement, they can be said to create an F-formation. The system of spatial and postural behaviours by which people create and sustain this joint-transactional space will be referred to as an F-formation *system* (Kendon, 1977, p.181).

It is noted that by establishing such a system of spatial and orientational relations, individuals create for themselves a context within which perferential access to the other's actions is established. Furthermore, such a system of spatial and orientational relations provides for a visually perceivable arrangement by which participants in a given focussed encounter are delineated from those who are outsiders. Indeed, it seems that the kind of arrangements that arise in the F-formation provide a means of clearly demarcating the 'world' of the encounter from the rest of the 'world'. Entering into an F-formation, thus, is an excellent means by which interactional and therefore social and psychological 'withness' may be established.

There can be considerable variation in the actual arrangements that individuals establish with one another within the framework that an F-formation provides. A roughly circular arrangement is common in free standing groups of three or more people, where all are participating in the same conversation, but it is by no means the only arrangement that may be observed. In F-formations of two individuals, for example, we may see arrangements that vary from a direct face-to-face pattern, to an L-shaped pattern, or even a side-by-side pattern. In F-formations of more than two participants we may see semicircular or rectangular arrangements as well as circular ones.

INTERACTIONAL RELATIONSHIPS

Different arrangements have different consequences for the kind of access that the participants have to each other. Thus different arrangements imply different kinds of interactional relationships. Hall (1964, 1966, 1968) pointed out that at different distances the senses make available different kinds of information, and this has consequences for the kinds of actions that can be used in interaction. At very close distances, for instance, touch may be used, whereas at greater distances vision and hearing come to play important but varying roles. As distance increases, because the participants are able to detect one another's behavior in an increasingly less fine grained fashion, Hall suggested that there are shifts in the style of language used, how listener behaviour is organised, and the uses to which vision is put in the interaction. Hall suggested, thus, that because the way p and q may relate, their behaviour alters according to the distance that separates them. The function of the transaction between them also alters with distance so that different distances are chosen by interactants according to the kind of transaction they are going to have.

Hall's analysis dealt only with distance, but similar considerations make it clear that the angle of orientation of the interactants also make a difference in how they interrelate their behaviour. Two people standing or sitting face-to-face, for instance, confront one another, and each, directing his eyes forward, looks at the other. The surrounding environment is less readily accessible. Two people standing or sitting in an L-arrangement, on the other hand, still sustain an exclusive interactional domain, but they also have ready access to the outside world, although which segment of the outside world each of them looks at is different. When two people are arranged in a side-by-side, both face toward the same outer world in the same way; they both can look simultaneously at the same segment of the outer world. They have a kind of mutual access to each other that is different from the access people in L-arrangements or face-to-face arrangements have.

Although studies of the relationship between the nature of the interaction and the spatial arrangement adopted by the gathering are sparse (see Batchelor & Goethals, 1972; Kendon, 1973; Sommer, 1969), there are enough observations, it would seem, to show that there is a systematic relationship between spatial arrangement and mode of interaction. This means that p will not only tend to adopt particular arrangements for particular kinds of interaction, but, by adopting a given spatial arrangement or by moving to a position and orientation that might suggest a spatial arrangement of a particular sort, can thereby propose an interactive relationship of a particular sort. Spatial positioning, is available as an expressive resource for interactants. It serves as a condition of interaction, and, for this reason, when used as an expressive resource by a participant to effectively propose an interaction of a certain sort, such propositions are treated as belonging to the unofficial or 'not-counted' stream of action. Spatial and orientational positioning, thus, serves well as a device by which expectation and intention can be conveyed.

The function of spatial orientational positioning in interaction is further illuminated by a consideration of the way in which spatial arrangements in F-formations may change. Such changes in arrangement occur in conjunction with changes in other aspects of the interaction, suggesting that they constitute one way in which frame changes in interaction are marked. It is common to observe that people maintaining an F-formation may alter their positions relative to one another, thereby changing the arrangement, sometimes several times, during the course of the encounter. These arrangement changes may be associated with external factors, such as a change in the environment of the encounter, or with changes in the participants of an F-formation. In the latter case they may be seen to reflect the adaptations to external changes through which the participants maintain or preserve the conditions of the interaction. On the other hand, such changes may also reflect re-arrangements associated with changes in the interaction itself. As the kind of interaction the participants are engaging in alters, so the spatial orientational framing appropriate for the interaction alters. This has been described elsewhere in analyses of opening encounters (Kendon & Ferber, 1973). Thus it has been observed how participants commonly frame their salutations with one spatial-orientational arrangement and move to another arrangement for the conversational interaction that follows. Examples have also been described in which shifts in conversational topic are accompanied by shifts in spatial orientational arrangements. In these cases, it would seem, the shifts appear to serve not so much as a means whereby different interactive conditions are created, as much as a means whereby different phases of the conversation are marked as distinct phases.

It is now seen how participants may employ spatial orientational manoeuvres as a means of testing out each other's alignments to a given interpretative frame or as a means of finding out if the other is willing to change to a new one. A participant wishing to change to a new frame may precede any actual change by small manoeuvres in the direction of the new position that would, if completed, constitute a position suitable for a different kind of arrangement. He may observe whether his co-participants will follow his lead. If they are willing to do so, instead of remaining in the same position or making manoeuvres that would compensate for the new move that p made, they will make incipient moves complimentary to p's own, thus indicating that they will move to the same new position. Such preframe change negotiations can be observed especially when the closing of an encounter is being negotiated. Thus one may observe how one or other of the participants in a standing conversational group begin to step back, increasing the distance between himself and the others. Such a move may be taken as an announcement of a wish for closure. Step-backs by the other participants may follow, and these serve to acknowledge the closure bid, thus making it possible for all of the participants to move into the closing phase of the conversation together.

Frame Attunement

By entering into and maintaining an F-formation, participants are able to keep each other continuously informed that they are present to a current occasion of interaction. Furthermore, as we have just seen, by showing themselves responsive to each other's adjustments in spatial orientational positioning, participants can show whether they are ready or not for alterations in the frame of the situation. However, spatial-orientational positioning (or postural arrangements, in seated groups, as dealt with by Scheflen, 1964, and McDermott et al., 1978), does not itself constitute the action of interaction. It functions as background. Spacing and orientation provide the scaffold for whatever it is that the interactants are to do together. It is for this reason that it can serve so well in the process of frame attunement.

What interactants do together is accomplished through actions, such as utterances, either spoken or gestural, or manipulative actions, directed at the other, that are regarded by the participants themselves as moves of some sort in the interactive process they are engaged in. Such actions always have an address. We now discuss some aspects of what is involved in establishing address for such actions.

ADDRESS

If p is to address an action to another he commonly will not do so unless he has reason to suppose that there is an audience for its receipt. Although fellow participation in an F-formation in itself usually provides p with good grounds for supposing that such a fellow participant will serve as an audience for any action he may address to him, it seems that usually more is required. Commonly what happens is that two or more participants establish an utterance exchange system between them such that any utterance produced within it by any of the participants is understood as being relevant for any other participant within the system. It is within such utterance exchange systems that we find the rules of turn-taking to have their application. Other sorts of action exchange may be set up, of course. For example, in an essay published in 1975, I analysed the pattern of action in a 'kissing round' (Kendon, 1975). Exchanges of kisses probably have a different sort of organisation from exchanges of utterances. Likewise, systems of action that can be observed in dancing may be different (consider the reciprocated but simultaneous swaying in the courtship dance of the Melpa of New Guinea, as described by Pitcairn and Schleidt, 1976). However, in these cases, as in the case of utterance exchanges, it would seem that the participants have to establish, within the frame of the agreement that is implied by the maintenance of an appropriate formation, a further agreement that their utterances or other actions are relevant for specific individuals in a particular way.

A number of studies have now been published which include detailed analyses of how utterance exchange systems are established and maintained. The main conclusions are summarised briefly here. It should be noted that all of the examples (Goodwin, 1981; Kendon, 1967, 1970, 1973) were taken from conversational occasions involving several people and concerning instances in which a speaker addressed his utterance to a specific other member of the gathering. Although all participants in the F-formation that constituted the gathering were able to hear what was being said, only two individuals were participants in the utterance exchange system at the time of the observation. What was at issue in these investigations was how speaker and recipient came to know that they were indeed together in a specific utterance exchange system.

It emerges from these analyses that participants in utterance exchange systems interrelate their behaviour in a number of ways that are distinctive for them and different from the way their behaviour is related to other participants in the gathering within which the utterance exchange system is contained. Typically both speaker and direct recipient orient their bodies at least partially toward one another so that one might say of them that they have established a sub-segment of their transactional segments in mutual overlap. They repeatedly focus their eyes upon one another and, from time to time, their eyes meet. The orientation of the body, especially the head, is toward one another but, it is the intermittent aiming of their eyes at one another that is one of the principle ways participants in utterance exchange systems indicate to whom their actions are addressed. It should be noted that it is insufficient to say of participants in utterance exchange systems that they 'look at one another'. The looking is rarely continuous, and sometimes it is very brief and takes up but a small proportion of the time that the exchange system lasts. At the very least we may expect to see such eye-address at the beginnings and endings of the system's establishment. What is characteristically observed, it should be noted, is that in aiming the eyes at another person, the speaker or listener's head repeatedly returns to the same position (oriented to the other member of the address system) and pauses. When the eyes are not directed to the other member of the address system, they are not directed to anyone else in the gathering. Indeed, one of the ways in which a recipient of an utterance may re-direct the speaker to another recipient is by looking away from the speaker and towards another member of the gathering. Goodwin (1981) reported some closely analysed examples that show how a speaker re-addresses his utterance in midstream if his initial recipient focuses his eyes elsewhere in the gathering. Sigman (1980) reported examples of what he called *conversational fission:* when two people speak at once, two separate utterance exchange systems may be set up within the same F-formation if other members of the gathering separately orient to the two speakers. I have studied a series of instances from a psychiatric case discussion film in which the chairman interrupts the case presentation from time-to-time to get complementary information on the case being discussed from the social worker who was involved. Having evoked replies from the social worker, he then re-directs the address of these replies by himself looking elsewhere in the group to another member.

If the utterer, then, can begin marking the address of an utterance by patterning his gaze in such a way that his eyes are aimed repeatedly at his addressee, the recipient must co-operate by maintaining an appropriate patterning of orientation on his part. Recipients, furthermore, are commonly observed to display a heightened congruency of posture with that of the speaker, and they also tend to exhibit a particular set of gestures, such as head nods and changes in facial expression that are patterned in systematic relation with the structuring of the speaker's speech. If the recipient ceases to display these actions and, in particular, as we have seen, if the recipient alters the target of his eyes to that of another member of the gathering, the utterance exchange system will alter in who it includes or it will come to an end. Since only those within a current utterance exchange system have rights as 'next speaker' within that system, if it changes its membership mid-stream, this also has implications for who may follow as next speaker.

RHYTHMICAL CO-ORDINATION

A further feature of the relationship between participants in an utterance exchange system may now be noted: It has been reported by several observers that speaker and recipient in such a system often exhibit rhythmical co-ordination in their flow of action. In an earlier report (Kendon, 1970), I described how, as an utterance exchange system got underway, the recipient's postural adjustments that ensued as he settled into a listening posture were rhythmically paced with the structure of the speaker's speech. Furthermore, as the speaker drew his utterance to a close, his recipient (who had evoked the utterance by a previous question) began to move again in time with the rhythmical organisation of the speaker's speech, anticipating the precise moment the speaker completed his utterance.

Rhythmical co-ordination of action with that of another, it would seem, is also part of the way in which participants display that they share the same perspective on the interaction. Elsewhere (Kendon, 1973) I have described an example of the establishment of an utterance exchange axis in which the participants established their orientations to one another prior to any exchange of utterance. What was at issue here was the observation that the head turns of the two participants were synchronised, as if the recipient of the first utterance in the system was already forewarned that she was to be the addressee. Close analysis showed how the recipient had begun to track the movements of the speaker well before he began to turn to her (while he was taking a drink from his coffee cup). Evidently, by following him in her movements, she was able to establish her attentiveness to him and thus establish her openness to an address from him. We suggested there, as we do here, that moving into synchrony with another person is one of the devices by which a person can indicate to the other that he wishes to establish an action exchange system with him, without making an explicit request. As we said in 1973:

> Initiating an axis of interaction with another person is always a somewhat risky business, since there is the possibility that the other party does not wish to reciprocate. By simply picking up on the rhythm of another person's movements one can establish a connexion with him which at the same time does not commit one to an explicit initiation. If, after having joined the rhythm of another, no reciprocal move is made, it is possible to continue as if no attempt had been made to initiate an axis. (Kendon & Ferber, 1973, pp. 59–60)

The point is that a person can modulate the rate at which he is carrying out any line of action that he may happen to be engaged in in such a way that it conforms to the rate of another. By allowing his actions to be performed at the same pace as those of another he lets the other know of his attentiveness and openness to him without in any way altering the nature of what he is doing.

SALUTATIONS

Such rhythmic matching can also be seen between persons who are not members of the same F-formation but who merely happen to be co-present, and here it appears to lay the foundations for an exchange of salutations between people. In a detailed study of greetings in which the aim was to analyse the way people organised their behaviour as they carried out salutational exchanges, the question of how greeting sequences are initiated was examined in some detail (Kendon & Ferber, 1973). It was recognised that before p could engage in a greeting with q, p would not only have to sight q and decide whether q was sufficiently unengaged to be open to a greeting from him, but would also have to receive some indication from q that q was ready to receive a salutation from him. Careful examination of a number of filmed greetings, in which the film record included a record of the activities of both parties before any salutational exchange could be observed, showed that in a number of cases, co-ordination of behaviour could be observed well before the salutational exchange. The greetings analysed in the study were recorded at an open-air party. The greetings in which presalutational behavioural co-ordination could be observed took place between guests at the party who were not well acquainted and who were, thus, not in a position to be certain of how each would recognise the other.

In several examples we were able to see how, prior to any exchange of salutation, p would place himself and orient himself in relation to q, but then not make any move toward q or begin upon any address until after q had begun to turn his head toward p. Often p would allow his gaze to meet q's gaze, and this seemed to provide the clearance p needed to embark upon an approach and a salutation. However one sometimes observed a carefully orchestrated eye-avoidance in which p, who has taken the initiative by orienting to q, leaves it to q to begin the salutational exchange, but not until he has let q know he is attentive to him by looking away from him synchronously with q's looking at him. Thus:

MG is standing talking to JF while about eight feet away from him at JF's right GG is standing, arms folded, not engaged in any focused interaction. At frame 71340 GG turns his head left slightly, focusing his eyes on MG while, at the same time, MG turns his head, focusing his eyes on JF. GG thus looks at MG as MG looks away from GG. Then MG rotates his head *away* from JF into an orientation in which he would catch GG's eyes. Simultaneously GG looks away from MG. MG then directs a distance salutation to GG, who looks back at him and replies with a salutation. Here, thus, GG, by synchronizing his head turns with movements of MG may be said to have signalled his wish for contact. However he consistently avoided catching MG's eye . . . thus making it possible for MG to take the initiative in greeting him, should he so wish.(Kendon & Ferber, 1973, p. 615)

Functions of Salutational Exchanges

The study of greetings just discussed showed that greeting encounters can be analysed into a number of stages, from the initial perception of the other, through announcement of intention to greet, acknowledgement of this and the management of the mutual approach, to the procedures by which the gestures of the close salutation are enacted. Through these stages we can see how the attention of the two participants is progressively calibrated as they come to agree upon a greeting encounter and upon the precise form that the close-salutation will take.

The close-salutation of greeting itself has a number of characteristics that are worth remarking upon from the point of view of the theme of this essay. Salutational exchanges, which can take a wide variety of forms, serve a number of functions. They serve to acknowledge a social relationship, and the form of the salutation itself also makes reference to the nature of the social relationship. They may be further modulated to reflect the degree of pleasure involved in the meeting of the greeters, the formality of the occasion, the amount of time that has elapsed since last meeting, and the like. We may also note that salutations also serve as a bracketing ceremonial. They come at a point of change in social access and often serve to establish the beginning of a social occasion of some sort. It seems that the peculiar character that salutations have are nicely adapted to this function.

First, we may note their very high degree of conventionalisation. The forms that are employed for any given kind of greeting within a given communication community are highly restricted. There is a high degree of conventionalisation of gesture, as in verbal forms. This has the important consequence of greatly reducing the degree of uncertainty of the participants about what may ensue at the moment of salutation. Second, it is to be noted that salutational forms, as acts, are often structured in such a way that the two participants do the same thing simultaneously (as in a handshake or an embrace) or in a closely co-ordinated sequential relationship (often observed in the verbal exchanges of salutation). Furthermore, the gestural forms of salutation often include rhythmically organised body contact such that the two participants come to share directly in the same rhythmical organisation of action. This has the consequence of rhythmically aligning the two individuals and, in consequence of the simultaneity of action, the salutational exchange is brought to a close simultaneously. This means that the two individuals are thereby placed upon an equal footing with respect to one other.

Not uncommonly, salutations are followed by utterance exchanges that, despite having the outward form of serving the exchange of information, either follow a set form or consist of informational exchange utterances concerning a topic on which all participants are already fully informed (as in weather conversation). Here again we may observe how use is being made of a ready-made format for interaction. The participants are thus able to further align the rhythmical organisation of their actions and their expectations in regard to one another.

It is often said that greeting exchanges, because they are so highly conventionalised, are good examples of *phatic communion*: they do not serve any informational function. It should be pointed out however, that because the forms of gesture and utterance are so highly conventionalised, the participants are able to pay careful attention to the manner of their performance, and from this much information can be derived. From the firmness or limpness of the handshake, from its prolongation or its curtailment, much can be inferred about the attitude of the other person. From the manner in which the conventional utterances are said and the readiness of responses, inferences can be made about many aspects of the person's social status, origins, background, current state of mind, and attitude in the present situation and toward his co-participant. This is a matter of widely held common knowledge in our own society, and ettiquette books are fully aware of it, often providing quite detailed instructions on how to perform salutations so that the proper impression will be conveyed. Youssouf, Grimshaw, and Bird (1976), in their account of Tuareg greetings, also bring this point out clearly. They show how the Tuareg, greeting one another in the lonely Sahara, follow a set routine. It is clear from their account, however, that this routine is of great informational value because it provides much opportunity for detailed observation of the other, thus allowing each to organise his expectations and thus his plans for action in the encounter that will follow.

When actions and interaction routines are conventionalised, they are provided with a detailed format for their performance. However, this format never amounts to a complete specification for action. The performer is always left with some latitude in how he may organise his actions in relation to the format. This means he has available to him a way of communicating in an inexplicit fashion that would not otherwise be open to him if the format were not conventionalised. Conventionalisation of salutational forms has thus a specifically informational function that it gains by virtue of its conventionalisation. By employing conventional forms, participants make available to each other a way of conveying information in just the manner that is needed if they are to convey to one another information about their interpretative frames.

Gradients of Explicitness

Hitherto we have written as if a sharp distinction is to be drawn between main-track action, on the one hand, and action that is treated as background and functions as communication "unofficially", on the other. It will be seen, however, that there is in fact no such sharp distinction. Spatial manoeuverings and orientation changes, for example, can be performed in such a way that they are regarded as incidental to whatever else a person is doing. However, they may be performed in a way that makes them more salient than usual, that draws attention to them in their own right. They can become, thus, attended to and regarded as explicit. We may also observe that actions such as gestures, which are usually treated as main-track actions, may be modified in their performance in such a way that they are perceived as tentative, incomplete, or even so ambiguous in their form as to be treated as incidental. Morris et al. (1979) have described circumstances in which obscene or insulting gestures may be modified in form so that they are recognised as gestures only to the person to whom they are addressed but which, to an onlooker such as policeman, may be explained away as an incidental, nongestural action. It would seem, in fact, that participants have considerable ability to modify their actions in such a way as to obscure them as merely incidental or to make them conspicuous as deliberately intended, officially meant actions to which the actor is officially committed. Participants may modulate their actions along what we might term *a gradient of explicitness,* according to circumstance.

We may sometimes observe such modulations of action along this gradient of explicitness when one member of a gathering wishes to induce a change in the working consensus of the interaction or, perhaps, to leave it altogether. Consider the circumstance where one participant wishes to leave ongoing interaction. We have already explained above why departures are sometimes very difficult to manage. The difficulty arises, because participants become jointly responsible for maintaining the working consensus so that the withdrawal of any one person may lead to the collapse of the whole occasion. For someone to take their leave it first becomes necessary for them to alter the prevailing agreement in the group so that their departure will be appropriately interpreted. This means, as we have seen, that the person must engage in actions of some sort that announce his intentions in advance, so that the other participants may adjust their own expectations to the point where an explicit departure becomes possible. Under circumstances of this sort one often observes the individual who would like to leave perform a series of actions, each one more explicit than the next. At small social gatherings where food or drink is being consumed, one may often observe the following sort of sequence. The guest who wishes to initiate a departure may begin by finishing up whatever consumable he may have. Draining one's glass, stubbing out one's cigarette, and cleaning the last crumbs from one's plate can all serve to announce that one has finished consuming and that, accordingly, this reason for remaining is removed. Such actions may then be followed by shifting posture to a sitting position from which rising to one's feet could very easily be accomplished. Further actions might include looking at one's watch or glancing at one's spouse to indicate wish for departure. Such actions may, of course, be performed with varying degrees of conspicuousness. Eventually, if the guest does not succeed in getting any acknowledgement of these moves from the others, he may have to resort to much more explicit actions. However, the point to recognise is that there can be many steps between action that is considered to be completely incidental and action considered by others to be explicitly expressive. It seems evident that participants have a lively appreciation of these differences and often can be observed to exercise considerable delicacy as to the place on this gradient of explicitness that they choose to operate.

Conclusion

Human interaction is built upon promises. As Peter Wilson (1980) wrote, because the human species is the most generalised of all primates, the forms of its social relationships are the least specified in advance.

In terms of adaptation, this means that it is possible for any individual to live with any others but, most important, it means that an enormous problem has to be met by all individuals, namely, that little information about another individual can be known in advance and hence an individual has little advance information that will help him coexist with others on a predictable basis. . . . if the human individual is to coexist with other such individuals, he must arrive at some ground for expectation and reciprocation. He must work out some common form of agreement about actions and reactions, one with some degree of reliability. (p. 43)

In this essay we have sought to show how various features of observable behaviour in face-to-face interactional contexts can function as a way of providing the advance information that anyone proposing to interact with another has to have. We have suggested that, in a number of different ways, people can make manifest their intentions, and they can reveal which of the situational principles they are responding to in advance of their taking any action that is explicitly addressed to another and would count as making a definite move in an interactional sequence. We have argued that for this to be possible, people must be able to deal with each other's behaviour either as fully intended and explicit or as unintended and inexplicit, and to treat the information they receive in this way as unofficial. There seems to be a tacit understanding that certain behavioural forms shall be treated in this way even though, as we have seen, participants are fully able to control much of their own behaviour that is treated as unintended; they are fully aware that the information that it may make available can be deliberately provided. It is our contention that the willingness and ability to treat each other's behaviour in this differential fashion is an essential component in the skill or competence of any normal participant in face-to-face interaction.

References

Batchelor, J. P., and Goethals, G. R. (1972). Spatial arrangements in freely formed groups. *Sociometry, 35,* 270–279.

Cutting, J. E., and Eimas, P. D. (1975). Phonetic feature analyzers and the processing of speech in infants. In *The Role of Speech in Language.* (J. F. Kavanagh & J. E. Cutting, eds.). MIT Press: Cambridge, Massachusetts.

Deutsch, R. D. (1977). *Spatial Structurings in Everyday Face-to-Face Behavior: A Neurocybernetic Model.* Association for the Study of Man Environment Relations: Orangeburg, New York.

Frake, C. (1964). How to ask for a drink in Subunam. *American Anthropologist, 66,* Part II, 127–132.

Frake, C. (1975). How to enter a Yakan house. In *Sociocultural Dimensions of Language Use*. (M. Sanches & B. Blount, eds.). Academic Press: New York.

Freedman, N., and Hoffman, S. P. (1967). Kinetic behavior in altered clinical states: Approach to objective analysis of motor behavior during clinical interviews, *Perceptual and Motor Skills, 25,* 527–539.

Garfinkel, H. (1963). Trust and stable actions. In *Motivation and Social Interactions*. (O. J. Harvey, ed.). Ronald Press: New York.

Goffman, E. (1955). On face-work. *Psychiatry, 18,* 213–231.

Goffman, E. (1957). Alienation from interaction. *Human Relations, 10,* 47–59.

Goffman, E. (1959). *Presentation of Self in Everyday Life*. Doubleday: New York.

Goffman, E. (1961). *Encounters*. Bobbs-Merrill: Indianapolis.

Goffman, E. (1963). *Behavior in Public Places*. The Free Press of Glencoe: New York.

Goffman, E. (1974). *Frame Analysis*. Harper and Row: New York.

Goodwin, C. (1981). *Conversational organization: Interaction between speakers and hearers*. Academic Press, New York.

Hall, E. T. (1964). Silent assumptions in social communication research. *Publications of the Association for Research in Nervous and Mental Disease, XLII,* 41–55.

Hall, E. T. (1966). *The Hidden Dimension*. Doubleday: Garden City, New York.

Hall, E. T. (1968). Proxemics. *Current Anthropology, 9,* 83–108.

Kendon, A. (1967). Some functions of gaze direction in social interaction. *Acta Psychologica, 26,* 22–63.

Kendon, A. (1970). Movement coordination in social interaction: Some examples described. *Acta Psychologica, 32,* 100–125.

Kendon, A. (1973). The role of visible behavior in the organization of face-to-face interaction. In *Social Communication and Movement:Studies of Interaction and Expression in Man and Chimpanzee*. (M. von Cranach & I. Vine, eds.). Academic Press: London.

Kendon, A. (1975). Some functions of the face in a kissing round. *Semiotica, 15,* 299–344.

Kendon, A. (1977). Spatial organization in social encounters: the F-formation System. In *Studies in the Behavior of Social Interation*. (A. Kendon, ed.). Peter De Ridder Press: Lisse, Holland.

Kendon, A. (1978). Differential perception and attentional frame: Two problems for investigation. *Semiotica, 24,* 305–315.

Kendon, A., and Ferber, A. (1973). A description of some human greetings. In *Comparative Ecology and Behaviour of Primates*. (R. P. Michael & J. H. Crook, eds.). Academic Press: London.

Liberman, A. M. (1980). An ethological approach to language through the study of speech perception. In *Human Ethology: Claims and Limits of a New Discipline*. (M. von Cranach, K. Foppa, W. Lepenies, & D. Ploog, eds.). Cambridge University Press: Cambridge.

McDermott, R. P. Gospodinoff, K., and Aron, J. (1978). Criteria for an ethnographically adequate description of concerted activities. *Semiotica, 24,* 245–275.

McDermott, R. P., and Roth, D. R. (1978). The social organization of behavior: Interactional approaches. *Annual Review of Anthropology, 7,* 321–345.

Marler, P. (1980). Development of auditory perception in relation to vocal behavior. In *Human Ethology: Claims and Limits of a New Discipline*. (M. von Cranach, K. Foppa, W. Lepenies, & D. Ploog, eds.). Cambridge University Press: Cambridge.

Morris, D., Collett, P., Marsh, P., and O'Shaughnessy, M. (1979). *Gestures*. Stein and Day: New York.

Pitcairn, T. K., and Schleidt, M. (1976). Dance and decision: An analysis of a court-
ship dance of the Melpa, New Guinea. *Behaviour, 58,* 248–316.
Scheflen, A. E. (1964). The significance of posture in communication systems. *Psy-
chiatry, 27,* 316–331.
Scheflen, A. E., and Ashcraft, N. (1976). *Human Territories: How We Behave in Space–
Time.* Prentice Hall: Englewood Cliffs, New Jersey.
Sigman, S. J. (1980). *An analysis of conversational "fission" and "fusion".* Paper for Amer-
ican Anthropological Association 79th annual meeting, Washington, D. C., De-
cember 6th.
Sommer, R. (1969). *Personal Space: The Behavioral Basis of Design.* Prentice Hall: En-
glewood Cliffs, New Jersey.
Wilson, P. (1980). *Man, The Promising Primate: The Conditions of Human Evolution.* Yale
University Press: New Haven.
Yousouff, H., Grimshaw, A., and Bird, C. (1976). Greetings in the desert. *American
Ethnologist, 3,* 797–824.

10

The Analysis of Human Action: Current Status and Future Potential

G. P. Ginsburg

The purpose of this chapter is to offer an assessment of the current status of human action research and to speculate about its future as a paradigm, especially with regard to social psychology. I start by identifying what I see as important themes in action research that tie it together in a coherent fashion, and then comment on the extent to which those themes are reflected in contemporary theory and research.

Central Themes in the Analysis of Human Action

As noted elsewhere (Ginsburg, 1980a,b,c), I think there is an emerging model of human action reflected in the research and writing of many people. The model differs in important ways from the conventional rhetoric of experimental social psychology. On the other hand, it seems to reflect developments that are already under way in that discipline but have not yet been articulated systematically (Backman, 1979).

The basic features of the emerging model will appear very familiar to investigators working within a human action perspective: Human action is situated, it is structured both temporally and hierarchically, and it is meaningful but the meanings are continually modifiable. Furthermore, the persons in whose actions we are interested are active agents, but their agency is subject to biological and social constraints; and these persons operate from the active agency or "first person" perspective of a continually present interval of reality. That reality is always partly specified but partly specifiable still further. In addition, many of the actions we wish to explain are joint actions, produced by the coordinated activity of two or more persons, and they can only be understood as joint products. Also, persons are capable of monitoring both their actions and the stylistic appearance of their actions. And finally, many of the purportedly intrapersonal processes of the person actually are social in nature, in both the rather obvious case of accounting and the less obvious cases of emotion and cognitive processes. It also is worth noting that the focus of the model is on action; that is, the phenomena to be explained are actions, not persons or organisms or societies.

The basic features listed above have several implications that further specify the model. First, to understand an action it is necessary to understand the situation in which it is known or believed to occur, and to identify the temporal and hierarchical structure of the action. This must be done from the active agency perspective of each of the persons involved, including that of the investigator. This leads to a second implication: namely, that first-person perspectives in human action include third-person perspectives regarding others in the situation. Therefore, any explanation of action must include both; if the theory operates only from the perspective of the observer, a third-person perspective, then that observer exists outside the theory and *his* actions are not explainable by it.

This in turn implies that the methodology of the analysis of action is part of the substance that theories of action are designed to explain. Therefore, the explanation of an action must include the investigative and explanatory actions of the investigator. In more concrete terms, the situation of investigation and the actions of the investigator must be included in the explanation of the actions under study.

Another implication concerns reductive and holistic theorizing. Since all actions occur in situations and as parts of acts, and since descriptions of the acts and situations are necessary for an adequate description of the constituent actions, the analysis of action involves holistic theorizing. Furthermore, since all actions are composed of constituent parts, at least some of which must be included in a description of the action, the analysis of action involves reductive theorizing as well. Both reductive and holistic theorizing are defensible; but the important point is that the analysis of action necessarily includes both.

The analysis of action has still another important feature. The analysis relies much more heavily on part–whole descriptions than on linear, cause–effect descriptions. This is tied to the point about reductive and holistic theorizing, and it also is reflected in the relatively greater reliance on descriptive research in the analysis of action and in the relatively less frequent use of the controlled experiment. This derives in part from the tendency to record whole episodes, in order to capture the act/action structure, and then to subject those records to detailed analysis. This can be contrasted against the experiment, which ordinarily involves an input/output, predictive orientation.

A comparison of these more methodological features of the action perspective with the conventional prescriptions and practices in social psychology is illuminating. In social psychology, causal explanations usually are emphasized; the rhetorical idiom of the discipline is the third person, as though the investigator were somehow above the world he is explaining; the methodology in general and the investigator's actions in particular are usually not part of the substantive theoretical statements; the situational and cultural contexts of the actions usually are ignored and not specified in the technical descriptions; and emphasis is placed on the discovery of context-free, universal processes. All in all, this adds up to quite a difference—at least, it seems to.

On the other hand, Carl Backman (1979) has suggested that these themes "constitute an emerging paradigm that already is evident in social psychological practice, even though most social psychologists may still think in terms of an earlier one" (p. 301). I think he is right, and I'd like to provide some examples.

Some Examples of Action Themes in Current Social Psychology

There are several general statements of human action theory in the current literature. Two volumes dealing with goal-directed action theory appeared recently (von Cranach & Harré, 1982; von Cranach et al., 1982). Harré has published a number of important statements about ethogenics that incorporate an action perspective, and two of them—his book with Secord (Harré & Secord, 1972) and his chapter in the Berkowitz *Advances* series (1977)—have received a fair bit of attention from social psychologists. My own discussion of the structural analysis of situated action was published a few years ago in the *Review of Personality and Social Psychology* (Ginsburg, 1980a). But these are isolated examples that have not truly been incorporated into the daily practice of social psychologists. On the other hand, there are many examples of human action themes emerging in particular substantive areas of research.

In the study of emotion, for example, James Averill's analyses of grief (1968) and anger (1977), and his recent statement of a constructivist theory of emotion (1980), are outstanding blends of concepts and processes drawn from physiology, ethology, evolutionary biology, psychology, sociology, and anthropology. He construes emotion as a transitory role—actually an improvisation—which includes the person's appraisal of the situation and which is interpreted by the person as a passion rather than an action. He distinguishes between impulsive emotions such as joy, conflictive emotions such as romantic love or anger, and transcendental emotions in which the self–other distinction is lost. Emotions are construed as complex biosocial phenomena that emerge and exist over time and serve important social functions, such as relief from responsibility; in essence, they are acts to be understood in terms of their sequential and hierarchical contexts of occurrence and their component actions.

Probably the most dramatic emergence of concerns compatible with a human action perspective in social psychology proper is in the broad area of attribution research. More and more attention is being given in the obviously social nature of attributions. They are coming to be seen as social acts with social consequences, as being tied to social roles, and as involving reflective stances; and questions are being raised about the importance of the contexts in which attribution data are generated and whether those data are generalizable to natural settings. Kelley (1980), for example, now acknowledges that attributions probably are made only rarely in the daily life of a person, and that the making of an attribution requires a reflective stance; he calls for further research into the conditions under which reflective stances are taken and attributions are made. In addition, several people have examined attributional activities as self-presentational phenomena and have found support for that interpretation (House, 1980; Sagatun & Knudsen, 1977; Tetlock, 1980), with the further implication that the context of study makes a difference in the outcome.

An interesting illustration of the importance of context and act/action structure when interpreting human activities concerns the currently popular "fundamental attribution error" (Jones, 1979; Ross, 1977), a putatively cognitive phenomenon wherein the cause of an action is over-attributed to the behaving person and under-attributed to situational factors. Several aspects of the common theoretical interpretation of the phenomenon have been called into question by Lee Hamilton (1980). Based in part on her earlier paper (1978) in which she links attributions to social roles and their interpersonal obligations, Hamilton argues that the fundamental attribution error is an error only from a particular perspective—that of a scientist, whose role-related task it is to *explain*. That is the role of a psychologist, and that is the perspective imputed by psychologists to research subjects. On those grounds, a subject's over-attribution of causation to the dispositions of the actor would be an error. However, the *lawyer's* role carries with it a concern about sanctions; the role-related task is the expression of a responsibility judgment. From the perspective of concern about sanctions, the over-attribution of causal responsibility to personal dispositions might not be an error. Instead, it could reflect a rational judgment, based upon the question, "Could the actor have done otherwise?" Hamilton's argument is important not only because it stresses context, but also because it brings the experimenter's actions into the world of phenomena he is investigating by emphasizing the fact that the experimenter usually assumes an underlying model of rationality.

A conceptualization of attribution of responsibility as social action also has been suggested by Fincham and Jaspars (1980). After an excellent review and conceptual analysis of the attribution of responsibility, Fincham and Jaspars end their paper by stressing the importance of language and of social context in attribution research. These same issues had been raised on occasion in the past (Ginsburg, 1976), but not in formal publications. Fincham and Jaspars cite earlier work by Kanouse (1971) that strongly implied that inductive and deductive inferences about responsibility were influenced markedly by the particular choice of verbs to express an action, and by the grammatical structure of the language. Based on that work plus some other studies, Fincham and Jaspars suggest that previous attribution findings should be re-evaluated because linguistic variables were ignored; that there is no single veridical description of an action sequence, so any particular description contains a selective set of implicit attribution material and emphasizes which cues will be used for attributions; and that even with nonverbal material, the subject's thinking processes have a linguistic structure that will affect his attributions of responsibility much as linguistic material might. And as to the social context, Fincham and Jaspars make several interesting comments: "attributions are necessarily situated in a context, which is often social, while the social nature of the attribution . . . is likely to be context dependent." Also, the attribution . . . judgment itself is a social act," but since most attribution studies are done in the laboratory, responsibility attribution generally has been "studied as a cognitive process and not as . . . a *social* act with all that . . . implies" (1980, p. 133). The compatibility of those comments with a human action perspective is obvious.

Self-presentation is another major and rapidly expanding area in social psychology that is compatible with a human action perspective. The compatibility stems largely from the self-presentation conception of the person as an active agent who tries to present himself in such a way as to achieve positive evaluations from a real, implied, or imagined audience and to avoid negative evaluations. A variety of phenomena ordinarily explained in terms of intrapsychic processes, such as attitude change and attributional behaviors, have been explained at least as elegantly using one or another of the current self-presentational theories (Baumeister, 1982; Schlenker, 1980, 1982; also see Paulhus, 1982, for a sophisticated experimental demonstration; and see Swann, 1985, for a closely related treatment of the self-verificational activities of the person). But active agency is not the only ground of compatibility with a human action perspective. Self-presentational models, in their focus on real, implied, or imagined audiences, necessarily draw attention to the contexts and the situated meanings of actions, themes that are important in action theory as well. In addition, the current self-presentational models share with action theory an interest in the processes of human action. In fact, there is a growing interest in processes, both social and cognitive, throughout social psychology; and there is a growing awareness of the importance of social context and the fact of joint action by active agents. As a further illustration, Krauss (1980), in a paper intended for presentation at the meeting of the Society of Experimental Social Psychology at Stanford, cited Grice, Searle, and a variety of experiments to make the point that face-to-face communication is an active, constructive process in which both parties contribute to the creation of shared meanings. Krauss expressed serious concern about the applicability of the information-processing metaphor, which appears useful in cognitive psychology, to the study of *social* cognitions and communicative processes; he felt that the metaphor does not reflect the reality of human communicative interaction. He suggested that social psychologists must capture that reality in their theories and research procedures if they wish to understand it, even at the cost of sacrificing some theoretical rigor and experimental control. That was an impressive message, given at the bastion of experimental social psychology by a productive and highly respected member of the experimental community.

Other areas, outside of traditional social psychology, which reflect movements compatible with an action perspective are child development and microsociology. In child development, there are at least three basic trends that contain action themes. One is the detailed analysis of interchanges between children or between mother and infant in an effort to understand the structure of the interchange itself (Kaye, 1982; Stern, 1977). Another is the longitudinal study of mother–infant pairs, using the interchange as the object of analysis; the interchange is examined for the development of patterns of closely coordinated actions, and these are used as a basis for understanding the emergence of later actions, such as speech acts (e.g., Bruner, 1975). The third trend is the use of rules and social conventions as central concepts in the development of morality among children (Turiel, 1979; Weston & Turiel, 1980).

In microsociology, explicit attention has been given to the structure of specific episodes, as in the classical paper by Kendon and Ferber (1973) on greetings and the papers by Albert and Kessler (1976, 1978) on ending social encounters. It also is in this area that some of the more interesting works on rules and on negotiated interactions have been published, such as Hochschild's (1979) discussion of rules that guide feelings and emotions, and Luckinbill's (1977) study of the negotiation of a homicide between the eventual victim and the perpetrator. In general, microsociology has been an important contributor to the content of theories of action (see Kendon, Chapter 9, this volume, for references to Goffman; also see McCall & Simmons, 1978, 1982), and it is not surprising to find action themes reflected in that literature.

In terms of substantive research, then, at least some of the themes of action analysis can be found readily in social psychology and related fields. But in addition, there is some indication of a more inclusive compatibility in the re-emergence of general systems theories in psychology (Powers, 1973) and social psychology (Carver & Scheier, 1982). Theories of human action and contemporary general systems theories differ in the explicit reliance of the latter on the reduction of discrepancies via feedback loops as the primary self-regulating control process; and they also differ somewhat in focus—systems theories serve as models of the behaving entity, while action theories attempt to model the activities and include the behaving entities in the model as producers of those activities. Systems theories are essentially monadic, while action theories need not be; and action theories give more sophisticated attention to the nature and contexts of human action (e.g., Harré, 1982). On the other hand, both approaches stress temporally extended processes of activity initiation and regulation, both make use of hierarchical as well as sequential structures, and both emphasize the importance of goals.

The similarities and compatibilities discussed to this point have dealt with substantive and theoretical themes; but we can also find examples of methodological and procedural features of action analysis that may turn out to be at least as important as the more substantive examples. Three or four of these are worthy of note.

First, there seems to be an increase in the number of studies that record interchanges, usually on videotape, and then analyze the tapes.

This is critically important; we are developing relatively permanent records of the detailed, real-world processes of interest. I return to this point below.

Second, social psychologists appear to be increasingly concerned about the generalizability of laboratory data, and many are moving out into the field while others are using simulated techniques in a more sophisticated manner to reveal role and rule structures.

Third, there has been a considerable increase in sophistication about the social nature of the laboratory experiment, including awareness of subject roles, experimenter bias, demand characteristics, implicit contracts between subject and experimenter, and so on (see *Personality and Social Psychology Bulletin,* 1977; also Ginsburg, 1979).

The one action analysis theme that is virtually unrepresented in current, conventional research is a metatheoretical one: the replacement of causal rhetoric by part–whole descriptions. Attention has been given to the relative merits of causal and reasons descriptions of such actions as attributions (e.g., Buss, 1978), but the value of causal descriptions and their status as ultimate scientific statements has not been seriously questioned, except by Ossorio (1978)—and by me (1980a,b,c), after having been persuaded by Ossorio's argument. This, too, is a point to which I return.

In summary, so far, many of the themes of action analysis are reflected in the current work and concerns of social psychologists and related scientists in North America. Both substantive and procedural or methodological features are apparent, but they have not yet been tied together in a coherent fashion.

The Future of Action Analysis in Social Psychology

Given that many of the major features of action analysis are represented in current, empirical social psychology in North America, it is possible that within the next decade, some form of action analysis will emerge as a dominant empirical paradigm in the study of social interaction. However, reason for the ascendance is unlikely to be recognition by our colleagues of the greater plausibility and elegance of human action theory, although such theories may indeed be more plausible and more elegant. Instead, the reason is likely to be technological—specifically, the emergence of a relatively inexpensive video technology. It is my view that video will become as important a tool for behavioral sciences as the microscope proved to be for the biological laboratory sciences (Bakeman & Ginsburg, 1981).

In 1981, I conducted a computer search of the *Psychological Abstracts* and found that in the preceding 5 years, over 100 studies were published that had made use of video. Video was used in two equally popular ways—as a recording technology and as a stimulus medium through which material was presented to subjects. The use of video to record interchanges not only offers the opportunity for analysis of interaction processes, but it also provides a relatively permanent record of what actually occurred and makes it difficult for an investigator to ignore those occurrences in favor of a more simple theoretical interpretation.

As to the stimulus use of video, investigators now have the opportunity to present whole scenarios to their subjects, instead of written descriptions that often were susceptible to multiple interpretations. However, as I have pointed out before, one must be very careful in the use of scenarios; there are several decisons investigators must make in order to use role-played scenarios effectively (Ginsburg, 1979; also see von Cranach, 1982, for caution in the use of role playing, and Cronkite, 1980, for further recommendations). Furthermore, I think that role-play scenarios, including those presented over video, are likely to be misleading if they are used to investigate subjective states of people; their real value is in shedding light on roles, rules, values, and other features of the situation (again, see Ginsburg, 1979, especially p. 143). Still, these cautions not withstanding, the use of video to present complex social stimuli, such as action sequences, in a controlled fashion is an important development.

Another important development is the continuing miniaturization of video equipment, making it smaller, lighter, more efficient—in short, making it portable. This was reflected in the fact that 28 studies using video were done outside of the experimental laboratory (including clinics, hospitals, and nurseries, however). The ability to obtain permanent observational records in the ordinary daily settings of the people of interest is certain to alter the basic nature of the data with which social psychologists work, and that in turn will alter the models through which we work with those data.

On the other hand, changes in scientific practice sometimes occur slowly in social psychology. If we look at studies that used video and dealt with infants and children, we find that half of them were done in natural settings, but of the video studies done with adults, including college students, only 9% were done in natural settings—the other 91%

were done in experimental settings. This is largely a difference between developmental psychology and social psychology. Nevertheless,
the increasing availability and portability of video equipment will have
what I think is its inevitable effect in social psychology, just as it is
doing in the developmental area, and within the decade the analysis
of videotaped episodes of action will become commonplace (Bakeman
& Ginsburg, 1981; Rosenfeld, 1982; Wallbott, 1982). Moreover, the
ability to present scenarios over video, altering them in carefully controlled fashion, will allow us to test a wide range of hypotheses concerning rules, roles, values, and character management. These two
major technological developments will require and facilitate analyses
of recorded episodes, involving hierarchical as well as sequential organization, rules, roles, shared meanings, personal and group identities, character management, and so on—in short, the structural
analysis of situated action.

   That is mostly for the future, although we see evidence of it today
in the study of such topics as social development, face-to-face interaction, speech and discourse, microsociology, and even collective behavior. However, the analysis of action as it has emerged to date has
a number of problems that require attention, and I would like to express my concerns about some of these.

Some Problems in the Analysis of Action

   There are several areas of concern in the human action paradigm as
I see it taking shape. The following sections give detailed attention to
the four that I think are particularly pertinent.

RESEARCH DESIGN AND THE
LOGIC OF INFERENCES

   The analysis of action, as actually practiced, usually involves the
recording of an episode on tape or film, followed by repeated detailed
analyses of the record at various levels ranging from situated acts to
micromovements. Such an analysis has been dubbed "structural" by
Duncan and Fiske (1977), who recommend it highly, as do I. In fact,
I consider it to be a *necessary* step in behavioral science research. However, the structural analysis of a completed episode carries with it a
serious threat to defensible inference, primarily in terms of the related
issues of verifiability and falsifiability. The structural approach contains no controls for the rejection of alternative explanations or even

for the accuracy of the description. A comparison of structural analysis with properly designed manipulative experiments will illustrate the problem.

A manipulative experiment assigns subjects randomly to the cells of the design, thereby protecting against unidentifiable biases being mistaken for experimental effects; it also builds alternative explanations into the design through the use of control groups; it clearly identifies the temporal order of occurrence of the manipulation and the dependent variable measurement; and it enhances the statistical sensitivity of the design to detect differences by maximizing the homogeneity of subjects within each cell and the heterogeneity of the subjects in different cells. The orientation of the investigator is predictive and synthetic.

In a structural analysis, the observed interactions seldom are assigned randomly to the conditions of observation, seldom are alternative interpretations built into the design of the study, and rarely is there a discrete and temporally controlled manipulation that allows for unambiguous inferences about direction of influence. Furthermore, the action investigator's perspective invariably is analytical and retrospective. There is no question about what will happen, since it already *has* happened. The investigator observes the tape of the action episode repeatedly, often until he develops a sense of understanding of the episode and its component parts. The understanding will strike him as plausible; it will "feel good"—but possibly only because of its familiarity. In fact, this is especially likely to occur if the investigator has a prior belief about the episode and searches the tape within the framework of that belief; such a self-fulfilling effect has been demonstrated experimentally (Snyder & Uranowitz, 1978).

There are very serious problems associated with the skeptical evaluation of the understandings we gain from structural analysis and with the consideration of alternative interpretations. I think it is a mistake to reject the predictive, experimental approach. Instead, those of us who are engaged in the structural analysis of situated action must on occasion use predictive designs to assess the adequacy of the understandings we gain from structural analyses. The two should be used in tandem.

My comments to this point have dealt with what some people call "internal validity" (Campbell & Stanley, 1966; Cook & Campbell, 1979), in contrast to "external validity" or "generalizability" (Cronbach et al., 1972; Mitchell, 1979). The structural analysis of human action actually has an advantage, at least in principle, with regard to generalizability because the actions of interest are construed as embedded in larger acts, in situations, and in a cultural matrix of meanings, values, and personal and group identities. Therefore, if we take seriously the specification of the hierarchical structure and social contexts of action, we automatically specify the circumstances to which our understandings apply (Argyle et at., 1981, make a similar point)—provided, of course, that our understandings are defensible in the first place.

An important procedure for identifying situational and cultural contexts of a situated action is role playing. I mentioned earlier that role playing can be quite useful if used carefully and with an appropriate objective. The objective is the identification of the roles, rules, and other situational and cultural states of affairs within which the actions of interest are believed to occur. The objective should *not* be the identification of cognitive or affective processes of the actors; that information, if it is relevent at all, is not accessible in reliable fashion to role playing procedures (see Ginsburg, 1979, especially pp. 127–144).

PERSPECTIVES

Another matter that needs clarification concerns perspectives. Both John Shotter (1980) and Ragnar Rommetveit (1980) have addressed this point, and my comments derive in large part from their discussions. A person is capable of two social perspectives: he can be an observer, either of himself or of another person, and he can have the perspective of an active agent. The active agent is *always* in a brief interval of reality, which, as I noted earlier, is partly specified and always specifiable further (see James', 1890, discussion of the specious present). Persons always have an active agency perspective, even while they are observing and commenting on someone's actions.

It is important to recognize that the active agent perceives the world—physical and social—within which he exists and upon which he acts; he perceives it directly. He does not infer its existence; he sees it, smells it, hears it, and feels it. And the world that he perceives as an active agent includes other behaving persons and their action. Sometimes, however, the active agent takes on an *observer* perspective with respect to the actions around him—whether someone else's actions or his own. The observer perspective does not involve merely "observing" (seeing, hearing, or otherwise perceiving) someone's actions, but also developing or offering commentaries about it. In other words, the observer perspective involves a reflective component, and that reflective component constitutes the necessary base for such acts as inference and judgment. This reflective component characterizes contemporary social psychological theories, to the relative exclusion of the continually present reality of the active agent. It also is a common feature of action theories. Yet, it probably applies to a relatively small proportion of time in the daily lives of most people.

In my opinion, the implicit assumption of an ever-present observer perspective is seriously misleading. Instead of assuming the ubiquity of the observer perspective, we must specify the conditions under which it is likely to occur. Kelley (1980) has now proposed exactly this issue regarding attributions, and I argued a few years ago (Ginsburg, 1976) that attributions are likely to be produced in the presence of actions that shock us or puzzle us—that is, in the presence of enigmatic actions, or when other people or the situation call for explanations or accounts. Furthermore, attributions that are offered as accounts for one's own actions are likely to occur under conditions of at least moderate self-focused attention, the conditions for which are fairly well known (Duval & Wicklund, 1972; Schlenker, 1980). More generally, any violation of expectations—but not their confirmation—might set the conditions for observer perspective (Kahneman, 1973, p. 131, makes the point about conscious experience, a concept closely linked to observer status).

In any case, I think that our efforts must be turned to discovery of the conditions under which the observer status emerges. Interestingly enough, we are well along in our specification of the consequences of the occurrence of observer perspectives, since that is what most of our social psychological theories deal with, and that is what most theories of action deal with as well. The ramifications of incorporating the active agent perspective into our theories have not been worked out and are not clear to me, but I think that this, too, must receive our attention.

SITUATIONS

The situation is still another problem area in action theory. The concept is central to any action analysis, but its technical definition and use have not become standardized. This may be due in part to a confusion over the implications of such ideas as the subjective definition of the situation and the life space, both of which imply that situations exist functionally only as they are construed by actors. A somewhat different approach might be helpful.

To begin with, situations should be conceptualized as if they really do exist, and not just as subjective entities in the mental worlds of persons. Argyle (1979; Argyle et al., 1981) takes the same position, and he proposes the existence of several component features, all mutually interdependent, which *constitute* a situation: constitute, not "produce." The features include goals, roles, rules, action elements and sequences, physical features, and requisite skills and knowledge. It is important to recognize that these features are features of situations, not of persons. This is quite different from recent attempts to characterize situations in terms of the reactions of people to them or in them—that is, to characterize a situation in terms of the affective and evaluative reactions of people (Forgas, 1982), or in terms of the kinds of people who would behave in specified ways in the situation (Bem & Funder, 1978; Bem & Lord, 1979).

The claim that concepts such as goals and skills can refer to features of situations rather than properties of persons needs some elaboration. Skills and knowledge are *required* by situations; in order for a particular situation to be manifested, the persons whose activities are bringing it into manifest existence must have the requisite skills and knowledge. Otherwise, a different situation will be brought into being. Goals present a different problem: they should be construed as accomplishments *afforded* by a situation (see Knowles & Smith, 1982; McArthur & Baron, 1983; Smith et al., 1983a,b—all apply a Gibsonian ecological model of perception to the social world). Once goals are construed as affordances, the conceptual difficulty evaporates, although we are then faced with the empirical problem of identifying the goals afforded by a given situation at various points in the flow of action. Argyle and his colleagues have dealt with this in their recent book on situations (Argyle et al., 1981).

On the other hand, different people have different objectives and different views with regard to a given situation. The constituent features of a situation may have very different meanings for the various people who are interacting within it. At first glance, these factors appear to militate against the position that situations should be conceptualized as real entities that exist independently of any particular individuals and to necessitate a retreat to the notion of subjective definition. However, on closer examination, individual differences in objectives and views are compatible with the realist position.

It certainly is true that people usually have reasons for entering a situation, and they may even have specific objectives in mind. Furthermore, there is considerable evidence that people differ in the kinds of situations they prefer to enter (Snyder, 1982; Snyder & Gangestad, 1982). Nevertheless, once a situation is entered, its participants operate under a variety of constraints. If the situation is highly routinized, such as a formal or informal ceremony or ritual, the participants act in accord with a relatively explicit framework of roles and rules, and have available to them a limited set of potential accomplishments that are fairly well known to the participants and to other members of the local culture familiar with such situations (this contention is compatible with the empirical studies reported by Argyle et al., 1981, especially in the sections concerned with roles, rules, and goals). Thus, the reasons that a person has for entering a situation may be important in his choice of the situation, but those reasons are eclipsed in their importance as determinants of his situated actions by the role/rule/goal structure of the situation, at least with regard to highly routinized situations. This argument is similar to the conclusion drawn by Kahneman (1973) that the task-related effort displayed by a person in task performances is related largely to the demands imposed by the task rather than to motivational variables, although the latter appear to be important determinants of the person's decision to undertake the task.

If a situation is not highly routinized, then negotiation among the participants may occur that will establish a set of jointly attainable goals and a related role/rule structure (Backman, 1981, and McCall & Simmons, 1978, 1982, discuss this under the rubric of negotiation of role identities). In any case, whether a situation is structured through prior routinization or contemporary negotiation, it indeed and necessarily has a structure as a fact of its existence, and that structure will include a set of acknowledgeable and to a lesser degree acknowledged potential for accomplishments and related role identities. The potential accomplishments afforded by the situation need not be mutually compatible. Some may be explicitly incompatible, as in a car sale situation: the salesman attempts, legitimately, to get a high price for it. In addition, as in the latter case, bargaining and compromise may be part of the characteristic structure of the situation. And obviously, some potential accomplishments may be attainable only by holders of certain roles in a situation; and some affordances may be known only to certain role holders. But nevertheless, the situation provides potential accomplishments to the participants and those potential accomplishments are not so mutually incompatible as to prevent the pursuit of coordinated lines of action by the participants.

To this point, I have argued as though there were only one situation for any episode of action; but in fact, different participants in the episode generally have different perspectives, and the situation may be somewhat different from each of those perspectives. In principle, there may be as many situations (usually differing only in small details) for a given situated action as there are perspectives involved in the action. However, most situations within a culture are common and recur frequently, and for such situations there will be a high degree of knowledge of a "generalized other" (Mead, 1934) sort, so that a common situation will exist as a core sufficient to the pursuit of coordinated action. That is, a temporarily *shared* reality will exist or will be negotiated. In fact, the attempts by interactors to establish temporarily shared realities in order to interact sensibly (Rommetveit, 1980) can be seen as part of the process of minimizing situational differences due to perspectives. Moreover, negotiations and the other efforts to establish a core situation or shared reality are not restricted to the start of an action episode. Instead, the unfolding situated actions have to be monitored continually to ensure that the situation as initially established continues to exist and be realized. Sometimes, a temporary "reframing" is necessary, during which repairs are undertaken. A nice example of such a re-framing is given by McAdam et al. (1981), who observed children in dyadic competition re-frame the situation from competition to cooperation to correct a feature that precluded continuation of the competition. After the repair, the children went back to the competitive framework.

The social psychological research situation is particularly interesting with regard to this sort of analysis. For example, we might have two interacting subjects and an investigator observing them on a video monitor. The two interactors will perceive each other and their relationship as parts of the situation, but neither will perceive himself as part of the situation unless he explicitly takes on a reflective, observer stance toward himself. For practical purposes, those two subjects may be operating within a temporarily shared reality, a common core situation, albeit an ambiguous one with considerable uncertainty. The experimenter, however, is part of a different situation that includes both of the interactors, toward whom he has an observer perspective, and himself, whom he experiences only un-self-consciously from an active agency perspective. Thus, the research situation actually is at least two situations, and the actions performed within the setting must be interpreted accordingly. Moreover, if the two subjects are required to act in a coordinated fashion, they will take steps to create a satisfactorily shared situation, even if one had not been established at the outset. But notice that, as a rule, the experimenter does not join them in the effort to create a shared understanding of the experimental situation, except occasionally at the end of the session during debriefing (and even then, debriefing only allows for the establishment of a shared reality after the completion of the session, rather than at the outset; see Ginsburg, 1979, pp. 123–124, regarding deception experiments). That may be an unfortunate omission, since, as Harré and Secord (1972) have argued, an adequate accounting for actions may require negotiation among the participants, each with his own perception and understanding of the situation.

Therefore, the setting for an episode of situated action will entail different situations for the different perspectives represented in it. One of the ubiquitous problems of interaction is the establishment of satisfactorily shared situations, and this often is accomplished by means of standardized situations, conventions, rules, rituals—and, of course, by negotiations. Does all of this reflect a sloppiness of the "situation" concept? No—it merely reflects the reality of our world.

INTRAINDIVIDUAL PROCESSES

Another matter that particularly concerns me is the common assumption of the existence and continuous operation of intraindividual processes—that is, of such cognitive processes as thinking, inferring, planning, and judging. This is an extremely complex issue, but I do think that the assumption of continuous operation of reflective cognitive processes is wrong. This already is being acknowledged with regard to other putative cognitive processes that are claimed to subserve our recognition of another person's intent or the meaning of his action. From my point of view, a much more exciting endeavor will be to search for the patterns in situated actions that constitute the intention, rather than to continue to locate intentions in the "minds" of behaving persons and to rely on cognitive inference processes by an observer to allow those intentions to become known.

Arguments along this line are beginning to appear in social psychology (Knowles & Smith, 1982; McArthur & Baron, 1983; *Personality & Social Psychology Bulletin,* 1980; Smith et al., 1983a,b), and they have existed for some time in psychology as a minority view variously labeled "direct perception" or "ecological psychology" and based heavily on the work of J. J. Gibson (1950, 1966, 1979; see also Shaw & Bransford, 1977). One line of research in this area is especially worthy of note because of its implications for the direct perception of intention and other dispositional features. Johansson (1973) studied the perception of motion by placing strips of reflective tape on the wrist, elbow, knee, and ankle joints, and along the hips and shoulders of an actor, videotaping the action in motion, and playing the tape back to observers using a monitor set at high contrast so that the observers could see only moving patches of light. The observers had little difficulty discriminating the kinds of biological motion involved, such as walking and running. Building on Johansson's procedure, Kozlowski and Cutting (1977) demonstrated that observers could readily recognize the gait of a walker (again using a dynamic light-point display), and the observers could identify their friends on the basis of the same sort of information. More recently, Runeson and Frykholm (1982) reported a series of dynamic light-point display studies that demonstrate that observers could perceive how heavy a person about to lift a box expected that box to be, simply from his preparatory movements (and those were revealed only as moving points of light). The studies also revealed that the weight lifter could not deceive observers about the weight of the box; and when he tried to deceive them, they were likely to perceive his deceptive intention. Finally, the gender of moving actors, adults and prepubertal children, was reasonably well identified (75%) on the basis of the moving light patterns, and it was found that the actual gender of the actor and the gender that the actor was trying (under instructions) to display were independently—but simultaneously—perceived.

This general line of work has important implications. First, the ordinary environment of events and objects changing and moving over time within contexts contains invariant patterns that can be detected—that is, perceived directly—without inference or other cognitive processes. Second, the perceiver may be incapable of identifying the invariant pattern to which he was perceptually sensitive, either because he doesn't have the words for it or because he literally is unaware of it. Third, dispositional qualities of active agents, such as a person's intended movements and at least some of his attempts at deception, are contained as complex patterns in the person's actions and are directly, non-inferentially perceivable. It is not necessary to posit reflective and inferential cognitive processes to account for this sort of knowing. On the other hand, it is necessary to discover the ecological invariants to which we are sensitive as perceivers and that are informative about such interpersonally important qualities.

The growing incorporation of speech act and discourse theory and research into the mainstream of social psychology (e.g., Clark, in press) might allow the extension of the ecological model to discourse as well. If so, then it might lead to the discovery that intentions are contained in the patterned structures of situated speech acts and are detectable— directly perceivable—without further inferential, cognitive processing. Although occasional and tentative moves in this direction have been attempted (Ginsburg, 1982, pp. 16–21), I am not aware of any concerted attack on the issue (but cf. Kreckel, 1982).

It should be noted that the detailed theory of goal-directed action presented by von Cranach and his co-workers (see this volume; also see von Cranach et al., 1982, for the full statement) deals forthrightly with the roles of conscious and non-conscious cognitive processes in the unfolding of action. From their view, action-related cognitions are not continuously consciously present but emerge into phenomenal experience sporadically, and it is to the credit of investigators that they attempt to specify the conditions under which that occurs. Von Cranach et al. also raise the question (1982, Chapter 8) of the sources of social knowledge that may be entailed in action-related cognition and make reference to social representations (*representations sociales;* see also Chapter 9 in von Cranach et al., 1982). This bears on an important matter in action theory and in social and general psychology. Specifically, it may well be that the cognitive contents and processes being revealed by contemporary research as causally involved in interpersonal transactions and individual experience and predispositions (e.g., equity, just-world, and consistency principles) are not causal generators of those phenomena. Instead, they may well be systematic statements of cultural criteria for giving intelligible accounts of action and of cultural strategies for conducting intelligibly accountable actions (see Ginsburg, 1982, pp. 6–9, for a more complete discussion).

This is not to say that people's actions are not guided by such rules as equity. Indeed, people may frequently employ those rules in making a decision or in choosing an action. But making a decision or choosing an action would be a discrete act in its own right, and the exercise of such a rule as equity would be part of the act rather than a cause of it. Discovery of the functions served by the phenomenal experience of a thought about such a rule in the generation of an act requires a simultaneously hierarchical and sequential conception of action, since the phenomenal experience must be located temporally in the action sequence, linked to other events and states in the sequence, and to the more grossly and more minutely organized levels of the action as well (the act being undertaken and the detailed movements, respectively). Action theory provides the opportunity for such an approach, even facilitates it; other, more conventional theories in psychology and social psychology do not.

CAUSAL EXPLANATIONS

Finally, I am concerned about the continued use of a causal vocabulary and the touting of causal explanations as being ultimately desirable. I find that incompatible with a conceptualization of situated action that embodies the themes I mentioned at the beginning of this chapter, including structural analysis as a preferred methodology. It seems to me that the embedded and retroactively revisable nature of the phenomena of interest—situated actions—simply requires a part-whole description along the line of what Ossorio (1978) calls a configuration description as the explanatory device. That is, a causal explanation or "cause-effect formulation" is in fact a form of description offered by the speaker or writer to an audience. Cause-effect descriptions are a formula for talking about the world, and within the scientific community and certain other subcultures, a particular status is conferred by convention on such statements. But that formula does not specify facts, is not a necessary formula, and has no special validity as a representation of the real world. It is most appropriate for prediction, unilateral manipulation of the real world, and representation of before/ after contingencies when we deal with processes that extend over time. It is not necessarily a useful formula for explanation.

In fact, Ossorio (1978; also see Ginsburg, 1980c, for a summary) notes two deleterious aspects of cause-effect descriptions. First, they are given in the traditional impersonal (third person) idiom. Second, they are seriously incomplete descriptions in that the fact that the experimenter had to produce the "cause" and that by doing so he subsequently caused the effect is omitted from the substantive causal description and placed in the methodology section. It is in that sense that the conventional causal description is defective as a representation of the real world, including the real world of the experiment.

On the other hand, a "configuration description" represents the state of affairs on which it focuses as either some sort of object with process constituents (e.g., a small group, with its communication processes) or as some sort of process with object constituents (e.g., ingratiation as a process, with relevant persons as objects). The investigator can start with either a process or object configuration description, and then compose and decompose to larger and smaller states of affairs, respectively. Translating to the vocabulary of the present chapter and volume, configuration descriptions specify the component parts and processes of a line of action, and the larger entities and processes of which the focal line of action is a component.

In other words, it is the configuration, or part-whole, descriptive formulation that is most appropriate for the hierarchical models that characterize human action theories—and in my opinion, any kind of explanatory theory in the behavioral sciences. Moreover, it has been argued by Peter Schwartz and James Ogilvy at SRI International in Stanford (no references available) that a new paradigm is emerging in a variety of fields, from physics and chemistry through the behavioral and social sciences. The paradigm involves interdependencies rather than linear causalities, multiplicity of perspectives, multiplicity of simultaneously existent hierarchies ("heterarchy"), and the absence of any single objective perspective. This clearly seems compatible with a part–whole descriptive approach to the structural analysis of situated action.

Conclusion

The objectives of this chapter were to review basic themes in the analysis of action, to comment on their appearance elsewhere in psychology and social psychology, and to look a little bit into the future. In closing, I want to reiterate some points I made earlier: the structural analysis of action is an exciting approach and it is developing rapidly, although its final shape is not yet clear. Moreover, there is a good chance that it will become a dominant paradigm for the analysis of interaction, in part because of technological advances that capture the details of interchanges over time. This makes it difficult for investigators to ignore the real activities in the process of producing an explanation. The enforced attention to reality will be frustrating, but ultimately it will benefit us all.

References

Albert, S., and Kessler, S. (1976). Processes for ending social encounters: The conceptual archaeology of a temporal place. *Journal for the Theory of Social Behavior, 6,* 147–170.

Albert, S., and Kessler, S. (1978). Ending social encounters. *Journal of Experimental Social Psychology, 14,* 541–553.

Argyle, M. (1979). Sequences in social behavior as a function of the situation. In *Emerging Strategies in Social Psychological Research.* (G. P. Ginsburg, ed.). Wiley: Chichester.

Argyle, M., Furnham, A., and Graham, J. (1981). *Social Situations.* Cambridge University Press: Cambridge.

Averill, J. R. (1968). Grief: Its nature and significance. *Psychological Bulletin, 70,* 721–748.

Averill, J. R. (1977). *Anger.* Nebraska Symposium on Motivation.

Averill, J. R. (1980). A constructivist view of emotion. In *Theories of Emotion.* (R. Plutchik & H. Kellerman, eds.). Academic Press: New York.

Backman, C. W. (1979). Epilogue: A new paradigm. In *Emerging Strategies in Social Psychological Research.* (G. P. Ginsburg, ed.). Wiley: Chichester.

Backman, C. W. (1981). Attraction in interpersonal relationships. In *Social Psychology: Sociological Perspectives.* (M. Rosenberg & R. H. Turner, eds.). Basic Books· New York.

Bakeman, R., & Ginsburg, G. P. (1981). The use of video in the analysis of human action. Unpublished manuscript.

Baumeister, R. F. (1982). A self-presentational view of social phenomena. *Psychological Bulletin, 91,* 3–26.

Bem, D. J., and Funder, D. C. (1978). Predicting more of the people more of the time: Assessing the personality of situations. *Psychological Review, 85,* 485–501.

Bem, D. F., and Lord, C. G. (1979). Template matching: A proposal for probing the ecological validity of experimental settings in social psychology. *Journal of Personality and Social Psychology, 37,* 833–857.

Bruner, J. S. (1975). The ontogenesis of speech acts. *Journal of Child Language, 2,* 1–19.

Buss, A. R. (1978). Causes and reasons in attribution theory: A conceptual critique. *Journal of Personality and Social Psychology, 36,* 1311–1321.

Campbell, D. T., and Stanley, J. C. (1966). *Experimental and Quasi-Experimental Designs for Research.* Rand-McNally: Chicago.

Carver, S. C., and Scheier, M. F. (1982). Control theory: A useful conceptual framework for personality-social, clinical, and health psychology. *Psychological Bulletin, 92,* 111–135.

Clark, H. H. (In Press). Language use and language users. In *Handbook of Social Psychology.* (3rd ed.) (G. Lindzey & E. Aronson, eds.). Addison-Wesley: Reading, Massachusetts.

Cook, T. D., and Campbell, D. T. (1979). *Quasi-Experimentation: Design and Analysis Issues for Field Settings.* Rand McNally: Chicago.

Cranach, M. von. (1982). The psychological study of goal-directed action: Basic issues. In *The Analysis of Action: Recent Theoretical and Empirical Advances.* (M. von Cranach & R. Harré, eds.). Cambridge University Press: Cambridge.

Cranach, M. von, and Harré, R. (Eds.) (1982). *The Analysis of Action: Recent Theoretical and Empirical Advances.* Cambridge University Press: Cambridge.

Cranach, M. von, Kalbermatten, U., Intermühle, K., and Gugler, B. (1982). *Goal-Directed Action.* Academic Press: London.

Cronbach, L. J., Gleser, G. C., Nanda, H., and Rajaratnam, N. (1972). *The Dependability of Behavioural Measurements: Theory of Generalizability for Scores and Profiles.* Wiley: New York.

Cronkite, R. C. (1980). Social psychological situations: An alternative to experiments? *Social Psychology Quarterly, 43,* 199–216.

Cutting, J. E., and Kozlowski, L. T. (1977). Recognizing friends by their walk: Gait perception without familiarity cues. *Bulletin of the Psychonomic Society, 9,* 353–356.

Duncan, S. D., Jr., and Fiske, D. W. (1977). *Face-to-Face Interaction: Research, Methods, and Theory.* Erlbaum: Hillsdale, New Jersey.

Duval, S., and Wicklund, R. A. (1972). *A Theory of Objective Self-Awareness.* Academic Press: New York.

Fincham, F. D., and Jaspars, J. M. (1980). Attribution of responsibility: From man the scientist to man as lawyer. In *Advances in Experimental Social Psychology,* Vol. 13. (L. Berkowitz, ed.). Academic Press: New York.

Forgas, J. P. (1982). Episode cognition: Internal respresentations of interaction routines. In *Advances in Experimental Social Psychology,* Vol. 15. (L. Berkowitz, ed.). Academic Press: New York.

Gibson, J. J. (1950). *The Perception of the Visual World.* Houghton-Mifflin: Boston.

Gibson, J. J. (1966). *The Senses Considered as Perceptual Systems.* Houghton-Mifflin: Boston.

Gibson, J. J. (1979). *The Ecological Approach to Visual Perception.* Houghton-Mifflin: Boston.

Ginsburg, G. P. (1976). *Attributions.* Lectures to NATO Summer School, University of Oxford: Oxford.

Ginsburg, G. P. (1979). The effective use of role playing in social psychological research. In *Emerging Strategies in Social Psychological Research.* (G. P. Ginsburg, ed.). Wiley: Chichester. pp. 117–154.

Ginsburg, G. P. (1980a). Situated action: An emerging paradigm. In *Review of Personality and Social Psychology,* Vol. 1, (L. Wheeler, ed.). Sage: Beverly Hills, California. pp. 295–325.

Ginsburg, G. P. (1980b). Epilogue: A conception of situated action. In *The Structure of Action.* (M. Brenner, ed.). Basil Blackwell: Oxford.

Ginsburg, G. P. (1980c). Psychology and the real world. *Journal for the Theory of Social Behaviour, 10,* 115–129.

Ginsburg, G. P. (1982). The structural analysis of primary relationships. Paper presented at the First International Conference on Personal Relationships, Madison, Wisconsin. July 18–23.

Hamilton, V. L. (1978). Who is responsible? Toward a social psychology of responsibility attribution. *Social Psychology, 41,* 316–328.

Hamilton, V. L. (1980). Intuitive psychologist or intuitive lawyer? Alternative models of the attribution process. *Journal of Personality and Social Psychology, 39,* 767–772.

Harré, R. (1977). The ethogenic approach: Theory and practice. In *Advances in Experimental Social Psychology,* Vol. 10, (L. Berkowitz, ed.). Academic Press: New York. pp. 284–314.

Harré, R. (1982). Theoretical preliminaries to the study of action. In *The Analysis of Action: Recent Theoretical and Empirical Advances.* (M. von Cranach & R. Harré, eds.). Cambridge University Press: Cambridge.

Harré, R., and Secord, P. F. (1972). *The Explanation of Social Behavior.* Rowman and Littlefield: Totowa, New Jersey.

Hochschild, A. R. (1979). Emotion work, feeling rules, and social structure. *American Journal of Sociology, 85,* 551–575.

House, W. C. (1980). Effects of knowledge that attributions will be observed by others. *Journal of Research in Personality, 14,* 528–545.

James, W. (1890). *The Principles of Psychology.* Holt: New York.

Johansson, G. (1973). Visual perception of biological motion and a model for its analysis. *Perception and Psychophysics, 14,* 201–211.

Jones, E. E. (1979). The rocky road from acts to dispositions. *American Psychologist, 34,* 107–117.

Kahneman, D. (1973). *Attention and Effort.* Prentice-Hall: Englewood Cliffs, New Jersey.

Kanouse, D. E. (1971). *Language, Labeling, and Attribution.* General Learning Press: Morristown, New Jersey.

Kaye, K. (1982). *The Mental and Social Life of Babies: How Parents Created Persons.* University of Chicago Press: Chicago.

Kelley, H. H. (1980). The causes of behavior: Their perception and regulation. In *Retrospectives on Social Psychology.* (L. Festinger, ed.). Oxford University Press: New York.

Kendon, A., and Ferber, A. (1973). A description of some human greetings. In *Comparative Ecology and Behavior of Primates.* (R. P. Michael & J. H. Crook, eds.). Academic Press: London.

Knowles, P., and Smith, D. L. (1982). The ecological perspective applied to social perceptions: Revision of a working paper. *Journal for Theory of Social Behaviour, 12,* 53–78.

Kozlowski, L. T., and Cutting, J. E. (1977). Recognizing the sex of a walker from a dynamic point-light display. *Perception and Psychophysics, 21,* 575–580.

Krauss, R. M. (1980). Cognition and communication. Paper prepared for presentation at annual meeting of Society of Experimental Social Psychology, Stanford University, October 11.

Kreckel, M. (1982). Communicative acts and extra-linguistic knowledge. In *The Analysis of Action: Recent Theoretical and Empirical Advances.* (M. von Cranach & R. Harré, eds.). Cambridge University Press: Cambridge.

Luckinbill, D. F. (1977). Criminal homicide as a situated transaction. *Social Problems, 25,* 176–186.

McAdam, D., Ross, D., Tanur, J., Uglow, D., Weinstein, E., and Zimmerman, D. L. (1981). Children's development of interpersonal resources. *Social Psychological Quarterly, 44,* 53–58.

McArthur, L. Z., and Baron R. M. (1983). Toward an ecological theory of social perception. *Psychological Review, 90,* 215–238.

McCall, G. J., and Simmons, J. L. (1978). *Identities and Interactions.* (Revised edition). Free Press: New York.

McCall, G. J., and Simmons, J. L. (1982). *Social Psychology: A Sociological Approach.* Free Press: New York.

Mead, G. H. (1934). *Mind, Self, and Society.* University of Chicago Press: Chicago.

Mitchell, S. K. (1979). Interobserver agreement, reliability, and generalizability of data collected in observational studies. *Psychological Bulletin, 86,* 376–390.

Ossorio, P. (1978). *What Actually Happens: The Representation of Real-World Phenomena.* University of South Carolina Press: Columbia.

Paulhus, D. (1982). Individual differences, self-presentation, and cognitive dissonance: Their concurrent operation in forced compliance. *Journal of Personality and Social Psychology, 43,* 838–852.

Personality and Social Psychology Bulletin, 1977, 3, 454–522.

Personality and Social Psychology Bulletin, December, 1980, 6.

Powers, W. T. (1973). *Behavior: The Control of Perception.* Aldine: Chicago.

Rommetveit, R. (1980). On "meanings" of acts and what is meant and made known by what is said in a pluralistic social world. In *The Structure of Action.* (M. Brenner, ed.). Basil Blackwell: Oxford. pp. 108–149.

Rosenfeld, H. M. (1982). Measurement of body motion and orientation. In *Handbook of Methods in Nonverbal Behavior Research.* (K. R. Scherer & P. Ekman, eds.). Cambridge University Press: Cambridge.

Ross, L. (1977). The intuitive psychologist and his shortcomings: Distortions in the attribution process. In *Advances in Experimental Social Psychology,* Vol. 10. (L. Berkowitz, ed.) Academic Press: New York. pp. 174–220.

Runeson, S., and Frykholm, G. (1982). Kinematic specification of dynamics as an informational basis for person and action perception: Expectation, gender recognition, and deceptive intention. *Uppsala Psychological Reports,* No. 324. Department of Psychology, University of Uppsala (Sweden): Uppsala.

Sagatun, I. J., and Knudsen, J. H. (1977). The interactive effect of attributor role and event on attributions. Paper presented at annual meeting of the American Sociological Association, Chicago, September 9.

Schlenker, B. R. (1980). Impression Management: The Self-Concept, Social Identity, and Interpersonal Relations. Brooks/Cole: Monterey, California.

Schlenker, B. R. (1982). Translating actions into attitudes: An identity-analytic approach to the explanation of social conduct. In *Advances in Experimental Social Psychology,* Vol. 14. (L. Berkowitz, ed.). Academic Press: New York.

Shaw, R., and Bransford, J. (Eds.) (1977). *Perceiving, Acting and Knowing: Towards an Ecological Psychology.* Erlbaum: Hillsdale, New Jersey.

Shotter, J. (1980). Action, joint action and intentionality. In *The Structure of Action*. (M. Brenner, ed.). Basil Blackwell: Oxford. pp. 28–65.

Smith, D. L., Knowles, P., and Ginsburg, G. P. (1983a). Conceptions of social stimulation and their effect on social perception processes. Paper presented at the annual meeting of the Western Psychological Association, San Francisco.

Smith, D. L., Knowles, P., and Ginsburg, G. P. (1983b). Reconsidering the information potential of movement and sound in social perception. Paper presented at the annual meeting of the Western Psychological Association, San Francisco.

Snyder, M. (1982). Understanding individuals and their social worlds. Address to the annual meeting of the American Psychological Association, Washington, D. C.

Snyder, M., and Gangestad, S. (1982). Choosing social situations: Two investigations of self-monitoring processes. *Journal of Personality and Social Psychology, 43*, 123–135.

Snyder, M., and Uranowitz, S. W. (1978). Reconstructing the past: Some cognitive consequences of person perception. *Journal of Personality and Social Psychology, 36*, 941–950.

Stern, D. (1977). *The First Relationship*. Harvard University Press: Cambridge.

Swann, W. B., Jr. (1985). The self as an architect of social reality. In *The Self and Social Life*. (B. R. Schlenker, ed.). McGraw-Hill: New York.

Tetlock, P. E. (1980). Explaining teacher explanations of pupil performance: A self-presentation interpretation. *Social Psychology Quarterly, 43*, 283–290.

Turiel, E. (1979). Social convention and morality: Two distinct conceptual and developmental systems. In *Nebraska Symposium on Motivation*. Vol. 25. (C. B. Keasey, ed.). University of Nebraska Press: Lincoln.

Wallbott, H. G. (1982). Audiovisual recording: Procedures, equipment and troubleshooting. In *Handbook of Methods in Nonverbal Behavior Research*. (K. R. Scherer & P. Ekman, eds.). Cambridge University Press: Cambridge.

Weston, D. R., and Turiel, E. (1980). Act–rule relations: Children's concepts of social rules. *Developmental Psychology, 16*, 417–424.

Author Index

Numbers in *italic* show the page on which the complete reference is cited.

A

Abbott, R. D., 117, *168*
Abelson, R. P., 87, 96, *112, 113,* 201, 202, *203, 205,* 208, 209, *228*
Ach, N., 119
Aebischer, V., 24, 57, *58*
Aebli, H., 22, *59,* 65, 73, *82*
Ajzen, I., 197, 198, *204*
Albert, S., 261, *275*
Allport, C. W., 124, 128, *167*
Allport, G. W., 116, 175
Alston, W. P., 86, *112*
Ammann, R., 19, 24, *61*
Anastasi, A., 130, *168*
Argyle, M., 95, *112,* 171, *185,* 209, 211, *227,* 266, 267–271, *275*
Arnold, M. B., 37, *59*
Aron, J., *252*
Ashcraft, N., 239, *253*
Atkinson, J., 218, *227*
Atkinson, R. C., 52, *59*
Averill, J. R., 88, 99, 111, *112,* 257, *275*

B

Backman, C. W., 255, 257, 269, *275*
Bainbridge, L., 68, *82,* 226, *227*
Bakeman, R., 263, 264, *275*
Ballstädt, S.-P., *83*
Bandura, A., 91, *112*
Barker, R. G., 179, *185*
Baron, R. M., 268, 271, *278*
Barthol, G., 117, *168*
Bartlett, F. C., 96, *112,* 200, *203*
Batchelor, J. P., 240, *251*
Baumeister, R. F., 260, *275*
Becker, W. C., 125, *168*
Bedford, E., 86
Bem, D. J., 268, *276*
Berelson, B., 53, *59*

Berlyne, D. E., 111, *112*
Bierwisch, M., 72, *82*
Bird, C., 248, *253*
Black, J. R., *203*
Black, M., 126, *168*
Blank, A., *205*
Bloom, B. S., 121, *169*
Blumenfeld, W., 63, 77, *82*
Blumer, H., 210, *227*
Bower, G. M., 87, 96, *112,* 201, *203*
Bradburn, N. M., 220, *228*
Bransford, J., 271, *278*
Brenner, M., 2, 14–16, 207, 220, 226, *227, 228*
Brewer, M. B., 194, *203*
Brody, B., 127, *168*
Bruner, J. S., 15, *18,* 261, *276*
Brunner, V., 58
Buhler, C., 127, 129, *133*
Bull, N., 37, *59*
Buss, A. R., 262, *276*

C

Campbell, D. T., 125, *168,* 265, *276*
Cannell, C. F., 216, 218, 227, *228*
Canter, D., 2, 11, 12, 14, 172, 174, 175, 177, 178, 180, 182, 184, *185*
Cantor, N., 172, *185*
Carlson, R., 116, *168*
Carr, H. A., 122, *168*
Cartledge, N. D., *83*
Carver, S. C., 89, 100, *113,* 191, *203,* 261, *276*
Cattell, R. B., 116, 124, 128, *168*
Cavallo, V., 70, *82*
Chanowitz, B., 202, *203, 205*
Chapman, J. J., 118, *168*
Chapman, J. P., 118, *168*
Charon, J. M., 211, 214, *228*

Christal, R. E., 123, *169, 170*
Clark, H. H., 272, *276*
Cohen, R. R., 87, 96, *112*
Collett, P., *252*
Constanzo, P. R., 211, *228*
Cook, T. D., 265, *276*
Coombs, C. H., 192, 198, 199, *203*
Cooper, J., *204*
Couch, A., 220, *228*
Craik, K. H., 172, *185*
Cranach, M. von, 2, 3-5, 6, 7, 9, 10,
    12-15, 19, 23, 24, 27, 28, 32, 38,
    47-9, 54, 55, 57, *59-61,* 67, 68, *82,*
    85, 90, *113,* 129, *171,* 172, 175, *186,*
    188, 190, 191, 225, 226, *228,* 257,
    263, 272, 273, *276*
Crockett, W. H., *205*
Cronbach, L. J., *130, 168,* 265, *276*
Cronkite, R. C., 263, *276*
Crowne, D., 220, *228*
Crutchfield, R. S., 130, *169*
Cutting, J. E., 234, *251,* 271, *276, 277*

D

D'Andrade, R. G., 123, 124, *168*
Darwin, C., 179
Davis, K. E., 194, 196, *204*
Dembo, T., 132-135, 140-167, *168*
Deutsch, R. D., 239, *251*
Deutscher, I., 218, *228*
Devaults, S., 180, 181, *186*
De Waele, J. -P., 2, 9-14, 16, 128, 137,
    168
Dickson, W. J., 179, *186*
Dörner, R. D., 22, *59,* 89, 103, 110, *113*
Douglas, M., 183, *185*
Duncan, S. D. Jr., 264, *276*
Duval, S., 267, *276*

E

Eckensberger, L. H., 90, 97, 106, *113*
Edwards, A. L., 117, *168*
Edwards, W., 197, *203*
Eichenberger, E., 55, *59*
Eimas, P. D., 234, *251*
Eiser, J. R., 2, 12-16, 193, 198, 201, *204*
Ellis, A., 117, *168*
Emminghaus, W. B., 90, 97, 106, *113*
Endler, N. S., 117, *168*

Engeli, M., 54, 55, *59*
English, A. C., 130, *168*
English, H. B., 130, *168*
Ericsson, K. A., 52, *59*
Etcoff, N. L., *206*
Eysenck, H., 116

F

Fazio, R. H., 187, *204*
Ferber, A., 241, 245-7, *252,* 261, *277*
Fillmore, C. J., 65, 73, *82*
Fincham, F. D., *204,* 259, *276*
Fischoff, B., 199, *204*
Fishbein, M., 197, 198, *204*
Fiske, D. W., 120, 125, 132, *168, 169*
Fiske, S. T., *206*
Flanagan, J. C., 130, *168*
Folkman, S., *113*
Forgas, J. P., 172, *185,* 268, *276*
Frake, C., 231, *251, 252*
Freedman, N., 234, *252*
Freud, S., 127, 128
Friedmann, A., 176, *185*
Fritsche, B., 77, 79, *82*
Frykholm, G., 272, *278*
Fuhrer, U., 26, *59*
Funder, D. C., 268, *276*
Furnham, A., 95, *112, 185,* 275

G

Galanter, E., *61, 113*
Gallistel, C. R., 89, 90, 100, *113*
Gangestad, S., 268, *279*
Gardner, R. C., 205
Garfinkel, H., 230, *252*
Gerard, H. B., 46, *60*
Gerngross-Haas, G., 182, *185*
Ghiselli, E. E., 117, *168*
Gibson, J. J., 271, *276*
Giller, E. S., 77, *83*
Ginsburg, G. P., 17, 18, 171, *185,* 255,
    257, 259, 262-264, 266, 267, 270,
    272-274, *275-278*
Gleser, G. C., *276*
Goethals, G. R., 240, *251*
Goffman, E., 2, 15, 21, *59, 60,* 230-233,
    252, 261
Goldberg, L. R., 120, 125, *169*
Gollob, H. F., 192, *204*

Goodwin, C., 243, 244, *252*
Görner, R., 71, *82*
Gospodinoff, K., *252*
Gottschaldt, K., 131, *168*
Graham, J., 95, *112, 185, 275*
Greenwald, A. G., 187, *204*
Greenwald, H., 128, *168*
Greenwood, J. P., 130, *168*
Grice, H. P., 260
Grichting, C., 55, *60*
Grimshaw, A., 248, *253*
Groat, L., 173, 178, *185*
Gugler, B., 49, 50, 58, *59, 60, 82, 113, 170*

H

Hacker, W., 2, 5-9, 12, 14-16, 21, 24, 26, 30, 31, *59, 60,* 70, 71, 73, 74, 80, *82,* 90, 100, *113*
Hackman, J. R., 64, 78, *82*
Hakel, M., 123, 124, *168*
Hall, E. T., 240, *252*
Hamilton, V. L., 258-259, *277*
Harré, R., 21, 24, 26, 27, 49, *59, 60,* 128, 129, 137, *168,* 171, 175, 183, *185,* 257, 261, 270, *277*
Harvey, O. J., 193, *206*
Heckhausen, H., 35, *60,* 74, 75, *82,* 90, *113*
Heider, F., 3, *18,* 21, *60,* 191, 192, 194, *204,* 208, *228*
Herrmann, M., 55, *60*
Herzlich, C., 200, *204*
Hewstone, M., *204*
Hilgard, E. R., 31, *60*
Hinde, R. A., 1, *18*
Hoc, J. M., *83*
Hochschild, A. R., 261, *277*
Hoffman, S. P., 234, *252*
Holmes, J. G., 195, *205*
Holt, R. R., 120, *169*
House, W. C., 258, *277*
Huang, L. C., 199, *203*

I

Indermuehle, K., 49, 50, 58, *59, 60, 82,* 113, *170*
Ittelson, W. H., *186*
Iwanowa, A., 80, *82*

J

James, W., 36, *60,* 266, *277*
Janes, A., 73, *82*
Janis, I. L., 104, *113*
Jaspars, J. M. F., 192, 195, *204,* 259, *276*
Johanssen, G., 271, *277*
Jones, E. E., 46, *60,* 194-196, *204,* 258, *277*
Joss, C., 55, *59*

K

Kahn, R. L., 216, 218, 227, *228*
Kahneman, D., 199, *204, 206,* 267, 269, *277*
Kalbermatten, U., 19, 47-50, 55, 58, *59, 60, 113*
Kaminski, G., 26, *60,* 68, 71, *83,* 90, *113*
Kanner, A. D., *113*
Kanouse, D. E., 259, *277*
Karasek, R. A., 79, *83*
Katkin, E., 118, *169*
Kaye, K., 260, *277*
Kellerman, H., *113*
Kelley, H. H., 15, *18,* 194, 196, 199, 200, *204, 206,* 258, 262, *277*
Kelly, E. L., 120, *169*
Kelly, G., 153
Kendon, A., 2, 16, 17, 233, 234, 237, 239-241, 243-246, *252,* 261, *277*
Keniston, K., 220, *228*
Kessler, S., 261, *275*
Kingsbury, F. A., 122, *168*
Kleinbeck, U., 79, *84*
Kleinmuntz, B., 130, *169*
Klinger, E., 54, *60*
Klix, F., 69, *83*
Knight, R. P., 120
Knowles, P., 268, 271, *277, 279*
Knudsen, J. H., 258, *278*
Kohler, W., 132
Kozlowski, L. T., 271, *276, 277*
Krampen, M., 178, *185*
Krauss, R. M., 260, *278*
Krech, D., 130, *169*
Kreckel, M., 272, *278*
Krenauer, M., 89, *113*
Kreuzig, H. W., *113*
Kriz, J., 53, *60*
Kuehne, K., 19, 49, 50, *61*
Kuhl, J., 91, *113*

L

Lalljee, M., 215, *228*
Lang, J., 51, 53, *60*
Lang, P. J., 96, *113*
Langer, E. J., 202, *203, 205*
Lantermann, E. D., 2, 8, 9, 12, 75, *83,* 85, 90, 106, *113*
Laucken, U., 21, *60,* 85, *113*
Launier, R., 87, 94, 97, *113*
Lazarsfeld, P., 129, *169*
Lazarus, R. S., 37, *60,* 87, 94, 97, 104, *113*
Leontjew, A. N., 21, *60*
LePlat, J., 68, *83*
Lerman, D., *114, 206*
Leventhal, H., 96, 99, *113*
Levy-Leboyer, C., 176, 179, *185*
Lewin, K., 116, 129, 132, *169,* 175, 211
Lewis, M., 117, *169*
Liberman, A. M., 234, *252*
Lisch, R., 53, *60*
Locke, E. A., *83*
Lompscher, H., 67, *83*
Lord, C. G., 268, *276*
Luborsky, L., 120, *169*
Luckinbill, D. F., 261, *278*
Luckmann, T., 21, *60*
Luria, A. R., 73, *83*

M

McAdam, D., 270, *278*
McArthur, L. Z., 195, *205,* 268, 271, *278*
McCall, G. J., 15, *18,* 211, 213, 215, *228,* 261, 269, *278*
McDermott, R. P., 239, 242, *252*
Mächler, E., 3, 19, 55, *60*
McNamara, W. J., 130, *168*
McNemar, Q., 120, *169*
Magnusson, D., 117, *168, 169*
Mandl, H., 70, *83*
Mandler, G., 87, 89, 97, 111, *113*
Mann, L., 104, *113*
Marler, P., 234, *252*
Marlowe, D., 220, *228*
Marsh, P., *252*
Matern, B., *82*
Mead, G. H., 15, 270, *278*
Meehl, P., 118, 119, *169*
Menninger, K. A., 120

Mento, A. I., 75, *83*
Michela, J. L., 196, *205*
Miller, A. E., 63
Miller, D. T., 195, *205*
Miller, G. A., 21, *61,* 90, 100, *113*
Miller, R. B., 63, 69, *83*
Mischel, W., 183, *186*
Mitchell, S. K., 265, *278*
Monty, R. A., 77, *83*
Morgenthaler, C., 51, 53, 54, *61*
Morris, D., 249, *252*
Moscovici, S., 24, 38, 57, *61,* 200, *205*
Moser, C., 55, *59*
Mueller, H., 19, 49, 50, *61*
Muliak, S. A., 124, *169*
Murray, H. A., 116, 119, 130, *169*

N

Nanda, H., *276*
Neisser, U., 31, *61*
Nisbett, R. E., 68, *83,* 195, 199, 202, *204, 205*
Norman, D. A., 71, 72, *83*
Norman, W. T., 123–125, *169*
Nowakowska, M., 171, *186*
Nüesch, F., 55, *61*

O

Ochsenbein, G., 53, *61*
Odbert, H. S., 124, 128, *167*
Ogilvy, J., 274
Oldham, G. R., 78, *82*
O'Shaughnessy, M., *252*
Osgood, C. E., 1, *18*
Ossorio, P., 262, 274, *278*
Österreich, R., 74, *83,* 91, 100, *113*

P

Pasini, F. T., 124, *169*
Paulhus, D., 260, *278*
Perkins, 86
Perlmuter, C. C., 77, *83*
Pervin, L. A., 117, *169*
Peters, R. S., 99, *113*
Phillips, D. L., 220, *228*
Piaget, J., 7, 70, *83,* 96, *113*

Pitcairn, T. K., 243, *253*
Pligt, van der, J., 198, *204*
Plutchik, R., 88, *113*
Potkay, C., 127, *169*
Powers, W. T., 100, *113,* 261, *278*
Press, A. N., 192, *205*
Pribram, K. H., *61, 113*
Proshansky, H. M., 180, *186*

R

Raaheim, K., 132, *169*
Rajaratnam, N., *276*
Rapaport, D., 120, 176
Raush, H. L., 130, *170*
Raynor, J. O., 71, *74*
Reither, F., *59, 113*
Richter, P., *82*
Rivlin, L. G., *186*
Roethlisberger, F. J., 179, *186*
Rogers, C., 116, *169*
Rommetveit, R., 266, 270, *278*
Rosenfeld, H. M., 264, *278*
Rosengren, W. R., 180, 181, *186*
Rosenkrantz, P. S., *205*
Ross, D., *278*
Ross, L., 199, *205,* 258, *278*
Ross, M., 195, *205*
Roth, D. R., 239, *252*
Rotter, J. B., 76, *84*
Rubinstein, S. L., 21, 35, *61,* 63, *84*
Ruderman, A. J., *206*
Runeson, S., 272, *278*
Russell, D., *114, 206*
Russell, J. A., 172, *186*
Rutenfrantz, J., *84*

S

Sagatun, I. J., 258, *278*
Saugstad, P., 132-4, 137, 141-167, *169*
Savage, R. E., 77, *83*
Schachter, S., 201, *205*
Schank, R. C., 96, *113,* 201, *205,* 208, 209, *228*
Scheflen, A. E., 239, 242, *253*
Scheier, M. F., 89, 100, *112,* 191, *203,* 261, *276*
Schleicher, R., 81, *84*

Schleidt, M., 243, *253*
Schlenker, B. R., 260, 267, *278*
Schmidt, K. H., 72, 79, *84*
Schnotz, W., *83*
Schönpflug, W., 89, *113*
Schulz, P., 89, *113*
Schwartz, P., 274
Schwarzer, R., 97, 104, *114*
Schweissfurth, W., 79, *84*
Searle, J. R., 260
Secord, P. F., 21, *60,* 129, *168,* 183, *185,* 257, 261, 270, *277*
Seligman, M. E. P., 196, *205*
Shallice, T., 52, *61*
Shaver, K. G., 195, *205*
Shaw, M. E., 211, *228*
Shaw, R., 271, *278*
Sheikh, A. A., *205*
Shiffrin, R. M., 52, *59*
Shotter, J., 266, *279*
Sigman, S. J., 244, *253*
Simmel, M., 194, *204*
Simmons, J. L., 15, *18,* 211, 213, 215, *228,* 261, 269, *278*
Simon, H. A., 52, *59,* 99, 100, *114*
Simoneit, M., 119, 120, *169*
Smith, D. L., 268, 271, *277, 279*
Smith, J. M., 218, *228*
Snyder, M., 265, 268, *279*
Sommer, P., 240, *253*
Staendel, T., *59, 113*
Stahelski, A. J., 195, *205*
Stanley, J. C., 265, *276*
Starr, B. J., 118, *169*
Staub, E., 208, *228*
Stein, M. I., 121, *169*
Steiner, V., 3, 19, 51, *61*
Stern, C. G., 121, *169*
Stern, D., 260, *279*
Stevenson, J. G., 1, *18*
Storms, M. D., 195, *205*
Streufert, S., 193, *205*
Streufert, S. C., 193, *205*
Sudman, S., 220, *228*
Swann, W. B., Jr., 260, *279*

T

Tajfel, H., 200, *205*
Tanur, J., *278*

Tarpy, R. M., 198, *205*
Taylor, M. S., 75, *84*
Taylor, S. E., 200, *206*
Tetlock, P. E., 258, *279*
Thayer, R. E., 99, *114*
Thibaut, J. W., 15, *18,* 199, *206*
Thomas, Dorothy, 214, *228*
Thomas, W., 214, *228*
Thommen, B., 19, 24, 38, 43, 57, *58, 61*
Thurstone, L., 126, *169*
Tomaszewski, T., 21, *61,* 63, 68, 69, *84*
Trower, P., 209, *227*
Troy, N., 77, *84*
Tupes, E. C., 123, *169, 170*
Turiel, E., 261, *279*
Turner, R. H., 15, 16, *18*
Turner, T., *203*
Tversky, A., 199, *204, 206*

U

Uglow, D., *278*
Ulich, E., 76, *84*
Uranowitz, S. W., 265, *279*

V

Valach, L., 38, 58, *59, 61*
Volpert, W., 21, 26, *59, 60, 61,* 71, 75, *84*
Vroom, V. H., 64, 78, *82*

W

Walker, E., 182, *185*
Wallbott, H. G., 264, *279*
Waller, W., 215, *228*
Ward, L. M., 171, *186*
Ware, R., 193, *206*
Weiner, B., 86, 87, 106, *114,* 195, 196, *206*
Weinstein, E., *278*
Welford, A. T., 209, *228*
Wertsch, J. V., 171, *186*
Weston, D. R., 261, *279*
Wicklund, R. A., 52, *61,* 267, *276*
Willems, E. P., 130, *170*
Wilson, P., 250, *253*
Wilson, T. D., 202, *205,* 68, *83*
Windle, C., 117, *170*
Wolff, S., 77, 79, *84*
Wolff, T., 77, *84*
Wong, P. T. P., 195, *206*

Y

Young, D., 178, *186*
Youssouf, H., 248, *253*

Z

Zajonc, R. B., 87, 99, *114*
Zanna, M. P., *204*
Zeigarnik, B., 74, *84*
Zimmerman, L., *278*
Zimring, C., *185*
Zube, E., *185*

Subject Index

A

Abilities, 90, 94, 196
Accounts, 132, 151, 154, 226, 256, 267, 270, 273
Achievement, 116, 151
Achievement concepts (*Leistungsbegriffe*), 126
Achievement motivation, 196
Act, 3, 24, 26, 33, 34, 39, 49, 57, 202, 230, 234, 248, 256, 265, 273
Act–action structure, 23, 53, 256, 258
Action, 1ff., 69ff., 78, 80, 85ff., 101ff., 106ff., 127ff., 151, 171ff., 184, 185, 189ff., 202, 208ff., 218ff., 227ff., 236, 239ff., 247ff., 255ff., 265ff.
Action, abstract vs. concrete, 22
Action analysis, 128, 151, 155, 226, 255ff., 261ff., 275
  problem-areas in, 264ff.
Action, communicative explicitness of, 246ff., 249, 251
Action control, 41, 45, 57, 89, 91, 93ff., 103ff., 109, 111ff.
Action, design of, 63, 66ff., 78, 80
Action exchange system, 245
Action, joint, 255, 260
Action, ongoing, 74, 88, 190
Action processes, 63, 65, 91, 128ff., 137, 151ff.
Action psychology, 115, 128ff., 152ff., 207, 216ff., 227
Action regulation, 3, 5, 7, 21ff., 63, 67ff., 80, 100
Action repertoire, 218ff.
Action research, 255
  levels of, 67, 69, 255
Action sequences, 34, 50, 54, 58, 72, 93, 100ff., 151, 154, 172, 190, 200ff., 209, 215ff., 235, 241, 245ff., 250ff., 256, 259, 263, 268, 273
Action slips, 72

Action, social, 171ff., 183ff., 187, 189, 191, 197ff., 202, 210ff.
Action steps, 46, 48ff., 53ff., 56
Action structure, 53, 91, 221ff., 225
Action style, 6, 66, 256
Action system, 210, 212,
Action taxonomies, coding, 73, 103, 152, 154, 226
Action themes, 255, 257ff., 275
Action theory, 1ff., 8, 11ff., 17ff., 23, 52, 55ff., 85ff., 89ff., 187ff., 190ff., 197, 199ff., 256ff., 267, 273ff.
Actions, complex, 28, 33, 73, 76
Activity, activities, 35, 42, 64ff., 71ff., 76, 80ff., 85, 91, 104, 109, 127, 129, 171ff., 174ff., 177ff., 232ff., 246, 261, 268
Actor–observer differences, 195
Adaptation, 40, 50, 55, 58
Addiction, 201
Address, 242ff.
Ageing, 72
Agency, 2, 5, 12, 16, 25, 57, 137, 151, 172, 255ff., 259ff., 266ff., 270, 272
Aims, 64
Anger, 257ff.
Animal learning, 198
Anxiety, 102, 106, 108ff., 116ff., 230
Arousal, 88, 99, 102ff., 105, 107ff., 111
Arousal reduction, 103
Artificial intelligence, 22, 189, 201
Aspirations, 6, 64, 66, 78, 136, 138, 174, 184
Attention, 4, 12, 16, 25, 32ff., 37, 136
  communication of, 235, 245ff.
  hierarchy of, 238
  selective, 200
  and spatial organisation, 235ff.
Attentional tracks, 17, 232ff.
Attitudes, 39ff., 45, 54, 56, 65, 72, 76, 78, 131, 136, 178, 188, 193, 197ff., 248, 260

Attribution error, fundamental, 258
Attribution theory, 12, 191, 194ff., 200, 258ff.
Attributional research, 196ff.
Attributions, 5, 11ff., 16, 21, 38, 44, 52, 56ff., 68, 106ff., 127, 132, 136, 195ff., 258ff., 262, 267
defensive, 195
Audiences, 139, 236, 242ff., 259ff.
Authenticity of verbal reports, 13, 190, 202, 225ff.
Automaticity, 13, 16, 73, 87, 109, 201ff.
Autonomy, 7ff., 10, 14, 72ff., 75ff., 81
Awareness, conscious, 36, 172, 190, 202, 272

B

Bargaining, 213ff.
Behaviour, 23, 29, 43ff., 47, 51, 55ff., 98, 128, 130ff., 136, 171, 176, 179, 188ff., 196ff., 201ff., 232ff., 243, 246, 251
Behavioural decisions, 191
Behavioural mapping, 180
Behavioural operations, 90ff., 100
Behaviourism , 13, 190
Behaviourist tradition, radical, 189
Bidirectional adaptation, 4, 6, 26
Bidirectional organisation, 48
Biographies, 10ff., 127ff.
Biographically situated experience, 153
Buildings, 177ff.
Bureaucratization of research, 116, 122

C

Categorization, 12, 193, 231
Causal description, explanaton, 1, 18, 67, 256ff., 262, 273ff.
Causal schemata, 200
Causality, internal vs. external locus of, 196
Charge, 6, 10, 63ff., 73
Children's interaction, 47ff., 260, 270
Choice, 198ff., 273
Clinical approach to personality study, 10, 122
Clinical psychology, 118ff., 127
Clinical setting, 115
Cognition, cognitions, 2, 4ff., 7ff., 12ff., 16. 20ff., 23ff., 29, 36, 39ff., 51ff., 68,

85ff., 104, 110, 112, 188ff., 196ff., 200, 202, 225ff.
action-accompanying, 5, 7, 13, 51ff., 57, 67, 69
action-related, 13, 29ff., 33ff., 39, 42ff., 47, 514, 55ff., 67, 69, 213, 225, 273
Cognitive appraisal, reappraisal, 87ff.
Cognitive balance, 191ff.
Cognitive bias, 192, 194
Cognitive commitment, premature, 202
Cognitive complexity–simplicity, 192ff.
Cognitive consistency, 191, 193
Cognitive dissonance theory, 187, 191
Cognitive ecology, 12, 177, 180
Cognitive effort, 99, 201
Cognitive events, 189
Cognitive operations, 99ff., 104ff., 107, 112
Cognitive processes, 67, 74, 85, 87ff., 97, 101, 103ff., 108ff., 112, 136, 151, 189ff., 199, 202ff., 214ff., 225ff., 259ff., 266, 271ff.
Cognitive psychology, 67, 71ff., 75, 86ff., 260
Cognitive structures, 177, 189, 191
Cognitive style, 78
Comfort, environmental, 176
Communicative acts, 46, 214, 229ff., 232, 235
Comparison, 12, 42, 44ff., 136, 202
Comparison level, 199
Conditional-genetic analysis, 154
Configuration descriptions, 274
Conflict between control systems, 103
Conscious cognition, 22ff., 25, 30ff., 36, 68, 74, 267, 272ff.
Conscious representation, 4, 21, 30ff., 37, 39, 43, 46ff., 49
Consciousness, 22, 30ff., 35, 37, 51ff., 55, 71
Consensus, 195, 215, 229, 232, 243, 250
in interaction, 229
Consistency, 195, 273, see also Cognitive consistency
Content analysis, 53, 55ff., 226
Context, physical and social, 1ff., 6, 9, 11, 13, 29, 42, 44, 46, 64, 70, 86, 88, 110ff., 122ff., 132, 171ff., 179ff., 184, 201, 239, 257ff., 266
Contingencies, 15, 46, 196

Control
  circularity of, 106ff.
  cognitive, 38, 56, 69, 74, 89ff., 99ff.,
    107ff.
  emotional, 38, 90ff., 99ff., 102ff., 107ff.
  levels of, 94
  locus of, 73, 76, 116ff.
  skips in, 106, 108ff., 111
  social, 25, 38, 41, 43ff., 47, 54ff., 81, 174
  voluntary, 87, 89, 99
Convention, 9, 21, 24, 38ff., 42, 56ff., 94,
    231, 261, 271
Conventionalisation, 247ff.
Conversation, 241ff, 248
Cooperators and competitors, 195
Correspondence analysis, 176
Cross-situational consistency, 123
Cultural socialisation, 203
Cyclic structure of actions, 7, 69ff.

D

Debriefing, 270
Deception, 272
Decisions and decision-making, 12ff., 21,
    23, 33ff., 43, 45, 53ff., 68, 70, 73,
    76ff., 81, 107, 189ff., 194, 198ff.,
    202ff., 210, 213, 216, 269, 273
Decision tree, 199
Demand characteristics, 225, 262
Dembo problem, 132ff., 140ff., 158ff.
Developmental psychology, 17ff., 74, 129,
    260ff., 263ff.
Description, see Causal; Part–whole
    description
Discourse, Discourse theory, 17, 264, 272,
    see also Conversation
Distinctiveness, 195
Distortions of data, 122
Drives, 188

E

Ecological psychology, 12, 179, 271ff.
Economics, 189, 197
Effort, 36, 64, 68ff., 71, 74ff., 78, 269, see
    also Cognitive effort
Emotion, 3ff., 6, 8ff., 13, 21, 30, 32ff., 40,
    46, 52, 55ff., 75, 85ff., 95ff., 104, 107,
    109ff., 136, 188, 196, 225, 256ff., 261,
    266

Emotion regulation, 104
Emotional quality, 99ff.
Emotional syndrome, 88
Encounters, 207ff., 210, 214ff., 230ff., 239,
    241ff., 247, 249
Energizing functions, 34ff., 37, 208
Environment, 2, 14, 51, 58, 89, 91, 94ff.,
    100ff., 104ff., 108ff., 111ff., 127, 131,
    172ff., 176, 179, 183ff., 194, 196, 201,
    208, 237ff., 240ff.
Environmental psychology, 11, 172ff.,
    175ff., 180, 185
Equifinality, 21, 111, 208
Equity, 273
Ethogenics, 257
Ethology, 1, 20
Evaluative beliefs, 198
Evaluation, 34ff., 37, 39ff., 42, 44, 46,
    54ff.
  emotional, 87
  environmental, 176
Expectancy, subjective, 197ff.
Expectancy of success and failure, 196,
    198
Expectancy value models, 12, 197ff.
Expectations, 91, 96ff., 101, 201, 215ff.,
    230, 241, 248ff., 267
Expected consequences, 191, 198, 208
Experiments, 131, 195, 197, 203, 207,
    225ff., 256, 257, 260, 262, 264ff., 270,
    274
Expressive behaviour, 17, 88, 128, 131ff.,
    136ff., 151, 153ff., 241, see also
    Communicative acts
External validity, 18, 124ff., 265ff.

F

F-formation, 239ff., 246
Fatigue, 79
Feedback, 1, 3, 8, 15, 22, 28ff., 69ff., 74,
    80, 100, 174, 182, 219, 222ff., 261
Field, psychological, 211ff., 216
Field theory, 211
Fire, 184
Flower problem, see Dembo problem
Frame, 230ff., 236ff., 241, 243, 249
Frame attunement, 16ff., 229, 233, 243
Frame of reference, 16, 192, 199
Frustration, 132, 136
Functional analysis, 48ff., 88

G

Gaze direction, 237, 243ff., 246
  in greeting, 246
Generalizability, 258, 262, 265ff.
Generating mechanisms, 125, 152, 154, 273
Genotypical modality, 152, 154
Gestures, 244, 247ff., 249
Goal as affordance, 268
Goals, 3, 7ff., 14ff., 21, 24ff., 28, 34ff., 40, 43ff., 53ff., 68ff., 90ff., 100ff., 127ff., 136ff., 172ff., 182, 190ff., 199, 202, 207ff., 261, 268ff.
  personal, 94, 98, 109
  step, 74ff., 79
Goal-directedness, orientedness, 1ff., 6ff., 10ff., 15ff., 25, 33, 64ff., 68, 73ff., 80, 85ff., 103, 107, 110ff., 129, 172, 175ff., 188, 190, 203, 207ff., 213, 216ff., 257, 272ff.
Goal setting, 65, 69ff., 127, 129
Grammar, 58, 65, 123, 125, 129
Greeting, 241, 246ff., 261
Grief, 257
Group, 41ff., 47, 49ff., 54, 73, 81, 129, 180ff., 183, 264, 274

H

Habit, 21, 28
Hawthorne investigations, 179
Health, 201
Heuristics, 69, 71ff., 89, 198
Hospitals, 180ff.
Housing, 182ff.
Hypotheses, 7, 70, 95, 97ff., 108, 200

I

Ideal point, 192
Identity, identities, 137, 211, 266, 269
Illusory correlations, 118
Imaginary gambles, 197ff.
Implicit personality theories, 118
Imposition of units, 131, 151
Improvisation, 12, 15, 220, 258
Individual differences, 5, 7, 9, 50, 72ff., 182ff., 193ff., 198, 215, 268
Inference processes, 12, 15ff., 259, 271ff.
Information-processing, 4, 7, 25, 29, 32,

34, 43ff., 46, 52, 56, 58, 67, 69, 87, 195, 200, 202, 209, 260
Input, 91ff., 100, 102ff.
Intention, intentionality, 6ff., 11, 13, 64ff., 68ff., 74, 76ff., 86, 90, 105, 129, 171, 174ff., 182, 188, 194ff., 197, 203, 207, 209ff., 229, 232, 236, 247, 249ff., 271ff.
Intentions, behavioural, 197ff.
Interaction
  departures from, 242, 250, 261
  focused, 230ff., 233, 235, 239, 241, 246
  rythmical coordination in, 245ff., 248
  social, 3ff., 10, 12, 15ff., 43, 46ff., 51ff., 80, 132ff., 179ff., 210ff., 229ff., 261ff., 268ff., see also Children's interaction
Interactional personality psychology, 117
Interactional relationships, 240ff., 247, 251
Inter-individual variation, 123
Internal validity, 18, 55, 265
Interpretation, 94ff., 98ff., 102, 107, 109, 132, 136, 208ff., 214, 216, 229ff., 237ff., 241, 249ff., 258, 263
Interview, 56ff.
  focused, 132ff., 155
  research, 14ff., 207, 212, 214ff., 225ff.
  self-confrontation, 4ff., 13, 15, 52ff., 225ff.
Interviewer effects, bias, 217, 219ff., 224, 227
Interviewer–respondent interaction, 212, 216ff., 225ff.
Interviewer-training, 207, 218, 225
Interviewing, 213, 217ff.
  non-directive, 217ff., 221, 224, 227
  style, 226
Intra-individual processes, 256, 271, 273
Intra-individual variation, 123, 129
Involvement, level of, 111

J

Job analyses, 121
Job characteristic models, 78
Job diagnosis survey, 78
Job, objective conditions, 80
Joint action, 216, 255, 260, see also Interaction, social
Joy, 111, 258

K

Kelly matrix, 153
Kissing, 243
Knowledge, 41ff., 57, 68, 81, 90, 95ff.,
    100ff., 107ff., 177, 183, 208ff., 216ff.,
    221, 268ff.

L

Language, 10, 86, 124ff., 128, 189, 202,
    226, 240, 242ff., 247ff., 259, 261, 264
Language-induced abstraction, 122, 126,
    128, 152
Learned helplessness, 196ff.
Life space, 267
Life-span psychology, 127
Life trajectory, 127
Light-point display studies, 271ff.
Lines of action, 207ff., 213ff., 230ff., 237,
    246, 269, 274
Looking and utterance address, 244, *see
    also* Gaze direction
Loud soliloquy, 5, 13, 54

M

Manipulation of antecedent conditions,
    130ff., 151
Meaning, 255, 260, 264ff., 271
    situational and environmental, 171ff.,
    177ff., 211, 260, 268
Measurement, 207, 216ff., 219ff., 226ff.
Melpa of New Guinea, 243
Memory, 34, 39, 44, 52, 69, 74, 87, 95ff.,
    200ff., 209, 225
Mental categories, 67, 68, *see also*
    Categorization
Mental representations, 69ff., 74, 80, 225
Method variance, 125ff.
Methodology, 9, 13ff., 67ff., 116ff., 119,
    122, 125ff., 129, 177, 190, 202, 217ff.,
    225, 256ff., 259ff., 267, 273ff.
    idiographic, 119, 128
Mindfulness, 194, 202
Monitoring, 25, 30, 32, 36ff., 55, 78, 81,
    215, 255, 270
Monotony, 79
Moral development, 261
Moral judgement, 194
Motives, motivation, 3ff., 6ff., 13, 21, 34ff.,
40, 55, 58, 71ff., 86, 89ff., 127, 188,
    194ff., 203, 208, 218, 220, 225, 269
Motor performance and skill, 209ff.,
    212ff., 218
Multidimensional scaling, 56, 178
Multiple-choice format, 153

N

Naive psychology, action theories, 3, 10,
    20ff., 68
Needs, 38, 64ff., 76, 176
Negotiation, 17, 212, 215ff., 224, 231ff.,
    242, 261, 269ff.
Nomothetic approach, 127ff.
Norm, 21, 24, 39ff., 44, 49ff., 54, 94ff.,
    109, 116, 198

O

Observation, 5, 10, 48ff., 51, 55, 57, 128ff.,
    180ff., 202ff., 234ff., 250ff., 263, 265,
    271ff.
Ontogenetic level, 88
Organisation, 4ff., 20ff., 24, 26ff., 30, 33,
    37, 43ff., 55, 57, 63, 68, 70, 73, 75, 80,
    89, 91, 94ff., 100ff., 104ff., 108ff., 171,
    192
    hierarchical and sequential, 1ff., 7ff., 22,
    26ff., 33ff., 43, 48ff., 71ff., 75, 89,
    94, 96ff., 127, 129, 145, 151, 255ff.,
    261, 264, 266, 273ff.
Orientational organisation of body, 237ff.,
    242ff.
Orthogonal factors, 123
Output, 91, 93, 103ff.

P

Pain, 32
Part–whole description, 256, 262, 273ff.
Path analysis, 79
Perceived responsibility, 79
Perception, 34, 38, 44, 46, 52, 56, 75,
    77ff., 87, 100ff., 109ff., 209ff., 212,
    218, 225, 272
    of action in interaction, 234
    direct, 266, 271ff.
Perception, sensory, and distance in
    interaction, 240
Person–environment constellation, 90,
    92ff., 104, 107ff.

Person perception, 118, 154, 194, 248
Person X situation interaction, 117
Persona, *see* Self-presentation
Personality, 2, 6, 9ff., 43, 56, 63, 65, 67,
    73, 78ff., 81, 115ff., 119, 122ff., 131,
    151ff., 155, 195
Personality assessment, 115ff., 122, 125ff.,
    128ff., 132
  criteria, 119ff.
  process oriented, 151
  systematic, 10, 117, 119ff., 126
Personality psychology, 72, 115ff., 119,
    122ff., 126ff., 152ff., 185
Personality research, 10, 115ff., 122,
    125ff., 128ff., 132
Personology, 115ff., 120ff., 128
Perspectives, 133, 229ff., 233, 245, 255ff.,
    266ff., 269ff.
  first-person, 255ff., 266ff.
  generalized other, 270
  observer, 16, 256ff., 270
  third-person, 256
Phatic communion, 248
Phenomenal causality, 194
Phenomenal experiences, 4, 174, 191, 273
Phenotypical modality, 152, 154
Phylogenetic level, 88
Physiological measures, 99
Place, 175ff., 179ff.
Place experience, 175ff.
Place-related activities, 174
Plans, planning, 2ff., 6, 23ff., 28, 34ff.,
    43ff., 46, 54, 58, 66, 72ff., 76, 78, 80,
    85, 91, 100ff., 104ff., 142, 148, 151,
    203, 213, 236, 249
Play, 5, 51
Positivism, 116, 119
Posture, 235ff., 239, 242, 244ff., 250
Preference judgements, 192, 197ff.
Preference space, 192ff.
Problem and conflict situations (PCSs),
    10ff., 129ff., 158ff.
Problem-solving, 11, 21ff., 104, 132ff., 209,
    224
Processes, 17, 67ff., 70, 99, 126, 151ff.,
    178, 184, 257, 260, 262, 272, 274
Process integraton, 174
Product–process fallacy, 126, 129ff., 152
Projective techniques, 117ff., 127
Prospect theory, 199
Protocols, 136ff., 158ff.

Psychodiagnostics, 117ff., 127
Psycholinguistic research, 18, 72
Psychopathology, 73
Psychotherapy, 43, 57, 115ff., 127
Purposiveness, 171, 188, 190, 202, *see also*
    Intention, intentionality

Q

Question–answer sequences, 217, 219, 221
Questionnaires, 117, 125, 180
Questions
  leading, 217
  open and closed, 221ff., 227

R

Rage, 103, 106ff.
Rationality, 85, 191, 193ff., 203
Reactivity, 207, 216
Realization, 100
Reductional concepts, 6ff., 66
Reflective stance, 258, 270
Reframing, 270
Rehearsal, mental, 66, 70
Reports of mental states, 189
Research design, problems of, 264ff.
Resolution, 36ff., 46, 54, 56
Respondent problems, 218, 224
Response, 189ff.
Response bias, 217, 225ff.
Response sets, 220, 225
Retroaction of concepts, 4, 21, 39, 57
Risk, 198ff.
Role, 9, 12ff., 88, 94ff., 111, 137, 181ff.,
    201, 215, 220, 245, 258ff., 262ff., 266,
    268ff.
Role-playing, 218, 263, 266
Role-rule model, 137ff., 141, 143, 145, 183
Role-rule structure, 269
Role-taking, 11, 15ff., 136
Routine, 4, 33, 51, 77, 269
Routinisation in interaction, 231, 248ff.
Rules, 4, 9, 11ff., 16ff., 21, 24, 38ff., 42,
    44, 46ff., 54, 58, 85, 94ff., 137, 173,
    183, 200ff., 231, 243, 261ff., 266,
    268ff., 271, 273

S

Salience, 195, 198

Salutations, 246ff., *see also* Greeting
   functions of, 247
Satisfaction, 12, 78ff., 136, 182ff.
Saugstad problem, 132ff., 137ff., 145ff.,
   151ff., 158ff.
Scenarios, 263ff.
Schemata, 12ff., 16, 44, 96ff., 199ff.
   emotion, 96
   motor, 72
Schools, 181ff.
Scripts, 4, 12ff., 38, 44, 58, 96, 199, 201ff.,
   209
Selectivity of theories, 187
Self-awareness, 52, 66, 89
Self-concept, 6, 15, 65, 68, 192
Self-control processes, 99
Self-development, 65ff., 79, 81
Self-esteem, 196ff.
Self-fulfilling prophecy, effects, 174, 265
Self-perception theory, 187
Self-presentation, 17, 42, 137ff., 148, 151,
   153, 231, 248, 258ff., 264
Self-regulation, 261
Self-report measures, 190, 202ff.
Self-talk, 47
Sequence analysis, 226
Shared reality, 214ff., 270
Situated action, 207, 214, 216, 255, 257,
   264ff., 269ff., 273, 275
Situated sequences of activity, 171,
Situation, 1, 9, 11, 14, 40, 42ff., 57ff., 74,
   87ff., 92, 95ff., 101ff., 107ff., 123,
   127ff., 130ff., 136, 151, 153, 172ff.,
   200ff., 208ff., 214ff., 225ff., 230ff.,
   256ff., 265ff.
   demand structure of, 94, 131
Situation test, 129ff.
Situational definition, 1ff., 11, 14ff., 24, 29,
   88, 95, 107ff., 131, 137, 139, 214ff.,
   219ff., 230, 267, 269ff.
Situational knowledge, 208
Skill, 15, 28, 64, 75ff., 79, 81, 90, 209ff.,
   212, 216ff., 227, 251, 268
Social and interpersonal influence, 38,
   207, 211, 213, 225
Social cognition, 187, 191, 194, 197ff.,
   201ff.
Social judgement, 12ff., 189ff.
Social knowledge, 4, 9, 12ff., 21, 38ff., 48,
   273
Social meaning, 23ff., 49, 55

Social processes, 174, 179
Social psychology, 171ff., 179, 183ff.,
   187ff., 191, 194, 197, 201ff., 255,
   257ff., 266ff., 270ff.
Social representations, 4ff., 12ff., 16, 24,
   28, 41ff., 57, 200, 273
Sociology and microsociology, 2, 260ff.,
   264
Spatial arrangements, changes in
   interaction, 241
Spatial behaviour, 12, 17, 49, 183, 235ff.,
   238
Spatial and orientational positions in
   interaction, 236ff., 239, 241, 245,
   249
Spatial component of place experience,
   176
Spatial positioning in interaction as an
   expressive resource, 240
Speech act theory, 272
Sport, 51
Stable vs. unstable factors, 196
Statistical reasoning, 198
Steering
   cognitive, 28ff., 34ff., 39, 42, 49, 55,
      152, 154ff.
   social, 38
Stereotypes, 200
Stress, strain, 76ff., 79, 89, 111, 130
Structural analysis, 48ff., 51, 66, 69, 257,
   264ff., 275
Subconscious self-regulation, 28, 37, 39
Subjective probabilities, 199
Survey research, 212, 226
Systems theory, 21, 25, 561

T

Task, 5ff., 8ff., 14, 53ff., 63ff., 67ff., 70,
   73ff., 121, 131ff., 196, 269
Theories, 187, 190, 203, *see also* Selectivity
   of theories
   categorization of problems, 187
   generalization of, 187
   monothematic, 116
   preference for, 187
Time, 2ff., 6, 10, 28, 30, 43, 49, 63, 69, 71,
   74, 91, 101, 116, 127, 129, 136, 151,
   172, 184ff., 190, 201, 235, 238, 241,
   246, 256, 261, 266ff., 273ff.
Timmy, game of, 233ff.

Tolerance of complexity and ambiguity,
    193
TOTE units, 71
Trait factors, 122ff., 152, 154
Transaction, person–environment, 95,
    97ff., 109ff.
Transaction schema, 91ff., 95ff., 100,
    107ff., 110
Transactional segment, 237ff., 243
Transition, state of, 94ff., 98
Tuareg, 248
Turn-taking, 243

U

Utility, 197ff.
Utterance exchange system, 243ff., 248

V

Valence, 75, 90
Values, value, 38ff., 54, 64ff., 197ff., 263ff.
Verification data, 226
Videotaping, use of, 5, 10, 52, 55, 57, 132,
    136, 153, 219, 261ff., 270ff.
Volition, 21, 25, 34ff., 64ff., 73ff., 77, 207

W

Work, 6, 65ff., 72, 75ff., 78ff., 137
Working agreement, 215ff., *see also*
    Consensus; Situational definition
World knowledge, 201

Y

Yo-yoing, 235ff.